ROVING COMMISSIONS 46

ROYAL CRUISING CLUB
JOURNAL 2005

Edited by JONNY CLOTHIER

Editorial Acknowledgements

More members than usual have departed over the horizon this year. I am hugely grateful to all of you who have so willingly written obituaries, encouraged others to write them or provided very helpful suggestions and information. What could be a burden for the Editor becomes an opportunity to get to know more of the Club's remarkable members by telephone and email.

We have done our best to edit contributors' work sympathetically. We do hope everyone who has taken so much trouble to write is happy with what appears in print. Jane Kimber has been tireless in her attention to detail. She handled a mistake I made in wiping out eight hours of her work with remarkable equanimity.

The staff at Footnote Graphics and the Bath Press continue to make our task easy, encouraging us to take advantage of new technologies whilst understanding our limitations. The high production quality is down to them.

ISBN 0-901-91626-9

Typeset by Footnote Graphics Ltd, Warminster
Printed and bound by The Bath Press

Contents

A JOURNAL FOR THE CLUB'S 125th YEAR

It is good to be celebrating the Club's 125th anniversary with a bumper edition. The Journal has grown by 32 pages this year thanks to the number of logs received, words written and the wide spread of areas cruised. Charles Nodder has marked the event with an examination of cruising trends. This was last undertaken by Robert Franks in 1977. Members have not resisted the temptation to increase the volume of their boats and the creature comforts which extra space permits. Nor have they eschewed the wonders of technology with microchips spreading through boats like a virulent army of cockroaches. The thirst for lonely adventure seems as strong as ever, particularly amongst time-richer older members. On the other hand, the thirst for other members' company seems to be growing. The Club Meet to celebrate the 200th anniversary of the Battle of Trafalgar was remarkably well organised and attended; a real triumph.

Last year Phil Sharp treated us to a thrilling account of preparations for the Mini-Transat in 2005. He sailed a remarkable race, finishing in fourth place overall without the benefits of the generous sponsorship available to many other competitors. Meanwhile Mervyn Wheatley and Paul Heiney were laying plans to take part in the OSTAR, a race founded in 1960 by Blondie Hasler, a member of the club. It was then considered an adventure fit only for lunatics. Paul's most readable account gives us the chance to assess whether this still applies. Mervyn went on to achieve remarkable success in winning his class. The OSTAR certainly sits very happily with the traditions of the club.

Although the Arctic Circle has again delivered some excellent reading this year, it does not predominate. Last year we shared Bob Shepton's agony over the loss of *Dodo's Delight*. *Iron Bark* was overwintering not far away. Annie Hill's account will undoubtedly tempt others to try. We have a very good worldwide spread. World girdling is represented by Richard Clifford outward bound to New Zealand and Graham Morfey returning to Europe. Katharine and Peter Ingram interrupted their voyaging for the birth of their son. He is with them as they are chased by a hurricane round the north Atlantic on the final leg back to Spain. Their three logs have been a joy to publish and to read as well as providing a wealth of pilotage information. As a complete contrast, we have no less than four accounts of canal transits. Those planning one should make Stephen Lennane's rueful account an early port of call.

Most contributors have moved to digital photography. The standard of photos has risen as a result, partly because you take and discard more pictures. There remains a problem. When I reluctantly told one member that his masterpiece couldn't be used because it was of too low a definition to print successfully, he sheepishly explained that he hadn't actually read the camera instructions. The more pixels, the merrier the editor. Electronic charts and chart software are also enabling members to generate track charts more easily. We plan to provide some tips on format and method in time for RC 47. Technology should deliver a better quality journal more quickly.

Ultimately the journal can only be the sum of what club members have written. I hope all those who have written in our 125th year will share a sense of pride in what they have achieved.

Jonny Clothier
February 2006

Galapagos Tortoise
Drawn by Richard Clifford

TOWARDS NEW ZEALAND

by Richard Clifford

The Royal Cruising Club Challenge Cup was awarded for this voyage

Gibraltar Straits proved typically difficult to negotiate and we had to anchor twice before finally crossing the shipping lanes and getting over to the African shore just before midnight on 10 October 2004. At last we were out into the Atlantic and heading towards Madeira. On this leg I had Alastair Grant who had last sailed with me across the Atlantic in 1972. The aim for the next year was to visit as many island groups as possible and to lay-up in New Zealand in November 2005.

Warrior Shamaal is a centre cockpit Warrior 35 that Jenny and I fitted out from a bare hull in 1978. A Haslar steering vane does most of the hard work, sometimes replaced by a belt-driven Autohelm when we are motoring. The engine is a Yanmar 30hp that is only five years old and the propeller has three blades. A large Delta anchor with 80 metres of chain provides the necessary security, backed up by a Brittany and a large CQR, each with 15 metres of chain. The working sails are seven years old whilst the spinnaker and other sails are over twenty. The last five years in the Mediterranean has taken its toll but with constant TLC we have kept ahead of old age.

Once clear of the African coast we had four glorious days reaching in F4-5. One night the spinnaker halyard parted at the block. Recovering the sail from the sea, it was damaged and I hand-stiched the eight-foot tear. We had decided on Porto Santo as the first port of call from where Alastair departed in a rush to get to his daughter's confirmation. I had five days gale bound with an on-shore wind, at anchor inside the breakwater but with rather too many other yachts. My next crew was due in the Canaries and I needed to move on. Time did not allow for a visit to Madeira.

Once at sea the wind became changeable and on each of the following four days we made less than 100 miles. The visibility was such that I could see the lights on the mountains of Tenerife from 60 miles away. With a day in hand before Guy was due I found a small rocky anchorage for the night on the west coast of Tenerife. Los Cristianos on the southern tip was busy and full of liveaboards and some cruising yachts. The airport is close by and Guy Sheridan, with whom I have mountaineered for years, arrived. Los Cristianos is good for provisioning and we hired a car to spend a day walking on the side of Mount Teide.

I had not thought to cruise in the Canaries but we decided to visit the southern anchorages on La Gomera before heading for the Cape Verde Islands where I planned to spend two weeks. The seas between the Canary Islands are often lumpy and the wind whistles around the northern sides. Our 26-mile crossing was not a pleasant experience for Guy. The open anchorages on the south of La Gomera were insufficiently secure for us to explore too far into the hills so after three days we weighed and headed south.

The Cape Verde Islands lie in latitude 15-17°N and are 350 miles from the West African coast. The archipelago is made up of 10 main islands all of volcanic origin and with limited or no vegetation. The shoreline is either rocky with volcanic cliffs or has white or black sandy beaches. They got independence from the Portuguese in 1975 and the population is a mix of African and European, but is increasingly added to by West Africans from trouble spots; some speak delightfully clear English or French depending on their country of origin. There is little work although there has recently been considerable investment in tourism with new airports and hotel complexes. The islands stretch 120 miles north to south and 100 miles east to west and the prevailing wind is from the northeast.

We approached the northeastern island in the archipelago, Ilha do Sal, at night, with the lights of the airport standing out well which was useful as there are no navigation lights on the north coast. The island had moved since my Admiralty chart, taken from the Portuguese government 1956 survey, was published but the Imray chart was accurate although a larger scale. The volcanic cones stood out in the moonless night as we slipped along the coast to enter the tiny port of Palmeira before first light on 6 November. Fortunately we spotted the masts of a sunken fishing vessel right in the middle of the anchorage, in which there was about 15 yachts. A short quay wall gave some protection from the northwest but the anchorage is open to the southwest, as we were to experience.

Clearance with the village maritime policeman was easy but of course he did not have change for the money I gave him for the meagre admission fee, so a small tip for him (which I did not begrudge). The main town on the island is seven kilometres inland and easily reached by open truck-taxis for a few pence. There the shops had sufficient supplies to keep us going. A visit to the new and impressive airport was worthwhile

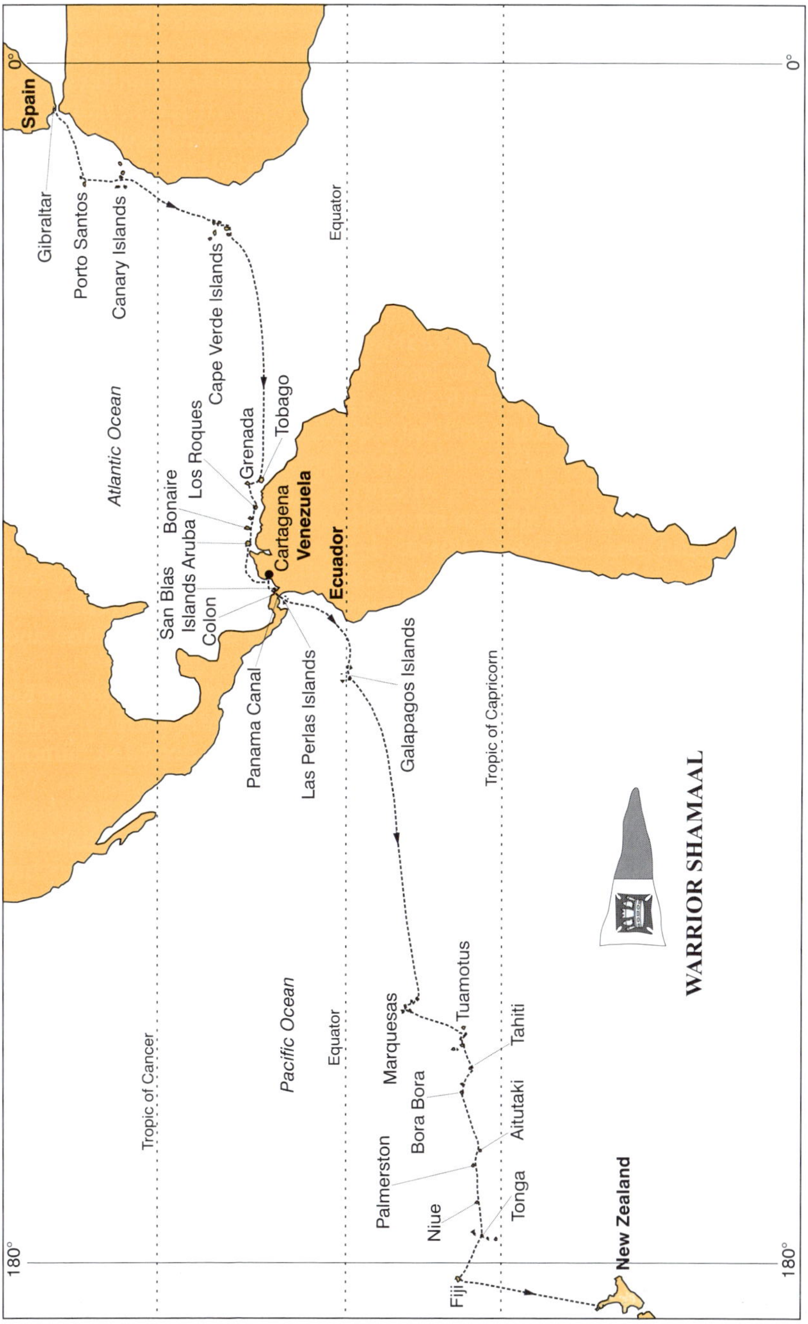
0°
0°
Spain
Gibraltar
Porto Santos
Canary Islands
Cape Verde Islands
Equator
Atlantic Ocean
Tobago
Grenada
Los Roques
Bonaire
Aruba
Cartagena
Venezuela
Ecuador
San Blas
Islands
Colon
Panama Canal
Las Perlas Islands
Galapagos Islands
Tropic of Capricorn
WARRIOR SHAMAAL
Tropic of Cancer
Pacific Ocean
Equator
Marquesas
Tuamotus
Tahiti
Bora Bora
Aitutaki
Palmerston
Niue
Tonga
Fiji
New Zealand
180°
180°

for exchanging money and getting tourist information. The island is almost devoid of vegetation and is largely volcanic sand and gravel; we saw and smelt a few goats. Desalinated water is available at the village pump.

The anchorage is small and crowded and with the wind going into the southeast the send caused dreadful rolling. It was time to leave what was becoming a dangerous anchorage. Going south was out of the question so we weighed with the idea of exploring the north end of the island and finding a lee. We heard later that everyone who stayed in the anchorage had a terrible night.

The north end of Sal has high volcanic cliffs with a number of little indentations. After a gentle run we rounded Ponta Norte and nosed into a calm bay 1½ hours before last light. It was rather dark and stark with high black cliffs but had a sandy-looking bottom in about 10 metres. It was just suitable so we anchored but a quick snorkel confirmed my fears that the bottom had boulders about three feet high with rounded tops. I needed to make a snap decision whether to stay and risk a fouled chain in an anchorage totally open to the north or to move on to the east side of the island and anchor in Puerto de Pedra de Lume, a recognised anchorage six miles away but unlit and in the dark. I knew if Jenny had been on board she would have recommended a move. Reluctantly we weighed and, motorsailing, rounded the northeast side of the island and headed south in the gathering darkness.

The port ('port' was an exaggeration) was used for nearly 200 years for exporting salt from a nearby crater into which seawater penetrates and the salt is gathered. The small rocky breakwater provided limited protection for the barges to load and carry salt out to waiting ships. We felt our way into the bay with rocks close to starboard and sand banks to port. The bay is open to the east and two hours after last light we anchored off the unseen breakwater 200 metres further inshore. We were the only yacht there. Next day we explored the salt mine, which now only employs 35 people. What obviously was once a thriving industry now largely lies in decay. The little church is immaculate and we felt guilty leaving our sandy footprints inside. Having explored, there was nothing else to hold us. In light airs we motored 12 miles to the lovely white sandy beach at the south end of the island off the town of Sta Maria. It reminded me of the southern anchorage off Isle de Houat in Brittany. A wide beach but in this case backed by a town to the east and a large chalet-hotel complex to the west. A dilapidated jetty provided a place to leave the dinghy rather than risk capsizing in the surf on the beach. Ashore we again found the influx of West Africans very noticeable, some trying to sell African art and others just 'chilling'. The hotels, rather empty, looked out of place. In the shops we found a few more supplies. The baker was particularly good and the ginger cake/biscuits lasted several months.

After a peaceful night off Sta Maria, we weighed with the aim of getting to the next island, Ilha da Boavista 25 miles south, before last light. The port, Sal-Rei, is on the west coast and we had a good run goose-winged in a northeasterly wind. There seemed to be room inside the breakwater but I chickened out at the last minute and headed for the recognised anchorage. We rounded the islet and anchored 5-6 cables off the beach well away from the only other yacht there. It was a long row ashore, supplies were very limited and water out of the question. The port was very run down; old Portuguese colonial buildings still in use but not maintained were in a dreadfully sad state. Lethargy hung in the air. When we returned to *Shamaal* we found a Frenchman anchored within 50 metres, in an anchorage twice as big as Studland Bay! That night it blew over 40 knots, fortunately off the land. We put out 40 metres of chain and a chum weight. The 14mm anti-snubber line broke and I lost the chain hook. Of note, the line was new and broke at the cleat.

There seemed little point in venturing inland on another rocky volcanic island and since there was a good breeze still blowing next morning we decided to move on to our next port, Porto da Praia on Ihla de Santiago, about 80 miles to the southwest.

A pleasant wind sped us along and at midday on 13 November we entered Praia, the capital of the island group. The commercial harbour is on the eastern side of the one mile wide bay and the recognised yacht anchorage off the beach on the west side close to a wreck just visible at

Warrior Shamaal at anchor in the San Blas Islands

low tide. We were the only yacht. We landed on the black sandy beach and were immediately set upon by locals to guard our dinghy. We cleared with the maritime police who wanted to keep the boat documents but I persuaded them otherwise. The town had a couple of fruit and vegetable markets and a modern supermarket (the size of a village store). It was a good place to stock up. I had my first meal ashore for over two months.

At 0300 that night Guy heard a noise on the aft deck, leapt from his bed and scared off the intruder whom we could see swimming to the shore. I had failed to put the long wire strop on the dinghy or take any other security precautions; we were lucky. We moved anchorage in the morning to be close to the fishing port and commercial dock; it was further to walk to the town but taxis were only a pound each way. That day was the only time in the whole cruise that I locked the saloon hatch on going ashore.

It was Remembrance Sunday and Guy and I listened to the Cenotaph Ceremony on the World Service and had our own two minutes silence. The last time he and I had done this was six years ago on top of a mountain ridge in Corsica.

With our trans-Atlantic passage looming we needed to top up with water and supplies. We made good use of the markets, but when we started to stow the two crates of beer we discovered that they were non-alcoholic. So back into the dinghy, row to the dock, taxi to the supermarket (fortunately we still had the receipt), swap the beer, taxi back to the dock and row back to *Shamaal*. It all sounds easy but when it is over 30° and seemingly airless and after several other trips it was very hard on the humour.

I have an SSB radio, which I link to my laptop with a Pactor modem. Using Winlink, I have a very functional method of sending and receiving emails. It is similar to Sailmail but free to radio amateurs. Using this system I get GRIB 5-day weather forecasts for about 8 kilobytes. They are excellent guides although they do not show the weather fronts. Whilst in Praia we were getting good indications that the trade winds were setting in south of the Cape Verde Islands so we decided to clear out as this was the last port of clearance on our route. Our only shortfalls now were water and an essential visit to the truck of the mast.

Thirty miles to the west lies the dramatic volcanic cone-shaped Ilha do Fogo. On its west shore is the tiny port of Cavaleiros. The Imray chart has a water tap marked there. So we gladly slipped out of Praia with its black sand covering our deck and the dinghy. Much of the night we lay uncomfortably becalmed between the two islands but the following evening we entered the port with the breakwater giving excellent protection. There was an abandoned yacht there and we anchored close by. Immediately, using the first calm water for two months, I went up the mast twice to do the work on my inner forestay. Then we went ashore to investigate the tap. The local fishermen denied that one existed but offered to take us to a town five miles to the south to collect water. This was not ideal so we returned to *Shamaal* for the night.

We would have liked to climb up the mountain (2800 metres with an active volcano near by) but it would have meant a night away from *Shamaal*, so we discarded this idea. Ten miles to the west is the tiny Ilha Brava, rarely visited and with Porto da Furna on the east coast, a high headland giving it protection from the prevailing winds. There had to be water in the village so we sailed over there and again anchored beside an abandoned yacht.

Going ashore, we were immediately befriended. The village freshwater tap was unlocked and for a tiny fee we did several trips topping up our tanks with fresh spring water. The place had such a friendly feel although the shops had nothing for us. The local policeman took our details in a correct and friendly manner. Having achieved our aim we weighed and headed for Tobago, 2100 miles to the west. We slightly regretted not going inland on this quite different island. A 12-hour delay would have made little difference, but by then we were keen to get on our way.

For the first nine days we made satisfactory progress initially heading southwest. Twin headsails did much of the work and under this rig we could use the bimini for some shade in the cockpit. Guy rigged a wind-scoop facing aft to give some reprieve in the aft cabin. We listened to Herbi's weather forecasts and were amazed at the naivety of some of his customers. He missed a small depression that gave us a short gale and a chance to fill up the water tanks. During that night Guy and I crouched under the back flap (a piece of material zipped onto the spray hood to cover part of the cockpit) reminiscent of the many nights we had spent in the mountains in tents. A good-sized king fish we caught severely upset Guy's stomach so subsequently he was reluctant to do too much fishing.

We crept into Man of War Bay on Tobago before first light on the nineteenth day at sea. The peace and stillness of this delightful anchorage was such a contrast to the rolling of the past few weeks. We spent a week enjoying the relaxed atmosphere before heading over to Grenada where I left *Shamaal* on a mooring in True Blue Bay and returned to England for Christmas.

Jenny and I flew back to Grenada in early January and had a windy but pleasant month in the Grenadines making the most of the warm water and good anchorages. Then Chris McDowall joined in Grenada; he had six weeks before he was booked to fly back from Panama. Getting the timing right is difficult and inevitably we did not spend long enough in some places and vice versa. A light downwind sail took us to the Venezuelan islands, Los Roques, a large archipelago with coral islands and good anchorages. Although it was very crowded we did have one anchorage to ourselves, tucked behind mangroves off a low-lying coral island in

Kicker Rock, Galapagos

excellent shelter. It would have been a place to stay but the wind picked up and it was time to move on to the Islas Las Aves, noted for the mass of birdlife. Our anchorage there was uncomfortable so after a night we decided to sail the 100 miles to Bonaire and make the most of the good wind.

You have to pick up a mooring in Bonaire's crystal clear water. This was one place we should have lingered and enjoyed the diving and quiet atmosphere. Chris speaks Dutch, which gave us some advantage in the ABC islands. We spent too long in Aruba although enjoyed the anchorage with a restaurant ashore. The next leg to Cartagena is renowned for its rough seas and the possibility of pirates. We had large seas and a dead run, often with just storm jib and trysail. We hove-to to wait for daylight to enter the tiny gap in the old defensive wall saving us 10 miles and anchored off the Club Nautico which is the centre for cruisers in Cartagena. Our five days there were well spent touring the historic city.

We decided to visit the San Blas islands of Panama next. These unlit coral islets with their primitive Kuna Indian inhabitants need to be approached with care. We covered the 200 miles in an uncomfortable cross sea with the wind abaft the beam but ran out of daylight so again hove-to. Next day we could see that we could have sailed in and anchored on a ledge without having to pilot around the reefs. We started our cruise here at the Holandes with several anchorages. The Kunas are sparsely scattered and live in small huts on the coconut-covered islands. On one visit I took bottles of water as a gift but later could see there was no need as most of the tiny islands have wells with sweet water. We spent several days there, piloting by eye and nosing into tight anchorages. Time was running out for Chris and it was 90 miles to the Panama Canal. We cut it fine but he got the opportunity to line-handle on a yacht passing through and to go straight to his plane.

Much has been written about the bureaucracy and transit of the canal. I found it easy and efficient and completed the paperwork and got my 'date' all within 48 hours. During the two weeks wait I line-handled for two different yachts and I consider this to be most important familiarisation. It just left me time to get tyres for fenders, hire two lines and get four yachtsmen to line-handle for me; not forgetting that I had to prepare food for them all as well as for the Advisor (pilot). We started in the evening and once into the Gatun Lake spent the night on a buoy. The next day we crossed the lake and dropped down into the Pacific. I kept my speed at 5 knots and was not going to be bullied into seeing how fast we could go. Amazingly the webcam enabled my family to watch *Shamaal* going through the lock. The most hazardous part of a transit is the arrival and departure of the Advisor in a high-sided pilot vessel.

Once on a mooring buoy off the Balboa Yacht Club my line-handlers departed and I was able to do the important final cheap shop for many months to come. Stocking up in Panama City on the Atlantic side is physically easier but there is a risk of mugging. We were at least two inches down on our marks as we departed for the Las Perlas islands 40 miles from Balboa. At 0400 a gentle sail through the anchored ships waiting their turn through the canal was a wonderful way to start out into the Pacific.

The Las Perlas islands are volcanic out-crops, some inhabited and all covered in jungle. The archipelago is about thirty miles by ten. Very few yachts seem to visit and there are some delightful, quiet and sheltered anchorages. A popular one called Espirito Santo had one other yacht and is totally surrounded by islands. In another I spent three days off a deserted beach with a freshwater stream. Getting ashore through the surf was sometimes a problem throughout my Pacific cruising. I have a two-metre GRP dinghy which I row and have had several capsizes, fortunately without injury or loss, except of pride. On Isla de San Josè, after wrapping chain round a coral head in a beautiful cove, I was looking for somewhere else to anchor, when I saw a signalling mirror in the jungle flashing at me. On the VHF I discovered there was a German living there. So I anchored off his house and met Dieter and Gerda who have lived the 'good life' there for many years. They had freshly picked fruit for sale.

My next passage was to the Galapagos, about 1000 miles; the recommendation is to get south before heading west. I set off with light southwesterlies that built over several days to give an uncomfortable sail and made getting west difficult. For seven days over the Easter period, we headed south until, within 40 miles of the Ecuador coast, a fisherman in an open boat disturbed my breakfast and the World Service news. It was time to head west. For the next six days I had one of those wonderful sails, just off the wind, sailing along the equator, although on some nights in the cold Humboldt current the air temperature dropped to 22°C and I needed a blanket.

I met Jenny and Chris and Maggie Elliott at Wreck Bay on Isla San Cristóbal Island. We were booked on an eight-day tourist trip and it was a good place to leave *Shamaal* at anchor. Clearing was a pleasure, but the sea lions took to using my dinghy for their snoozes usually filling it with water. If you sail to the Galapagos and do not do a guided tour you miss 90% of what these wonderful islands have to offer. It was a remarkable and memorable experience. After Jenny's departure I decided to visit Villamil on Isla Isabella as this is a good anchorage and another possibility to see more of the hinterland. I arranged with others to go by horse into the world's second largest crater. Then it was time to head towards the Marquesas, 3000 miles away.

This well-worn trade wind route is never straightforward. Boats a week ahead of our departure were becalmed for days. I headed south, as

Hiva Oa, Marquesas

recommended, and after several light days off the wind with numerous sail plans from spinnaker to cruising chute to twin head sails and goose-winging we finally got into the trades and for twelve days averaged nearly six knots with little effort under twin headsails. But then the trades went light and I would will the squalls to come in my direction. I joined an SSB net that was well run by several American yachts and 25 of us spread over 1000 miles clocked in daily, which gave me the chance to plot positions and compare daily runs.

Highlights included good daily runs of over 150 miles and catching fish for the pot. Since there is no fridge I grill a fillet on the day of the catch and make a curry in the pressure cooker, which lasts two days. I do not fish when there is fish in the pot. I use lures made from a pink plastic bag, with a double hook, a hand line and bicycle tube as shock absorber, leather gloves and a bottle of gin to kill the catch. The moon was full the day I left the Galapagos and the day I arrived in the Marquesas. Those wonderful long tropical nights brilliantly lit with the wind abaft the beam are very special.

The landfall on Fatu Hiva is spectacular and to see the green, steep and deeply-ravined hills after 27 days was very satisfying. Since I was keen to arrive in the unlit anchorage before last light I started the engine for the first time on the passage and motorsailed for the last few hours. Anchoring in the Bay of Virgins with its steep sides and volcanic towers

Twin headsails in the Pacific

was awe-inspiring. Much has been written about the friendly people of the Pacific. I spent a month visiting five of the islands. The two main ports of Atuona on Hiva Oa and Taiohae on Nuku Hiva had little appeal so I visited many of the isolated anchorages and had a few to myself. Some were well protected and out of the swell, in others the send was inconvenient. Good walks to waterfalls, with cool fresh water, and to ancient dwelling sites were very rewarding. At anchor the social life was unexpectedly good and I met like-minded people from many countries.

It is about 500 miles to the Tuamotu atolls where the entrances and anchoring require good timing and care. You need to select which of the many atolls to visit and I decided to start well to windward with Makemo. The four-day reach across the southeast trades was at times uncomfortable with breaking seas. On the final night I reduced to trysail, to slow down. Timing the passes with over six knots of ebb and two to three knots of flood is critical. The Admiralty Pilot has a formula using moonrise and set and coupled with tide tables that means you can make a fair estimate. But I was early at Makemo. The pass looked like the Swinge off Alderney at springs. After a short wait I gave it a go but chickened out in the approaches so headed back to sea and handed the main, which I later regretted. Then against a strong ebb, I crept through the seething mass under engine and foresail with the speed over the ground reduced to a knot and standing waves jumping into the cockpit. The main would have helped.

Anchoring in the lagoons is not easy. It is either very deep or very shallow with coral heads. A change of wind can turn what was a calm anchorage into a lee shore with a 20-30 mile fetch and breaking waves with coral close astern. In one of my atoll anchorages the coral heads were three metres high, not good for the chain to wrap around. A diving set is an essential item for clearing the chain. The highlight of my week in Makemo was a tiny enclosed lagoon near the northern entrance where I assisted a copra farmer for two days; hard work for him for little reward.

The second atoll was Kauehi, which has pearl farms. I joined in a First Communion service taken by a roving priest. Unaccompanied singing by 150 locals was followed by an amazing feast of seafood and other local delicacies such as coconut crab and terns' eggs. From the pearl farmer I learnt that the black pearl industry within many of the lagoons is booming and largely run by the Chinese.

I had heard about a blind pass on Toau atoll, which has a tiny population. Again an overnight downwind sail brought me off the entrance to the pass, which has not broken right through the reef into the lagoon. Entry was straightforward and I found a lovely enclosed anchorage bounded by reefs and a small palm-covered island on either side. Here I spent 12 days, initially carrying out maintenance, socialising with the few other yachts and playing volleyball every evening with the sum total of the local population. Once the other yachts had left I worked alongside the fisherman, Gaston, for eight days. This was a wonderful experience, helping gather fish, shellfish and lobster, butchering them for sale and loading them onto the monthly trading vessel. I helped the family with several tasks and they visited *Shamaal.* It blew up to 30 knots but the anchorage was calm and as the stream was always ebbing we did not swing.

After this I thought any other atoll would be an anti-climax. It was also time to head for Tahiti and prepare for Jenny's arrival. The 250 miles in pleasant off-wind conditions was typical of much of my Pacific sailing this year. I had noted an anchorage on the isthmus joining the two islands of Tahiti and I headed to this deep inlet, Port Phaeton. Tahiti has a barrier reef round most of its coastline and I selected a pass at the southern end of the island and decided to use the inshore passage to make my way to Port Phaeton. The pass was tame after my Tuamotu experiences. I looked for somewhere to anchor and found there was 20 metres right up to the land. Fortunately just before last light I found a narrow shelf within a few yards of the shore. The next day I went into Port Phaeton and anchored in mud for the first time in months. It was flat calm and there were trees close by on either side. Throughout the Society Islands we found the same difficulty with the depth rarely less than 20 metres. Without a windlass, this is a consideration! In Bora Bora we had one anchorage which was 30 metres, a lee shore and blowing F5; most unpleasant but the only place with a supermarket.

Jenny and I had a month together in the enchanting Society Islands. Geographically they are similar with a mountainous interior and a barrier reef with navigable passages surrounding most of the islands. We found some excellent anchorages at the head of long inlets and also on some sandy platforms near the reefs. The clear water and coral reefs teeming with fish make for good diving and snorkelling. We also enjoyed delicious fruit. After four months without fresh lettuce and tomatoes it was a treat to have salad again.

At the end of August Jenny returned to England and I set off immediately towards Aitutaki about 500 miles away. Initially the wind was F6-7 and we had a couple of good days rolling downwind, bypassing some seamounts. The pass through the reef into the harbour at Aitutaki is 20 metres wide, just over two metres deep at high water and not well marked. On the fourth day as we closed the small island the wind dropped and we missed the evening window. That night I hove-to knowing that I would not be able to get into the harbour the next day as strong onshore winds were forecast. In the morning we sailed into the lee of the atoll on the eastern side and just to break the monotony decided to anchor close into the reef and surf. This was a costly decision as during the afternoon the wind shifted back into the normal trades. It was time to weigh and heave-to again. However I could not shift the anchor. The water was 32 metres deep and in that depth I use a Brittany anchor, 15

Bora Bora, looking across from near the Bloody Mary restaurant

metres of chain and sufficient line just to keep the chain on the bottom. After 30 minutes of pulling and pushing under engine I grabbed my facemask and started to prepare the diving set when the line parted at the stemhead roller. At first light the next day we scraped into the Lilliputian harbour touching the bottom once. There was room to anchor fore and aft in shallow water, almost unheard of bliss in the Pacific. I enjoyed cycling round and chatting to the friendly people. There were more smallholdings with fruit and vegetables than I had met so far.

On all cruising trips you have to make difficult decisions on the route, where to go and what to miss. My next choice was quite easy. I did not like the look of the docking arrangement in Rarotonga and I knew that Palmerston was a fascinating place. It was an easy 200 miles downwind to Palmerston and I rounded the southern part of the atoll at first light after 48 hours at sea. I sailed along a line of yachts anchored on the edge of the reef and was met by a member of the Marsters family who showed me exactly where to drop the anchor. It was 12 metres deep and crystal clear. As we drifted back in the trade winds the stern had over 50 metres under the keel. We were on the edge! For the next week Paul and Kai Marsters included me in all their family activities. With some other yachtsmen we cleared a pass so that a British catamaran could scrape into the lagoon, one of the first yachts to achieve this since Victor Clarke's memorable experience in the 1950's. We laid a few moorings; we visited other islands in the atoll and collected arrowroot, taro and coconuts. We fished: first catching large sleeping flying fish before dawn and then using them as bait for a big catch using eight lines over the stern. We had lunch together everyday. I spent one day making Polynesian drums out of solid mahogany logs. In return I gave what I could and held a singsong in the school with the RCC songbook and donated a copy. Sadly it was time to move on.

On 12 September I weighed for the 400-mile downwind passage to Niue. It was a slow sail only interrupted by a few squalls on the third night. We closed the north coast on the fourth dawn and paralleled the high coral cliffs down to the port of Alofi. Fortunately there was a mooring buoy free. Anchoring here is a lottery in over 20 metres with deep gullies and coral boulders on the bottom. The surge is so bad alongside the jetty that you have to use a crane to hoist the dinghy onto the dockside. Niue is a large lump of coral about ten miles by six with remarkable geological features including coastal arches and chasms and caves in which you can duck dive from one to the next. Like many Pacific islands it is suffering from de-population. Also recently it was struck by a cyclone and the waves wrecked houses over 60 feet above sea level. It was an interesting and friendly stop but again after a few days it was time to move west.

The northern group of Tonga islands lie 250 miles downwind and I was keen to visit them. It was another slow passage under spinnaker or goose-winged main and foresail. A dawn arrival off the high cliffs along the northern coast of Vava'u coincided with the wind starting to pick up which would make clearing alongside in Neiafu difficult. So like several others we selected a sheltered attractive anchorage and sat out a three-day blow enjoying the scenery and the company of friends. The Tonga archipelago needs time and I decided to return next year. However I did spend a week at anchor in a lagoon at Hunga where I got to know the villagers in a very poor and unsupported community.

I thought I would do a brief visit to Fiji to whet the appetite. The passage is about 500 miles with some fearsome reefs. Lieutenant William Bligh RN sailed through here after the mutiny with fewer aids than we have and I initially planned to take a similar passage through the reefs in the Lau island group but we had had a slow sail and it would have meant a night transit so instead on the third evening we rounded the southern end of the reefs with surf riding high. The following day a volcanic island lay in our path and I decided to try to anchor in its lee. Totoya Island is a crater breached by the sea with a surrounding reef with a few unmarked passes. I was not prepared to use the engine and so we entered the pass exactly as the sun set. In the diminishing light, with 30 metres still under the keel as we approached the shore, I reluctantly decided to head out to sea again. At dawn two days later we entered the totally enclosed harbour at Suva. I had avoided the weekend but found I had arrived on Independence Day. No one seemed concerned about clearing and I dealt with the vast amount of paperwork the following day. Suva has a wonderful, typically colonial yacht club, which is the focal point for the cruising fraternity and is only a 20-minute walk to town. It was a good place to do odd jobs and stock up before heading south towards New Zealand.

Forty miles south of Suva lies Kadavu Island and the Astrolabe Reef. We left Suva on 18 October with the aim of visiting North Astrolabe Reef, which is a ring of coral about three miles in diameter. However once we got into its unmarked passage I became uneasy as even at low water none of the reef was exposed and with F4 blowing there would have been little protection from the seas. Reluctantly I sailed out of what looked a very interesting, rarely visited spot. With six hours of daylight remaining I sailed on to a passage in the Great Astrolabe Reef and spent several days visiting a number of small islands as well as Kadavu Island and their delightful inhabitants. There I did *servuservu*, an important Fijian custom in which the visitor presents some kava root to the Chief and in return is given permission to visit the village and have its protection.

The passage from either Tonga or Fiji to New Zealand is just over one thousand miles of open ocean. Timing for departure is important in order to try and avoid strong southwesterly winds once one is clear of the southeast trade winds. I picked my window and after church on 23 October made my excuses to the kind Fijians who had invited me to lunch, weighed and sailed along the coast of Kadavu Island. The island remained in sight for 48 hours. There was no wind but it was sunny and I was able to get on with maintenance and even dived on the hull to give it a good scrub. Suddenly the wind came in and the daily mileages picked up. So did the wind, which slowly went round to the south to give six days of beating into F4-7. A foul 1-2 knot current made tacking through 160 degrees very painful. I had two major concerns: firstly the bearings in the reduction gear box on the steering system were seizing, making the wheel hard to move and secondly, splits were appearing in the foresail where I had removed the rotten ultra-violate protective strip. Both needed nursing.

Later when the forecast southwest winds came in I was able to lay North Cape, an area that should be avoided with a disturbed confused sea. Once in the lee of North Island the seas flattened. The landfall was well and truly cheered. Off the Bay of Islands the wind disappeared. Again for 48 hours we either crept along or hove-to to sleep. Starting the engine was an option but I saw no point. Finally a good spinnaker run down the coast and at 0100 on 8 November we entered Whangarei River to clear customs and to lay-up for a spell on land.

The highlights of this amazing year must be meeting the delightful people that inhabit these isolated islands and the good company of the cruising fraternity. Excellent sailing generally down wind in warm temperatures. Also not having a programme and deadlines to meet made for flexible departures and no pressure to move on except the need to reach New Zealand prior to the cyclone season.

Gibraltar to Whangarei, New Zealand
Hours underway 3581.5 hours
Engine hours 311.5 (none during ocean crossings)
Gallons of fuel used: 64
Average speed: Ocean passages 4.7 knots. Overall 4.2 knots
Mileage: 14,302
Nights at sea: 132
Nights at anchor: 209
Nights on a mooring: 21
Nights alongside: 1

Breakages/defects
Spinnaker halyard parted (26 years old)
Spinnaker sheet parted (26 years old)
Inner forestay tack fitting parted after several thousand miles. Poor fitting (my fault)
Engine water pump replaced (5 years old)
Whitlock reduction steering gear box bearings out of alignment (27 years old)
Ultra-violate strip on foresail disintegrated (9 years old)
GRP dinghy many glass fibre repairs to gunwale and bottom (27 years old).

CANAL DU MIDI

by Stephen Lennane

Right now seems to be an appropriate moment to write up the log of the first part of our cruise this year towards the Trafalgar meet.

I am alone on board, Sue having just thrown me some lunch across the three metres that separates the stern from the *quai d'attente*. We arrived last night at Menton on the Franco-Italian border where we have a house, with a warning of strong northeasterly winds arriving next day. Having made secure to the heavy harbour chain at the bow, leaving an alarming distance to jump to the shore, we went home for a bath and bed. Early in the morning realizing that the wind was getting very serious we went back to *Arcadia* to find various kind people trying to keep her off the pontoon in a gale that had arrived from the southeast and had allowed the harbour chain to move. As I write the wind is subsiding and all that is left is to count the damage – an indented toe rail at the bow and a bent stern ladder. The hydrovane rudder is locked in such a position that, were we to leave, we would miss Trafalgar and describe a circle towards Barcelona or even worse to Agde at the end of the Canal du Midi, which is where our problems began.

There is a new tendency in advanced surgical circles to give a lecture along the lines of 'My mistakes and where I went wrong'. Quite properly, given behind closed doors and with an American lawyer detector humming away on full power, it is an opportunity for colleagues to learn from others' mistakes. In this spirit I offer an account of our experiences in the Canal du Midi, which is summed up in the title 'Don't'. Put in a nutshell, we were the wrong boat for the passage and all our problems stemmed from this. However I would like to point out that many RCC boats have passed through the canal with no problems. Better judgment and, I hope, better luck. We did have our doubts but the first lockkeeper on the Canal Lateral du Rhône assured us we would get to the Mediterranean easily.

Arcadia draws 1.4 metres; the official depth is 1.6 metres though they do occasionally say it is 1.5 metres. We waited until April to make the transit on the basis that there would be more water then after the winter rains. Mistake number one. Fuller research would have revealed that the water levels are entirely artificial and any variation in level comes from the individual lockkeeper's control of the water. Judging by exposed tree roots the levels can vary by 0.3 metre in adjacent reaches. Thus we went aground several times. Downstream of all the locks there is a shallow patch but this was not generally a problem as we learnt to drive through the soft mud. Perhaps we should have had an echosounder that read in minus metres. In one lock near Carcasonne we were left high and dry by about a half a metre and the lock had to be re-flooded to allow us to get out into the middle and afloat again. Not our fault this one. They need to dredge the locks more frequently.

The real problem is not the depth but the underwater debris – reputedly there is a car somewhere in the canal but given the lack of water even a Deux Chevaux would show. More likely is the presence of old fridges, supermarket trolleys and so on. When the boat was lifted scratches along the keel up to about 12 inches above the lowest part and a chunk out of the leading edge of the keel were revealed. Occasionally the boat would rise gently out of the water as we went over a tree root but only once did we hit something really hard.

Arcadia leaving Pauillac for the Canal du Midi

Mistake two was not taking on board the fact that the canals were built for metal barges. The edges are pretty unforgiving to GRP and the oval shape of the locks ensures that there is a knuckle that has to be negotiated before coming to rest in each lock. Given some 159 locks, if you only makes an error in 1% then there is bound to be some damage. I had ample time later to polish out most of the scratches in the gel coat. We had fenders and a tyre but really should have had twice the number. In fact we should have resembled the Michelin man after a good lunch.

Mistake three was to take the mast with us. A lot of boats do seem to do this but we took ours because we weren't sure which exit from the canal we were going to use. With an overhang of more than a metre at either end the boat is significantly longer than before. The protruding delicate equipment made manoeuvring into locks with other boats interesting. It would have been sensible to have reversed the radio aerials and removed the masthead lights though there is little we could have done to protect the furling gear.

The next miscalculation was to underestimate the ability of hire boats to cause damage. To be fair, most of the users were doing quite well for the first time afloat and after only ten minutes instruction they had to learn fast. Unfortunately they seem to treat a boat like a car and anyone who has driven in France will be able to visualise the scene. They seem to forget that a boat has no brakes and is subject to the wind. Having lost the masthead lights into the waters of a lock as a result of being hit for the fifth time by one hire boat, we would not thereafter follow one into a lock until we had seen the stern line made fast. The hirers had no trouble with the bowline as they just steered for the side. Then they turned round to find the stern somewhere else, usually across the lock. With the protection of dodgem-like all round rubber and a no-excess insurance policy they don't need to mind too much who or what they hit. Going through the canal in the French holiday season does not bear thinking about.

Following on from this we should never have left the boat unattended but we had to go back to England for two weeks. We berthed her in the wide basin at Carcasonne but when we returned the side of the hull was marked all along with black rubber where hire boats had obviously lost control. I'm glad I wasn't there.

I suppose our biggest problem was just bad luck. We had stopped for the night with the bow gently turned towards the bank and just aground as usual. Because of the shallow water it is rare to be able to go alongside the bank. Next morning the water level had dropped by about six inches and we were hard aground. Going astern did not free us but something must have been drawn onto the propeller, there was a nasty clunk and the coupling of the shaft to the engine gave way leaving the engine merrily going round but no wash from the propeller. Here was the true meaning of up a creek without a paddle.

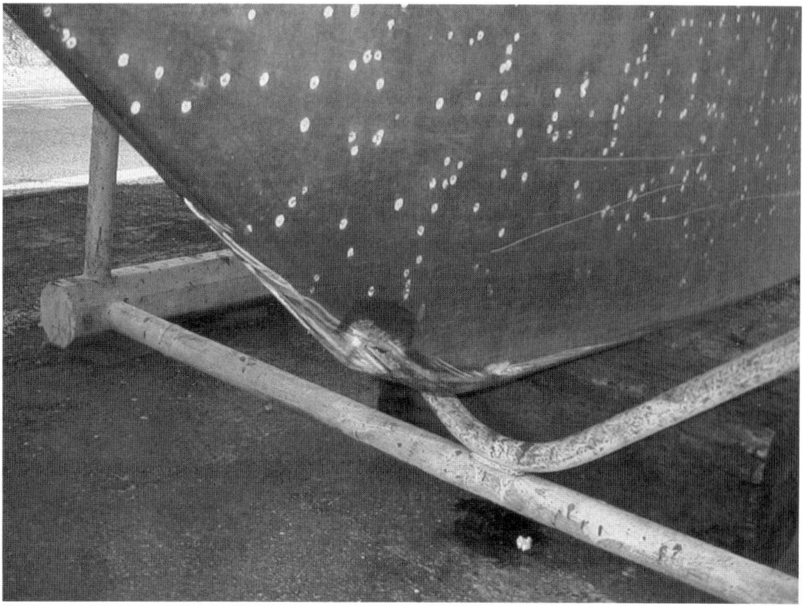

Arcadia showing the damage from underwater objects

We hitched a tow from a passing hire boat full of Americans. They were delighted to help but I could not get it across to them that we weighed eight tons, had no brakes and that all the furling gear would be badly bent if they suddenly stopped. They were very enthusiastic but I am not sure that the American psyche is capable of appreciating the need to travel at only one knot. We tried an alongside tow but of course the many narrow bridges stopped that. After an exciting trip we came to a yard where there appeared to be a crane and we stopped there as I thought that *Arcadia* would have to be lifted. We tied up temporarily alongside a large Dutch barge and there, fortunately, our luck changed. It turned out that amazingly the barge owner and his wife were both master mariners and ship's engineers. A quarter of the barge was devoted to an engineering workshop. The Dutchman agreed to make us a temporary repair but he first insisted that I dived down to check that the propeller was not fouled. The waters are somewhat murky but it is nice to know that the discharge of sewage into the canal is absolutely forbidden. It is not so nice to know that not one of the many hire boats has a holding tank and in any case there are no pump-out stations anywhere. Never have I appreciated a shower more. The kind Dutchman got us going, albeit slowly. We were only allowed low revs and could not to go astern, which made stopping in the remaining 25 locks quite a test of judgement. However I was very grateful, as I had had visions of having to hire a boat so I could tow *Arcadia* to the nearest proper shipyard.

We limped down the remaining 30 miles to Agde at the mouth of the river Hérault where at last we could see the Mediterranean. The boat was lifted to reveal that the A-frame supporting the propeller shaft was twisted and there was a large chunk out of the leading edge of the keel. The yard was very busy and we had to wait our turn. We lived on board on the hard for 10 days before they found time to do the repairs but not before, in desperation, Sue and I had started the awful job of removing the rudder.

When we did at last get out to sea I noticed that the GPS and Autohelm had stopped working, possibly because the electrics had been damaged during the repair work but no matter, the south coast of France is not difficult to navigate. And the heads blocked at the same time.

I am sorry for this catalogue of setbacks, so unusual amongst the daring and successful exploits that usually appear in Roving Commissions. Some years ago a Flag Officer who shall be nameless came on board calling for gin after an extremely trying passage. During the ensuing conversation he made a remark, which has stayed with me and seems relevant now. 'Members of the RCC seem to be good at getting themselves out of situations they should never have got themselves into'.

And should an American lawyer read about my errors I am afraid he will have to go away empty handed as I would like to point out they damaged no one else and I blame only myself.

Arcadia is a Vancouver 34 long-keeled cutter, which eventually arrived in time for the Trafalgar meet somewhat worse for wear but at least with new hoses in the heads.

SOUNDS FUN: A CRUISE AROUND THE MARLBOROUGH SOUNDS

by David Mitchell

The Claymore Cup was awarded for this cruise

I had to be in Florida for a family wedding in April and before that I wanted to spend four weeks trekking in the hills and mountains of north South Island, New Zealand. This left February to explore the Marlborough Sounds. I thought it might be a bit of a rush, but then we retired folk are used to rushing around.

The Marlborough Sounds are one of New Zealand's four great cruising areas – the others are Fiordland and Stewart Island in South Island and the Bay of Islands and the Hauraki Gulf with the Mercury Islands in North Island. The Sounds are on the northeast corner of South Island and lie like a broken, arthritic hand pointing northeast across the Cook Strait towards North Island and Wellington. This would be my third visit to the area, though my first by sea, and would be another opportunity of following in the footsteps of The Great Man (TGM), Captain James Cook. I had my fair share of gales but the sun shone almost every day. The steep sides to the sounds generated winds that created a wide gamut of feelings from exciting and exhilarating to frustrating and boring, throwing in enough 'Shit!' moments – when buttocks crimp, palms sweat and knees weaken – to keep me on my toes. Taken as a whole, it was a fun three weeks.

The Cook Strait is New Zealand's second windiest area, after the southwest tip of South Island. Look at a chart and it is easy to see why. The strait is shaped like a lavatory on its side. The bowl, here known as Tasman Bay, is about 60 miles across and wide open to the Tasman Sea – next stop Australia. Beneath the bowl, the pipe narrows and goes 'round the bend' to the south, passing the Sounds, before bending back to the east and exiting the strait. At its narrowest point, only 14 miles separate the Sounds from the Wellington mainland. The prevailing wind is from the southwest; the combination of the high ground on both islands and the bends squeeze and accelerate the wind so that a benign ten knots off Cape Farewell on the west coast can become 40 knots on the east coast. Sixty knots is not uncommon and wind against tide throws up the usual horrid, short seas. Overfalls off the principal headlands create conditions more akin to the Channel Islands than the South Pacific.

I left Auckland on 3 February taking the long way around the north coast and down the west side of North Island, as the odds of having an easterly through the Cook Strait are about the same as finding a pearl in your oyster. TGM also went anticlockwise but I have a nagging suspicion that this was more luck than judgment.

There are no real anchorages on the west coast; in fact it is low lying and shallow and must have been a pig to sail down as TGM surveyed the coast. He sighted North Cape on 10 December 1769 and sailed non-stop to Admiralty Bay in the Sounds. I too sailed non-stop but to Nelson, a thriving port and yachting base on the northwest of South Island. In 2004, on my circumnavigation of New Zealand, I had experienced three gales by the time I reached this latitude. This time I was lucky, kicking off with a gentle broad reach north in an easterly ten knots. This veered to the southeast on day three and life became lively, as the wind increased to over 20 knots. Reefed down, *Ondarina* charged on over the blessedly calm sea at six knots. A 'champagne moment' came when the perfect, snow-capped cone of Mount Egmont, 2518m, (named by TGM after John Percival, Earl of Egmont) appeared above the clouds and haze. The trailing white cloud, perhaps the one that inspired the first Maori settlers to give New Zealand the name of *Te Aotearoa* (the Land of the Long White Cloud), indicated a northerly wind. This came in later and helped *Ondarina* to run down the final 70 miles into Nelson. Actually, the conditions were horrid. Thick haze obscured the land, making it tricky to pick out any landmarks, the bay was shoaling and I was running onto a lee shore. On top of this, the entrance to the harbour requires two sets of leading lines and both the harbour and the town are set back behind a low shingle bank.

The Sounds are about 30 miles east of Nelson and stretch for another 30 miles from D'Urville Island on the west to Cape Koamaru on the east. The longest sound (Pelorus) runs inland for about 25 miles. Haverlock and Picton are the only places where stores and fuel are available, so I stocked up in Nelson and left on the ebb the next afternoon. I had hoped to make D'Urville Island, but the wind veered to the northeast and we tacked slowly up the coast. Slowly was the word and with less than an hour of daylight left I ducked into Croisilles Harbour on the mainland, passing my first green-lipped mussel farm to port before anchoring in seven metres in the company of one other yacht.

Although strictly not in the Marlborough Sounds, the anchorage (grandly named Oyster Bay) was typical of those I found later. Through the bush

I could pick out the line of a rough track linking a clutch of single-storey timber-built 'baches' (the term for a New Zealand holiday cottage, which could be a hut with no water or electricity or a six-bedroom house with swimming pool and helicopter pad). The grey-green bush rose to a variety of steep-sided ridges that glowed in the setting sun. Peace reigned. Dark green and brown-striped plantations of pine trees (New Zealand's highest export earner) scattered the hillsides. There were no power cables, no telephone wires, no rumble of traffic; just the occasional whine of a fizz-boat returning from a fishing trip.

The holding was good. This is not always the case and I came warned that anchoring could be a nightmare because of the depth and poor holding. For flooded river valleys, the sounds are surprisingly deep and can drop quickly to over 40 metres. Because of the steepness of the hills, when it rains the run-off is so fast that it carries the silt out into the bay but drops the gravel forming a shallow shelf. My first 'gravel-moment' was a novel experience – but more on that later. Fortunately, most anchorages are ringed by moorings laid by bache owners, yacht clubs and the odd hotel. The New Zealand yachtie's respect for buoy ownership is such that few will pick up an obviously empty mooring if it is not theirs. I have no such scruples and grabbed as many as I could, muttering a grateful thanks to the absent owner. February is a good month to be in the Sounds – the weather is warm and the summer holiday crowds have gone

Jules-Sébastien-César Dumont d'Urville, to give him his full name, led a French naval expedition to the Pacific from 1826 to 1829. In 1827, fifty years after Cook, he arrived off D'Urville Island, naming Croisilles Harbour after his tutor. The west coast of the island is jagged and rugged, battered by the westerly swell sweeping in across the Tasman. There are two main harbours, Greville on the west and Port Hardy on the north. I sailed up the west coast in a gentle, five-knot westerly (so gentle that at times I had to motor to keep way on in the swell), admiring the rocky-brown islets and the rugged cliffs. I kept a wary eye on spots where the occasional splurging white sea marked rocks lurking unseen below the surface. Then I ran into Greville Harbour – just a circular bay with sides of pale yellow-green pasture and what looked like a farmhouse tucked in low behind a sandy bank and sheltered by a few trees. I aimed for the southeast corner, where a post marked the end of a shallow reef and a bar into the inner anchorages. Here I picked up a club buoy. The bush lay thick around the anchorage. There were no baches and no paths, just the splash of a small waterfall. It was a funny feeling, hanging there with little to see except for the steep-sided bush and nowhere to go for a walk ashore. I could see the clouds zipping over the ridges but down in the anchorage all seemed still. That was until the first vortex came whistling down, ruffling the water. It spun *Ondarina* around and just as quickly shot off leaving us wondering 'What caused that?' It set the pattern for most anchorages.

TGM thought D'Urville Island was a peninsula. Jules d'Urville knew better. He discovered French Pass. Here the channel narrows to about 300 metres but just below the surface a shallow reef reaches out from the island leaving barely 50 metres through which the water runs at up to eight knots. The underwater profile is a serious mess. The depth in the narrowest part varies from 18 metres to six. From the west, the approach is around 60 metres deep but to port a bank rises to 2.4 metres, marked, thank goodness, by a green buoy at its western end. To the east of the pass, the seabed drops into a massive 100-metre hole ringed like a doughnut to a depth of 15 metres, except for a long bank that rises to four metres. Anyone who has sailed into the Morbihon in South Brittany on a spring flood can imagine the effect the seabed has on the water sluicing over it at eight knots.

I arrived two hours after low water, about an hour too late for slack water, and already the water was pouring through the pass. I was running the engine in case the swirling mass carried *Ondarina* into a back-eddy. In Auckland, I had seen the damage to a 30-metre gin palace where the professional skipper had 'got it wrong' and was swept onto the reef. We shot through in that heady euphoria that balances precariously on the knife-edge between excitement and terror.

D'Urville Island's east coast falls less steeply to the sea. In places, the bush remains cleared and there are baches and the odd hotel. I hoped to anchor in Catherine Cove and climb D'Urville Peninsula. When he had finished his coastal survey TGM anchored just outside in Admiralty Bay and, according to his biographer, climbed the D'Urville Peninsula to spy out the land. When I reached Catherine Cove, I realized that he could not have landed here as he would have seen French Pass and realized

Tribute to Cook

that he was on an island. This was his third survey mistake – the other two were thinking that that Banks Peninsula was an island and that Stewart Island was a peninsula!

After lunch, I pressed on, keen to tuck into Port Ligar at the head of Pelorus Sound before the forecast westerly gale arrived. The 12-mile trip was a frustrating mixture of sailing and motoring. Mussel floats ringed Port Ligar taking up more space than shown on the chart and limiting the shallow space to anchor. My attempt to anchor off the old timber-pile jetty provided my first 'gravel-moment'. I gave up and picked up a buoy in Waterfall Bay. It was a boisterous night with the wind whistling down the narrow cove. My fear was that the buoy's owner would return. There was a second buoy but at low water it looked horribly close to the beach. I spotted another in an adjoining bay, which was even more open to the northwest; this was Plan B.

The next morning's forecast gave another gale warning and with the pressure down to 996mb, I thought they could be right. I left under a beautiful clear sky to explore Pelorus Sound, which winds inland for 25 miles. Initially the sailing was tedious and frustrating as we ran, gybed, beat and reached, all within about 200 metres! Once out in the sound, conditions settled down slightly and we had a glorious sail that at times was fast and furious. I learnt the hard way how the wind can blast out of innocent-looking bays at about 30 knots, throwing in 180° wind shifts for fun. There was no time to reef. It was a question of holding on and hoping for the best. We tore down the sound under full sail, the lee-rail under and spray from the bow-wave flying across the foredeck. With no fetch, it was like sailing on a lake. The prevailing wind was west to northwest but it could come from anywhere influenced by the neighbouring high ground that rose to just under 800 metres. Once past the offending bay, life returned to normal until the next blast.

I had meant to move about 14 miles to another anchorage to sit out the gale but the sail was so exciting that I kept going and going, threading between the mess of interlocking peninsulas. The wind followed the valley as I gybed *Ondarina,* spying out bays and coves for possible anchorages on the return journey. Instead of following Pelorus Sound to Haverlock, I hardened up and turned east into Kenepuru Sound. The attraction was Portage Bay, where I had parked my camper van during my first visit in 2002 and where I had spent a night whilst walking the 80-kilometre Queen Charlotte Track in 2003. As Portage is open to the northwest, I tacked into Mills Bay on the north side and anchored in a lovely cove. The crescent-shaped beach promised a sandy bottom and a wealth of tree ferns and the bush looked liked a decent habitat for birds.

After a peaceful night, I woke to more sun. The glass was up to 1006mb and there was no more talk of gales. Brilliant. In a northwesterly ten knots, I pulled up the anchor and enjoyed a lovely exploration to the head of the sound. I could see the rough track I had taken in Hannibal

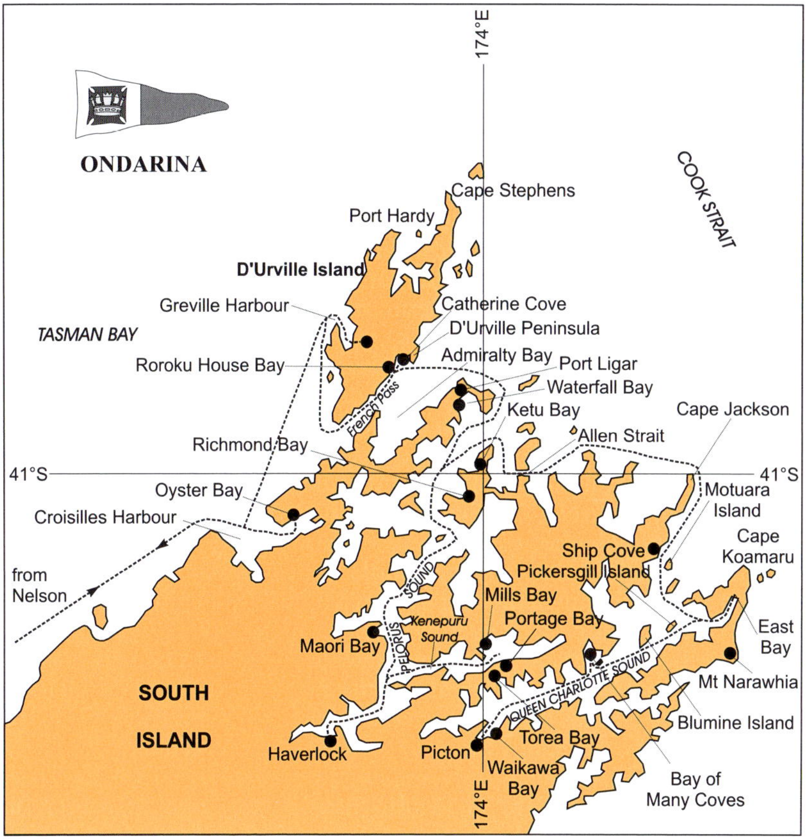

(so named as he had trouble getting over the hills) when I walked to Ship Cove and back in a day (56 kilometres, a personal record that I have no intention of beating). I could see the ridgeline I had walked on the Queen Charlotte Track. I returned and picked up a buoy in Portage Bay. This completed my personal, travel-trilogy by vehicle, foot and now by sail. The emotion of the moment surprised me. The Maori manhandled their canoes (*wakas*) over the Torea Saddle that divides Kenepuru Sound from Queen Charlotte Sound, saving a round trip of about 60 miles – well worth the effort.

The sail out of Kenepuru was the most fun of the cruise. We were hard on the apparent 15-knot wind all the way. I expected to have to tack but every time I neared the south shore we picked up a 50° wind-shift, which allowed *Ondarina* to point up to the north side. Here we were headed and bore off until freed again. A scattering of posts marked the channel up to Haverlock but the mud banks move and I followed a line of returning motorboats and zigzagged up the channel. Haverlock claims to be 'The Green-lipped Mussel Capital of the World' – not difficult when the mussel is unique to New Zealand. Flat-bottomed, aluminium work-boats loaded to the gunwales with vast white sacks of mussels are a common sight in the sounds. Haverlock is tidal and has a small, dredged marina with space for a few visitors. Like most marinas in New Zealand, it belongs to the local council. Facilities are what you might expect in a tourist village – garage, fuel dock, small store, post office, clinic and a few places to eat. I had a 'chef's gourmet selection of grilled green-lipped mussels'. The mussels are vast, seriously chewy and the less said about that particular meal, the better.

I caught the afternoon ebb and motored back the way I had come in – well, not exactly, as without any lead-boats I had to execute a few hasty pirouettes in the channel to avoid the hidden mud. Then we tacked slowly up Hikapu Reach finally anchoring at the head of Maori Bay, a delightful, two-mile, low-lying inlet. I could see two small baches that blended with the trees – unlike many, which are amazingly painted in unsympathetic colours (reds, blues, white and yellows). The post motor-boat chugged slowly into the inlet and a timber dinghy pulled out from the shore. Both stopped, floating as if on a mirror; there was a short chat, hands reached out passing over in-coming and out-going mail and they parted. I thought I could hear a fast-flowing stream and peered through my binoculars. Eventually I realized the noise came from the massed ranks of male cicadas – a bright green, hard-skinned insect the size of a ten-penny piece that claps its clear, spotted wings together to attract a mate.

I spent one more night in Pelorus Sound, this time on a buoy in Richmond Bay after a tedious afternoon with more motor than sail. The 40-miles round and into Queen Charlotte Sound was an excellent sail with fun pilotage amongst the islands. We twisted round them and sneaked through a narrow, shallow channel ridiculously called Allen Strait – most likely an illustration of wry New Zealand humour. Rounding Cape Jackson reminded me of a sleigh-ride down the Swinge in the Channel Islands, as the two-knot flood tide hurtled through the overfalls caused by the rock shelf that rises from 66 metres to five and extends for nearly a mile. A few years earlier, a Russian cruise ship had tried the same route in the dark. 'Not a good move, Boris!' Now it lies in about 30 metres and must be a great dive.

TGM came to Queen Charlotte Sound on five separate occasions between 1770 and 1777, staying a total of 200 days. He first arrived on 16 January – I was there on 16 February – naming the sound in honour of George III's wife. He anchored off Ship Cove where the local Maori made him welcome – unlike the Maori on the south side of the sound who ambushed and killed nine crew off HMS *Adventure*, captained by

Tobias Furneaux. I passed between Ship Cove and Motuara Island where Cook raised the Union flag claiming the country in the name of George III.

The afternoon forecast gave another gale warning. On the chart, I selected East Bay as a sheltered anchorage from where I could climb Narawhia (558m). This was the most likely hill that TGM climbed to discover that New Zealand was two islands. I beat up to the head of the bay. By now the wind was gusting around 25 knots and anchoring proved a major 'gravel experience'. In fact, the 45lb CQR slid through the gravel so smoothly that there were no vibrations up the chain. I gave up after the second attempt by which time the plough had a brilliant, shiny sheen. Later I heard that East Bay has the reputation of being the worst anchorage in the Marlborough Sounds. I ran back out of the bay under main, gybing at times, slipped through the narrow passes inside Pickersgill and Blumine islands and ended up in the Bay of Many Coves. This looked more promising and a cluster of smart new mooring buoys off a hotel beckoned me over.

The gale arrived the next day. Gusts up to 40 knots shook *Ondarina* and pushed her over whilst the Ampair wind-generator spun so fast I thought I should plug it into the national grid. I watched as each vortex, scarcely ten metres wide, shot over the water lifting spray and occasionally rattling the tree ferns when it touched the steep, bush-covered cliff only 15 metres off our bow. I looked up at the masthead and was surprised to see the club burgee hanging there like a bedraggled daddy-long-legs. I switched on the wind instruments, which showed three knots, illustrating just how local these squalls can be.

Typically a day of calm followed the gale-bound day and I had to motor the nine miles down the sound into Picton Harbour. This is the ferry terminal from Wellington and a major tourist hub. There is a small marina and a better selection of shops than Haverlock. The main marina is over the peninsula in Waikawa Bay.

For two days, I explored other anchorages in the sound, including Torea Bay, which is the south side of the portage. On my walk up to the saddle, I passed a mass of Maori school children, here to learn about their roots. Various *iwis* (tribes) from North Island settled the sounds in the seventeenth century. After Cook's last visit in 1777, few *pakhia* (white people) visited the Sounds, as there were no whales or seals to attract them. The farming settlers arrived in the early 1900s. They burnt and cut the bush but the soil is light and sandy. Some tried to plough but by the 1960s, most 'pastoralists' had given up. I welcome the return of the bush to the abandoned land and despair the lack of mature trees. However, the good news is that numerous *rimu* trees (a native evergreen and excellent nurse tree) are standing above the bush and so in time the bigger hardwood trees may return.

The reason for hanging around Picton was to wait for Valerie and

David Mitchell with David and Valerie Dobson

David Dobson who were touring South Island by car. We had a fun time exploring the vineyards around Marlborough and I introduced them to the vagaries of sailing in the Sounds. Richard, a friend and keen sailor, also came along. His family settled the Marlborough area four generations previously. As we tacked out of Picton Harbour, we watched the local dinghies and cruisers racing around the buoys. Richard said that racing could be tricky. He had once gybed accidentally in a squally windshift then gybed back at which point his timber mast snapped below deck. We returned under staysail and reefed main and watched a young, wet-suited boy in an Optimist running down the harbour alone and without a watch-boat. He gybed repeatedly, clearly just for the hell of it. No wonder the country produces such good sailors.

On 24 February, I headed back towards Nelson. First stop was a proper visit to Ship Cove. The holding is horrible but there is a club buoy. This was occupied by *Moonlight Express*, a 34-foot sloop that I had met before. Chrissie and Mike welcomed me alongside and later a sleek 45-foot motorboat came alongside *Ondarina*. It is easy to see why Cook liked Ship Cove: the sandy, crescent-shaped beach is an excellent landing place, the shore is flat and ideal for tents for the sick and for the carpenters, sail makers and other specialists who would be kept busy during each refit. There is a bubbling stream for fresh water, timber for spars and cooking, plenty of fish and most importantly, a friendly *iwi*, who made Cook welcome.

In 1913, the people of New Zealand commemorated Cook's visits by erecting a memorial – they called it a 'tribute'. It is not original in design, nor pretty. It is a five-metre high, white-painted, roughcast concrete trig-point guarded by a pair of cannon. On top, is a reproduction fisherman's anchor. Each side has a grey marble plaque. The front has what purports to be TGM's crest, which the good people made up. It is bizarre. At the top, a hand on a bent right arm, dressed in a captain's blue jacket and white shirt, rises out of thick yellow rope. The hand clasps a flagstaff flying the Union Jack. A banner with 'CIRCA ORBEM' straddles the flagstaff. All this is obvious but the branch of leaves rising out of the rope on either side of the arm has me beaten. Below the arm, sitting on a blue shield (the same colour as the arm, saving paint) is half a globe showing the Pacific Ocean with glimpses of the fringing land painted brown. The vertical line through the centre of the globe, I assume, depicts the International Dateline. (In reality, the 180° meridian passes just east of New Zealand.) Above and below the globe is a single gold star. And at the bottom are the words *'nil intentatum reliquit'* (which loosely translates to 'never give up'). I beached my dinghy where The Great Man must have stood, walked where he walked and drank from the same stream. All good stuff.

I waited until the afternoon to catch the flood back to Pelorus Sound but made a mistake and had some current against me. In the flat calm, there was no alternative but to motor and at 2000 I picked up a buoy in a cove on the north side of Ketu Bay. The forecast for the next day was northwest 15 knots, but the outlook was an unfriendly 40 knots, so I chose Catherine Cove again. There I was asked to leave, as the hotel was running a fishing competition involving 23 motorboats. The next bay had a selection of buoys. I ignored the smart club buoy and picked up an alternative whose mussel-clad mooring-line indicated an absent owner.

I sat out the next day, gale-bound. White clouds skimmed over the ridge and *Ondarina* spun to the occasional 35-knot gust. I wondered about the mussel-clad line even though the mooring licence requires that the line be checked every two years. I watched the fishing competitors moving out. Nothing stirred around the bay; the neighbouring baches stared at me through closed curtains. I read.

In spite of another gale warning I decided to leave in the afternoon of 28 February and catch the flood through French Pass. I slipped the buoy at 1400 and sailed around the southern half of Admiralty Bay, killing time. The wind was a gentle breeze from the northeast and whilst it was fun tacking around the bay it had little to offer: a few farms, only one mooring-buoy and no anchorages, as the depth is over 40 metres. By 1600, I was impatient to reach Nelson in daylight and bore away for the pass. I had memories of sneaking back into the Solent against the ebb, as I hugged the mainland shore to avoid the tide. An eddy gave us a little push. Eventually, we had to come out for the narrow pass and I engaged the engine to push us through against the two-knot current. Three dolphins joined us for 30 fun minutes. I sang, clapped my hands and beat the topsides to encourage them. One, with several nicks in his dorsal fin and scratches down his flanks, came right out of the water on several occasions and eyeballed me. What wonderful moments. A pod of about ten came leaping up through the pass and my three joined them.

The wind filled in from the south and we were on the wind for the last leg, eventually following the low shingle bank that leads down to the harbour. As the sun set, I motored down the leading lights and came alongside in the marina. Then I prepared for four weeks trekking in the mountains. The 19-day cruise around the Sounds had produced some testing sailing. There had been frustrating moments and great moments. Above all, it had been fun.

Ondarina is an Ohlson 35 fitted out for single-handed sailing. She is now back in Auckland looking for a buyer and David has bought a Bowman 48.

A COUPLE OF GEMS

by Keith Holland-Gems

Time for Bed

Boats were asleep, spars bare, cockpits covered, the yards crowded with cradles – a sea of bottoms. The September cruise cut short by reality – Pam's rehearsals, a first night and the return of the prodigal daughter. Nobody sails in November! It was Wednesday 3 November 2004, St Malo. A grey misty dawn, south-southwest F4 with poor visibility gradually improving to five miles as the mist lifted into thin stratus under a watery sun too weak to burn it off.

In order to catch the tide east of the Minquiers, 0800 was the right time to leave. We were frustrated by a bloody-minded Frenchman in a dirty grey motorboat who followed us for a mile before crossing our bows and demanding that we return to pay our harbour dues. We offered €20 but he was adamant and lifted his phone to call the police. One hour later and only €5 lighter we were in the same spot. We made up the delay with a strong wind on the port quarter, centreboard up and an easy motion. Leaving the SE and NE Minquiers buoys to port, we were through the South Channel and into St Helier an hour before dusk, to lie on the outer pontoon excluded from the port by the tidal step.

Thursday, up and away early, a southwest F4-5 to take us westward round La Corbière light on the southwest tip of Jersey, then east of the Channel Islands with a quartering wind in time to clear the Alderney Race on a fair tide and with two hours to get through the west-going shipping lanes before dark, well on the way home to Christchurch.

Not so! The wind was westerly so progress was slow. As we rounded La Corbière, it veered to northwest and finally north. No hope of getting to the Race in time – and who would want to tack across the Channel in lumpy seas in a cold northerly, losing way at each crashing wave. Where to go? The Channel Islands' tides dictate direction and there are only three tenable harbours in the entire group. We had an exhausting tack to

Guernsey arriving tired, cold, wet and demoralised as a grey night enclosed St Peter Port. Forecast northerly F4 occasionally 5. We decided to eat well for the first time since leaving London and to fly home the next day.

'Geoff,' I said, when creaking out of my sleeping bag at 0700 next day, 'do we really want to chicken out?' We didn't. Refuelled and stiff with thermal clothing, at 0900 we left port into the north wind.

Dangers at sea seem to be exaggerated. Tales of the Alderney Race strewn with the drowned bones of seamen are mostly folk law, based on creditable fact but fed by the imagination. Wind against tide produced a few juddering stops but nothing worse than yesterday's conditions and we were clear of Sark and Alderney, through the Race and making a slant on a port tack that would have landed us at Brighton Marina had we held it all the way.

We had plenty of sail up without using the jib and settled into a groove at 4½ knots, slowing dramatically when our bow kicked spray high into the night. The first ships crossed us in daylight but soon we were fumbling bearings in our gloved hands and dodging our way through them. The barometer needle was against the stop on the 'High' end of the dial and the air was so crisp that it sparkled in the head like champagne bubbles. In mid-Channel we could see lights on both sides, 40 miles in each direction. The red, green and white of the big ships were easy to see.

Our little boat heeled steadily, our wake white in the beam of our stern light and best of all, the wind slowly backed until we were pointing first at Portsmouth and finally directly at Christchurch. Geoff, heated by the Tilley lamp, juggled sublime savoury pasta on a stove whose gimbals failed to balance the pans.

The wind, now northwest, provided shelter in Christchurch Bay so we attempted a night approach on the unlit channel, relying on an exact GPS position and a powerful searchlight. There was nothing wrong with this strategy, the long dark arm of Hengistbury Head gave us smooth water, the tide was half-flood and we were spot on, but.... no channel buoys!

They had been removed at the end of the season. Fishermen had marked the eastern sides of the three salient sandbanks with white floats but this only became plain as we zigzagged between them in a maximum depth of two metres. Eighteen hours for a windward journey from Guernsey to Christchurch Bar at 4½ knots was good going. The remaining mile took 2½ hours. It was then 0500. We crashed out amid a chaos of wet gear and tumbled odds and ends, to wake at 1000, sort ourselves out and return to London on Saturday afternoon.

The Salute

This is less of a log and more of a 'yarn' – as my father used to say when he recounted, yet again, his story of the used matches that appeared on the cabin table when he was single-handing his engineless cutter *Marjorie* in 1906! He was anchored at Dunmore East near Waterford, Ireland where this account ends.

At 2200 we groped our way out of Christchurch, picking up unlit buoys with a torch in a minimum depth of 0.9 metres. June was near but summer had not realised it. God, it was cold! The quest: homage to my father. A pale pink dawn was telling of the shepherd's warning – but how could shepherds know about the sea? The wind, just south of west, gave us a chance to motorsail. Our boxy centreboarder has not heard about slicing through waves. St Albans Race, wind against tide, is calm when you are hugging the point in a boat drawing only 0.8 metres.

All was going well and thoughts had turned to a night passage inside Portland Bill, then another fair tide past Start Point. Alas! The engine struggled and stopped. A heavy woven plastic sack had enveloped the prop. It took four hours instead of one to tack into Weymouth. The wind died but a friendly sailor towed us to the town wharf below a thriving farmers' market in full swing. Shallow boats have shallow propellers – a sharp knife disposed of the bag and a long arm picked the bits out of the Maxprop. It was time for healthy fare from the jolly farmers and away, this time for a daylight navigation of the Bill.

The wind, now with some north in it, served us well as we sailed night and day to Falmouth. It was then 'weather forecast time' because it's

Jan Van Gent 2

a long way round Land's End and across St Georges Channel with a barren lee shore to starboard. Yes, we were bound for Ireland.

A complex low in mid Atlantic was promising a sustained south-westerly F5-6 airflow for the next three days – the right direction and duration but the wrong strength and sea state. If things became too rough in the Atlantic we could run for the open arms of Pembroke Dock. We sat in Mylor fully found, had our 'last supper', put waypoints on all the buoys and departed at 2200 in almost nil visibility. The only light we saw was the Manacles buoy because we hit it with the GPS. Otherwise there were no lights from the Lizard to Longships.

A close circle of grey for two nights and nearly two days. Ships appeared as suddenly as they went, grey on grey, the bow wave the only other tone. We tooted our pump-up foghorn feeling foolish. It was a relief to bear away at Lands End, furl the job, reef the main and tramp north with the Atlantic rollers sliding sideways under us. No tides to help us now – the numbers on the log jumping about but averaging 5½ knots. At 1050 hours on 2 June we saw the massive bulk of Hook Head lighthouse, its light still on in the poor visibility. We were in time for the flood up the 15 miles of river to Waterford.

Inside Hook Head a darker grey to port marked the little harbour of Dunmore East. At 1135, abeam four cables, I dipped the ensign. No point in talking about moist eyes – we were moist all over!

Jan Van Gent is a 24-foot Dutch shallow draft centreboard cutter with a mast that can be lowered for river or canal excursions.

THE ROYAL CRUISING CLUB'S COMMEMORATION OF THE BI-CENTENARY OF THE BATTLE OF TRAFALGAR

by Christopher Thornhill

On 21 October 1805 the Battle of Trafalgar and the destruction of the combined fleets of France and Spain confirmed England's maritime supremacy for more than a hundred years. The huge growth in yachting throughout the Victorian era was surely a by-product of Britannia's rule of the waves. Yacht clubs proliferated and in 1880 the Cruising Club was born. So the bi-centenary year of the Battle was also the 125th anniversary of the Club. We decided to celebrate both with an ambitious plan to be off Cape Trafalgar on 21 October 2005; other clubs expressed interest in joining us but nothing came of the discussions and the RCC was, with a sigh of relief, on its own.

In 2002 Trevor Wilkinson proposed a cruise that included gatherings at Gibraltar and Barbate and sailing off the Cape on the day, all to be preceded by a meet in Morocco and a trip into the Rif Mountains. This is how it happened, three years later, after much planning by dedicated people.

On Thursday 13 October we gathered at Marina Smir, a small harbour on the coast of Morocco, ten miles south of Punta Almina and only 24 miles from Gibraltar. The ten yachts were *Arcadia, Gas Pirate, Golly-wobbler, Namaqua, Octavia, Talisker, Wombat, Yoquese* and two guests, *Sky Hunter* (RTYC) and *Sunbird* (RWYC). The following morning the crews were persuaded into a coach. The Commodore commented that trying to get the RCC to move is like herding cats!

We were driven for an hour and a half to Chefchaouen, a pretty Berber town high up in the mountains. The inhabitants are rather inclined to sell their goods to tourists but it is definitely the real thing, very ancient and unspoilt. All assembled for rooftop drinks and dinner, the whole

The Trafalgar Trio

journey and proceedings overseen by Trevor's masterstroke, Aziz. The perfect Mr Fixit, Aziz was always there when needed and shepherded us round the town; at the same time he seemed to be on holiday with his wife and small child. In the morning the bus took us back to Smir in good time for an excellent sail to Gibraltar where the rest of the fleet was gathering, victualling and socialising.

On Sunday we turned out en masse for the 1030 service in the Cathedral and in the evening the Royal Gibraltar Yacht Club opened its doors to us. We gathered for drinks on the terrace and met our Hon Representative, John Isola, and his wife Tazy. The Commodore presented a burgee to the RGYC Commodore, Patrick Canessa.

On Monday the cloud was down on the Rock and it poured, the only wet day we had. Many of us inspected a rather good exhibition about the Battle; combined with a visit to the town's museum we got a very good idea of Gibraltar from the beginning of the nineteenth century right up to modern times. The few who climbed the Rock were glad of the shelter of the tunnels. The apes performed in spite of the rain and the cloud lifted in the evening so the view of the harbour and across Algeciras Bay put the history into context.

Our Trafalgar Commemoration Dinner at the Garrison Library was a

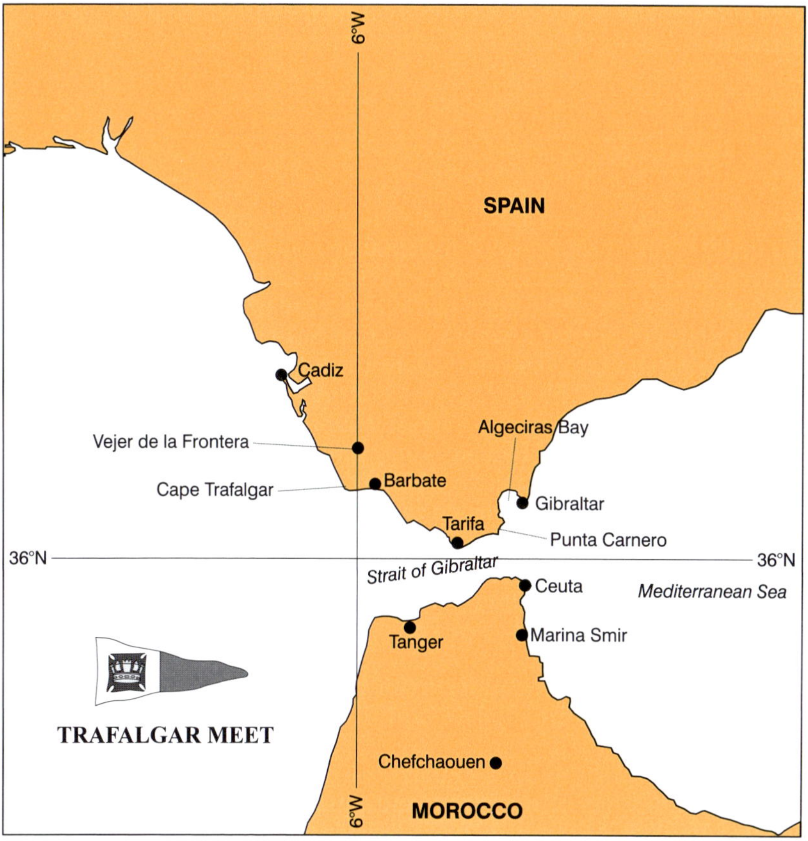

high point of the cruise, excellently conceived and organised by Nicko Franks. Eighty three of us sat down to an excellent meal surrounded by shelves of books going back to the eighteenth century. The Isolas were our guests and Jim and Catherine Pitts flew down specially. Geoffrey Nockolds and Dick and Sheila Trafford arrived and later joined *Wombat* and *Namaqua* respectively. The Rooke Volunteer Band (formerly the band of HMS *Rooke*) played and at the end we were issued with the words of *Land of Hope and Glory*, *Rule Britannia* and *Hearts of Oak* which were sung, standing up and accompanied by the band. The volume was impressive. Sandy Watson gave a short and lucid talk about the political and military events leading up to the Battle and Robin Whiteside, one of our guests who was sailing on *Jessamy*, gave an exciting account of the *Pickle's* dramatic race to England with the news of the Battle, leaving us in suspense as Lieutenant Lapenotière boarded a coach at Falmouth.

The evening was a perfect mixture of a light-hearted meal, a feeling of patriotism and an introduction to the commemorative purpose of our cruise. Our time in Gibraltar reminded us vividly how many members of the RCC have a naval background. Some have served there and others have family connection going back through the world wars to the eighteenth century.

It was an early start on 18 October to catch the west-going eddy between Punta Carnero and Tarifa. The skippers and navigators had all studied or cribbed the Straits of Gibraltar Handbook and the fleet was under way at 0730. There was no wind so we all motored to Barbate but at least we got the tides right! Barbate is a huge harbour, built by the Andalusian authorities; a separate section has pontoons for yachts but few marina facilities. A meagre shower is a long walk and it is a bleak trudge to the town. The redeeming feature is a very nice bar and restaurant, run by an enthusiastic Belgian couple, who can get taxis. The advantage for us was that Barbate is only seven miles from Cape Trafalgar.

The fleet arrived in a bunch, which confounded the harbour authorities but all were found berths on two pontoons. *Kokiri* with Katharine, Peter and baby Robert (eight months) Ingram had arrived at 0700 from Canada via the Azores, a spectacular feat of timing and baby minding that caused much admiration and dramatically reduced the average age of the gathering. 19 October was a lay day. Some stayed in the marina, others explored inland and many found their way to Vejer de la Frontera, a pretty white Andalusian hilltop town, and to the Restaurante Trafalgar where quite a crowd gathered for lunch.

On Thursday 20 October, the eve of Trafalgar Day, the whole company was driven to Cape Trafalgar in two coaches. The coastline between Cadiz and Tarifa is low and sandy; it is rather disappointing that the Battle is not named after a dramatic headland. There is a lighthouse on an outcrop that looks like a separate island from some directions, with a low sandy cliff behind and nasty shoals off it. White beaches stretch away in both directions and it is a pleasant place on a nice day.

We assembled on the beach in bright sunlight with a brisk southwesterly onshore breeze and were joined by the Rev Stewart Lamont, the Church of Scotland minister at Gibraltar, who led us in a short commemoration service. We began by singing *Eternal Father* and ended with *I vow to thee my country* accompanied by the RCC accordion and concertina band (Judy Backus, Mike Pidsley and Christopher Thornhill). Nelson's prayer before the Battle and three well-chosen readings by the Commodore, Nicko Franks and Dick Trafford stirred everyone to a proper remembrance while the minister's white hair blew in the breeze and waves crashed on the beach behind him. It was a very dignified and appropriate ceremony.

We walked two miles or so along the deserted shore to a small hamlet where we had lunch and the coaches were waiting to take us away.

The whole expedition including the service had been arranged by Rear-Commodore Anthony Wells who struck exactly the right balance between solemnity and fun.

In the evening we dined at the Yacht Club, the restaurant at the Barbate marina. The Commodore proposed the toast, 'The Immortal Memory', George Ehlers (RTYC) thanked the Club on behalf of the guests and proposed a toast to the Royal Cruising Club, Mark Adams gave a well-researched account of the Battle and Robin Whiteside completed his account of the delivery of the news of the victory to the Admiralty in London. It was a full and interesting day.

Friday 21 October, Trafalgar Day. At 1100 the fleet assembled at 36°07′N, 006°11.5′W, five miles west-southwest from Cape Trafalgar and formed two columns, representing Nelson's and Collingwood's divisions as they approached the Battle. There was almost no wind and conditions were very like those described 200 years before but the ominous swell that warned of the gale after the Battle was missing. Yachts slotted into their pre-arranged order with remarkable efficiency and kept station pretty well throughout. Unfortunately we were motoring. The two divisions proceeded at 3½ knots on a course of 045° while Nicko Franks gave a really excellent commentary over the VHF, recounting the course of the Battle right up to the victory. At 1315 the yachts formed a circle with *Wombat* and *Octavia* in the centre. As we

Cape Trafalgar

circled, *Wombat* dropped into the sea a replica of the bullet that killed Nelson and *Octavia* dropped a garland in memory of all those who died and in particular of Peter Parker, Captain of HMS *Weazle* and ancestor of a member. Before the Battle he had been despatched by Collingwood to warn Gibraltar of a possible invasion.

Namaqua (Victory)	***Enki IV (Royal Sovereign)***
Acquest (Temeraire)	***Rapscallion (BelleIsle)***
Arcadia (Neptune)	***Semiramis (Mars)***
Gas Pirate (Euryalus)	***Sky Hunter (Tonnant)***
Gollywobbler (Leviathan)	***Standeasy (Bellerophon)***
Jessamy (Conqueror)	***Summerbird (Colossus)***
Kokiri (Britannia)	***Sunbird (Achilles)***
Octavia (Ajax)	***Talisker (Revenge)***
Pastime (Sirius)	***Wombat (Defiance)***
Pemandia (Agamemnon)	***Yoquese (Swiftsure)***

The fleet in two divisions off Cape Trafalgar, 21 October 2005

The fleet sailed close past Cape Trafalgar taking the shallow inshore passage. A white ensign was flying on the Cape surrounded by a group of naval officers who had come to watch us and to be part of the ceremony.

That was the end of the Royal Cruising Club's nine-day cruise and commemoration of the Battle of Trafalgar and the fleet dispersed. It had been tremendous fun. It was a most congenial group and we were delighted to have with us two yachts from the Royal Thames, one from the Royal Western (with Jonathan Trafford on board), one from the RNSA (with Sandy Watson) and one from the RCIYC (with Colin Barry). The formal events in Gibraltar and at Cape Trafalgar had moments of great dignity and solemnity. We didn't just celebrate the victory; we remembered the loss of 5000 lives and the extraordinary seamanship and heroism of both sides during the Battle and in the storms that followed.

The organisation was impeccable. Trevor Wilkinson, whose original plan it had been, took charge of the Moroccan expedition. Anthony Wells arranged the service. Nicko Franks, who has served in Gibraltar, undertook the mammoth task of co-ordinating all the participants, arranging the berthing and the dinners. After much consultation he devised the sail in two divisions, took command of the fleet and provided the commentary. It involved months of work, a great many emails and visits to Gibraltar and Spain. It was a complete success. Thanks to Nicko and to all who took part, the Royal Cruising Club's celebrations of the bi-centenary of Trafalgar were thoroughly enjoyable, completely appropriate to the occasion and a memorable part of our 125th anniversary.

Postscript

Why did we have the sea off Trafalgar to ourselves? We fully expected a crowd but we were the only yacht club there. The Oyster Owners' Association, which held its annual racing in Cadiz, had a similar ceremony but by agreement kept clear of us. The TS *Lord Nelson* was with them. One small British yacht briefly attached herself to us but otherwise no one else was visible. It was disappointing that neither the British, French nor Spanish navies sent their ships out until late in the day so no one saw them (although they did appear on the television at home).

The next day Spanish yachts appeared en masse off the Cape and were joined by *Namaqua, Kokiri* and *Summerbird.* There was a gentle breeze and a long line formed, sailing towards the Cape. 127 yachts were reported but my count stopped around 80. It was an impressive performance. Yachts sailing in close order with little fuss, minimal bunching and no collisions. When the parade reached the shoals off the Cape we all turned smartly to seaward in line ahead and a wreath of flowers in Spanish colours was dropped into the sea by the leading yacht. It was a simple and impressive way of commemorating the Spanish heroism and losses.

OOTSTAA TO STARBOARD

by David Vass

The Royal Cork Yacht Club Vase was awarded for this cruise

Our cruise really began at Stromness, which we reached in a comfortable three days from Ardfern. A brisk overnight passage from Loch Laxford to Orkney saw us in the fine new marina behind the ferry pier. Here we were greeted by the harbourmaster on the pontoon as old friends because he *kent* the boat.

While we had passed down the east coast of Shetland some years back returning from Norway, we had long wanted to spend more time there and we had, over the years, explored Orkney to the full. So it was that we sailed from Stromness for Westray on 6 July at 0400, right at the last half hour of the ebb – the classic timing to avoid the overfalls in Hoy Mouth. Unfortunately our elegant departure was spoiled by a gentle grounding on the sandbank behind the northernmost pontoon but we were soon away. There were no significant overfalls remaining and we made good time to the northwest on the young flood. Close northwest of Braga Skerry we came upon the (very small) cardinals marking the experimental wave generator and investigated them more closely, rapidly establishing that they are not there for fun but surround various large semi-submerged bits and pieces. We retired discreetly towards the Yesnaby cliffs and Birsay, concentrating on the birds and scenery.

A gentle northeasterly pushed us nicely down Papa Sound to reach Pierowall just before noon with help from the flood all the way. As expected we were greeted by Tommy Rendall, the remarkable harbour-master. The co-owner's birthday was celebrated properly next day with an evening meal at Cleaton House with pick-up and return courtesy of the hotel. This finished a fine day that included taking on board the maximum sensible stock of crab from the Westray packing station and also diesel from Tommy.

We sailed for Shetland at 0600 on 8 July passing south of Papa Westray. The conditions were beautiful and visibility good so that we could enjoy the spectacle of Fair Isle to starboard and Foula to port as we rolled gently across the Fair Isle Channel. We were at anchor on sand in Bigton Wick, on the northern side of St Ninian's Isle at 1900 amidst spectacular cliff scenery but surprisingly few sea birds. Rain fell overnight and the wind had gone to the southwest offering a chance to idle up to Scalloway at a gentle speed enjoying the approach or so we wished! Within an hour the visibility had closed right down and we both needed and appreciated the radar for safe navigation, as the approaches to Scalloway are quite tight from either direction and strewn with hard lumps. We were alongside the pontoon of the Scalloway Boat Club by lunchtime in time to explore the castle and make the very friendly acquaintance of the Boat Club. The castle is in good order and is yet another legacy of the Stewarts, an altogether evil dynasty responsible in the seventeenth century for many acts of gratuitous nastiness throughout Orkney and Shetland.

Next day the weather was stable, the barometer steady and the forecast passable so we thought it best to take the chance to see Foula. Once clear of Scalloway harbour it was thicker than we realised, with visibility less than two cables on occasion. We groped our way out by the South Channel and turned west into fine cotton wool, encountering a moderate swell and a dying westerly wind. Apart from a very strong tide on the Foula Shoal, which we skirted nicely with the aid of the GPS, we were hardly aware of Foula until about a half-mile out when some of the darkness ahead intensified and then solidified. The next problem was finding the harbour at Ham Voe. Ahead of us seemed to be a uniform, murky cliff stretching evenly in both directions with a generally unaccommodating appearance. Careful study with binoculars suggested a crack and we approached this circumspectly. The swell diminished rapidly as we advanced into the lee of Foula, a short concrete wall materialised and we slid through a very small entrance to see the ferry suspended on davits above us and a space so small that we did not think we could turn *Borealis*. We did and moored bows out on an old RNLI lifeboat. The harbour was now full!

After a good chat to some of the locals who showed us terrifying photos of the harbour in winter, we set off to explore. There is an astonishing amount of scrap on the island, some of it mobile and some not. There are many Soay-like sheep, a fine community centre and amazing numbers of great skuas full of the usual aggro. We retired to the boat deciding the island merited another day.

It was not to be! During the night (well, twilight) we were assaulted by 40-knot gusts and a steady 25-knot westerly. In the harbour all was more or less well but in these conditions a prudent retreat to the Mainland of Shetland seemed wise. We scurried out with two reefs down at 0830 next morning with Foula shrouded in mist. A mile out we were utterly becalmed and in thick fog again. Visions of a rapid trip to Scalloway vanished and we returned cautiously by the North Channel in foggy conditions with visibility down to a cable on occasion making the benefits of GPS and radar only too obvious. Moira thought surf a useful aid at times!

We left Scalloway on 13 July intent on making progress up the west coast. A F5-6 southwesterly took us quickly round Russa Ness into Sandsound Voe and then to Tresta Voe where we found excellent holding. It got steadily windier and wetter but at least the views were different from Scalloway. After a day at anchor in unremitting rain and wind, we ventured forth again. The sun was visible and its presence duly noted in the log. Outside Sandsound Voe we found a northerly F4 and a big swell. We tacked north all day with a steady wind and a slowly clouding sky towards Papa Stour, visible as a craggy object on the horizon. A short but interesting piece of pilotage saw us in Hamna Voe on Papa Stour, with slightly frayed nerves. A trip ashore revealed a very neat and tidy island, a very hairy airstrip, a notable lack of scrap and a harbour in the main bay with a solid-looking new pier and breakwater under construction on the north side.

We left Hamna Voe gingerly next morning but were relieved to find 2.5 metres on the bar at low water neaps. We had been a bit off track on the way in! Outside there was still a big swell and an excellent southwest F3-4, just right to allow us to circumnavigate Papa Stour. Even with these light conditions it was quite bumpy with moderate overfalls at times but the scenery is worth the effort. Papa Stour is a bit like a ripe cheese with fine cliffs, a large number of arches, stacks and caves and great variety of rock colour. Once we had rounded the western extremity we had the tide with us and enjoyed a brisk sail inspecting Housa Voe, site of the big new pier. We then reached across to Swarbacks Minn, past Vementry and into sheltered water where we enjoyed a fast sail into Olna Firth.

As we approached Voe at the head of the firth we noticed it had acquired a breakwater and what looked like a wee marina not mentioned in the pilot. What luck, we thought – we will moor at the outer end and enjoy a quiet night. We set ourselves up, began the approach but lost sight of the pontoon itself in a sheet of rain. Moira stepped off in great style only to find the pontoon was 25 centimetres wide and very slippery. She completed this exercise lying on her back, one leg each side, both feet in the water and, with impressive sang-froid, passed the breast line through a metal ring and back to the skipper. Twenty minutes later we were more or less fast and she was back on board. She wondered if she might change her shoes! By then we had grasped that the 'marina' was incomplete but secure. A further bonus was the mussels in the pub. By next morning it had become profoundly wet and windy and we replaced

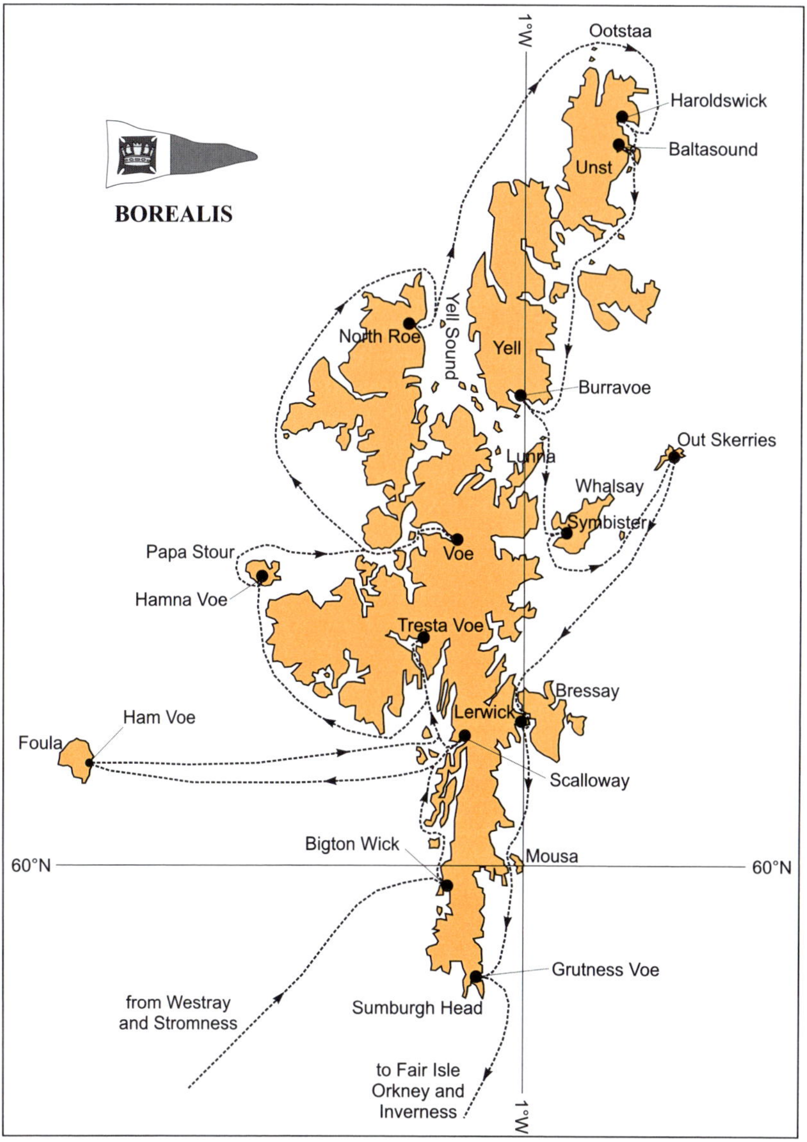

the faulty VHF aerial. The old one emerged in two parts, explaining a lot! The day ended with thunder and lightning and a lot more rain.

Next day the wind was south and fresh and would serve well to take us to Yell Sound. Once into outer Olna Firth the conditions were brisk and we took down two reefs and set off enjoying the scenery and complexity of Swarbacks Minn. The iron sail was needed on and off to take us out to Eshaness past a fascinating seascape with drongs, stacks, caves and surf in abundance. Uyea and Ramna Stacks were generating even more surf and did not look at all inviting in the rain. The flood gathered us up and swept us past Point of Fethaland into Yell Sound and we found secure anchorage at North Roe late in the afternoon. We were now nicely positioned to get round Muckle Flugga and Out Stack if the weather was kind or to go down Yell Sound to the archipelago round Sullom Voe if we were thwarted.

The forecast at 0600 on 19 July was more encouraging than for some time. It spoke of fair winds, little rain and a hint of sun. (Shetland forecasts, in contrast to elsewhere, are only valid for 12 hours and the outlook likewise so there is always a frisson of uncertainty for the next day!) We left at 0700 for the top of Britain, delayed a little by a batten repair but in dry weather and clear sky to the south.

We enjoyed a morning of spectacular scenery and bird life, especially after crossing Bluemull Sound. We reached Unst and closed Muckle Flugga to see the remarkable position of the lighthouse perched on the top of an isolated rock, another Stevenson engineering masterpiece. Shortly afterwards Ootstaa (Out Stack), the very last bit of the United Kingdom and immediately south of 61°N, was a cable south and to starboard of us. We bore away to the east. The swell rapidly eased, the weather improved and the big yellow thing came out. The scenery was dominated by the cold war radar on Saxa Vord and the cliffs of North Unst. The pilot had grave warnings about Skaw Roost at the northeast corner of Unst and we gave it a wide berth before approaching Haroldswick, where we anchored close to the shore shortly after 1400. We were soon ashore to visit the Unst Boat Haven, an outstanding museum recounting the history and development of traditional Shetland working boats. Beautifully laid out and supported by accounts of life at sea in dialect, this is unmissable. If only the anecdotes had been available in book or leaflet form!

We moved round to Baltasound where we found secure anchorage off the pier with the spectacle of a Viking longship left there four years ago by its Scandinavian crew who had decided that rowing this beast any further was too serious a business.

Next day we left Baltasound shortly after 1000 and reached down the Unst coast at a steady seven knots, fast going for *Borealis* but Hamish the Autohelm coped well and required little attention. Within an hour we were down to the island of Haaf Gruney and recognised we could leave it to port with advantage. The wind had veered further north and made this manoeuvre easier and we took the opportunity to furl the genoa and carried on with the staysail and reefed main. *Borealis* became even more docile than usual and we maintained six knots in a northwest F6 while leaving Haaf Gruney to port, Wedder Holm to starboard and Urie

Lingay to port in a neat slalom which delivered us into Colgrave Sound. By 1400 we were under the lee of the Stack of the Horse where we lowered sail and began the approach to Burravoe, a landlocked harbour at the southeast corner of Yell. The pilot enjoined us to approach using an old storehouse, two doors and four windows as marks. It works and feeds you into a very sheltered narrow voe extending to the northeast. At the end of the pier is another Shetland mini-marina, this one complete! We were only 10 miles from North Roe, our anchorage of two nights ago, having sailed 67 miles.

The next morning could only be described as unpleasant. At the top of our mast it said F6 but outside it was significantly stronger. We decided to stay put. It was cool and we gave thanks to Herr Eberspächer. Taken little and often he did the trick. Having noticed a small museum, the Old Haa, en route to the erratic shop the previous day, we returned there to find a real gem. Everything a local museum should be and a café too. That took care of the morning.

Stores were now a bit low so Whalsay with its big fishing community seemed a better bet than Burravoe. The distance was small but the overfalls and tide off Lunna Holm looked worth avoiding and we planned our departure to pass at slack water. It had been quiet in the voe but outside there was a solid northerly F6. The course was almost south so we used the genoa and ran down towards Lunna Holm. With about a third of

Borealis in Foula Harbour

the genoa we felt in control for the seas were rather big and short and she was smashing through them. Once clear of Lunna there was only the swell to contend with and we reached the top of Linga Sound just as the tide turned south letting us enter Symbister on Whalsay with ease. Mooring at the marina was not available so we eyed up the main inner breakwater where we were directed to a secure berth labelled 'No berthing'.

Next day we paid a visit to the Bremen Boed, a small timber building where the Hansa traders used to exchange grain and cloth for salt fish, and around noon sailed for Out Skerries with the young flood. Rounding the south of Whalsay we picked our way through the assortment of baas, flaeshans, stacks and holms to the northeast and found a northeasterly breeze which showed every sign of freshening. It became a hard beat but *Borealis* thrived on it. The pilot suggests the Sooth Mooth should only be attempted in light wind and minimal swell but it was a choice between this entrance or surfing or worse through the northeast entrance, so in we went. It is well marked but tight and delivered us to another very secure pier berth. Moira reappeared from a reconnaissance to announce that the showers were heated by a Dimplex heater and had a shower mat. She was away a long time!

We were soon ashore for a quick exploration. Welcome advice on the Sooth Mooth was offered by a local waiting for the ferry. Summarised as 'leave so as to touch the marks', this served us well next day. The arrival and departure of the ferry by the northeast passage and the state of the in-bound passengers convinced us we had come in by the correct channel.

24 July dawned sunny but still with a stiff northeast wind. Mid-morning we sailed for Lerwick experiencing sustained bursts over eight knots but as we came under some lee from Whalsay the thrills diminished and dodging the hard bits became easier. After running down the southern side of the Stepping Stones we were off the Mull of Elswick and could set course for Lerwick Harbour. We moored in the small boat harbour where we were the only British yacht in 12; the others were mostly Scandinavian. The next day Moira did ancestor research and the skipper fixed unreliable wind and speed indicators.

26 July was best described by that fine Scots word, *dreich*. It was dull, damp and cool with an overcast sky but we were anxious to see Mousa and Jarlshof. Off Bressay the breeze freshened a little and gave us an excellent sail to an empty anchorage at Mousa. The broch, the best-preserved example of its genre, is absolutely superb. The sun emerged and we enjoyed a very pleasant reach to Grutness where we anchored well in, beside the Fair Isle ferry pier and clear of the construction work extending one of the Sumburgh Airport runways. We had a good grip on sand but some swell found its way in with the northerly wind and we rolled gently.

27 July was an altogether better day and we were ashore early. Jarlshof is only a half-mile from Grutness. We arrived before 0900 and as it looked closed, we climbed the fence. A light shone from the office so we knocked. A delightful Historic Scotland official greeted us with the words, 'We're closed so you don't have to pay but do come in!' We got our audio sets and off we went. If Skara Brae is amazing then Jarlshof with 2000 years of continuous settlement is remarkable. We were underway by 1030 and had a nice reach in sunshine over a lumpy sea, mooring alongside the old jetty in North Haven, Fair Isle.

The ferry leaving for Grutness at 0600 was a good alarm. A stiff northeasterly blew straight in the entrance of North Haven and it took some time to unmoor without leaving the crew ashore. Our engine needed full power, such as it is, to force the exit into a hefty swell and rough sea. Outside the breakwater things were messy. We got the main up and escaped the worst with only a few seas on the foredeck. A mile north of The Skroo we were in calmer water and were able to turn towards Westray.

Borealis

Now we enjoyed one of the best sailing days. The breeze rarely faltered and maintained a steady 15-17 knots from the northeast all day; the tide was with us almost all the way, the sun came out and Hamish did his duty. We were alongside at Pierowall at about 1500. Preparations were well in hand for the Westray Regatta. We had an invitation to crew on a Vega. Tommy arrived to update us on everything and finished the gin. We were back in Westray and felt very welcome.

The next day was spent on maintenance and restocking including crab! Parts of the racing fleet began to trickle in. The ferry from Kirkwall arrived on 30 July carrying 25 dinghies free of charge. Racing got underway by 1100. Our extra weight forward going to windward in the fresh breeze must have helped get two firsts in our class. The subsequent hospitality from Westray Sailing Club was quite extraordinary and festivities slackened only slightly with the departure of the re-loaded ferry in the late evening.

We sailed for Kirkwall on 31 July with another brisk northerly. A very fast trip downwind was thwarted when we noticed a wedge had jumped from a batten end. A repair didn't endure so we dropped the main and continued under the genoa alone. Even with much less canvas up we made good progress and caught the tide in Westray Firth as we emerged from Fersness Sound. A moderating wind helped us take the Vasa Sound passage into Kirkwall Bay and we were soon inside the breakwater extension. Though only partly finished there was a radical improvement in conditions inside the marina. We found a berth close by *L'Acushla,* the only club boat seen in our travels apart from a very brief encounter with *Slioch* in Gairloch. We exchanged news over tea and then settled down for a distinctly quieter evening than the previous one.

Overnight the wind veered south and there was no prospect of reaching the Canal or indeed crossing the Pentland Firth in sensible conditions so we re-stored, made an adequate repair to the batten, took in some archaeology and enjoyed an exceptionally good meal ashore for our wedding anniversary. The next three days were even less auspicious with very fresh southerly conditions and heavy rain. Being forced to spend time in Orkney is fortunately a pleasure as there is plenty to do if you have even a minor interest in archaeology.

We had a better forecast for 5 August. Heavy rain greeted us early on but the wind was already northwest F4. We left at 0645, caught the young flood in The String, goose-winged and ran down quickly to Mull Head. The overfalls can be nasty but the wind and tide had flattened them and we were able to pass close to the Head, taking advantage of the strong stream, before gybing and heading outside Copinsay for a point on Sandy Riddle about four miles southeast of Pentland Skerries, some 20 miles away. The wind was steady at west-northwest F4-5 and we made good progress with Hamish in full control. Once clear of the shelter of South Ronaldsay the swell was heavy but on the beam and we crossed Sandy Riddle as planned, avoiding the welter of white water to the northwest and southeast and thus a longish diversion to the east. We reached Tarbat Ness at 2000 and passed into Inverness Firth at about midnight. We had been discussing what to do. The canal would not open until 0900 at the earliest and not before 1100 if outbound traffic was waiting. Inverness Harbour was well-lit but a couple of hours away while right inside Chanonry was Skate Bank covered by 3-4 metres for a large part of its northeastern area and protected by two red buoys sending in-bound ships to the west. So we sneaked inside the buoys till a decent distance onto the bank and enjoyed a very quiet night with outstanding holding on sand. Such was our level of comfort that we overslept. No matter as a call to the Caledonian Canal revealed that entry would not be before 1100! Soon we were snug in Muirtown Marina where a stiff cleaning regime was enforced by Moira to prepare for the arrival of our elder grandsons. Comments such as, 'They are grubby creatures anyway,' carried no weight!

The junior crew joined at about 1800 on 7 August delivered by their father. We enjoyed a better than usual canal passage enlivened, entertained and exhausted by the crew and emerging at Corpach on 10 August in good time to take in the steam train from Mallaig and take their mother aboard. All accomplishments acquired on canal duty were demonstrated and peace broke out as they abandoned us at 0845 on 11 August. We were at sea by 0850 to meet a southwest wind off Fort William. The tide was with us and we made good speed under power to Appin Narrows where we found a westerly breeze but a mere F2, which was more of a frustration than an impediment. We forced the tide at Luing using the back eddies and were anchored at Shuna by 1800 in heavy rain to await the RCC mini-meet next day. 12 August dawned quiet and overcast. At first we thought we were in the wrong anchorage or had the wrong date but just before the appointed hour six yachts, one carrying Christopher and Valentine Thornhill, appeared from Craobh and a fine lunch was enjoyed. Time demanded our return to Ardfern while the others continued to the Bay of Pigs in Corryvreckan.

Shetland had been a very good cruise and will be repeated. The absence of other yachts in this fine cruising area was notable; we saw only one other British yacht in Shetland and three in Orkney and Fair Isle. It is a fair distance north but it is certainly worth the effort.

Borealis is a Rival 36, deep keel version and cutter-rigged. She was launched in 1985 and we have owned her since 1995. For our longer cruises she is usually sailed by Moira and me.

MILLING AROUND MULL IN A HUNGRY *BROWN BEAR*

by Mary Max

A ten-hour drive from the smoggy bustle of London brought four of us one Saturday morning in September to a peaceful dawn at Ardfern and the welcome sight of Jonny Clothier and Jane Kimber aboard *Brown Bear*. From previous experience of sailing together (and as this was our one cruise of the year, we were determined to make the most of it) we knew that our priority lay in sourcing food. Most importantly, we required enough roast potatoes to keep the boys quiet and provide ample midnight feast material.

The excellent butcher in Lochgilphead was raided successfully, along with Co-op and Threshers, and soon every last item on our substantial shopping list had been ticked off. With all supplies stowed, we had sufficient nourishment for a voyage of considerable duration, despite the fact that we were only going to be away for a week. After a hearty lunch and a thorough briefing on how to keep *Brown Bear* dancing we got underway until it was time for supper (a beautiful butcher's steak pie which we would heartily recommend), and made the epic voyage to Goat Island, two miles away.

With Sunday on us, we rose to blue skies and the scant remains of the previous evening's steak pie. We were mildly baffled by the volume of technology around the chart table but knowing we had 30 minutes to sail to the Dorus Mhor before the tide turned against us we decided to use trusty paper and leave the electronics to the next day. As we successfully negotiated the choppy water, the sun came out to shine on our first glimpse of Mull as we passed Corryvreckan and exchanged tales of the angry tidal waters in the sound.

We set off at a gentle pace through the Sound of Luing. It became immediately apparent that *Brown Bear* is loth to sail at anything like a gentle pace and wasn't happy unless she achieved a minimum of eight knots even with the briefest of breezes. This brought us very efficiently to the beautiful anchorage of Puilladobhrain and gave us plenty of time to start on the roast potatoes. We were too busy devouring a succulent cut of roast beef, accompanied by so many potatoes and Yorkshire puddings that there was barely room in the oven for the meat, even to succeed in walking over the hill to the pub by Atlantic Bridge. (We did make a late attempt to get to it but found that two Mini-Maglites were no opposition to the Grimpen Mire we got lost in as soon as we rowed to 'dry land'!)

Monday was once again sunny and as we set out towards the Sound of Mull we were provided with a dolphin escort. Once again cruising at eight knots and to many sighs of 'Ah, this is the life!' we headed towards Tobermory, keeping a wide berth of the Caledonian MacBrayne. We knew that the tail of hurricane Maria was moving speedily in our direction (having already chased Mary's sister, her husband and their baby son across the Atlantic for three days) and with F8 expected we needed to be sure of a safe mooring. As the wind picked up, we settled down at Tobermory to the comfort of bangers and mustard mash and wondered whether we'd have a chance to raise a sail the next day.

Sure enough, the weather turned grizzly overnight but spirits aboard *Brown Bear* were still high (and plentiful). A quiet day was had with a gentle tour around the town. The brightly painted buildings along the harbour wall were dazzling despite the storm. We enjoyed an excellent lunch of haggis with whisky and cream in the Mishnish, followed by a visit to the distillery. Having bought several bottles of whisky we headed to the teashop for a hot chocolate. A couple of pints and a game of pool later we returned to *Brown Bear* rather depressed that we were unable to keep up with our university drinking days. We did, however, re-live one tradition and cooked up a large tureen of Thai green curry for supper.

Another fiercely windy night made us glad that we hadn't been anywhere near to Maria at her worst but the next day's sail more than made up for the lack of sailing the day before. *Brown Bear*, happy to be out in the wild again, did us proud with her usual eight knots as she cut through the swell on a series of long tacks around the north of Mull. We passed beneath Ardnamurchan Point with Janey trying to lure the local minke whale with excellent whale impressions. We rounded Ulva and anchored amongst the islands in Cragaig Bay. A colony of seals greeted us in this tranquil place, blissfully ignorant of the panic down below that we wouldn't be able to find a dish big enough for a *Brown Bear*-sized shepherd's pie.

Skipper Mary was woken on Thursday morning by the creaking onset of another year and a great deal of squeaking and giggling as the rest of the crew filled *Brown Bear* with balloons and banners. Particular trouble was also taken to pipe the icing onto Mary's chocolate birthday cake. Jane Asher would have been proud. Well aware of the tantrum that would have ensued had they not been suitably prepared, the crew had also laid out a HUGE pile of presents (many somewhat hastily wrapped

The Max Mafia pilots Brown Bear through the Sound of Iona

in newspaper) and thrust a mug of birthday tea in Mary's hands to get the day off to a splendid start.

As we waved goodbye to Ulva – once more in fabulous sunshine – we again tried our best to summon the minke (well, it had worked in Finding Nemo) but to little effect. Our thoughts instead turned to taming *Brown Bear* sufficiently to negotiate the rocky Sound of Iona. With a sliver of jib unfurled, we convinced her to cruise at a mere four knots against the tide as Daniel skilfully helmed her through the Sound, avoiding the coach-loads of tourists being deposited by Iona's sturdy cathedral.

Having hit warp speed (8.4 knots, with very little heel) and raced along the south coast of Mull, we knew that the skipper's birthday supper needed care and attention and with this in mind, we decided that 43 miles in seven hours was enough to constitute a good day. Moreover, in order to avoid a grizzly Bear skipper, there was a roast to prepare and onion gravy to create. Although Daniel did his best to produce a culinary masterpiece for his new wife in the five hours left before midnight, it was 2215 and half a birthday cake before we started the roast lamb. Incidentally, it was lunchtime two days later before we had ploughed all the way through it!

Having spent another gluttonous evening in Ardinamir Bay to the east of Luing, we used the bright Friday morning to explore the area and eventually set sail when the tide was high enough to leave the anchorage and make our way into the Sound of Shuna. After a re-pass through the Dorus Mhor (and our one and only glimpse of a very lost-looking puffin), we re-anchored by Goat Island ready to return to Ardfern early the next day. We feasted that night on macaroni cheese and tried not to think about how much we still had to eat before our return to London on Sunday morning. Needless to say, we made a valiant attempt to reduce the leftovers.

Saturday was soon on us, bringing grey skies and lashing rain to accompany our final leg into Ardfern and ensure that everyone was drenched by the time we'd finished cleaning and tidying. Having fully laundered *Brown Bear* and ourselves, the only thing left to do was to head to the Galley of Lorne and enjoy a good, solid pub meal and a few drams of single malt. Well, we city folk had had a hardy week after all!

Brown Bear is a 45-foot cutter designed by Michael Pocock and built of epoxy resin over a cedar core by Stephen Etheridge at Sway. She was launched in 1999.

MY HUSBAND PINCHED THE BOAT

by Libby Purves

So what's a girl to do, when her husband inconsiderately pinches the boat for the single-handed transatlantic race? Next year *Ayesha's* return will give me a great cruise but for 2005 urgent action was needed to blast some sea air through my head. As often before, the Tall Ships Race was the answer. I signed up as supernumerary aboard the Jubilee Sailing Trust's newest ship *Tenacious* for the leg from Newcastle to Frederikstad. Beside the Tyne, the banks were heaving with keen spectators for the largest fleet of tall ships to assemble there in modern times.

I am fond of the JST, with its philosophy of getting people with disabilities to sail alongside able-bodied crews of all ages. In Tall Ships Races half the ship's company must be under 25, but the rest meandered up to 72. The first time I sailed with them, on *Lord Nelson* in a Baltic race, I was dubious. I thought the style of sailing would be soft and cautious and polite: prone to reef, run off or retire early for the sake of the wheelchair users. This illusion was shattered when Captain Barbara Campbell, a slight but steely figure, put the novice crew of this thundering square-rigger through a horrifyingly hairy start-line tack right on top of the committee boat at Gdansk, thus winning three hours over the nearest competitor. Nothing soppy there.

So I was pleased to find her commanding *Tenacious* and busily ordering anybody fit to get aloft and be lit up fetchingly by the pre-departure fireworks. The kids descended dazzled, 'Oh, wow! It wasn't just the fireworks, but all those cameras flashing...' In the morning we peeled ourselves from the hospitable banks of the river, were instructed by an elderly Geordie crewmate to cheer as we passed Swan Hunter, the last working Tyne shipyard and headed out to sea with a forecast of strong headwinds all the way.

If you think beating is hard work in a yacht, try bringing a 580-tonne square-rigger through a F7, even if there are 40 of you at it. As often as not, in a big sea you have to wear ship rather than trying to tack. We started out second in class with much whooping but fell overnight to fourth. At 2000 we wore ship for the first time, fortified by a large roast dinner. Then at 0230 in spiky rain all hands were called on deck to do it again. There is something very endearing about a first-night watch below. Confused figures lurched and clung their way from their bunks with their hoodies on backwards or had to be prodded from the huge beanbags that lie around the frames of the bar at the stern for those who can't face climbing into a bunk. We heaved and yawned and shuddered, turning the ship round. Unfortunately, as the yards came slowly round so did the wind, boxing the compass and giving new crew a fine demonstration of the origin of the expression 'taken aback'. A brief interlude of violent hauling ended with the ship on a most satisfactory heading, whistling along at six knots in a F7, heeling hard, on course for the northern waypoint. Then, clutching lumps of cold Yorkshire pudding left out by a thoughtful cook, the watches below slunk back to their pits.

At some stage on the second day the rain stopped. The northeast headwinds returned and with them an angle of heel which made it necessary to do the washing up by leaning forward at an angle of 50° with our chins in the suds. *Tenacious* is a lively ship, a Tony Castro design who, despite her dignified appearance, sails like a yacht and likes to heel. My good friend Jason took a spectacular dive out of his wheelchair on the bridge and dragged himself back up observing 'a new way of polishing the deck'. However there was a sneaking satisfaction in learning that out of a fleet of over a hundred, 23 had already retired, either turning back or abandoning attempts to reach the infernal waypoint off Scotland. In the end, less than half completed the course.

On the second night we rounded the damn thing. The wind had freed just enough to let us point at it for the final few hours and at 2320, with the weird flaring towers of the Triton oilfield all around us and the wind rising to a full gale, we passed it at 12 knots and plugged on upwind. By now safety ropes were criss-crossing the ship – even across the mess – and water was sluicing across the waist of the ship. We were still carrying royals; so much for soft sailing. One upper topsail blew out. Jason crashed his wheelchair again and light teenagers in the for'ard-most bunks reported rising bodily from their mattresses as we crashed down a wave and claimed to have hovered briefly weightless before landing again. As for the mess, many a plateful of baked beans slid majestically onto the owner's crotch. You soon learned to sit uphill of other people's food and to pick alien peas from your clothing.

It was one of those nights when exhilaration tips over into crisis management. The main topgallant had to come in quickly, with a scrabbling, lurching, sitting-standing-crouching line of haulers toppling over on each other in the dark in a sort of *Carry On Conrad* scene. Then the upper spanker had to be handed, which proved difficult and took over an hour. In the middle of this a radio call came from another vessel requesting medical advice from Lucy, the doctor in our voyage crew. Seasickness had swept through the crew and I finally located her hunched in a companionway with a sick-bag in her fist. However, when hauled up to the radio moaning all the way, she astonished onlookers by giving crisp, precise professional advice in a voice that sounded as if she was back at the Chelsea and Westminster in a sharp white coat. Only then did she relapse into head-spinning sickness and flake out for the rest of the night under a pile of oilskins in the upper mess.

Back on deck, the anchors needed securing and the gangway lashings replacing, all in biting rain and darkness with waves rolling over the waist. After a chaotic breakfast at 25° of heel with flying toast and a gallant attempt at cleaning ship, the wind suddenly dropped away almost completely. We were in the middle of the low.

The captain and the bo'sun at this stage kept fretting loudly about losing our lead. The crew refused to worry about such competitive fandangles. From Thursday to Sunday, *Tenacious*' crew had lived, worked and eaten at a steep angle; to add to the frustration of the wheelchair users the only two lifts viable in bad weather suffered malfunctions. However this led to a historic first. Marion, paraplegic veteran JST watch leader and upholder of general morale, was persuaded to stay safe in her bunk for 18 hours solid. By morning, her watch and other fans were gathered round her awaiting orders, like courtiers at a medieval levée. Within six minutes of the wind dropping she was back on deck.

We spent eight restful hours drifting in the wrong direction, removing up to three layers of clothing whenever the sun peered doubtfully round a cloud and having much-needed showers. Watches on deck smugly watched wussy fellow-competitors in the distance motoring past towards Frederikstad. Hands went aloft to bring down the tattered remains of the upper topsail, while Steve the bo'sun conducted ropework lessons on the bridge (interestingly, the first newcomer to grasp the principle of finding the lay of a rope was the blind boy). A light wind returned towards evening, ideal for *Tenacious* and her yachty acceleration; speed and spirits rose and new sports were developed in the dawn by the teenagers, including precision spitting on jellyfish from the bridge wings. The able-bodied young who were doing the JST Leadership at Sea ticket tried out various impediments, such as experiencing life in a wheelchair and trying to do a whole watch blindfold, including steering with the audio compass. A survey was taken to work out who we all were: ages ranged from 16 to 72, occupations from school student and plumbing apprentice to telecom engineer, cleaner, deputy head, doctor, chiropodist and pub licensee. There were seven wheelchair users, two MS sufferers, one with muscular degeneration, one epileptic, one post-stroke, one with sleep apnoea who uses an oxygen mask at night, one blind and various other disabilities entered as 'old age' 'seasickness' and 'intermittent stupidity'. As for me, I admitted to a bad knee and cowardice. A third had never been on such a race and several never been afloat. Between us, under a permanent crew of eight including cooks, we had hammered that big ship across the widest, nastiest bit of the North Sea to Norway with barely a cross word.

When the race was ended at sea with positions declared at 1500, we were within twenty miles of the finish. We came fourth in Class A and ninth overall, having sailed 640 miles to travel a course of 480. Within two minutes of the official end the first fair wind of the trip sprang up astern and we were making 10 knots under low sails as we sailed into our final night at sea, rolling like a good trade wind ship instead of heeling and banging like some vulgar racing yacht. Graham the cook made slabs of chocolate embedded with cherries and bits of marshmallow and anything else lying loose in the galley. We guzzled. I am sorry to say that in a most ungentlemanly manoeuvre, while young Ross was blindfolded in his visual-impairment exercise, the rest of his watch scraped the bowl clean while mendaciously assuring him that there was none left. The ship gave one last huge roll at dinnertime and deposited Lucy the doctor's gravy-soaked broccoli in her lap, to a ladylike squeak of 'Bollocks!'

It was a lovely final dusk: the gunmetal gleams of afternoon gave way to a clear sunny view of the wide northern sky and the sunset painted the topsails pink. The wind held, and in creaking peacefulness we stayed under sail until after 2300, talking quietly in the dark, aware it was the last night and happy to recognize the now familiar silhouettes of shipmates against the stars. The wind died, headsails were furled, the unfamiliar

The Jubilee Sailing Trust's Tenacious

sound of the engine broke the spell and a young trainee managed to fall asleep at the helm (motoring is so soporific). The mobiles began to work and one student got her degree result and whooped. Jason, almost recovered from his last two falls, nearly took a header into the lee rail while using two deck brooms to try out a new way of punting his wheelchair along the poop deck at speed. Jason is not 16. He is a grown-up civil servant at the Ministry of Defence.

One final drama as the anchor went down. A cry of horror went up from the captain because (the shame) we had lost the Norwegian courtesy flag. A team with needles and thread began to assemble, reminding me of the last time I sailed with Cap'n Campbell and we had to make an Åland Islands flag out of a hippie shirt. However, the watch on deck had a better idea and hailed a passing Norwegian yachtsman on an immaculate little gaffer. 'Please sell us your flag!' they cried in several languages. 'We will give you anything! T-shirts! Vodka! Many virgins!' The chap considered for a moment and agreed; we hastily lowered a goodie-bag containing the captain's own Tall Ships T-shirt and recovered a frayed ensign to fly in triumph from the crosstrees.

Then, after the uniquely Jubilee Sailing Trust ritual of Assisted Climbing – hauling the wheelchair users to the fore-top while the Norwegians gaped from a fleet of spectator boats – the Captain looked around the grey dusky fjord for more fun, spotted *Shabab Oman* anchored nearby also waiting for the morning pilot and invited 20 of them aboard for a barbecue. A local with a RIB offered to ferry them across, so he (and his children and eventually his neighbours from the edge of the fjord) joined the party. The Omanis came aboard in formal style in smart naval jumpers and black chequered *shamaghs* worn turban-style, presented us with two panfuls of curry and shook hands with everyone aboard. There were polite conversations with these gentle souls about the cold, the headwinds and how tired everyone was.

However, by 2045 fuelled by the barbie, the Omanis had hauled out bagpipes and skin drums and there was a bit of genteel clapping along to the rhythm; sort of sensible, F2-3 sociability. By nine, the dancing had started (say, F5) and within ten minutes the party rose to F10 after a number of teenage girls of the rave generation cottoned on to the manic drumbeat and started shimmying at the young Omani cadets. Soon, few of the Omanis were wearing *shamaghs* and most of the *Tenacious* girls were. There may be a market for photographs of Captain Campbell, ornament of the British merchant marine and Younger Brother of Trinity House, doing a dervish whirl in a garish palm-tree shirt with a turban falling down over her eyes.

And so it was that, while I may not have sailed the Atlantic single-handed like my gallant spouse, I can claim to have been in possibly the only singalong Omani line-dance involving wheelchairs, bagpipes and random Norwegians ever to take place in a chilly fjord by night....

GULLS AND GIRLS OF THE GÖTA CANAL

by Tim Barker

Mina² cruised extensively in the Baltic from early June until returning for the Beaulieu Meet. Tim Barker has written a log of no less than 33,000 words. He has chosen the passage through the Göta Canal for publication in the Journal.

Mina² is not used to tranquil pastoral surroundings, but as part of our summer cruise round the Baltic we had decided to cross the middle of Sweden through the canals and lakes. Having brought the boat from London and through the Limfjord at the top of Denmark, our transit started in Göteborg on the west coast.

5 June Nigel Fawkes and I were on our own at this stage, intending to rendezvous with our respective wives somewhere in the middle of the country. We left the Lilla Bommen marina in the middle of town and headed upriver towards the Trollhätte Canal. The first obstacle is the Götaälvbron bridge which, with a closed height of 19.5 metres was just too low for us. We hoisted flag P (the signal indicating you require the bridge to be opened), a call on Channel 09 and the traffic was stopped, the bridge lifted and we were on our way – but not far. Half a mile up river was another low railway bridge. We had to hang around for 35 minutes whilst a couple of trains crossed before the bridge opened, after which our journey resumed and we found ourselves passing through the industrial outskirts of the city with a graveyard of half-sunken wooden fishing boats lining the shore. The further we went (motoring as the wind was light from behind) the more rural the landscape and eventually we were passing farmland on either side. The river is extremely well buoyed with boomed marks every 100 metres either side of the channel, each marked with the distance from the head of the river/canal at Vänersborg.

There were very few places where we could moor up for the night, so we decided to tuck into Kungälv, a little island with an imposing castle and a small guest harbour up a narrow channel, a delightful and secluded spot. We were within a few feet of our destination when we suddenly went aground. As there wasn't enough room for us to turn round in the narrow channel, I started to reverse between the mooring piles to give me room to turn. This technique is guaranteed to work if you don't have a one knot current pushing 18 tons of boat onto the flimsy mooring piles and pinning you there (I had been lulled into a false sense of security in the non-tidal Baltic and had completely forgotten we were in the current of the river). For good measure I then jammed one of the piles underneath our dinghy which was hanging off the davits at the back of my boat. The next few minutes are a bit of a blur, but with Nigel effectively lifting 18 tons of boat off the pile and me manically gunning the engine forward and astern, we eventually managed to claw free and retreat shamefaced back out of the channel. Nigel thereby acquired super-hero status.

Having disgraced ourselves at Kungälv, we headed further upriver to Lilla Edet. We tied up for the night against the waiting pontoon below a lifting bridge. We went for a walk and came back to the boat an hour later to find that the sluice gates had obviously been shut, the water level had fallen by at least half a metre and we were hanging onto the quay with bar taut lines.

6 June In a freezing cold northerly, we donned full foul weather gear, hats and gloves and entered, alone, the first of the locks in the Trollhätte Canal. These ship locks are carved out of granite from the very mountain. With an enormous rise, the top of the lock, with battleship-sized bollards standing like sentries, towered four stories above us. Keeping us alongside the lock wall by heaving on the rungs of a slimy rusting ladder with a boat hook, I ordered Nigel to the top, mooring line in teeth, to make fast to the bollards. Now covered in slime, he hauled himself over the parapet and found himself looking at a pair of boots. The boots belonged to a faintly embarrassed lock-keeper who had just emerged from his hut and said it was totally unnecessary to climb up the wall; using the little hooks recessed into the lock wall (which neither of us had noticed) would be quite sufficient.

Having subjected Nigel to this unnecessary ordeal, I made amends by authorising the issue of a tot or two of my treasured and diminishing supply of sloe gin (or should it be slø gin here?). Feeling this might not be quite enough, I had the brilliant idea of appointing Nigel Chief Fire Officer and presenting him with our newly acquired fire gloves (a present received in Göteborg) as his badge of office. This clearly did the trick. Nigel took his new responsibilities very seriously and kept the gloves on all day – even whilst he ate, which was quite a feat. Eventually we arrived at Vänersborg on the edge of Lake Vänern. We spurned the marina as the pilot book indicated it had a maximum depth of only two metres (although I later found out from the girl in the harbour office that the outer wall of the marina can take 2.4 metres) and we headed for the town quay.

Nigel's recently acquired status of super-hero had obviously gone to his head. As we approached the quay and just as I was saying to him that

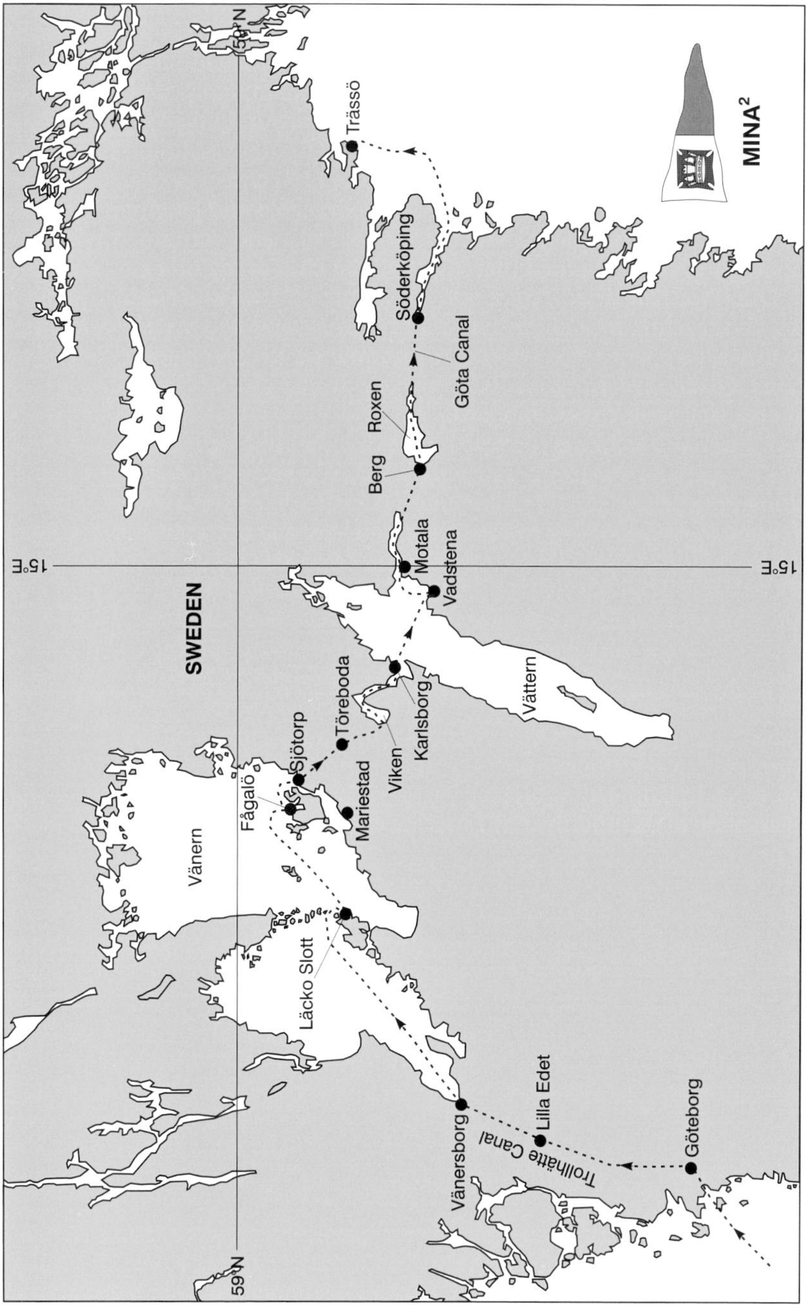
SWEDEN
59°N
58°N
15°E
15°E
Vänern
Vättern
Trässö
Söderköping
Göta Canal
Roxen
Berg
Motala
Vadstena
Karlsborg
Töreboda
Viken
Sjötorp
Fågalö
Mariestad
Läcko Slott
Vänersborg
Lilla Edet
Trollhätte Canal
Göteborg
MINA²

it might be easier to step ashore from amidships, he launched himself from the bow, Superman-style, whilst the quay was still six feet away and a good two feet higher than the boat. His feet just made the edge of the quay, but his body ran out of momentum. The outcome was inevitable. When Nigel finally surfaced he was still valiantly holding onto the mooring line. It was a fat lot of use in the water. By now it should have been secured to a bollard on the quay. Just before I ran him over Nigel managed to haul himself onto the quay, looking bedraggled and laughing hysterically with embarrassment (which I was as well) and continued tying the boat up. He later claimed that it was all the fault of my sloe gin. Rubbish.

Once we had dried Nigel out, we went for a walk around the town. There are some nice older buildings here in wood and brick but it is not worth a diversion. We walked to the marina in which there were just three boats, one flying an RCC burgee. It was *Ben Mor* owned by Ted Watts, but no one was on board.

*7 **June*** We awoke to a clear blue sky – the first sight of the sun for a week – and a very strong northerly wind. We had obviously done something to upset the local gull population as the decks were covered in bird droppings. The foredeck crew obligingly cleaned up, counting no fewer than 100 direct hits. We left the town quay at about 1030 beating across Lake Vänern to Läcko Slott. The final seven miles of the 38-mile passage was through a wonderful skärgård. It was very, very pretty, and made all the more exciting by seeing our first white-tailed eagle flapping over, as ever being harassed by outraged gulls. One bit of the twisting passage was a particularly tight turn through the rocks and there were four stone-built blocks, with granite bollards on, lined with wooden staves for springing larger ships round the tight bend. Eventually we got to Läcko Slott – a magnificent imposing castle with a little marina under its walls. Slap bang in the middle of the marina entrance, we hit a rock, quite hard. They obviously don't expect 2.2 metre draft boats to come in. We backed up and tied up to the end of the ferry quay, blocking half the entrance. Nigel prepared dinner and as it was being put on the table two young ladies turned up, wearing aprons and chefs' hats. They explained that they were the cooks in the castle and they were catering for a party of 40 people that evening. We exchanged pleasantries and then made our excuses to go below and eat the cooling meal. The final question from one of the girls was, 'You have to pay to stay here?' to which I replied, 'I presume so. Doubtless someone will come and ask us for money'. Apparently she was not asking a question but making a statement. 'No' said one of the girls, 'you have to pay us. It will be 80 crowns'. Well, I'm used to paying harbour dues to people in uniforms but pinafores and chefs' hats was a first.

So, to summarise the docking successes of the previous three days: we ran out of water and nearly destroyed a marina trying to extricate ourselves, later in the day we nearly left the boat hanging from a quay by its warps, the following day Nigel fell overboard and this night we hit a rock. I fully expected to sink the boat next.

8 June We went round Läcko castle which was a revelation. Whilst it looks run down from the outside, inside it was spectacular. Originally built as a fortification, it was then developed into a baroque palace by the De la Gardie family. Of the 248 rooms the most spectacular are the enormous state rooms, beautifully gilded with flying cherubs hung from the ceilings.

In the afternoon, we crossed 16 miles of Lake Vänern and passed down the narrow sound between Brommö and Fågalö, two islands in middle of the lake, and into a very pleasant, large shallow bay at the top of Fågalö where we anchored for the night.

9 June We awoke to another hot and sunny day and the nine mile trip to Sjötorp and the start of the Göta Canal proper. We arrived to find that the convoy (the canal did not open fully until the following day) had already left. This was something of a problem as we had arranged to meet our wives the next day in Karlsborg and there was now no chance we could make the rendezvous. But a few phone calls later, all their plans had been reorganised and we were to meet them in Töreboda instead. Unable to enter the canal we now had a free day. Nigel was keen to visit the cathedral in Mariestad, a 20-kilometre bike ride down what looked on the map to be a pleasant lakeside road. It turned out not to be the tranquil pastoral cycle he had hoped for but instead he found himself on the main Stockholm-Göteborg motorway, the busiest road in Sweden. For the return journey, Nigel sensibly folded the bike up and caught a bus.

Meanwhile, I spent the day sorting the boat out. Walking down the pontoon I noticed some gull chicks nesting below. All of a sudden, and without any warning, there was an incredibly loud shriek in my right ear and something hit me hard on the head. I ducked sideways only to see mother doing a tight turn and lining me up for her next bombing run. Not wishing to be batted over the head a second time, I rapidly retreated back to the boat, rubbing my neck which I had ricked whilst taking evading action.

10 June At last we entered the first of the 58 locks of the Göta Canal. We were to take five days for the transit. Apart from the two massive ship locks of the Trollhätte Canal this was the first lock experience for all of the five boats which managed to squeeze in. Being the first day the canal was fully open, it was also the first experience for the pretty young lock girl. But she nannied us all into position and waited until we had all gone to the office and paid our dues (just over £300 which included the locks and all marina fees). The lock gates were closed and the sluice opened. A maelstrom of swirling bubbling water hit the boats like a brick wall. For the next five minutes it was like being in a washing machine, desperately trying to fend off lock walls and the other boats as the roaring water pushed us first one way then the other. Eventually the waters calmed, the lock gates opened and in a state of catatonic shock we motored out of the lock knowing that we had to go through the traumatic experience another 28 times before we reached the summit.

But the management of the Göta Canal is canny. They employ a clearly sexist recruitment policy and most of the lock keepers were extremely pretty young girls who provided mainly male skippers a delightful distraction from the trauma of the locks. Having tied the boat up, Nigel was in the habit of swanning off to chat up the Gorgeous Göta Girls, photographing each one and marking them out of ten for pulchritude, leaving me in the washing machine to wrestle with the mooring lines.

At one point we swung round a bend to find a vintage passenger ship, the SS *Sandon*, pretty much blocking the canal. Hanging down the sides of the ship were old tree trunks which they use as fenders, rolling down the hull as they squeeze into the locks. Adhering to the international rule of the road, I moved to the starboard side of the canal and stopped to let her pass. She gave two loud blasts on her horn and turned directly towards us. Obligingly I moved over to the other side of the canal where as we almost went aground it became obvious why the ship wanted to use the 'wrong' side of the canal. Edging past us, the captain of the *Sandon* opened the bridge window and, much to the amusement of his passengers, shouted to me, 'Not only do you have lots of money and a

Läcko Slot

beautiful boat, you have lots of common sense too!' and with a farewell blast of her horn she steamed on her way.

By late afternoon we had reached Töreboda where we were reunited with Jane and Maria, long-suffering wives of the Chief Fire Officer and Skipper respectively. I was now experiencing considerable discomfort in my shoulder and arm, the consequence of my encounter with the maternal gull.

11 June We left Töreboda and passed through the last of the uphill locks, reaching our highest point of more than 300 feet above sea level, certainly the highest our ocean-going vessel had ever been or was ever likely to be. We had been passing through lovely soft countryside with pretty well-kept canal-side properties. It was a bit like motoring through somebody's back garden. We then headed across Lake Viken to the town of Karlsborg on its eastern side. The enormous castle is still a garrison and walking round it reminded me of Aldershot. A hangar full of camouflaged snowmobiles reminded us that this part of the world is completely frozen over in the winter months.

By the marina was a crazy golf course. I had thought they had gone out of fashion in the 1950s. Not so in Scandinavia apparently. There had been a crazy golf course by every marina we had visited in both Denmark and Sweden. Here it remained a passion. The reason I mention this one in particular was because of the bizarre sight of a car drawing up, a man getting out and opening the boot, and taking out a pair of golf shoes and his own putter. We speculated whether he was the local professional come to give lessons or perhaps a member of the Swedish National Team, keeping his hand in until crazy golf was made an Olympic sport. The other surprising sporting feature of the region is *petanque* or *boules*. I thought this was restricted to France apart from the occasional pitch in trendy places like Docklands.

12 June Although we were heading across Lake Vättern to Motala, everyone told us that a diversion to Vadstena, a little further down the lake, was pretty much obligatory. And when we got there we understood why. The moorings are in the moat of Vadstena Castle. Built in 1544 by Gustav I, it is a magnificent building – absolutely spectacular. We immersed ourselves in the history of the Brigittine Nuns in the impressive new museum housed in the old convent dormitory (part of the castle grounds remain an active convent). The other local attraction is the Museum of Insanity, which sadly was closed. But through one of the windows we could see the cast iron bath with its strapped-down canvas cover and a hole for the patient's head. You shared the bath with a large number of electric eels. This was only one of the instruments of torture on display. If you weren't insane before these treatments, you certainly would be after!

As we left for our overnight stop in Motala, the skies blackened, thunder rolled and a triple rainbow arched perfectly over the ancient spires and turrets of Vadstena. Motala is rather dull in comparison although Nigel and Jane did go to a rather whacky motor museum. Even though they were the only visitors, the curator was determined to make everything as authentic as possible, including giving a fresh cup of tea to the mannequin who was in charge of the 1940s switchboard!

That evening, the Downstairs Skipper treated us to a gastro-dinner, producing a whole fillet of beef which she had brought in her luggage firstly from Argentina to London, thence to Stockholm and onwards by train to Töreboda – breaking countless international laws of which we all professed ourselves entirely ignorant. Delicious!

13 June From Motala we were back in the canal again, heading for Berg on the west coast of Lake Roxen where there is a staircase of eight consecutive locks. The accommodation looked better at the top than at the bottom so we stayed put for the night and decided to tackle the flight of locks the following morning. Having seen only two other British boats since leaving London three and a half weeks earlier, we bumped into four Royal Southern boats cruising in company and heading in the opposite direction. We discovered that a number of them lived in Hamble and knew my parents. By now my shoulder and back were pretty constant agony and all the fingers of my right hand had gone completely numb, even though I was eating Ibuprofen like popcorn. I hadn't been able to sleep for a couple of days and I was becoming exhausted. Clearly the demon gull of Sjötorp had inflicted more damage than I had originally thought.

14 June We awoke to another hot and cloudless day. We had a late start as a flotilla of boats had to make their way up the staircase of locks before we could head down. Standing on the boat at the top looking down 100 feet to the lake below was bizarre. Having crossed Lake Roxen we had one final stretch of canal before making our way out into the Baltic. This included the lifting bridge that carried the main Stockholm to Göteborg railway line. Responsibility for manning the bridge fell to a young lad who was obviously as new to the job as his more attractive lock-keeping colleagues. He was clearly terrified by the vision of his raising the bridge only to see an intercity express doing an Evel Knievel across the Göta Canal. Every time an opportunity presented itself, he lost his bottle and rushed back to report to us that there would be a further ten-minute delay. Meanwhile the boats kept on coming down the canal. By the time he had steeled himself to open the bridge, the canal was as busy as the Hamble on a bank holiday weekend. As there was no time to allow more than five boats through at each opening, I should think some of them are still there. Going through you had the novel experience of looking at eye level at the railway line stretching out over the horizon. Even more weird was the experience a little further along of going over an aqueduct and looking down on the motorway below.

With the delays it was touch and go whether we would get to Söderköping before 1800 when the lifting bridges stopped lifting for the night.

Göta Lock

We failed. Three miles short of our destination we met a small road bridge which was remotely controlled and resolutely failed to open so we, along with a boat with a young couple and their child, tied up to the waiting pontoon and settled down for the night.

One of the features of the Trollhätte and Göta canals was the bridges. Some swung vertically up to the left, others to the right. Some swung horizontally from the shore, others pivoted horizontally in the middle of the canal. Some were cantilevered, others on cogs. There was the one that lifted vertically between two enormous towers, another that moved horizontally along rails and a further one that lifted vertically in two parts into bascules like Tower Bridge. Most were single but some were twin bridges. It was as though there was a rule 'We are building a new bridge and you are invited to tender for the design but it has to be like none other on the canal'. But it sure makes it interesting.

15 June We looked at our watches waiting for 0900 when the remotely-controlled bridge was due to open. At two minutes to, the bells started to ring and the lights flashed red, warning the non-existent traffic that the barriers were about to close. A driving school car, the first car we had seen for half an hour, cruised to a halt, not behind the white line but directly under the barrier. We all waited with bated breath. On the stroke of 0900 the barrier fell with a resounding clang onto the roof of the car. A very large lady flew out of the car, screaming hysterically. As the barrier was not down properly, the bridge was not going to rise. The bridge operator was looking at the scene on a closed circuit TV screen some miles away and was not in the best position to help. So our neighbour walked round, and gently lifted the barrier whilst the driver (presumably the hapless student) reversed the car back. With the barrier now lowered, the bridge at last started to rise and we motored through to the sound of the continuing hysteria of the fat instructor.

The evening before, our new neighbours had joined us for a drink and told us that the great attraction of Söderköping was the best ice cream parlour in Sweden. I had better explain that the Swedes were not the sylph-like beauties we had expected but like the British they all seemed to be running to fat. Whereas in Britain it is chips, beer and junk food, in Sweden it is ice cream. You may be in a village so small that it has no corner shop or petrol station, but you can guarantee that it will have at least two ice cream shops and you rarely see a Swede without an ice cream. So in the land where ice cream is a national obsession, the best ice cream parlour in the country had to be worth a visit. And it was. The menu of gargantuan and bizarre concoctions of ice cream ran to several dozen pages and included 'The Vesuvius' that was presented steaming like a cauldron in a bowl of dried ice. Unfortunately for Nigel he chose the one that seemed to be made from Domestos-flavoured ice cream. The others were exquisite but of such an obscene size that we were all defeated. We tried to walk it off with a stroll round the town, the big feature of which is the largest wooden bell tower in the country. Very tall and thin and apparently propped up by ill-assorted spillikins, it is almost contemporary in design and would not look out of place in the Tate Modern. Unbelievably it was built in 1582. Replete with ice cream we went through the last of the Göta Canal locks and enjoyed a brisk sail to a lovely anchorage at Trässö.

Our transit through the middle of Sweden was a complete change to the coastal and offshore cruises we are used to. Whilst we were sprinting through as part of our 3500-mile Baltic marathon, the canal systems and the lovely inland lakes (some of them enormous with hundreds of islands and anchorages) are a cruising ground in their own right. We could happily have spent weeks there and would still only be scratching the surface of this delightful and different area.

Mina^2 is a cutter-rigged Oyster 485 drawing 2.2 metres. She was built in 1997 by Windboats in Norwich.

A whale of a tale (Kellett)
Previous page: HMS *Diamond Rock*, Martinique (Brunyee)
Male orang-utan at Kumai (Morfey)

Fishing boats near Bali (Morfey)

Condor at Brecknock (Melling)

Restless in Maine (Lennox-King)

Flight of Time (Morfey)

FLIGHT OF TIME HEADS HOME

by Graham Morfey

This voyage was awarded the Romola Cup

Sitting in Opua at the beginning of August 2004 we had been promised a 'sling shot' departure by Bob McDavitt, the New Zealand weather guru, but on leaving it seemed more like being shot from a cannon. The low that was generating a southerly wind had decided to stall and deepen just east of New Zealand giving Wellington the strongest winds for 50 years. Seven hours out darkness closed in, Cape Reinga and the open sea were ahead and the wind was gusting to 50 knots. With the wind on the quarter the staysail was all we needed. The drama of the night was soon behind us although the Orion that flew over us was a grim reminder of the Mayday when two fishermen had lost their lives just west of us.

Craig had sailed with us to Vanuatu and I was glad to have his strength and experience for this passage. As the wind eased, the sail area increased, the Monitor was set and meals became more civilised with an evening drink accompanied by music. A week and nearly 1000 miles from Opua, we and the boat were well into ocean passage routine. Despite turning north there was no sign of the trade winds and we were making generous use of the engine. The plus side was that the watermaker was running. Even 200 miles from land there were reefs to avoid but our Maxsea navigation system combined with C-Map made life much easier. We still carry a huge quantity of paper charts kindly lent by fellow members, but only as back up. Sailing with the wind astern means poling out the yankee for maximum speed but a wind shift entails gybing and foredeck work, so during the night we revert to main only so that the other crew can get some sleep.

On 1 September in a light wind and smooth sea we were sailing at 2½ knots aiming to enter the Barrier Reef soon after dawn. Yet again we marvelled at navigators finding these entrances in pre-GPS days. Suddenly we could see the edge of the reef. In the clearest of water we got a sounding of 700 feet then the entrance led us into smooth water and 70 feet. With 50 waypoints set up we threaded our way through the Blackwood and Pollard Channels before joining the main inshore channel as darkness fell.

Now in smooth water we had the best sailing of the passage. A day and a half later we were anchored at Thursday Island. In the next four hours we cleared customs and quarantine, who kindly let us keep all our New Zealand food, took on diesel, spoke to *Ocean Song* and got under way with the course due west. The Gulf of Carpentaria stretches for 250 miles and with depths of only 30 metres has a reputation for being uncomfortable. In the continuing light winds we had no problems and 320 miles from Thursday Island the light of Cape Wessel was abeam and Darwin was only 414 miles away. The relaxed sailing was now over as we turned south into Dundas Strait passing Cape Don. Fortunately and totally by luck we had six knots of favourable current and swept past the Abbott Shoal buoy. We could smell the wood smoke off the land and briefly the tide was against us. We spoke to the Fisheries officer and were given clearance to go straight into the marina at Darwin avoiding the usual 24 hours of 'treatment' for foreign molluscs. At the lock, Merryl who was joining me for the rest of the voyage was looking down at us. At 1830 on 8 September we were safely moored in Cullen Bay marina 3090 miles and 23 days from Opua. It had been a wonderful voyage and Craig had proved himself yet again to be an ideal companion and invaluable crew.

I had not realised how tired I was, but in the next five days Merryl organised our travels around Darwin, which seemed to be spread out over many miles. We cleared customs, bought new yankee sheets, got the kicker reattached to the mast, stocked up with provisions (in many cases for six months) and stored all the wine and beer for which we could find space. We were unlikely to be able to get spares or repairs until Singapore, 2000 miles away. In Darwin we met up with *Keeshond* and *Solent Venture*, who were to be our companions for much of the next six months.

Our departure on 14 September was a bit of a disaster. I misjudged the wind and we blew sideways onto a very unyielding pontoon and damaged the toe rail; our first crunch in nine years. It got worse; while filling the tank and cans with 563 litres of diesel it seemed to get everywhere and all under a relentless Northern Territory sun.

Wind was not expected on this leg so it was no surprise to be steadily motoring on a glassy sea. One dawn was enlivened by a fiery glow, not the sun but oil rigs. The more interesting hazards were the unlit abandoned ones. Due to a misunderstanding I had not got visas for Indonesia and so we were making our entry at Kupang, West Timor to put things right. It was dark by the time we anchored off Kupang and we were grateful to those who had gone before and given us a waypoint for the

Rice paddy fields in Bali

anchorage, which otherwise we would never have found. Just before anchoring a problem developed which was to plague us over the next 1500 miles to Singapore. The engine overheated and would not respond to the normal treatment. Over the next four weeks we tried everything. There was plenty of advice over the airwaves but the problem remained.

Merryl went ashore and with the help of the local agent cleared the formalities and got fresh food. The wind allowed us to sail to Rinca, 200 miles away, and soon after dawn the anchor was down. We had joined *Solent Venture* in a beautiful bay. As we finished anchoring we saw a large black Komodo dragon swaggering along the white crescent of a beach.

Log extract: 'This is a beautiful bay. We are surrounded by hills and white sandy beaches. In the morning the fishermen come and lay nets to the shore, a wonderful stretch of white sand. Yesterday we had a very convivial evening on board *Solent Venture*, an English boat we met in Darwin with a young couple Alex and Caryl on board. We are travelling the same route, so will probably see quite a lot of them. The morning was hot and still and I read and drank tea in the cockpit. Merryl was serving up breakfast, which was interrupted by two fishermen coming on board to chat. Our book of home photos and the Indonesian phrase book proved invaluable so that we just about managed to communicate. They departed with some diesel and plans to meet us on the beach at 1300 to take us to see monkeys, dragons and their village, but they never turned up. Whether it was a language problem or a change of heart on their part we shall never know. I then returned to the engine. Yesterday I had stripped down and checked the whole cooling system and found a considerable amount of old anode in the heat exchanger, hopefully this was the cause of the overheating. The alternator had been dying and only putting in 20 amps so this was also replaced. The small reef in the bay over which Merryl snorkelled was full of healthy-looking and colourful coral and plenty of small reef fish, not the usual dead and decaying corals destroyed by anchors and pollution. Rinca is part of the national park with neighbouring Komodo Island and we have seen a monitor lizard, several fish eagles, deer, heron and other seabirds. We think we could hear the monkeys on shore shrieking their alarm calls but have been too chary of venturing inland to find out, as the Komodo dragon can be fearsome. The sea is turquoise over the white sand and the land is very arid with sparse low vegetation except for a few straggly palm trees marching across the tops of the lower hills. At night the bay is dotted with the occasional lonely light on board local fishing boats.'

The next stop was Bali, 250 miles away but meanwhile we were enjoying sailing past these beautiful islands. Sumbawa was green and mountainous but still very visibly volcanic. At dusk the cloud ahead turned out to be Sangean Island, 6000 metres high. We had six days in Bali and wished we could have doubled that. Merryl had been doing her research and discovered that we had arrived at full moon and the most important festival of the year. So we and the crew of *Solent Venture* found the principal temple in Denpasar, bought our offerings (small banana leaf dishes full of scented flower petals and rice plus incense sticks) and joined the huge throng waiting to enter the temple. Graham was whisked off into the crowd by two very pretty girls who were intent on ensuring he was blessed with holy water and rice. He found his way back to the taxi with slightly damp hair and rice stuck to his forehead.

We arranged for a driver to take us around and each morning he would collect us, frequently not finishing until ten at night and all this for £20 per day! Our minds are still full of the varied and beautiful sights and the friendliness of the people and their good humour. We saw traditional dancing and visited several temples, one by Lake Bratan and another by the sea at Tana Lot. We ate in a variety of restaurants from the posh with dancing to a transport cafe, Balinese style. We ate sucking pig correctly (with our right hands). We saw mountains and volcanoes and watched rice being planted and harvested. The hillsides were covered in terraced paddy fields just as in the picture books. We saw monkeys, fruit bats and even a python. We saw *ikat* and batik cloth being woven and coloured in the traditional way, wood being carved and canvases being painted, albeit now with modern acrylics from Yugoslavia! We swam in the hot springs. The markets were always fun and bargaining is a way of life. This was all done with great humour and side talk, quite tiring after the fourth purchase. The market in Denpasar was our final call and this was vast with huge piles of spices, vegetables, clothing and local artefacts.

We left Bali Marina on 3 October. Coming south we had had a favourable tide, sometimes up to 5 knots so we were not looking forward to going north. However, by keeping inshore along the 20-metre contour we picked up the counter-current which ran in our favour virtually all the way until the last few miles around the northeast headland where we fought our way with the aid of 25 knots of wind on the beam against the 3-knot tide. As we sailed along the north coast in the dusk we could see fires on the sacred mountain of Agung and realised that these must be natural fumaroles. What I thought was white sand in the small coves turned out to be line upon line of fishing craft nestling together. In the gloaming, dark clouds loomed behind the mountainous outline and below a necklace of little lights indicated the fishing communities along the lower slopes. The Balinese consider the north to be a holy place and the home of God – on that evening it certainly looked special.

Before darkness on the evening of 6 October we just made it into the Teluk Kumai, the shallow bay at the entrance to the river leading to Kumai, Borneo. The shoreline was not far away but completely hidden by the perpetual smoke haze caused by burning rice stubble. It was a weird sensation anchoring apparently in the middle of nowhere in 13 feet. The wind was blowing straight into the bay, so it was a bit bouncy but superb holding in sticky mud. The next morning we were underway by 0620. The course is difficult and because of the poor visibility it was not easy to see the leading marks. We were very grateful to John Whyte of the Cruising Association for his invaluable waypoints. It took us four hours to get to the anchorage and it looked as if we were going to be late for our meeting with Harry with whom we had booked a two-day river trip. Fortunately Kumai has its clocks at GMT+7, so we had an hour in hand! The passage up the river was fascinating with lots of local craft, jungle on either side, murky water, a wooden boat careened on a sand bank and long fast boats laden with pandanus leaves. It was very Somerset Maugham.

We grabbed our walking/mosquito/overnight gear and together with Alex and Caryl boarded Harry's boat and set off on what was to be one of the most memorable events in our eight years of cruising. The boat wound its way up the narrow and sometimes shallow river. One side of the tributary is a national park whilst the other had been deforested for farming. The agricultural side was peppered with inlets and very basic huts on stilts. Glimpses through the trees revealed a landscape reminiscent of the Somme with a few dead trees standing gaunt in a barren landscape. The national park side was lush and full of wild life. Ahead we would see branches move and then two or three proboscis monkeys would climb the trees or swing from one branch to another. A flash of blue was the hawksbill and we saw a crocodile in the water. A wonderful lunch of Indonesian food was served on the shaded upper deck of our gaily-painted narrow boat.

At a landing stage our guide set off at a galloping pace and within a few minutes we were meeting orang-utan on the path. He knew them all by name and sometimes we had to take a detour as the ape was sitting firmly in the path; after all it was his jungle! At the feeding platform there was a solitary piece of blue rope to show us our boundary and the apes approached from all directions, sometimes high up in the trees, sometimes from behind us and we had to move to let them through. They are fed bananas to make up for the loss of their natural food because logging has destroyed so much habitat. A full diet is not supplied and this encourages them to forage for themselves. As dusk began to fall we followed the path back to our boat, very hot and tired but realising how fortunate we had been.

We woke early at 0600 and after a visit to a rehabilitation camp for orphan orang-utans recovered from poachers we carried on down river. Travelling at a butterfly pace to join the main river we lounged under the canopy and watched out for the wildlife. Periodically local canoes powered by simple raucous engines with no silencers roared past with coolant water spraying from the stern. We reached our anchorage just before nightfall. Harry arrived with our passports and with all the paperwork done, he joined us for a beer.

In the morning after a brief tour of the town we set off for Singapore, 600 miles away. After four days we crossed the equator at 1100 on 13 October, some four and a half years after our first crossing. The Inmarsat C was giving us steady reports of piracy against commercial vessels only 50 miles away but a more immediate problem was to avoid the fishing boats with their extensive nets and, even more dangerous, the tugs and barges. The latter appeared to be lit with a candle and had half a mile of towline attaching them to the tug. Our course up the Selat Riau west of Bintan was a short cut but a night passage in company with a multitude of other vessels was pretty exhausting. We joined the Singapore Strait, which despite the dire warnings was a joy with all the ships on clearly defined courses. We scuttled across to the Singapore side, wound our way up the channel helped by an up-to-date C-Map and at 1415 moored in Raffles Marina at the western end of Singapore. It was 59 days and 5297 miles since New Zealand. With the help of Neil on *Keeshond* the engine overheating problem was finally cured. The back plate of the seawater pump was rotating, so a new pump was fitted. The problems of long distance cruising are not as everyone imagines gales and pirates but keeping everything working. Self-sufficiency in spares and skills is vital but the help provided by fellow cruisers is overwhelming.

We stopped for 12 days in Singapore. The boat was lifted out for a quick check, two alternators were repaired and stores replenished. After Indonesia, Singapore was very different. We enjoyed the markets, the

Graham Morfey in the galley

restaurants, the Asian museum and the Botanical Gardens and mastered the superb underground system. Merryl flew home for two months and Margaret joined for the next stage to Thailand.

The Malacca Strait presents four major hazards. Pirates operate on the Indonesian side but fortunately concentrate on commercial shipping, there is a steady flow of traffic, the fisherman have very long nets and take them right up to the shipping lane and there is lightning more dramatic than we had ever seen. We decided that the prudent tactic was to travel only by day and so we started a steady pattern of long day passages in company with *Solent Venture*. On the third day we tied up in the very smart Admiral's Marina, Port Dickson, Malaysia, and made a very worthwhile visit to Melaka, an old city that has been at the centre of Malaysian history for centuries. The Portuguese, the Dutch and the British have all ruled here and left their mark.

We departed early from Port Dickson for a 12-hour day with plenty of excitement passing through Port Klang with thunder and lightning all around. After an overnight at Pangkor and then a peaceful anchorage at Penang we caught the tide up through Penang and under the bridge. The city is dominated by high-rise blocks but there was just a glimpse of old Penang at the junk anchorage with a few yachts anchored off. This is a very busy port with cargo vessels, tugs, ocean liners and several highly coloured passenger ferries zipping to and fro across the fairway, all in the brilliant early morning sunshine. The northern channel was dominated by a flotilla of fishing boats and their nets. We managed to avoid them all but were not so lucky later on. There was a horrible clunk and the engine slowed dramatically. We had collected a plastic sack on the propeller. The cutters got rid of some but we were still going slowly and the temperature gauge was rising. Alex from *Solent Venture* very nobly dived in and cleared the bag which was wrapped around the prop and well clear of the cutters. We reached the beautiful bay of Langkawi with its tall wooded islands just as the sun was going down and Alex and Caryl joined us for dinner and a large quantity of red wine.

The next day started with clearing in followed by serious shopping. We managed to load up with enough drink to last us until the Mediterranean and got fresh vegetables and salad at the supermarket. After a very idle day at Langkawi we made an early start and by 1400 were anchored at the beautiful island of Koh Lipe, Thailand. Graham managed to inspect the propeller. The clacking sound which had followed us since the plastic sack incident had ceased just before we anchored and he discovered that the stationary cutter had broken.

As we approached Phuket we saw amazing tall islands rising from the sea, not one but dozens of them, all extraordinary shapes. After finding our way up the winding channel we entered the Yacht Haven Marina at 1700 on 8 November. It is well laid out and the managers were incredibly helpful. There are few facilities but all the tradesmen will come to the marina. We organised outboard repairs, laundry, re-stitching the spray hood and the repair of the teak toe rail.

Graham spent a day wrestling with the gearbox, the problem being that it would not engage astern. Fortunately help was at hand and the very capable Wasan diagnosed that the clutch and bearing had gone and it needed a major rebuild. He then negotiated a space on the hard at the Boat Lagoon to investigate the stiffness in the prop shaft. The entrance wanders through mangroves with a few poles to mark it. Like most boats we went hard aground at the shallowest and trickiest corner but were pulled to safety by the dockmaster's launch. The yard was incredibly hot, noisy and dirty. Wasan checked the shaft and the problem was identified as a minor misalignment of bearings, which he undertook to correct.

The charms of boating had definitely faded by this stage and we set about booking flights. We visited Bangkok and Angkor Wat and trekked on elephants in Chiang Mai. We returned to Phuket to find Wasan had done all the work he had promised and then we flew back to England for Christmas. Little did we realise that by the end of Boxing Day the whole world would have heard of Phuket.

Merryl and Graham returned on 16 January. Our exit from the Lagoon was even more dramatic than our entry but fortunately the dockmaster was at the wheel and we ploughed on through the mud. That night it was wonderful to be at anchor away from the heat and noise and to realise that we were clear of the shore. The next day we followed the coastline down to an anchorage at Nai Harn and met up with Alex and Caryl. They had been anchored there when the tsunami came in. After eating at a local restaurant we adjourned to a bar where the locals were fund raising to help those affected by the tsunami. A DVD played chilling footage of the wave as it hit only three weeks earlier.

On 22 January we made a leisurely start and soon were enjoying beautiful trade wind sailing towards the Maldives. We rounded Pygmalion Point at the southern end of Great Nicobar in the company of many very large ships. Now we were really in the Indian Ocean with 808 miles to the tip of Sri Lanka and a further 450 to the Maldives. Conditions were perfect with a steady wind of 18 knots from astern. The genoa was boomed out to starboard, the main to port. The wind shifted yesterday evening with some dark clouds overhead. Here is an extract from the log: 'Twelve hours of life aboard, late afternoon and we are charging along with full sail so as to catch up with *Solent Venture* and get some photos of her before the sun goes down. We make it, get the photos and I notice that the cage on the furling gear is chafing the line. Fortunately it is not too wet and I am able to use the Allen key and get it in the correct position. We suddenly find we are doing 10 knots over the ground thanks to a surprise 3-knot current. Put the second reef in the main ready for the night. Pour some red wine and relax with it in the cockpit. Although we are west of 90° I have not adjusted the clocks so we get an extra hour of daylight. Merryl sets to and produces steak (imported into Thailand from New Zealand), mushrooms, onions, boiled potatoes. We eat in the cockpit wearing our head torches. At 2100 Merryl goes down below and I am left on watch. First coffee and chocolate, then listening to *The Planets* on my walkman. The moon is astern and is shining a brilliant light on the sea behind us like a wide silvery wake. Ahead I can see the red light of *Solent Venture*. The clouds are gentle and puffy with the stars shining in the dark sky ahead. The temperature is perfect and shorts and shirt are adequate, although at night we always wear a harness. 0030 and it is time to call Merryl and within five minutes I am asleep. Roused at 0330 for my watch, the moon is now lower and ahead on the starboard bow. At this hour something strong is needed, so it is Verdi's *Requiem* turned up loud. We are north of the main shipping lane but one ship passes astern heading for some port on the east coast of India. Only an hour to go and time for my midnight feast. Everybody has their favourite and it alters according to the conditions but for me tonight it is asparagus soup. 0630 and I call Merryl for her watch and leave her to see the dawn.'

We managed to sail most of the time but the wind was light at night. In the mornings it picked up and was on the beam, which was great; there was a lot of shipping but they all seemed to keep a good lookout. Six days

Merryl visits a school in the Maldives

out and we had very little wind but the sea was smooth so we managed to make good 118 miles in 24 hours. At midday we turned southwest to cut across the shipping lanes before nightfall when we would turn west again. It was very hot and we had been motoring since the turn. There was a minor disaster when we found that 50 gallons of fresh water had emptied into the bilge. The accumulator tank had rusted through. We ran the watermaker to make good the loss and the next day I managed to bypass the accumulator tank so pressurised water and our showers were restored. Two days later we were motoring and the engine suddenly slowed. Merryl harnessed up and went over the side and spent 40 minutes clearing coconut fibre that had encased the prop. There was a gentle breeze, which made it difficult for Merryl as even with the sails down we were doing one knot. With the prop cleared we stuck to sailing very slowly through the line of tree trunks and other debris including a huge tree complete with roots. We were very glad we had encountered this while it was still light. Once clear we started the engine and had several rum punches! On 1 February we anchored at Uligan, Maldives, a beautiful atoll with a brilliant white beach. All the officials came out to us; there was the usual volume of paperwork but it was all very efficient and courteous. Uligan was a delightful place and we relaxed there after completing the various chores including ferrying a considerable quantity of diesel which took several dinghy journeys.

We left on 6 February and enjoyed peaceful sailing in a gentle breeze

on a calm sea, which is always a pleasant way to begin a passage. At midnight the wind died and we motored with three other yachts for company. The next night was enlivened by being overtaken by a huge aircraft carrier travelling fast. The following day the wind picked up at dusk and we roared along on a close reach with two reefs and several rolls in the genoa. Five days out and we were on a broad reach. It was colder at night and we had to wear trousers and sweaters for first time for many months. Oman was 507 miles ahead. We were fortunately sailing when we got hooked on a fishing line in the night. The boat had been calling us on the VHF telling us to 'turn 30° to red' and giving us the position of his line. Unfortunately both *Solent Venture* and ourselves misheard the latitude, but even with the turn we made we were well inside the length of net, which stretched for over 10 miles. After a considerable effort we lowered the sails (we had been running goose-winged and poled out) and eventually managed to depress the buoyed line so that it slid past the skeg. I remembered to centre the wheel and I think the modification made in Maine for lobster pot protection saved the day. Getting the sails up again took some effort but soon we were under way. The next day provided some excitement when we were hailed by a French warship.

At 1300 on 15 February we anchored in the harbour at Salalah, Oman, having passed massive container ships and oil tankers in the outer part. The approach was enlivened by the attention of patrol craft and helicopters. We enjoyed our few days in Oman and were well looked after by Mohammed, the distinctive tall figure in white *disdasha* and skull cap who ran his business, as agent looking after all the yachts' needs, from his car on the quay. We drove inland to see the desert; it is not sand dunes as in Lawrence of Arabia but sandy coloured sedimentary rock, in places carved dramatically by rain and wind. The day ended in a traditional Omani family restaurant, seated on floor cushions in front of a TV in a small plywood-lined windowless room. On the menu were 'bull's eyes' and 'whole goat's head in spicy soup'. Having eaten well at lunchtime we chose less ambitious but otherwise very tasty dishes. We left Salalah on 20 February with a departure delayed by entangling with another boat's kedge warp; they had chosen to use floating rope which created a hazard in the crowded anchorage.

After 24 hours we stopped the engine and were able to sail, though rather slowly. It was very peaceful but that would not last. Boats ahead entering the Red Sea were reporting winds of 30 to 50 knots and very big seas. Hopefully the weather would have eased by the time we got there. We were getting closer to the pirate zone but our radio contacts ahead had no problems and there were three warships in the area so we were keeping our fingers crossed. We continued to sail goose-winged with full sail. There was a frustrating current of nearly a knot against us and our speed over the ground was only four knots. We had a bit of excitement in the morning when a dhow came fast straight towards us before turning, slowing and then departing. Fortunately *Solent Venture* was only half a mile away. In the next 24 hours we would be going through the worst pirate area, then we could relax before the winds and currents of 'The Gate of Tears' (Bab al Mandeb). As we approached the straits the wind picked up and the current gradually changed from adverse to 1.5 knots in our favour. The wind was dead astern but with slight fluctuations so we had to gybe three times in 15 hours including once at night. With a pole on the yankee, running backstay, preventer and downhaul it took quite a time. We reached the entrance to the Straits at 0800. From then on we had an exciting ride northwards but the wind never went above 30 knots and the seas were modest. We stormed up with three reefs in the main and one in the yankee. The goose-winged rig is very stable and the

Autohelm coped magnificently. Most of the day we were doing between 9 and 10 knots over the ground. We were running up the west side of the shipping channel and it was quite frightening at the turns to see big ships pointing straight at us. We continued sailing at a fast speed into the night but the wind and seas gradually eased. At 0800 the wind was down to 5 knots and we motored very gently until the sea breeze kicked in just after lunch. All afternoon we enjoyed a beautiful sail on smooth seas, fishing trawlers around and birds wheeling above us. On a close reach with full sail the cutter rig is perfect. At midnight the wind had died and so we motored gently to arrive at dawn on 28 February at Massawa, Eritrea.

As we went through the busy main port into the inner harbour in the early morning calm there was still evidence all around of the epic struggle the Eritreans had had to free their country. Along the starboard bank were a couple of ships' graveyards with the rusting skeletal remains of half-submerged coastal traders slumped in the shallows. On the opposite bank the most spectacularly damaged building was the bombed-out dome and arches of the Imperial Palace. The peeling facades of the Arab-influenced terraces and ruined Italianate port buildings stood in sharp contrast to the few quite brutal experiments in modern architecture visible on the neighbouring Taulud Island. We slowly picked a route through the brightly painted fishing dhows, each with a colourful box jutting out from the rail and teams of fishermen carrying out their morning ablutions or waving to us sleepily through the open sterns from their bunks. We had plenty of space and down went the anchor on the African continent. We knew we had little time in the country and through Mike, Mr Laundry-and-general-fix-it-all man, quickly arranged a shared taxi with an English speaking driver for the following day to take us up to the mountain capital of Asmara. Just as with many Eritreans we were to meet over the following days, there was a book to be written about Mike's experiences during the war and as a refugee in Sri Lanka. We found the Eritreans friendly, gracious, hospitable and tolerant of the nine tribes and several religions within the country. Even with the obvious poverty there was optimism for the future. Crime was low and we heard that hassling tourists was not tolerated. After lunch we returned to the anchorage and downloaded the boat's email to learn that Graham urgently needed to return home. It was fortunate that we had booked the trip to Asmara as from there Graham could get a flight. The evening was spent preparing the boat and making sure Merryl was up-to-date with all the systems so that she could maintain everything while Graham was away. The journey up through the mountains was interesting with wonderful views and stops whenever we wanted to photograph camel trains or breathe in the clear mountain air. Graham did not get to see much of Asmara but he did experience the laid-back ambience of the city with its café society and enjoyed a traditional communal Eritrean meal in

Close encounter in the Suez Canal

the evening. It was composed of several spicy and non-spicy meat and vegetable dishes on a huge platter with *injera* pancake bread, which served well in lieu of cutlery and reduced the washing up.

Graham returned on 8 March and the following day we weighed anchor at 1430 after the immigration official had come on board to check that we had no stowaways. We picked up a gentle breeze and were soon sailing with full sail at five knots in smooth water. Then followed a beautiful 24 hours of sailing with the wind on our beam, never more than 15 knots. The seven boats in our little fleet were all British and in touch with each other on our private radio net. By the evening of the second day the wind had gone into the north and the following morning we had north-northwest 25 knots on the nose and we were tired. It was time to stop and fortunately Khor Shinab, Sudan, was close. At midday we found the entrance to the anchorage, which was perfect timing for visibility. It is essential to have the sun high and behind to be able to see the shallows and coral as you negotiate the gap in the reef. It was overcast but the sun was shining through. We wound our way through the channel edged with low sandstone cliffs. We anchored well inland surrounded by hills and dunes. It was beautiful in a barren sort of way. Three other boats with whom we had been in close company joined us.

We knew that we would now have predominately northerly winds until we reached Suez but there were occasional shifts. The problem was that there were no adequate forecasts. This was solved by my son and grandson getting the information from the web and emailing us every day. After four days the forecast showed some improvement and we departed on 15 March. The light was perfect and we could enjoy the colours as we came down the channel. As we cleared the land the wind was still 25 knots north-northwest. We were sailing 60° off the wind making 6.5 knots with two reefs, staysail and a minute yankee. The waves were not bad; the only problem was that the next port was 280 miles dead upwind. Two days later we had logged 280 miles but were only 98 miles closer to our destination. With big seas, an adverse current and winds on the nose it was hard work. We had three reefs most of the time. As the wind decreased it also backed so that on the port tack we were able to make good a course close to north at 6.5 knots. On the Saudi side we had to tack to avoid a military exclusion zone and then found we were going south.

The shipping was quite a hazard. Whilst the big tankers and container ships were fine and obviously had good radar, this was not true of the smaller freighters. They never responded to the VHF (I suspect that there was no English speaker on board) and tended to pass us very close. We could never be sure that they had seen us and often had to take avoiding action ourselves. On the evening of 18 March we were approaching the Egyptian shore and the wind died so we motorsailed towards Port Ghalib, Egypt. Very soon the wind came back and that night was the worst we had experienced. A true wind of over 25 knots gave us more than 30 knots over the deck. We continued to motorsail but 30° off and still did barely three knots. The seas were big and it was very wet. Gradually the wind direction improved so that we were able to lay the course. It eased slightly but it was hard going and the seas remained big up to three miles off the entrance. We managed to enter Port Ghalib after four days, having logged 520 miles to achieve 282 miles from Khor Shinab.

The entrance to this new marina was easy and well buoyed and could be safely entered at night. The authorities had introduced new regulations to encourage yachts on the Egyptian coast. Although facilities were minimal and it was very dusty, it was a joy to be moored in still water. This is a huge project covering a vast area of the desert and will be another Port Grimaud when completed.

We left at midday on 22 March and had pleasant light winds to start with. At midnight the wind came up suddenly, a lovely time to be reefing! By 0400 it had eased and with *Solent Venture* we enjoyed a great sail across the Red Sea towards Saudi. The coastline was very dramatic with big mountains. Unfortunately the wind veered which made our tack less and less efficient. The next day saw some vigorous sailing, but not as uncomfortable as we had had. We were again zigzagging across the Red Sea trying to keep to starboard of the shipping lanes. We entered the Gulf of Suez at 1630 on 24 March and initially the wind and waves were bearable. We had decided to motorsail and had three reefs in. This was partly in preparation for the night but also so we could set up both running backstays without fouling the sail. We had decided to keep to starboard of the shipping lane so we had a very narrow corridor between it and the reefs. Life was soon to be made more complicated by the numerous oilrigs and exclusion zones. We were tacking every few miles and were glad that we had a simple system set up with the Autohelm doing all the hard work. As the night progressed, the wind increased and the seas built. We were in close company with *Solent Venture, Keeshond* and *Neva*. At 0320 we recorded 31 knots and frequently the apparent wind was over 40 knots. We took one big sea into the cockpit. We had no choice but to continue as there were no anchorages. It was a night to forget! A mutual decision was taken to head for the anchorage at El Tor. It had taken us 30 hours to achieve 44 miles.

We anchored at El Tor, which is on the Sinai side of the Gulf of Suez and 120 miles south of the canal, and collapsed from exhaustion. It is the only really safe anchorage in the Gulf. We heard that the winds were so strong that the canal was closed to all traffic including the biggest cargo ships. One yacht, considerably bigger than us, went out but returned nine hours later after battling against the winds and failing to make progress. We had tried it the day before, but even leaving early in the morning we only achieved seven miles north after four hours so gave up and returned to this safe but windy anchorage. All the other yachts were waiting to see how we managed before poking their noses out. Unfortunately we could not even go ashore as it is a military town and some yachties have been arrested for doing so. The fresh food was running low and it was tedious to be sitting at anchor day after day with the wind howling.

We finally managed to leave on 29 March. The winds had eased and the seas had gone down. Even then there was a sting in the tail and at midnight I had to put the third reef in again and we resumed our slow and uncomfortable fight to get north. Fortunately this wind was short-lived and by the morning we were in contact with our agent from Felix Maritime and weaving our way through the anchored ships waiting to transit. By 0940 on 30 March we were moored comfortably at the Suez Yacht Club. Felix smoothly and efficiently organised the paperwork, but we declined their offer to go through on the next day, as the forecast for the Mediterranean was horrible. In the next two days the anchorage filled up, mainly with the Blue Water Rally boats that were all due to transit at the weekend. We managed two excursion days to Cairo seeing the museum, the Pyramids and the Sphinx.

We returned to the Yacht Club ready for our departure on Monday. Following the spectacular mountainous Gulf and the sight of serried ranks of vast tankers accumulating at Port Suez, the low level view along the actual canal was not great – no camels, no pyramids, no lock gates – so, unlike the Panama, there was not the same sense of a spectacular engineering enterprise. Although it was narrow in places, small local boats still managed to fish as the huge tankers passed. Military presence was obvious along both banks with regular manned lookouts, barracks and the occasional burnt out vehicle. Plenty of access roads had been carved through the banks and stacked on both sides of these were pontoon bridge sections ready to assemble when needed. Also, unlike the tropical heat of Panama, at this time of year the cold wind funnelled down the Suez bringing out our woolly hats last used in New Zealand. Our one night stopover in the small marina in Ismailia was disappointing. The only meals available in the restaurant were rather overblown pizzas and fizzy drinks but this was tempered by the last chance to converse with our partners-in-sail before the final leg to the Mediterranean. An early departure at 0600 meant that some with deep keels had to drag through the mud in the rising tide or risk missing the piloted passage. The view became more interesting as we approached Port Said with historic maritime architecture mingling with mosques lining the main city quays. The atmosphere was quite lively as the canal fell behind us. The sea within the port acquired a heave and chop from the Mediterranean that the local boats enjoyed riding as they rakishly landed and collected pilots from the vessels entering and leaving the canal. Men shouted between boats and a sharp lookout was needed to maintain any rules of the road, as if this was their last chance to engage visitors to stay awhile. Even as we cleared the breakwater and entered the Mediterranean itself, fishermen seemed desperate to land us in their nets. It was an emotional time for us as we waved farewell to our fellow travellers as they bore away towards Cyprus and Greece. With no further westing to be made at the end of this circumnavigation we set course north towards Kemer in Turkey. Suddenly we discovered how pleasant sailing can be. With a fair wind and smooth sea we set the Monitor and settled down to enjoy the last 300 miles. We arrived at Kemer Marina, Turkey at 0350 on 8 April. We had logged 11,194 miles since we left New Zealand eight months earlier.

Flight of Time is a cutter-rigged Bowman 45, designed by Chuck Paine and built by Bowman Yachts.

CRUISING TRENDS

by Charles Nodder

The Club's 125th anniversary seemed an appropriate occasion to publish a brief analysis of cruising trends within the RCC. The last to appear in the Journal was by Robert Franks as long ago as 1977.

The main sources were the Blue Book for details of members' current yachts and the articles published in Roving Commissions for records of cruises accomplished. Extrapolation from the latter was fraught with danger because many members do not write for the Journal. As the Editor observed last year, a man from Mars reading Roving Commissions 45 would have concluded from the evidence presented that 25% of us spend part of the year within the Arctic Circle! Happily, the excellent Millennium Record provided a more complete picture and I therefore drew from that as well.

The first thing to emerge was that our yachts are getting larger. In 1977 the average size was 10 tons TM. We don't include Thames Measurement in the Blue Book any more so a direct comparison is impossible, but we do record overall lengths. These show that yachts in the region of 40 feet predominate today and most of these must be significantly larger than 10 tons TM. Reasons could include the pursuit of comfort or speed. A more prosaic explanation could simply be that the Club is getting older. The Millennium Record shows clearly that members tend to sail in progressively larger boats as they mature and the average age of members has certainly risen over the period in question.

What are all these boats made of? GRP dominates (74%), although a solid 18.5% are made of wood. Several of the latter have been recently built, including 12 in variations of wood epoxy. Nineteen of our total fleet of 389 yachts are constructed of steel and six of aluminium but only two of ferro-cement. Perhaps members are sceptical about the buoyancy of concrete. When it comes to rig, a tenth of the RCC still favours the gaff, whilst the 41 ketches in the fleet easily outnumber the 14 yawls. Robert Franks noted in 1977 that multihulls were very much in a minority and despite the considerable development of the form, they are still less than 2% of the total.

Moving on to the cruises themselves, the 10-yearly indexes in Roving Commissions enabled a comparison of members' cruising activities in successive decades. The range of destinations has always been impressive and has increased further since 1977. In the previous ten years no member had recorded a cruise to East Africa, Tunisia, Russia, East Germany, Japan or the Philippines. Since then there have been notable cruises to all these places.

In some cases (East Germany, Russia) the reasons for increased popularity are clearly connected with changing politics. Less obvious is the cause of more visits to a destination such as Chile. There were just two recorded cruises to the Chilean canals in the 20 years before 1987; there have been 11 since. In part such trends will be due to favourable word getting back from pioneer members – a happy confirmation that an original objective of the Club is alive and well. Another factor must be the increasing ease of travel by other means, allowing a boat to be left and re-joined. These days a circumnavigation can more easily be conducted in bite-sized chunks, whilst a popular cruising ground, such as Croatia, may become the base for a member's yacht for several years.

Cruises to high latitudes have grown in popularity. There were only three logs relating to Greenland in the period 1977 to 1988 and nine in the following decade, but there have been ten already in just five years between 1999 and 2004. As far as I can ascertain, no member had ever written about going far into the Arctic before the year 2000, yet there have been five logs from very high latitudes since. At the other end of the world, Antarctica has also seen more RCC burgees. Mutual encouragement must again be a factor but surely improved comfort and heating aboard the larger modern yacht, more certain navigation and the availability of ice forecasts have all played their part?

Is there anywhere that members no longer go? Not really. The logs submitted do suggest a slight decrease in popularity of the Baltic and a dramatic fall in visits to the Low Countries. I suspect, however, that this has more to do with members' reluctance to write about what they regard as less glamorous cruising than with where they actually sail. This seems a pity as the Millennium Record clearly shows that the often-silent majority of members are regularly occupied in interesting if less dramatic cruising about which it would be good to hear more.

Robert Franks analysed the cruises written up for Roving Commissions in the period 1967 to 1977 and calculated averages for duration, distance travelled, speed on passage and engine use. I have subjected the 82 logs submitted in the period 1999 to 2004 that contain tables of statistics to a similar analysis. The comparisons are as follows:

Average (Mean)	**1967-1977**	**1999-2004**
Cruise Duration	32 days	44 days
Cruise Distance	1050 nm	2750 nm
Speed on Passage	4.15 knots	4.8 knots
Use of engine	27% hours underway	33% hours underway

These figures may well be misleading as an indication of average RCC activity in that they are drawn largely from cruises submitted for competition and therefore have an in-built bias towards exploits that members regarded as noteworthy. However the same was true in 1977 so a comparison between the two periods is valid.

The time available for journal contributors to go cruising would appear to have increased by a third, something we might perhaps expect from general socio-economic trends. This of course means members can go further but the analysis also shows that they tend to press on much more than they did, going faster on passage and spending fewer lay days in port or at anchor.

One clear reason that RCC members go faster, apart from their larger, more comfortable boats, is that they use their engines more than they did and this too may explain why they spend less time in harbour waiting for a fair wind. The 27% engine use in the period 1967–1977 was itself an increase from 19% in the decade before. Robert Franks ascribed it to 'better engines or more impatient owners.' I make no comment on the further increase to the current average of 33% of time underway, although to be fair to all, I did also find that the variation around the mean remains considerable (0-60%).

Of course, there have been other notable changes since 1977. Navigation has altered out of all recognition. The survey of RCC members conducted for the Pilotage Foundation a few years ago found that the vast majority now use some form of electronic system. Reading contemporary logs it is clear that as a result almost no one gets lost. On the other hand, as equipment in general becomes more and more complicated an increasing amount of time does seem to be spent trying to mend things or waiting for spares to arrive.

Conditions on members' yachts have certainly changed. Simpler reefing, better oilskins, fridges, central heating and showers have made the quality of life aboard easier, although some might question whether they have actually made it better; it all depends on your rationale for going to sea. However, one definite consequence of easier sailing is that members now tend to write less about their experiences at sea and much more about the places they visit. The emphasis in cruising reportage, if not in cruising itself, has changed.

In 1977 Robert Franks' conclusion was that cruising feats were becoming more spread around the Club. That trend would appear to have continued with more members going further afield, aided by abler

Our yachts are getting larger

boats and equipment. My assessment is that the proportion of members engaged in what we might call extreme cruising has changed little but that these days you have to take a modern boat somewhere pretty remote in order for that description to apply. The majority of RCC members remain content, as they were 30 years ago, with the gentler pleasures of cruising.

LA CHASSE AUX CUISSARDES
or
TAKING TEENAGERS SAILING

by William Bourne

I brought *Iseult* back from Japan in autumn 2004. After a refit I sailed her from Portsmouth home to Newhaven on a bitterly cold February day – and in northeast F7 to boot. The summer plan was an old-fashioned Channel cruise whose main objective was to give my son Robert and Imogen, daughter of Justin Wood, both in their early teens, ten days enjoyable cruising on the way back from Falmouth. A secondary objective was to buy some size 12 *cuissardes d'huitrier* for a friend who dredges for oysters for a living. They are cheaper in France than Cornwall.

Iseult left Newhaven at 1300 on 27 June with my mother and brother aboard to take in the Trafalgar celebrations off Portsmouth. Northeasterly winds gave us an easy passage and we anchored just west of Gilkicker Point at 2145. The following day, after a brisk sail up and down the fleet of yachts, we anchored for lunch close to *Apprentice* with Simon Butler, Charles and Elizabeth Nodder and assorted children and then cowered in our cabin as a spectacular thunderstorm blotted out almost all the assembled warships. We had planned to return to Newhaven but the forecast of northeast F7 tempted us into going on to Weymouth and we upped anchor at 1830. In the event, the fog closed in off St Albans and the wind moved to the southwest. *Iseult's* unstayed mast and single sail mean that I mount the radar reflector on the pulpit. The torch slipped from between my teeth and I watched torch and clevis pin go to the bottom. Under Plan B Johnny held the reflector in his hands. The plots on the chart resembled shark's teeth as we thrashed to and fro against the tide. Progress was slow until the latter relented and we ghosted into Weymouth at 0800 on 29 June.

The next leg with Eddie Colfox, tried and trusted stalwart, and Robert began when we left Weymouth at last light on 3 July with westerlies forecast. We were soon foaming towards Portland at 8 knots. I chose to go five miles out to avoid the race and we only took one breaker over the bows. There was a brief interlude of northwesterly winds just as a front went over, which Eddie, our weather expert, said was 'textbook' but within the hour the winds backed westerly again. We were close-hauled to Start and beating from there on. By the time we were in sight of the Mewstone the next afternoon, the wind was up to F6, though the sunshine made for pleasant if tiring sailing. We tacked up to the Lynher River under one reef and a local yachtsman who had enjoyed watching us showed us to the perfect anchorage under Trematon Castle.

The next day began with rain and wind and re-anchoring at 0730, as we had swung over a mud bank. We then sailed down to the Mayflower Marina, where we were charged £9 for three hours, a sum that can only put visitors off. We dropped Eddie and after showers and shopping Robert and I ran back up to Cargreen for minor maintenance while the weather passed. We set off at 0945 the following day for Falmouth against a forecast northwest F4-5. It turned into a close haul under reefed mainsail (OK, I shook it out for all of 25 minutes) and we ended beating into and anchoring off Portscatho as the wind blew up in the evening to the top end of F6. *Iseult's* bow sections are narrow and there were some complaints on the foredeck when I gybed just before anchoring. We sailed on to Helford the following day to pick up *Sequester's* mooring and *Iseult* spent the next three weeks being used for local sailing only.

Robert Bourne at the helm off Alderney

The leg back began on 8 August after some careful logistical planning with the help of my mother and Justin and Liz Wood. We dropped the mooring off Mylor at 1445 with a forecast of light winds – a trade that I was happy to make given my inexperienced crew. In the event, over the next 33 hours the log records wind F0-2 with only one bracketed mention of a F3. We motored for five hours in the middle but otherwise kept sailing. *Iseult* will sail if there is a breath on the waters and I only turned the engine on when the instruments logged less than F1. Dolphins, phosphorescence, shooting stars and the Milky Way all put in an appearance to keep the teenagers engaged.

Les Sept-Iles appeared as expected, though we found it hard to believe the GPS when it told us that the west-going tide would sweep us past the islands before we could pass inside them. Once we had sorted out which was Ile Roisic and which Ile aux Moines, the gadget turned out to be right and we turned on the engine to ensure that we beat the tide. I am a relative latecomer to electronic navigation and use a handheld GPS with Bluechart cartography. It makes rock dodging in strong tides so easy. Without it, I doubt we would have realised that our direction made good was insufficient and would not have got into Ile aux Moines that night. As it was, a happy crew anchored off the quay in the gloaming.

The following morning I cajoled two teenagers ashore at 0715 and we were rewarded by a magical visit before the arrival of the vedettes. I got close enough to a chough to take a meaningful photograph. We went on to Port-Blanc in light winds and anchored off Ile St Gildas at 1040. The afternoon was spent walking round Ile de Chateauneuf (muddy, not recommended), cleaning the Mylor mud off the boat and finally a game of Cheat. I regret to report that the skipper proved almost invincible.

With fresh croissants and baguettes, we left Port-Blanc at 0745 the following morning in poor visibility bound for Lézardrieux. The light wind got up to F3 from the west and we shamed a number of other boats into sailing as we passed La Jument and Les Heaux before taking the Chenal de la Moisie into Lézardrieux. The marks were not easy to identify until we were actually on them but with the leading line marked on the electronic screen it was hard to go wrong. We enjoyed a fabulous sail against the ebbing tide into what must be one of the most beautiful rivers in the world. We only took our sails down right by the marina and were alongside at 1250.

Lézardrieux provided showers, wine and stores, but for *les cuissardes* we were told to go to Paimpol or Tréguier. So on 12 August we set off at 0620 for Paimpol where we were also to meet the Allouis, French friends of Justin's and mine. Considering this was between three and five hours earlier than their customary rising hour, both Robert and Immy were remarkably understanding of my love of early starts. As they said, 'At least we're getting up for something.' Lézardrieux to Paimpol is a fun passage, involving at least ten different transits and if you are travelling at

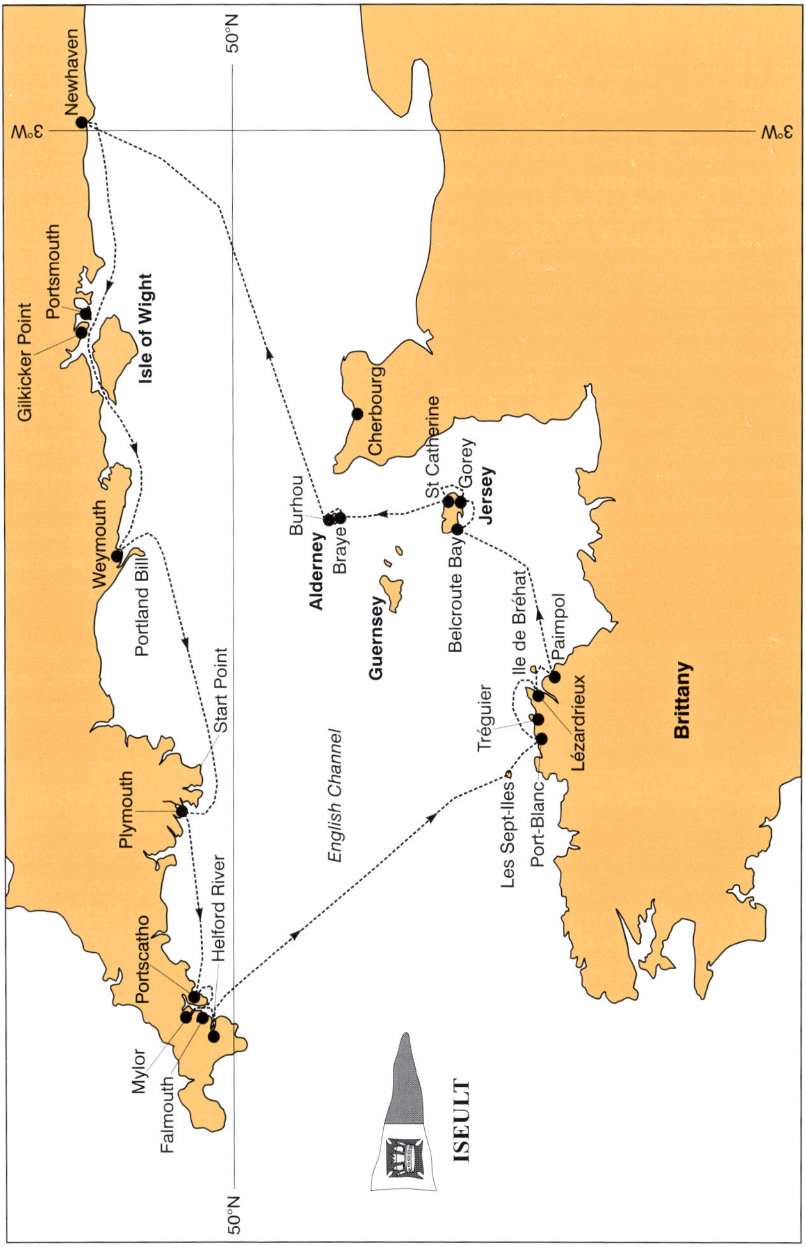
Newhaven
3°W
50°N
Portsmouth
Gilkicker Point
Isle of Wight
Weymouth
Portland Bill
Start Point
Plymouth
Helford River
Portscatho
Mylor
Falmouth
English Channel
Cherbourg
St Catherine
Gorey
Jersey
Burhou
Alderney
Braye
Guernsey
Belcroute Bay
Ile de Bréhat
Paimpol
Lézardrieux
Tréguier
Les Sept-Iles
Port-Blanc
Brittany
ISEULT

close to eight knots over the ground it all happens in about 30 minutes. We overtook a much larger Glénans sailing school boat off the Ile de Bréhat before trusting ourselves to Malcolm Robson's transits and branching off among the rocks. In the event we were too early for the lock at Paimpol and anchored off at 0820 for breakfast before entering harbour at 1000.

The rest of the day was devoted to the *chasse aux cuissardes*. The local maritime cooperative had been converted into *la boutique cooperative maritime* and no longer sold practical items such as size 12 waders. I was then directed to the *ancien cooperative*, which in my rather rusty French means the ex-cooperative and so it turned out to be. A couple of chandlers later, I had failed until I mentioned my problem to Pascal and Liliane Allouis. *La chasse* was on again and after one false start we ran them to ground in the Tréguier cooperative, which is incidentally a treasure trove for any yachtsman.

In the evening we visited the Musée de la Mer, dedicated largely to the Iceland fishing industry. Seeing boots and oilskins made out of oiled canvas we realised how much difference modern clothes make to the comfort of sailors. I was able to add to the museum's knowledge of one particular photograph that showed a Cornish rather than an Icelandic wreck.

We were bound for Jersey the following day with a forecast of west or northwest F4 and we were looking forward to a fast passage. We took the Chenal de St Rion out, again using Malcolm Robson's transits. There is a single stern transit between rocks for about a mile and then a small dogleg. The challenge is to know when to make the dogleg and it was not made easier by my, admittedly vintage, version of the pilot misnaming the Grande Moisie as Petite Moisie.

We had a frustrating sail in the morning with the wind dying before lunch before picking up from the west in the afternoon. Rain clouds and what looked like a line squall started to appear. At 1715, although only logging the wind as F4, I took in a reef, 'To be in control,' as the log records. We were all glad I did, as the 1750 forecast was west or southwest F5-6, perhaps 7, which materialised within minutes. Rain soon brought the visibility down to a mile or less as we closed the south coast of Jersey. *Iseult* has a large sail even with a reef in and three somewhat nerve-racking gybes later we had rounded Passage Rock and were heading for Belcroute Bay. I compounded things by both misreading high and low tide and then anchoring almost on top of a rock that was marked on the paper chart but not on the GPS. A black mark for the skipper who consoled himself with a large rum punch. The GPS redeemed itself by telling us that we were sufficiently clear not to have to re-anchor in the pouring rain.

Despite a roll in the anchorage until the wind went northwest later in the night, we slept well. The next morning the wind was still blowing the top end of F6 and we left with two reefs in the main bound for the drying harbour of Gorey. We took the Brett Boat Passage round the rock-strewn southeast corner of Jersey before a boisterous beat up the east coast. Later a couple of boats left Gorey and returned saying conditions were too tough but *Iseult* performed splendidly under two reefs. After a visit to Mont Orguiel Castle we left Gorey before the tide left us. We beat the two miles round to St Catherine's, where we took advantage of the neap tides to anchor in Belval Cove inshore of the moored boats in almost complete calm. We blackberried ashore and the log then reports that the skipper was defeated at Cheat by the combined crew. I call that cheating!

From St Catherine's onwards, *Iseult* was almost continually on the wind all the way to Newhaven. We set off for Alderney at 0725 to visit Annabel Finding, Immy's aunt. The wind was a very light easterly and when in the adverse tide we were stationary by a fishing buoy for 15 minutes

Iseult

off Les Dirouilles, I switched on the engine for an hour and a half. The wind eventually filled in from the northeast though still no more than F2 and, once again the only yacht actually sailing, we beat gently through the Alderney Race to anchor at Braye Harbour at 1815.

We had a high old time the following day in Alderney with Annabel. The teenagers got to sleep in until 0930; we took her and her two children over to Burhou; we traversed the transit towards the Lug of Burhou sideways because of the tide; we clambered over rocks in what is clearly avian rather than human territory, though Burhou was apparently farmed in the last century; the skipper and the children swam; there was just enough of an overfall on the way back to give the younger ones a thrill. After a leisurely afternoon and supper at Annabel's house it was a rude shock to get back to the boat rolling as the northeasterly swell came into Braye.

Departure on 17 August was at first light to catch some of the east-going tide. We were hard on the wind the whole way back, making one tack to just west of St Catherine's Point followed by a tedious almost dead beat to Newhaven. Visibility was poor to start off with and we had a number of sudden appearances of steamers. However, at least there was wind, if only F3, and it was not unpleasant sailing. By the evening the wind had died and we failed to get round the Owers buoy and inshore before the tide turned. As a result, Robert and Immy spent two night hours each making very little progress. We arrived back at *Iseult's* berth at 1015 on 18 August, exactly on schedule.

Apart from the prerequisite of a good boat, my criteria for a good cruise are threefold: crew who know what they are doing and are good company and weather that is possible rather than impossible. 2005 passed with flying colours on all three counts. The weather was kind, and in particular the first night passage was, like my first Channel crossing 33 years earlier, one to remember for a lifetime. Robert and Immy are both thoroughly competent and great fun to be with, even if conversation between the two of them tended towards the subject of chavs, the behaviour and expressions thereof. We also experienced some of the downs of cruising: slow passages, a lot of close-hauled work and a little taster of rain and wind off Jersey. *Iseult* showed her wonderful sailing qualities though I am still working on improving some of the interior and deck arrangements. Overall I think I can say that objectives were achieved: the teenagers got a taste of cruising and we achieved *les cuissardes,* size 12.

Iseult is designed by Tom Wylie and built in California. Her (fairly) conservative hull is 30 feet long and displaces 2.5 tons, of which her lead keel bulb accounts for more than half. Her construction is high tech with a 42-foot carbon fibre mast, designed to bend to reduce heeling forces, stepped right forward with an aluminium wishbone boom. In short she is a large windsurfer with a cabin. She also has a single cylinder 8hp Yamaha engine but given her dinghy-like manoeuvrability it is not much use. Facilities below are basic.

THE VIKING TRAIL

by Andrew O'Grady

The Cruising Club Bowl was awarded for this cruise

What is it that repeatedly draws RCC members to cold and rugged places? Some yearn to climb rugged mountain peaks; others thrive on the taste of danger or the chance to explore new waters. For us it is the empty anchorages, wild beauty and fascinating people we meet ashore and afloat. Newfoundland, Labrador and Greenland have an added interest for us. Our Viking forebears (yes, with my Irish ancestry I use that word deliberately; besides Ulla is Swedish) sailed these waters in open boats, without motors or any of the navigation aids we take for granted. They explored, colonised, thrived and then disappeared, all before the time of Columbus, leaving many questions unanswered.

Exactly 1,005 years after Leif Erikson set out for his exploration of Markland and Vinland (Labrador and Newfoundland) and established the first European settlement on the North American continent, we were sailing in his wake. Almost nothing had changed from Leif's day; the large glacier in Bredefjord (Sermilik) still regularly releases enough ice to fill the adjacent fjords and make navigation challenging. The hills have a little less vegetation due to grazing by sheep and thoughtless cutting of wood. The small town of Narsaq can just be made out nestled at the foot of a mountain where Norse longboats had once been beached. Sailing boats still arrive regularly from Iceland or Labrador following routes pioneered by Norse adventurers.

We had sailed *Balæna*, our 42-foot gaff cutter, with a design ancestry running back to the Vikings through William Atkin and Colin Archer, from her winter quarters in Labrador. We passed Leif's settlement at L'Anse aux Meadows on the northern tip of Newfoundland. Ulla and I set out across the Davis Strait from the lonely outport of Henley Harbour. In May there should still be lots of ice on the coast of Labrador and icebergs in the open sea. We were taking a chance by leaving so early but we wanted to have the maximum time in Greenland. This year we found not a single piece on the whole voyage. Winds in Davis Strait are notoriously variable; we were lucky enough to have mainly following winds with just a couple of days of strong head winds. As we don't like beating into big seas, we lay a-hull and waited for the winds to change. In two days of drifting we only lost 30 miles. One clear evening the midnight sun lit up the mountaintops just near the Arctic Circle, not far south of Sisimiut. What a magnificent landfall! Now we were ready to spend the summer exploring southwest Greenland.

Cruisers we met in Greenland were surprised by how mild and settled the summer weather was. Most yachts arrive around the beginning of July; in June we had the waters to ourselves for nearly a month as we cruised Disko Bay where the Ilulissat ice fjord calves 20 million tons of icebergs each day. Here we discovered that the weather is even better north of the Arctic Circle with long sunny days and many blue and yellow flowers dotting the green hillsides. We had to pinch ourselves to believe that we could be sailing amongst the bergs in summer clothes.

Twenty-four hours of sunlight does not slow down the relentless pace of the glacier, which fills the sea with flows, growlers and icebergs. To cross the bay we had to weave though the densely packed ice. It was inevitable that we would bump into some; with just two people it is hard to keep a continuous lookout a few feet ahead for 18 hours on a stretch.

'Oh! Oh! Help!' Ulla screamed. I jumped up from my sleep and rushed on deck to see one of the worst sights imaginable to a sailor. A few feet ahead and towering high above, was an enormous iceberg. Ulla was struggling to disengage the self-steering but there was not enough time to manoeuvre and within seconds *Balæna's* bowsprit crashed into the ice. Fortunately the berg was so big that it had cut off the wind and slowed us down, as had the backwash of swells on the face of the berg. Amazingly there was no ear-splitting, boat-shaking crash and we rose up a foot or two on the chain bobstay and then slid back into the water. By that time the helm was engaged and we could fall off to leeward and sail by.

'What happened?'

'It came up so quick,' said Ulla, severely shaken. 'I saw it and thought it was miles away. When I next looked up it was right ahead.'

In the clear arctic air and at two in the morning following a busy day, it is very hard to judge distances and from the shape of an iceberg it is impossible to tell whether it is a small one close by or a large one miles away. Of course there is no excuse for failing to keep a proper watch but if we had been using the radar it would have alerted Ulla to her misjudgement. With hindsight, I believe that despite the perfect visibility we should have had the radar turned on.

Luckily no major harm was done; the decorative tip of the bowsprit was shattered and the mooring bits that support its inboard end were shifted but not broken. We scurried south, being careful not to put too

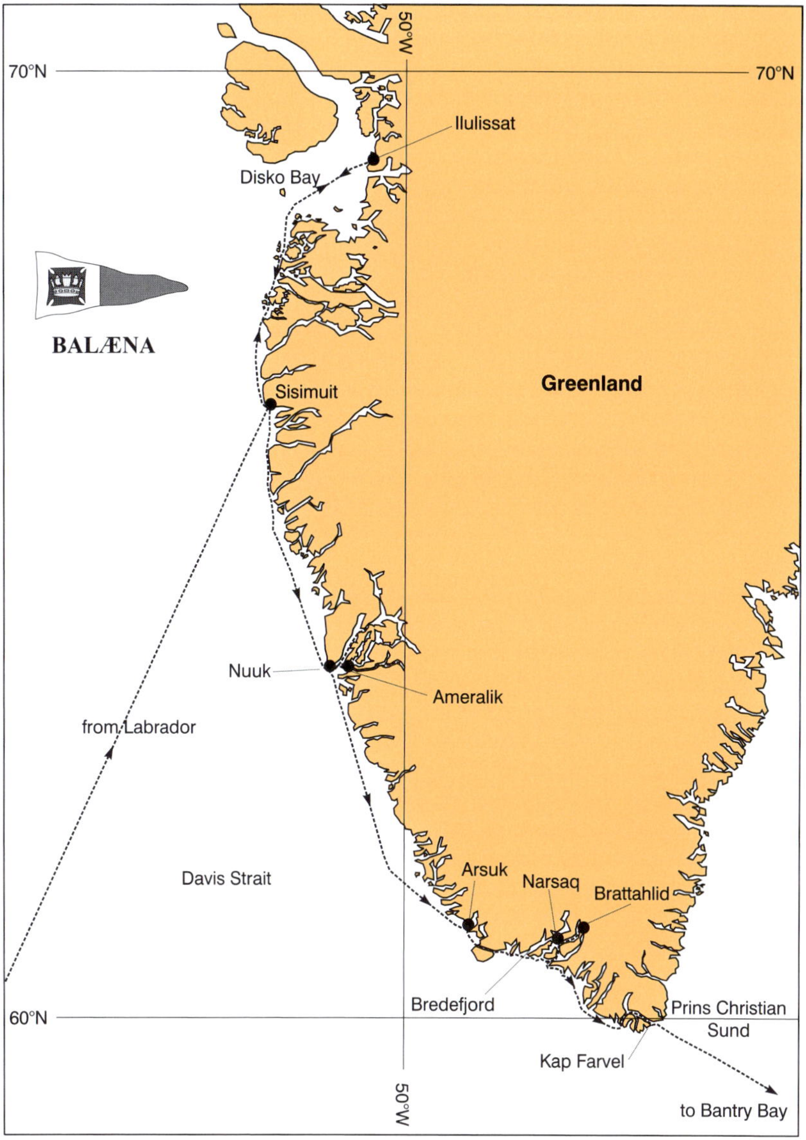

much strain on the bowsprit, to lick our wounds and find a quiet spot to get out the epoxy and woodworking tools.

Sometimes we sailed the intricate but sheltered inshore route past small communities and attractive anchorages where the cod were waiting to snap at a jigger. At others we took advantage of a favourable wind to make a big jump along the coast. There are so many fjords and inlets to visit in the 700 miles of coastline between Disko Bay and Kap Farvel that cruisers need to select a few places to linger and explore rather than to try to see everything. As the southern area near Kap Farvel is often subject to dense arctic ice until late July, the best way to cruise is to start in the north near Disko Bay where there is little sea ice and to work south. We chose to spend two weeks exploring the extensive fjords in the Nuuk area. Nuuk (Godthåb in Danish) has good boating facilities. Motor launches are popular; there are no local sailboats and the marina is unable to accommodate them. Visiting yachts often make this their first port of call, anchoring just outside the commercial harbour or tying up with the workboats inside.

Shortly after we anchored, a large ketch hove into view flying the Stars and Stripes. 'What do we do about clearing in?' they called. 'Go to the harbourmaster's office on the commercial dock,' we replied. 'He will welcome you to Greenland and ask if you need any help. Then, almost with embarrassment, he will ask if you have an excessive amount of alcohol. He won't be interested in your papers or passports. If you want a Greenland stamp you will have to visit the police station in town and ask them nicely.'

We had heard that the Godthåb Bådeforening (Nuuk boat club) had a map of recommended anchorages. I rowed around to their office to enquire. 'Here is the map and our burgee for you to fly,' said the officer in good English. 'Most of the anchorages marked have a mooring with a nine ton weight, you are welcome to use them.' 'Is there any charge?' I asked, looking at the notice on the wall that said: Maps 60 Kronor. 'Absolutely not,' he replied. 'This is our way of thanking you for visiting our country.'

This area would be a worthwhile destination for an entire cruise. We enjoyed the steep mountains falling into placid waters; encountered whales feeding amongst the ice-flows and explored little-visited Norse ruins. Occasionally, at the boat club moorings, we met some of the friendly locals who were netting delicious arctic char. We learnt more about their country and culture and gratefully received as much fish as we could eat.

Beating back to Nuuk on an overcast day we heard the VHF call: '*Iron Bark, Iron Bark,* this is *Seal.*' We had been hoping to meet *Iron Bark* sailed by Annie Hill and Trevor Robinson. Trevor had spent a winter frozen into the ice of Antarctica and wanted to experience the Arctic winter. Later we learnt that we had crossed tracks in Disko Bay without seeing *Iron Bark* as she sailed south from her frozen winter home well north of Disko.

We realised that the caller on the VHF must have seen our gaff sail and thought we were *Iron Bark*. Imagine our surprise when we discovered that *Seal*, a 57-foot Chuck Paine pilothouse cutter, was skippered by

Hamish Laird from my childhood home, the Isle of Wight. Hamish and his wife Kate, both of whom have many years sailing experience on Skip Novak's *Pelagic*, had built *Seal* in New Hampshire for sailing in high latitudes. We agreed to meet up in a couple of days in Ameralik fjord, which lies just to the southeast of Nuuk.

Leif Erikson's brother Torstein had a farm at Sandnes at the head of Ameralik (Lysefjord to the Norse). We hoped to visit this famous site, a stopping point on his route to North America, but were frustrated by the extensive shallows that fringe the head of the fjord. Instead we anchored in the shelter of Equaluit Ilordlit (which means the inner bay with many arctic char). The name proved to be accurate as locals were setting their nets and landing huge numbers of these delicious fish. We had them fried, smoked and as gravadlax, made caviar from the roe and relaxed in the sunshine that is typical of the inner fjords. *Seal* joined us and we visited their impressive aluminium boat that with the experience gained over many years in Antarctic waters is one of the strongest, best thought-out and soundest boats in the world. Needless to say the skipper and crew were also outstanding.

Leaving the Nuuk area we put to sea and sailed directly south to Arsuk fjord. We had a fresh northerly breeze and poor visibility so the radar was important as we started to meet icebergs drifting north. As happened so often in Greenland, when we made our landfall and came inside the headlands the fog dropped away and sun started to beat down. From here on we kept to the inner leads all the way to Prins Christian Sund.

Andrew O'Grady on the Viking Trail

'Modern Vikings showing the reckless courage and adventurous spirit of their forebears'

Sailing down the fjord from Brattahlid (today called Qassiarsuk) where Leif's father, Erik the Red, had established a prosperous farm, we came across some modern Vikings showing all the reckless courage and adventurous spirit of their forebears. The Norwegian steel ketch *Peregrine*, from Bergen, had docked in a cleft in the side of an iceberg and the crew was taking turns clambering and sliding on its sides. We came as close as we dared, wondering if they had ever seen an iceberg capsize or had a serious brush with one of these unpredictable sea monsters. At least they were wearing life vests.

We had the sort of conversation normal to yachts that meet at sea: 'How long have you been out sailing? Where are you heading next? Are there really six of you on that little boat?' Expecting to meet up in a few days, we parted ways but never saw them again as the ice became even heavier and caused us to change our plans.

August came and brought unsettled weather, especially in the south. It was time to think of leaving for Ireland. We wanted to sail through Prins Christian Sund, the waterway that runs across Greenland's southern tip, just north of Kap Farvel. Here mountains rise straight out of the water and climb to multiple sharply pointed peaks. In many of the valleys there are glaciers slowly making their way to the sea and in the water are small iceflows from the glaciers as well as huge icebergs that have drifted in from the ocean. One sunny day we were able to stop and take pictures of *Balæna* looking insignificant amongst the grandeur of the mountains. The scenery was every bit as impressive as in the Beagle Channel and for us the weather was just as stormy as we had experienced around Cape Horn.

We reached the weather station at the eastern end of the sound. This has been the jumping-off or arrival point for many yachts and we poured over their visitors' book finding old friends and even an entry on 31 August 1970 by Bill Tilman and the crew of *Sea Breeze*. Here we had to wait for several days as one depression after another brushed past Cap Farvel bringing easterly gales. Eventually we left with a less than ideal forecast. A three-day gap seemed to be opening up between the lows.

Balæna sailed rapidly southeast in the swells left over from the last gale. All caution went to the wind as we pushed her as hard as possible to be 450 miles from Cap Farvel by the time the next low, reinforced by an ex-hurricane arrived. Luckily our tactic succeeded and we only had F9 winds and a day lying a-hull. We thought we had got off lightly.

It was not all plain sailing to Bantry Bay and on to the Beaulieu meet. We had another strong gale and then took a rudderless 45-foot Swedish boat in tow for 80 miles. It was satisfying to be able to help another yacht in distress and also make some good friends who coincidentally came from very close to where we plan to spend the winter. Nonetheless it was a fast passage and after eleven days we were in Berehaven and relaxing with a pint of Guinness and a toast to the fearless Viking Leif the Lucky.

Balæna is a 42-foot gaff cutter designed by Denis Brown and built by Andrew O'Grady in 1988. A pilothouse with an internal steering position has recently been added.

LEARNING IN LOWER LATITUDES

by James Nixon

Last year we set out in *Scilla Verna* to follow the route taken by Lord Dufferin in 1856 in his schooner *Foam*. In *Letters from High Latitudes* published a year later, he describes the very rapid passage south from Spitzbergen and almost coming to grief on Røst, the most western of the Lofoten Islands. He ends this stirring tale with his departure for home, overland from Copenhagen.

I came home by air, leaving *Scilla Verna* for the winter at Skattora, just north of Tromsø at 69°42′N. Leaving a boat through the Arctic winter was a new experience and some useful lessons were learnt from that and from the voyage homewards along the Norwegian coast and beyond.

I visited in April to check on progress and found that although all the deck snow had melted, the spectacular surrounding mountains were still covered and there were skiers about. During the winter a friend had cleared the snow from the deck and centre cockpit and I was to learn from a problem that arose from this. As we had decided to leave the boat in the water, the boatyard staff had been assiduous in closing all seacocks and putting anti-freeze into the lavatories and sinks. Thanks to the Gulf Stream the sea does not freeze but the air temperature drops to well below zero. However the cockpit drains pass through seacocks in the engine compartment and these were closed also.

The life raft is a heavy brute in an unwieldy canister but it seemed excessively so when we lifted it from the locker under the cockpit sole and heaved it into position on the quarterdeck. The cause was obvious when I reached home and left it for servicing. The engineer reported that it was full of seawater and therefore unserviceable; I tasted the water and it was fresh, almost certainly from melted snow. The cockpit locker must have filled with melt-water that then leaked into the canister. The life raft is now back in service.

The second lesson was 'read' by the Russian Government. On the journey home I had hoped to go northwards and east around Nordkapp to the White Sea and Archangel, and then through the White Sea Canal to St Petersburg. Vladimir Ivankiv in St Petersburg, who has been of great assistance to yachtsmen entering Russian waters, had been working on my behalf. All visas had been arranged up to about two weeks before our proposed departure, when the Russian government changed the regulations without warning; any passage through a waterway by a foreign-registered vessel would now require a chain of requests starting from me to the Foreign Office in London. The request would pass to the Russian Foreign Ministry and thence in turn to the Russian Ministry of Transportation, the Provincial Government in Karelia, and finally to the Karelian Department of Transportation which would issue the permit to enter the canal at Belomorsk near the Solvietski Islands. Obviously there was not enough time to arrange this, so sadly I abandoned those plans and looked forward to a voyage south along the spectacular Norwegian coast.

Jarlath Cunnane and Paddy Barry of the Irish Cruising Club had hoped to use the same canal in completing their voyage in *Northabout* through the Northeast Passage from Alaska. They were awarded the RCC Medal for Seamanship for a rescue during the unfinished expedition in 2004. I explained to Paddy that I was having permit problems but he told me to just turn up at the first lock and demand entry. As a diplo-

James Nixon, Russell O'Neill and John Witchell in Trollfjorden

matic wimp I have to express a little relief that they did not do this either and were forced to leave Russian waters at Murmansk and follow us to Tromsø.

We left Tromsø in late May and came south in cold blustery conditions through the Lofotens to Svolvær, the attractive capital of this archipelago. Trollfjorden is spectacular and worthy of a visit, despite the cruise ships and rock graffiti. The temperature rose slowly as we motored and sailed across the broad Vestfjorden to Bodø and along the complex leads and sounds of the inner passages on this coast, protected by the offshore rocks and islands. We would particularly commend the lovely and relatively undiscovered island of Bolga.

Further south we crossed the Arctic Circle. We learnt that the globe-like metal sculpture on Vikingen is in fact about one minute of latitude south of the circle. It is not a point of any navigational significance but this did not stop us raising a glass in celebration on a sunny morning as sea eagles soared above.

Crew changes are a problem for most skippers and we had difficulties. The first was at Sandnessjøen, just south of the Arctic Circle, where John Witchell and Russell O'Neill left for home. They had helped greatly in re-commissioning *Scilla Verna* and bringing her out of the Arctic. This busy town has an airport and Keith Seybert flew in via Stansted, Trondheim and Brønnøysund. Unfortunately his luggage remained in Stansted. I was able to fit him out with spare oilskins and warm gear and we sailed south that night to reach Brønnøysund just after midnight. We kept in touch by mobile telephone with the local airline, Braathens. Thankfully the Norwegians have developed a very efficient mobile network, so much so that we learnt that pay telephones were no longer in use. We had to keep moving and eventually the errant luggage was safely delivered at Rørvik, the next good harbour to the south. Full marks to Braathens.

The same situation arose when Paul Bryans joined us in Stornoway from London, where his luggage had stubbornly remained. The Stornoway airport staff arranged for it to be delivered by taxi to Scalpay. The mobile telephone network coverage is less than 'Norwegian' in the Outer Hebrides.

Another lesson was one that I had nearly forgotten. Leaving Sandnessjøen, I noticed a familiar rattle when reversing under engine, and I feared that one of the two anodes on the propeller shaft had worked loose. They had been put on by divers in Tromsø. The efficient harbour master in Brønnøysund was able to contact a diver who went down and said that 'the anode is loose and I have tightened it thoroughly'. I asked what had happened to the second one and he said there was only one! Obviously one had dropped off and the other loosened and the re-learnt lesson is to ensure that sacrificial anodes are applied properly. These were the good quality MG Duff devices that had never failed for me before. It was still cheaper than lifting the boat out.

An aesthetic lesson: Ålesund is a gem. Continuing southwards, we berthed in the Brosundet, in the centre of this city. Keith and I had time to enjoy the art nouveau delights of this historic town while preparing *Scilla Verna* for the North Sea crossing. The centre was largely destroyed in a fire in 1904 but has been restored. Brosundet is a convenient berth from which to explore and shop and there is a bracing walk up the hill north of the city to a viewing point. The aquarium is exceptional, especially when a scuba diver feeds the large and varied specimens. Crew change was efficient and Michael McKee and Ed Wheeler joined by air, landing at Vigrø airport on an island to the north of Ålesund. A rapid bus journey through two tunnels delivered them quickly to the centre of the city.

Equally delightful in its own way is Fair Isle. After Shetland we crossed in fog to North Haven, spending two days exploring this attractive island. It is owned by the Scottish National Trust and is an important ornithological site. I had been there before, but the crew, now including Peter Minnis, had not. We were able to see and feel the attentions of the many arctic and great skuas and we used the recommended trick of keeping a stick overhead to reduce the accuracy of their attacks. Keith was able to start his return home to Ireland using the Shetland ferry, the *Good Shepherd.*

Other lessons arose from my failure to read instructions. We had a calm exit from Norway, leaving Ålesund by the lovely Vartalsfjorden, and resisting the temptation to dally at Geirangerfjorden further inland. As we headed for Shetland, the wind freshened from the southeast and we had quite a boisterous passage, enlivened by spotting an orca. The confused sea, fresh wind and fog persisted into the next day as we approached the oilrigs in the middle of the North Sea.

Near the Snorre rig a RIB appeared out of the fog at great speed, manned by armed Norwegians in survival suits. Their leader was cross with us for not contacting them by radio. We then realised there was a problem with our VHF. Also we learnt that we should have made contact before approaching within 20 miles of the rig. During our shouted exchange the fog lifted slightly and we could see the huge concrete legs of the rig but its platform remained invisible. After grovelling apologies we sped on though they continued to shadow us for a while. The Brent rigs in the British sector were passed without any such encounter.

A similar lesson was learnt when leaving Orkney. We had been weather-bound in Kirkwall and I felt under pressure as we had connections to make at Stornoway. After assessing forecasts and barometer and studying (some) directions and tidal information we left Kirkwall shortly after midnight. On a dark night with the gathering ebb, I opted for Eynhallow Sound to make our departure westwards. All proceeded well until we approached the western entrance, where in the early dawn gloom we could see a line of breaking water across the whole sound to Eynhallow, the islet in the centre. We had, correctly, chosen the south side of the islet, but the appearance was worrying. Ed was navigating and I shouted below to ask if he thought we were on the right track. As we entered the breaking water another shout became more anguished. The depth decreased to about four metres although this may have been caused by turbulence. Little water came aboard and suddenly we were out into calmer and deeper waters to the west of Orkney. Unhelpfully, my old edition of the Clyde Cruising Club Sailing Directions was at home, and later I read of the dangers, with phrases like 'hazardous' and 'no one without considerable experience of the area should...' There is a helpful diagram but the prudent navigator would use Westray Firth further north. Ed had read the Admiralty Pilot but did not mention this as he 'knew it would put me off from doing it'. Perhaps the skipper should beware of selective reading by adventurous (however experienced) crew.

A pleasant lesson was that the west coast of Scotland remains a marvellous cruising ground. After the Orkneys, we enjoyed solitary splendour in Loch Laxford, with Arkle and Foinavon, two of the bold landmarks on this mountainous Sutherland coast, close by. We then crossed the Minch to Stornoway where Michael and Peter left us, and we were

Bosun's chair spotted at Vinsand

joined by Paul Bryans (whose problems with luggage have already been described). Here also Russell O'Neill came back for more.

Stornoway was a final link to Lord Dufferin who had anchored here on his way to Iceland and rode out a gale that 'increased to a perfect hurricane'. He records the resultant sad loss of life in the local fishing community. His passage further north was stormy too.

In calm sunshine we berthed alongside the fish quay. The pontoons further up the harbour had been damaged in January storms (as had also happened in Kirkwall). Bill Spiers gave us the benefit of his great experience of the Outer Hebrides with advice about trout fishing and special anchorages. We had lonely and lovely nights in Risay Sound in Loch Leurbost and in the Witches' Pool in Loch Mariveg. After Loch Maddy we had a fine sail back across the Minch to Loch Harport on Skye, the mizzen staysail making its first appearance since leaving Ireland. We were alone again in sunshine at Acarseid Mhor on Gometra, another secluded anchorage to the west of Mull. My favourite remains Bagh Gleann nam Muc, the bay on the north end of Jura, open to the *son et lumière* of Corryvreckan. After a spanking reach to Craighouse, we dropped Paul off at Port Ellen to fly home. The little airport is a short taxi-ride from the village.

Our final anchorage was in North Bay, Sanda, at the south end of Kintyre. This little-visited spot gives good shelter and holding in all winds except a fresh northerly. There are fine walks, and storm petrel nest there. Bird-watchers are frequent visitors. The island's owner farms sheep, and has now opened a friendly pub which we had helped 'christen' on an earlier visit. As a result this haven will probably become more popular as a good temporary anchorage when making a passage through the North Channel.

Next day in calm conditions we motored on the flood the 40 miles south to Bangor. *Scilla Verna* was safely home after a memorable two-year voyage. This year she had covered another 1510 miles, again much of it under engine. She has since been lifted out for a re-fit. Time, heat and cold have taken their toll especially on the teak deck, and this provoked debate aboard. Russell's remark, 'I would think twice before lifting that deck, James. Teak doesn't grow on trees you know,' still makes me smile.

Some lessons were learnt or re-learnt. As always the most important truth of all is that none of the planning, nor the doing, nor even the reminiscing would have been possible without a good boat and a willing, able and often agreeable crew, John Witchell, Russell O'Neill (twice), Keith Seybert, Ed Wheeler, Michael McKee, Peter Minnis and Paul Bryans.

Scilla Verna is an Oyster 435 ketch, built in 1983.

ALONE TO ÅLESUND

by Christopher Clothier

This passage won the Sea Laughter Trophy

There are lots of members of this club for whom a four-day, single-handed sail from Scotland to Norway would be an entirely everyday affair and not worth writing about. I hope this account goes some way towards demystifying it for the rest of us.

Some time last winter I was at home with my parents and sister. Jonny was explaining his summer cruising plans for *Brown Bear*, a trip from Scotland to the Lofoten Islands and back again. He wanted volunteers. I said that I should like to sail the boat there single-handed. I had always wanted to sail alone and this seemed a good opportunity. It had the benefit of sounding suitably impressive – sailing to the Arctic Circle – while in all probability being a quite gentle, downwind trip. Back in London I spent the next couple of weeks telling everyone I knew that I was going single-handed sailing. Shame is a very strong motivator and I thought the most effective way to stop me backing out.

As the summer got closer the plans took shape. The trip was shortened as the insurer would not allow me to take the boat into northern latitudes alone. This struck me as a little odd. Surely the crowded waters of the North Sea and Channel are much more dangerous? I was to take the boat from Ardfern to Stornoway and from there to Ålesund. Then my parents would join and we would sail up to Bodø. Apart from a couple of weekends, I hadn't sailed in two years. My father, in an act of parenting beyond the call of duty, volunteered to come with me to Stornoway to help me get used to the boat again. He was then condemned to the tedious journey from Stornoway to Ålesund by public transport. There were two things that made me nervous. The first was what impact the lack of sleep would have on me but there was no way to prepare for that. My second concern was that I was very unfit. I never think of sailing as a particularly physical activity but I am used to splitting the work four ways; doing it all myself could get very tiring. Fortunately I was unemployed for the month before I set off and was able to go to the gym and sweat away my laziness on a rowing machine.

We set off on 4 June. If I had wanted to slip away unnoticed, I couldn't have picked a worse place. At teatime the cockpit filled with a veritable Hello-list of RCC celebrities – Willy Ker, Bob Shepton, Hugh Read, Anne and Andrew Fleck. It took three days to get to Stornoway, stopping at Isle Ornsay and Gair Loch. My father lay slug-like in his bunk ostensibly allowing me to sharpen my single-handing skills. The days were long and to windward but with good sailing. I hadn't realised how much I had missed all the funny idiosyncrasies of being on boats: salty coffee, rope burn and the warble of the weatherfax. We tied up in Stornoway alongside a fishing boat in the evening. Audrey and Bill Speirs came round for a drink and offered the old man a cooked breakfast and a lift to the airport on the following morning. I spent the evening doing some navigation, in particular planning the approach to Ålesund thinking I would be tired by the end of the passage. The course was quite short, around 460 miles with the rhumb line running straight through Shetland. I decided to leave Shetland to starboard, where there was probably less traffic and I would be clear of any oilrigs. Also the forecast was for the wind to swing to northwest over the next couple of days and I didn't want to find myself on the wrong side of the shift, fetching to Norway.

I set off at 0830 the following morning motoring out of the harbour, waving to the Stornoway seal and a gin palace of Abramovitch proportions. Outside the breakwater it was blowing quite hard from the south with gusts hitting 28 knots. If I had been braver I would have put the mainsail up inside the breakwater; as it was I went through a much slower, wetter and bouncier process in the channel. The wind soon settled down to 20 knots, almost directly astern. I shook out all the reefs and poled out the smaller of the two furling headsails. I spent a very pleasant morning reading *The Observer* from cover to cover, something I realised that I had never done before. I also began making inroads into jasmine tea and ginger nuts.

At lunchtime I learnt my first lesson about sailing alone – procrastination is actually a virtue. The wind dropped to around 15 knots and the *Bear* slowed down. I went onto the foredeck and began changing headsails. This turned out to take a long time by myself. The small jib had to be furled, the pole dipped and the sheets re-led through the ends. Just as I was ready to unfurl the larger jib the wind jumped back and I spent another 20 minutes on the foredeck reversing what I had just done. The wind edged round to the southwest over the afternoon and I gybed onto port tack. I think I set a new record doing this manoeuvre; the whole process took nearly an hour. It was surprisingly tiring and I found myself taking a five-minute breather in the middle. So much for all the afternoons at the gym.

At six o'clock I had a gin and tonic. This was the first time that I really noticed that I was alone as normally six o'clock is happy hour. One of the real pleasures of going sailing is having the time to cook, something I almost never do in London. But for this trip I was very pleased that my mother, Jane Kimber, had made me several shepherd's pies. I ate one with fried courgettes – very nearly my perfect meal. Soon after supper I had my first sleep. As it was a short trip and the waters were quite busy, I used the radar most of the time that I slept. I set an alarm to go off if anything came within a range of four miles. This mostly worked well. Occasionally the alarm continually tripped and I had to switch it off. Every time I went to sleep I set my alarm for about an hour and a quarter ahead. In practice I found that it rarely woke me up. So I suppose that, on average, I slept for about 40 minutes at a time. I did most of my sleeping at night and if when I got up there weren't any boats about and the wind hadn't changed I would go almost straight back to my bunk. That way I had around four or five short sleeps that night.

Christopher Clothier

The next morning was one of those days that I am sure only exists in the north Atlantic. The visibility was down to around a mile, the sky was perfectly grey, the sea was petrol black and despite a 15-knot breeze, everything seemed completely still. A chattering VHF and radar told me that there were lots of fishing boats about but none came too close. On the way from Ardfern I had caught my trousers on a winch and ripped them from the hem to the knee. I am very fond of those trousers not least because their existence means that sailing cannot ruin any of my other pairs. So I decided to repair them but as I am very bad at sewing this took most of the morning.

The rest of the day and night passed pretty uneventfully; a mixture of caution and visibility meant that I saw neither Shetland nor any oilrigs. The sailing conditions were perfect. There was a following southwesterly breeze varying between 15 and 25 knots and the seas had built up to a good size. I spent a lot of time on the wheel enjoying the surfing conditions. When I wasn't steering I read my book or listened to Radio Four on the SSB. I was disappointed that there wasn't a test match to follow. I had another supper of shepherd's pie and courgettes and washed up to the sounds of *The Postal Service* and *Britney Spears*. On reflection that is something you probably shouldn't confess to in print.

I was genuinely surprised at how much I was enjoying myself. I had thought before that sailing single-handed would be one of those things that I would hate while doing but would be pleased to have done. Of course the conditions were ideal; I am sure that if I had been beating into F6 I would have felt very differently. The whole experience was deeply relaxing. It made me realise that all of the stress of skippering a boat comes from responsibility for the crew. If you remove the crew, you remove the worry. Of course, you do feel responsible for the boat. (I have always dreaded having to make a call to the old man and explain that I have just sunk his favourite and most expensive toy). Clearly the ultimate for stress-free sailing is to be single-handed in your own boat.

Another big change that I noticed was a total lack of urgency. People who sail with me are occasionally a bit frustrated by my continual tweaking and changing of sails (a hangover from racing dinghies as a child). Before leaving I had teased my mother that I would put the spinnaker up as soon as I had the chance. Yet even though the conditions were perfect, I simply didn't have the urge. Procrastination was another side of this; I would regularly wait half an hour after thinking of shaking out a reef before actually doing it, just in case the wind blew back up. If you are with other people, you often feel *obliged* to make a decision, to take action. Once a sail change is suggested, the rest of the crew never fully relax until the decision is made. This is a luxury of being alone. The other great freedom is the release from the tyranny of a watch system. When alone you are unable to keep anything approaching a complete lookout and so it is only rational, when out of sight of land, to give up completely and

The inner harbour at Ålesund

not worry about how often you step on deck to look around. Then there is the very best bit. I am sure that everyone has their favourite point of sailing – for me it is working on the foredeck when sailing downwind in a good breeze. That favourite moment is completely magnified when you can pause in the middle of what you are doing, turn completely around and realise that you are all alone.

Of course, there are lots of things that I missed. I missed the afternoon bridge sessions that were a staple of my last trip, bringing the *Bear* home from Brazil with friends. (That trip was mostly spent on our collective ear, fetching through the northeast trades. Some seats around the table were much more comfortable than others and became so prized that we adopted a strict rotation system). I missed changing watch on cold nights, hugging the person coming on deck, swapping gloves and smugly going below. And of course I missed the company. There is another downside to being alone, the lack of urgency turns into lethargy. The sink would fill up with mugs and plates but I couldn't bring myself to wash up. And sometimes as I lay dozing on deck it took all my energy just to stand up and look around.

On the third night I began to approach the coast. Fortunately, being summer and high latitudes, it didn't get dark, which meant that I wouldn't have to stand off. When it did appear, the coast was very dramatic, all jagged rocks and cliffs. The wind also had a sense of occasion. It blew up to a steady 28-30 knots and the seas built. I put the headsail away and went down to three reefs. By this point I was getting quite tired, I wasn't able to sleep at all, partly because I was excited at arriving and partly because of that particular unease of approaching a lee shore. Several pots of coffee and the rest of the ginger nuts were very helpful.

The marina in Ålesund is in the very centre of the town. Most of the town burned down in 1904, a lot of care and money went into rebuilding it and the result is very pretty. Once in mobile range I called ahead to Jonny. I didn't feel guilty about calling him in the middle of the night. He hadn't tried to book a hotel until a couple of days before setting off, only to discover that there was a convention that night in Ålesund and there wasn't a single bed in the whole city. He spent the night in an armchair in a hotel lobby. I think we were equally pleased to see each other. The *Bear* was tied up by 0345 and we sat down in the cockpit for a cup of tea and a glass of whisky. Shattered, I went to bed soon after. Three hours later I was woken from the most delicious sleep I had ever had by my father, insisting that I go and check in with customs and immigration. I swore at him continually for ten minutes, pointing out that customs really wouldn't mind if I wasn't waiting on their doorstep when they opened at 0830. But, now awake, I grumbled my way to their offices. They were, inevitably, almost entirely indifferent.

999 MILES IN CROATIA

by Colin Barry

Sundance had been in Croatia for the past three seasons, but I had not managed to take in the northern islands and the Istrian peninsula. For 2005 I planned an extended eight-week cruise. After completing the maintenance in April, Jane and I flew out to Dubrovnik on 15 May.

Our first guests had already spent several days sightseeing and their time was short so the next day we slipped at 1100 and headed north. A pleasant southerly wind meant that we actually got the cruising chute up for one of only three occasions in the season, before the wind inevitably dropped. Our first port of call was Okuklje on Mljet, where we visited one of our favourite restaurants, Tim's Place, before making a very early start the next morning with a 50-mile passage to Hvar. We had a day with variable wind strengths, mainly from the southwest. In the narrows between Korčula and the mainland we had 28 knots. An hour later, as so often happens in the Adriatic, the wind died and we were motoring.

One of the marina hands at Dubrovnik had given us his unofficial weather forecast saying we had three days before a bora set in. He proved to be right. After a rolly night at anchor off St Klement island we set out on the Wednesday morning in oily weather that boded ill. We had about 25 knots to start with and made the Kremlik marina in the early afternoon where we met up with the Beisers who were fitting out. Thursday was a write-off, but Friday saw us tearing up through the Kornatis, close reaching in F6. The wind died later in the day and we made Goran's restaurant at the top of the amazing Telescia inlet. Goran's speciality, slow-roasted lamb, proved irresistible. Jane had a copy of the Croatian Gourmet Guide, which lists 28 of the nicest restaurants in Croatia, most of which are small and family owned and usually won't take credit cards. We seem to have visited a great number of them.

By now the weather had reverted to a steady summer pattern and for the next two days we threaded our way through the islands to Zadar, where our first crew left us. We decided not to take the narrow passage between Ugljan and Pasman though we looked at it and it seems to have more height than in the guidebooks, which record it as 16.5 metres.

The next few days Jane and I worked the boat through the islands to Pula. At Premuda the water was unbelievably clear and the walk across the island to the town remarkable. After we picked up Bill and Heather Howard at Pula, we headed for Lošinj to meet up with the Carnegies. Unfortunately we were entering a period of thoroughly indifferent weather, although we were now in early June. After Lošinj we went to Cres and were holed up for a couple of days before heading north and around the top of the island and south to Krk, a most delightful harbour and a splendid town.

Our next port of call was Rab. We stormed towards it in F7, until inevitably the wind dropped and we found a pleasant bay for lunch. However, the weather was deteriorating fast and we were glad to make port, particularly as the next day it was blowing F9. The following day we were able to get going again and it was time to head back to Pula for a crew change. We made the passage between Lošinj and Cres, which is an adventure, and spent the nights in two almost deserted bays (these days unusual in Croatia) on Cres and the east side of the Istrian peninsula. After a change of crew at Pula we were Venice-bound, spending nights at Rovinj and Novigrad on the way. Venice was the highlight of the whole summer. We had two nights in the marina at San Giorgio,

Roman amphitheatre from Pula Marina

leaving in the early hours of the morning in clear and spectacularly calm conditions.

On returning to Istria we cruised gently south along a magical coast before spending two nights in the Brijuni islands. These had been Tito's summer residence and had strong connections with the pre-war British navy, who used to go there largely to play polo. There are no cars and an enormous variety of facilities and they have been kept very exclusive, largely by making them very expensive. We still thought the £60 a day we had to pay for a berth was worth it.

After going home for a week for my grandson's christening we had two weeks to get the boat south 350 miles to Dubrovnik. To start with there were five of us aboard and we had some interesting weather. The first day we had considerable wind and heavy rain. The people with whom we had dinner the night before had told us that they had never had their oilskins out in the two years they had been in Croatia but when we texted them that evening to say how wrong they were, they replied that they had not had any rain at all. How the weather varies in the Med!

We tracked south through the islands, spending a delightful night at the northern end of Dugi Otok and another at the northern end of Kornati, before tracking towards Split for another crew change. After Split it was southwards through the islands to Dubrovnik, revisiting Brač, Hvar, Korčula, Mjlet and Sipan Luka. At Polače, we sent our guests off to visit the superb monastery set in the middle of a seawater lake in the National Park.

The return to Dubrovnik marked the end of the summer cruise and we were amused to find that we had grand total of exactly 999 miles. We had some tough sailing and as always in the Mediterranean we did an awful lot of motoring. I had been swimming up to four times per day, seen a number of interesting places and taken in a lot of local culture.

Sundance is a 38-foot Beneteau 381. Designed for coastal cruising and living on board in comfort, she has sailed to the West Indies and logged some 25,000 miles in the last six years.

THE EAST MEDITERRANEAN RALLY

by Peter Price

Kemer, Turkey

In April we were fitting out *Lectron*, our faithful Moody 376 at Kemer where we have wintered for three years. We were preparing to join the sixteenth East Mediterranean Yacht Rally. It was the brainchild of Hasan Kacmaz, who accompanied us in his own small boat. It had collected boats from Istanbul southwards but the real start was at Kemer. We were feeling very uncertain, as we are not 'rally people'. We were all given a copy of the handbook, various trinkets, a haversack, a coloured neckerchief so we could recognize our group and the all-important 'rally bag' used for handing over passports and crew lists when appropriate.

We were very fortunate to have Jeffrey and Sal O'Riordan as our crew and they were a constant source of fun. They had sailed with us before in Turkey so knew the ropes. Jeffrey had a new knee and Peter was recovering from a broken ankle so we were lucky to have such a competent female contingent. Having said that, the male crocks met every challenge!

The proceedings started with what one can only describe as 'bonding'. We were arranged by boat size into six groups. The Skipper with his wobbly ankle was able to avoid the tug of war but was a wow at tying bowlines blindfolded behind a pretty blonde's back (so he was told). All good fun and no one was damaged. A cocktail party was followed by a dinner where 270 people were well fed and we had the chance to get to know our group and to bump into new faces. Many were most interesting people and experienced seamen and women; all boat owners as charter boats are excluded. We had survived test one!

14 May, to Alanya, Turkey

The first stage was east to Alanya. We carefully read the instructions in the excellent handbook, as did 270 sailors on 78 boats of 16 nationalities.

Boats were dressed overall immediately

The main message was that whatever happens, 'Keep smiling' and whenever there was a minor crisis some wag would trot out the line and we would all laugh. With a passage of 66 miles we set off at 0400 for a day sail with a carefully calculated time of arrival. We had a lovely sail with some motorsailing later to keep to our schedule. We appreciated that it was going to be interesting seeing 78 boats all anchoring and pulling back to the quay. We were called in and entered in our groups and, bingo, the seamanship was immaculate helped by Umut in a dinghy as rally co-ordinator. We were impressed and on our metal! In each harbour all boats were dressed overall immediately. That evening we had a 'pot luck' supper on the shore. We were a bit concerned as Sal had a new passport that made her a British citizen rather than Irish, so there were panic emails by our efficient rally team to the countries to be visited. The next day we explored the castle where prisoners had been thrown to the rocks below – only avoiding this if they could throw a stone direct into the sea, an impossible feat. We looked over the Red Tower, built in 1222 and an impressive 35 metres high. On by bus past oranges, yellow plums, bananas and fig trees to a lunch of trout and salad by a rushing river with 130 people being served in quick time. Then to the Dripping Caves, part of a huge underground complex some 15 metres high and 360 metres long, first explored in 1986. Back on board we had about two hours to gather ourselves together before being whisked off for a cocktail party and dinner. This time the buses were ordinary city dolmuses as the cocktail party was being hosted by the city council. A straphanging crowd of well-dressed yachties arrived at the base of the Red Tower where drinks and small eats were laid out on tables in the square beside the sea. We were still trying to get to know each other and all had nametags and coloured scarves to help this. Into the dolmuses again and we were taken to a seashore restaurant for a very good meal of typical Turkish fare with gentle music in the background. Some speeches and then the music increased and people started dancing. We were exhausted and took one of the waiting dolmuses back to the boat where we dropped into bed at about midnight. And that was just the first day!

16 May, to Girne, Northern Cyprus

This was the first overnight trip of about 98 miles. Leaving at 1330 we duly reported to our group leader every four hours – a chore at first, then quite fun as we got to recognise voices and little innuendoes. David, our leader, was a comic at all times. When problems arose there was an expert on every subject somewhere in the fleet. We had a good sail between spells of motoring. That night one of the larger boats lost power and was rescued by the US boat *Pooh Bear,* the smallest boat with one of the oldest crew, who turned back five miles and towed them for some 20 miles.

Because of numbers our group was directed to the new harbour, which was not as picturesque as the old one but had more space. We bussed round to admire the old harbour and witnessed *Pooh Bear* towing in the large boat. As the rescuers came to moor, their gearbox seized and, crunch, a bent stanchion or two. Two days later a substantial sum had been raised to help offset the cost – their seamanship had been much appreciated. We were amused at nice letterboxes, good old UK power plugs and driving on the right. A reception in the lovely setting of the castle was followed by dancing in traditional dress, the boys with upturned glasses of water on their heads. We slept well.

Next day we boarded buses and our first stop was a steep climb to St Hilarion Castle and monastery overlooking Girne. The crew overcame their disabilities and managed to climb all over it, though guess who kept the bus waiting! After Bellapais Abbey, made famous by Lawrence Durrell in *Bitter Lemons*, we went to the old part of Nicosia, where we saw a caravanserai (staging post for merchants and their animals) and thirteenth century St Sophia Cathedral, now a mosque. We were turned loose to find our own way back to the buses for about a mile through the old streets. Everyone made it!

We returned in dread of the Pirates' Party but it turned out to be fun. We had been warned and all dressed up a bit. We sat with the crew of *Iwanda* whom Peter had often heard on the Med Net and an interesting

Swedish crew and compared notes on our various past adventures. Danced the night away and watched a rather good belly dancer.

19 May, to Mersin, Turkey

The rally now returned 107 miles to Turkey. A lovely night with boats all around but well spread out. We were getting into a routine of four-hour watches so as not to arrive too tired. Jeffrey, our master cook, served his usual excellent breakfast and on arrival we were mostly able to go alongside jetties. We were directed to a desk ashore where they would sort out all problems. We had been using our watermaker as we felt it safer to avoid unknown sources but unfortunately the compressor had broken.

With little hope, notwithstanding the usual Turkish confidence, we passed it over and were told it would be ready the next day. A short bus journey took us to the cocktail party in a huge new sport complex, followed by some colourful dancers and their castanets.

The tour next day was to Tarsus, birthplace of St Paul, where we took part in an unexpected church service. After lunch we saw two large holes said to have harboured dragons and serpents and then viewed the Kanyteleis and Elaiussa Sebaste Roman remains. On our return Peter was delighted to get the watermaker back in working order. A small plastic cogwheel had shattered and they had enterprisingly made a replacement out of brass. That evening we had a good dinner in the smart military barracks where the staff did an excellent barbecue.

22 May, to Iskenderun, Turkey

It was now time to move further east with another 80 mile run. Light head winds to start with but then it freshened and we had a lovely sail. We cheated, as we had spotted a tiny harbour half way and stopped from 2000 to 0400. Luckily only about six others did as it was very small. Entering at dusk using Jeffrey's hand-held IPOD navigator was a bit hairy! Next day in Iskenderun we had to double-bank but it was all achieved with no fuss. An impressive sight. Iskenderun is near the terminal for the Iraqi pipeline but we saw no evidence of it or the tankers. The town still shows on Syrian maps though it was taken back by Turkey in 1939. The dinner was at the local yacht club. They struggled a bit but we all got fed in the end.

There was heavy rain in the night. We decided to go off on our own, breaking from the arranged tour, and took a local bus to Antakya (biblical Antioch). Locals were very helpful, pointing us in the right direction or stopping the bus for us to get on. One was a university lecturer who had a degree from Bath. We visited the magnificent Roman mosaic museum, a mosque and St Peter's church cut into the rock face. It was here that St Paul preached for a year and founded the first Christian community before being discovered. Unfortunately we did not follow one of the small boys asking for *baksheesh* or we would have seen the escape tunnel.

25 May, to Lattakia, Syria

Another 85 miles and a night passage but the excitement was rising. We were given waypoints and dire warnings should we stray. The wind was blowing strongly as the first boats left reporting 30 knots. However, Hasan had heard from local fishermen who said it was less offshore and we decided to give it a go. Others returned and set off a few hours later but we motorsailed into a headwind and uncomfortable sea. A Turkish coastguard boat kept watch over us until we reached Syrian waters where we reported to the Syrian Navy patrol vessel. The harbour coped with all

Girne Old Harbour

of us as a lot of boats had been moved from the quay to make room. We took a taxi to the town but it was very dilapidated and we were glad to be taken to a beach restaurant for a good meal.

The next day at 0715 we boarded our buses for the 'Road to Damascus'. Probably not the same as taken by St Paul as ours was mostly dual carriageway and we were comfortable in our air-conditioned coaches (or at least to start with). Our guide was very enthusiastic and seemed determined to convince us that there was no desert and it was all fertile. True we did see some green valleys but also enjoyed the desert and roaming camels. The bus needed some air in the tyres so we stopped at a kiosk and a tall man placed some crock clips on two bare wires with a great flash and air was duly delivered.

Our first visit was to Krac des Chevaliers crusader castle. It is high in the mountains guarding the Homs gap. Built in the twelfth century, it is remarkably complete and you could imagine 2000 knights sitting in the huge rooms with their horses in the stables below. We walked round the immensely thick walls with marvellous views. Lunch was in a Bedouin tent surrounded by hubble-bubbles. Arabs in traditional dress (but with plastic gloves) pulled apart a whole roast sheep.

Refreshed we moved to Palmyra, a Roman city built in an oasis on an old trade route. The remains are stunning. A double line of columns leads to a triumphal arch, temple, theatre and agora. There has been a lot of restoration so it was easy to imagine it as a key stopping place on the Silk Route from China. A four-hour drive took us to Damascus to stay in a 5-star hotel, which was to have been bliss *but* we were already supposed to be at supper so off we all went laughing to dinner in a new restaurant complete with a wedding party, a dreadful belly dancer and a good whirling dervish. Then back for showers at 2330 and so to bed.

Next day, off at 0900 to tour Damascus, said to have been continuously inhabited since 4000BC. We walked through the large covered souk to the Great Mosque (Mosque of the Omayyads). The women had to wear white gowns covering them from head to toe and men in shorts had to put on skirts before we all took off our shoes to admire the inside of the building. We were then let loose in the souk. Catnaps on the coach made up for sleep lost on night passages.

A late start at 0800 for Aleppo to the north. We explored the citadel, which is largely ruined inside the outer wall except for the ornate Sultan's room with beautiful ceiling and windows. We then had the chance for a more relaxed tour of a souk before returning to the marina. However, that was not without its fun as the air conditioning broke down and we had to stop to cool down alongside the road. Luckily we were able to hitch a lift on the French bus. We had learnt a lot about Syria and its ambitions but felt that the people were not free to say what they wanted and that our guide had fed us the party line.

30 May, to Jounieh, Lebanon

For this trip of 105 miles we were again given strict instructions and waypoints and a plea for boats to observe the rules concerning lights. A few boats seemed to insist on both tricolour and main lights and one would have his beastly strobe light on all night. They never did succeed and at times you were not sure where people were going. We set off early to have a better chance of sailing the whole way and still meeting our scheduled arrival time. Quite a bumpy night. We had to keep our eyes skinned to avoid a collision – easily done with so many boats but people were generally very alert. Once when we stopped the engine to sail the boat behind came roaring up. We had been warned before the rally never to go straight for the waypoint and people did spread out. We arrived safely at Jounieh just north of Beirut. Though we were squashed into a very small space this was a first class marina. There were good showers, laundry, an Olympic-size swimming pool and a good restaurant. All a joy for the travelling yachtsmen and we slept and swam. Next day we saw another crusader castle at Byblos and could date Phoenician, Roman and Byzantine ruins all on the same site. It was in Byblos that the precursor of our alphabet was developed in 1000BC. We visited the best set of caves we have ever seen; a trip in a cable car and then pure magic underground but unfortunately we were not allowed to take any photos. On the way back we saw the statue of the Virgin of Harissa that the night before we had seen lit up on the horizon.

Up early to be whisked off to the Bekaa valley. Hezbollah yellow flags fluttered on poles along the streets although Lebanese soldiers manned the old Syrian checkpoints. At Baalbek the Romans built the greatest temple complex in the Roman Empire and you can only marvel at the magnitude of the task. Six granite columns of Jupiter's Temple stand 22 metres beside foundation stones each weighing over 1000 tons. The temple of Bacchus has most delicate carvings. We also visited Anjar, an Arab city which had been buried in sand since 700AD but is now uncovered with its stone and brick construction well-preserved. A wine tasting at Kasara and so to bed.

The next day we visited Beirut where there has been much reconstruction although there are still quite a lot of bullet-holed buildings. We were there on 3 June, the day after a journalist had been assassinated, and a small demonstration was taking place in Martyr's Square. Only a few weeks before the ex-Prime Minister had also been assassinated and there were memorials to this remarkable man everywhere as well as living testimony to the way he had encouraged rebuilding of this beautiful city. Lebanon is a lovely country on the crossroads to everywhere. We all liked it but felt that as all it has to sell is tourism and banking, the future is bleak.

On the way back we stopped at a huge supermarket and filled the bus with stores. That evening there was an excellent dinner in the marina, good French food and an impressive belly dancer. Our computers were going like mad and emails were easy as the marina had broadband. On leaving harbour each boat had to present itself and its crew at the dock to be checked. They needed to be sure we all actually left. We felt they were relieved that we were all safe and everything had gone well.

4 June, to Haifa, Israel

Haifa was 85 miles away. Another night passage and again the waypoints had to be followed exactly to avoid prohibited areas. We were instructed to call the Israeli navy when reaching the border and every five miles thereafter. Each boat was likely to be visited by a high-speed patrol boat and asked a series of questions. Most of that did happen and we got to loathe the monotonous voice of the poor girl representing the navy. More interestingly, in the middle of the night they changed the position of a critical waypoint. The system worked nearly perfectly. The group leaders were informed and they in turn informed their chickens. The result was amazing. Imagine 78 boats all with twinkling red lights more or less in a row and suddenly they all became green, all that is but about three. Suddenly the rebels were on the radio wanting to know what had happened. After much leg pulling they duly turned as well.

We were packed into the fishing harbour. Passports were looked at but not stamped and passes issued. On the first day Peter visited Haifa hospital to get an ear problem sorted and afterwards joined the crew to visit the Baha'i gardens on the steep slope of Mount Carmel. An amazing place, which cost $27m to build and $2m each year to maintain, all donated by members of the sect from all over the world.

The next evening every crew was entertained to supper by an Israeli family – except us. Jeffrey and Sal had friends in Haifa and we were invited to stay the night. We marvelled at their ingenuity. Almost everything we ate came from the garden. Every plant had a measured quantity of water applied daily and even the morning dew was collected.

In Nazareth we saw the Church of the Annunciation and the Church of St Joseph on the probable site of his carpentry shop. We were ushered onto a boat for a trip on the Sea of Galilee (212 metres below sea level) with biblical sites and the Golan heights in the distance. In the River Jordan a number of our party decided to be baptised with a full immersion; they might have changed their minds if they had seen the mink(?) swimming by. We had an excellent lunch in a kibbutz.

7 June, to Ashkelon, Israel

After our skippers' briefing session we set off for Ashkelon, another 85-mile night passage but we were hardened to it by now. Some were not

Gill Price and a reluctant racing camel

too keen on going in quite strong winds but Hasan, the diplomat as always, was most anxious not to have a split fleet and in the end everyone left. A speedy, rolly but fun sail with wind mostly fair as we went round waypoints until the wind died in the morning. We were greeted by a fire tug with hoses squirting in two arches. The main trip here was to Masada. This city is perched high up on a rock reached by an impressive cable car. The fortress was a palace of King Herod where a Jewish community later held out against the Roman invaders in 66AD. When it was apparent that they would be overcome they committed mass suicide rather than be taken alive. A few people who hid in the tunnels lived to tell the tale. It was all brought alive by a wonderfully enthusiastic guide. Bringing us back to reality we then swam in the Dead Sea, 400 metres below sea level. Next we had a completely free day, spoilt when Peter spilt a pan of boiling water down his tum. He lay with an ice pack on it for over an hour, not just five minutes, and there was no scarring except for a small area that had been missed. A salutary lesson but also we will know what to do if it happens again.

11 June, to Port Said, Egypt

52 yachts sailed the 124 miles from Ashkelon to Port Said, overnight yet again. We had a very exact arrival time and had to congregate at the

Race! We would never do such a thing

entrance to the Suez Canal just after dawn. We anchored out of the channel waiting for stragglers, dressed overall and at 0630 set off in line down the canal for about two miles. Two anchored tugs hooted loudly as each yacht passed and finally we moored in an old naval basin under some rather faded British Empire buildings. A big effort was made to clear us in easily while a small band paraded along the quay.

Next morning we set off in three coaches at 0615 to visit Cairo and the Pyramids. No slacking allowed! Throughout our journeys in Egypt we were escorted by army jeeps, often police sirens and each bus had an armed guard on board – they are determined that no harm will come to their tourists. It was interesting to see the fertile Nile valley, ships on the canal and then barren desert up to the outskirts of Cairo. Three hours later we parked by the Pyramids, surprisingly close to the city. The exact angle of each wall is stunning; the Great Pyramid is 146.65 metres. The views out to the west over rolling sand dunes are also worth seeing. We were taken down to the Sphinx (much larger than expected), which is out of view from the Pyramids.

After all that we were dumped outside MacDonald's for lunch, perhaps a safe place for a group of foreigners! A quick visit to the Egyptian Museum for the Tutankhamun exhibits (amazing, we never saw them in London) was followed by a sail on a felucca on the Nile. Our group of offshore sailors thought this might be a waste of time but actually it was good fun. The skill of each single-handed helmsman/sailhandler was staggering and the 25-foot boats sailed very fast. We stayed in a hotel by the Pyramids that had originally been built to house visiting heads of state at the opening of the Suez Canal in 1869 though our rooms were in a more modern annex. We drove through the crowded nighttime streets of Cairo to a restaurant for an Egyptian meal.

Luxury next morning, when we were allowed a leisurely and really good breakfast (the eggs were tossed in front of us) on an outdoor terrace before setting out for a tour of Cairo. We visited the Citadel and Mohammed Ali Mosque built about 1830 on a height overlooking the city and were then let free in the bazaar. Our final visit was to a much older mosque/university/school for the blind and we learnt that the Muslim muezzins who shout prayers from the top of minarets used to be blind so they could not pry on the houses below. Nowadays they just speak into a microphone at the bottom and presumably can be sighted.

Back in Port Said we had a welcome free day and explored some of the nearby old town. 'Faded elegance' sums it up with many old buildings of the shipping, import/export and insurance businesses of earlier days. It was hot on board and we were glad to have our big canopy set up. Showers ashore were cold but no worry; everyone was very kind and helpful and a big effort had been made to clean up some old buildings for us. Even the quay had 'Welcome' painted on it. Fuel was very

Just a taste of Petra

cheap but as it was only delivered in cans we decided we had enough to get us back to Israel.

16 June, to Herzilya, Israel

Checkout was easy and we marshalled at 0700 to motor in line out of the canal. We sailed back to the very modern Herzliya marina just north of Tel Aviv, once again being monitored by the Israeli Navy chattering almost continuously on VHF radio. We had to shorten our watches to three hours, as we were so sleepy. By 1430 we had a grand wind and enjoyed sailing past another Moody 376.

Our tour from there was a day trip to Jerusalem, the Mount of Olives, the garden of Gethsemane and the Wailing (now Western) Wall. On a walk through the city we saw so much of biblical interest and the old, old streets leading to the Church of the Holy Sepulchre.

The rally itself formally ended in Herzilya on 18 June with a final dinner and presentations of plaques and certificates to everyone. We were quite sad to say goodbye to friends we may never see again. It is an amazing affair and this year had an excellent committee and group leaders who helped everything to go smoothly. Reasonably good weather throughout was a bonus.

20 June, to Petra, Jordan

Several people wanted to go to Jordan and we joined a small group for a three-day trip. We managed to visit the remains of a huge Roman city in Jerash (north Jordan), the ancient sixth century floor mosaic of a map of the known world at that time in Madaba followed by a night in Amman. The highlight was the visit next day to Petra. However many pictures you see, it is such a surprise to enter through a narrow canyon of multi-coloured rocks. We walked to the far end passing the huge treasury building and other tombs and temples carved in the cliffs in the third century BC. It was pretty hot so we rode donkeys up the 800 steps to the monastery. It was a long walk back again but all looked different in the late afternoon light.

After a night in a hotel we drove further south through the desert and were taken in jeeps for an off-road trip in the desert at Wadi Rum. It was a mixture of sand dunes and high rocky outcrops of red stone. Bedouins were waiting to give us rides on their camels and tea in their tent. (Another group did a two-day camel ride sleeping in the desert!) We crossed back into Israel via Aqaba and Eilat and had a long drive back to the marina mostly through desert in the dark. A huge part of all those Middle Eastern countries are desert. Bedouins still roam around with their sheep and camels but they are now being persuaded to move into houses and towns.

Our crew flew home the next day. We had enjoyed their jolly company and did not have to say 'Keep smiling' at all!

26 June, to Finike, Turkey

After three days rest we set of for Turkey and an easy 71-hour passage brought us to Finike again. The winds were light and mostly fair so we had some sailing and it was good not to be in a rush or among a crowd of other yachts. Amazingly we could still hear the 'Israelee Navee' on channel 16 when we arrived in Turkey some 330 miles away.

The whole six-week cruise had been a wonderful experience and we recommend it to anyone who gets the chance. We were not as tired as we might have expected but then we had a super crew!

Ayesha (Heiney)

Warrior Shamaal (Clifford)

Dinghy ride in the San Blas Islands (Clifford)

Bed for the night, San Cristóbal, Galapagos (Clifford)

In *Pemandia's* cockpit at Barbate, the Trafalgar Meet (Hill)

Service beneath Cape Trafalgar lighthouse, 20 October 2005 (Power)

Midnight sun at Kirkenes (Lomax)

Stunning icebergs in the Vaigat (Hill)

QUIVER'S FIRST CRUISE

by Anthony Browne

When I retired in June 2004 we decided we should simplify things. We sold our flat in London, got rid of a lot of old furniture but somehow ended up a year later with three boats when we had started with one. This was not the plan. I thought we had sold our dear Bowman 40 *Quiver* to a friend, but she pulled out the day she was due to complete the deal. It was also the day the new *Quiver* was launched.

The new *Quiver* is a Hallberg Rassy 48 designed by German Frers. She has a simple sloop rig and most of the sail handling is done from the cockpit with push button electric winches. She handles well under power – even astern. She has large water and diesel tanks and plenty of stowage space. She has a clever Raymarine electronic navigation system with a chart plotter in the cockpit as well as at the chart table. Combined with the large protective sprayhood, this makes sailing at night or in bad weather safe and comfortable.

Quiver was launched in Ellos, near Göteborg, on 25 May, the date agreed more than a year earlier when we had signed the contract. Monique cracked a bottle of champagne over the bow while our daughters, son-in-law and grandsons shivered in the cold. We returned with a car load of equipment and stores in mid June. Our first sail was on my birthday. It was a very exciting moment. We sailed up and down the Ellos Fjord trying her out on different points of sailing. It was soon clear that we had a fast and close-winded boat and we enjoyed tacking up the coast to our first Swedish harbour.

Fiskebackskil is a charming picturesque village with cobbled streets, pastel-hued houses and a busy marina. As we approached a pontoon several people came to help us. When I thanked them one of them said, 'There will always be people to help you with a beautiful boat like that'! We found that in Sweden and Finland people were invariably friendly and helpful; rather than waiting to see how you would get on, they would come to take your lines.

We had dinner in an excellent fish restaurant on the waterfront and fell into conversation with a young family with a doting grandfather. They came for a drink on board and invited us to visit their house in the village next morning. They live in the old bakery and we were very moved when they insisted on giving us a beautifully illustrated book about the village with a touching inscription.

We spent a week sailing north along the inner passages up to the Koster Islands, near the Norwegian border, enjoying *Quiver's* good sailing qualities and appreciating the chart plotter which made navigation in these complicated waters much easier. On midsummer's eve we found a delightful anchorage in Testholmarna. We walked through a wood behind the rocky foreshore and came upon three Swedish yachts secured alongside the rocks, as if the rock were a harbour wall. The Swedes told us about the local way of securing to rocks. They also told us about the importance of midsummer's eve and the associated rituals. The children were picking wild flowers and binding them into garlands for their hair and to hang from the crosstrees. In Lango Island off Smögen we rode out our first gale. After that we felt more confident about the holding properties of our Delta anchor.

We returned to Ellos to have a few snags sorted out, then set off to the south. We sailed to Marstrand and to Falkenburg, a town which became popular with British fly-fishermen in the 18th century. In Helsingør we lay in the shadow of Hamlet's castle. Copenhagen was a short sail to the south; on a Sunday morning the Sound was like the Solent, with hundreds of yachts out sailing, racing and pottering about, ferries charging across to Sweden and huge tankers lumbering up and down the channel.

We decided to go into the centre of Copenhagen. We passed the Little Mermaid, which is so small I almost ran aground as we tried to get close enough to see her. We headed gingerly into the Christianshavns Canal. A large tour barge astern grew impatient and yelled at us, 'Get out of the way – there is no room in there.' As we went up the crowded canal I was very conscious that I was approaching a dead end and there was very little room to turn round. Eventually a kindly Dane invited us alongside his 85 year old trading ketch, and all was well.

We were joined in Copenhagen by Chris and Di Hoare. Chris had been on a boat building course with me. They loved the canal life; people bring their picnic tables and bottles of wine and just sit by the side of the canal all day. Chris is restoring a 50-year old Folkboat and he found the neighbouring boat of great interest. Like many up the canal she was undergoing a long, slow restoration. There did not seem to be much sense of urgency about the work but there were plenty of opportunities to exchange ideas and just have a chat.

We sailed to Ystad, passing through the Falsterbo Canal, which was built in the Second World War to enable Swedish ships to avoid the German mines that covered the south end of the Sound. Ystad is a lovely

mediaeval town and we decided it was a place which deserved more time. Then we headed out to the island of Bornholm, where we secured in the harbour of Hasle and had a lovely walk along the coast to the small fishing harbour of Helligpeder. The village and its smokery went out of business in the 1950s when the authorities demanded white overalls for all the staff and the installation of white tiles.

Our next stop was the naval port of Karlskrona, which has a superb maritime museum with an interesting boatyard attached to it. We anchored for a night at Kristianopel. The sea was covered in yellow-green algae which stretched as far as we could see. It did not stop Chris having a swim. He came out looking like a Martian and had to be washed down before he was allowed back on deck.

A gentle beat took us to Kalmar. It was so hot that we put up the bimini to shade us from the sun. We enjoyed our stay, visiting the splendid castle and the interesting town museum. Chris and Di left us here and we continued to beat gently northwards, carving a wake through the spinach soup-like sea. We found a lovely anchorage at Paskallavik, tucked up a channel where we saw a huge wood pulp factory gobbling up forests of wood delivered by incredibly run-down Russian ships.

The next day we entered the Stockholm skägård and enjoyed sailing with some beautiful yachts, including a fine old twelve metre. The Swedes sail seriously and as we tacked up the narrow leads we could see why so many Swedish boats are narrow and deep and built for going to windward. We found some interesting anchorages in the skägård. Although the weather was fine and it was by now high season there was always room to anchor and we found that everyone behaved well, not anchoring too close to other boats and respecting the peace of the anchorages.

Approaching Stockholm the islands became more populated and the frequent ferries made the scene almost suburban. We had been advised by a Dutch couple to make for Navis Hamnen rather than the noisier Vasa Marina. It is situated in the diplomatic part of the city, a pleasant residential area with some good walking nearby. The harbourmaster is friendly and helpful. The good weather came to an end. The rain set in and we were very pleased to have a sprayhood extension – a sort of cockpit tent that meant we could sit in the cockpit in the heaviest rain without getting wet.

Alan and Vanessa Watts, friends from Dorset, joined us in Stockholm. We spent a couple of days enjoying this wonderful city. The highlight was the fantastic Vasa museum. We were examining an exhibit when I felt a tap on my shoulder and heard someone saying, 'Are you Anthony Browne?' It was Charles Gorer. He and Elizabeth were touring Scandinavia in their motor home. They came for a drink on board later – our first RCC meeting this year.

The sun shone as we motored to Paradiset for lunch, then continued on to Tjocko. This is a handy jumping-off spot for the Åland islands, where we headed next morning in wind and rain. Large high-speed ferries ply between Stockholm and Mariehamn. As we entered the channel leading to Mariehamn two ferries were leaving and two were racing in to take their place at the quay. They set up a huge wash and a wave swept the whole of our deck, swamping the deck lockers out of which we were fishing fenders and lines. The harbour master found us a inside berth and we enjoyed this historic shipping port.

Over the next few days we sailed through the Åland islands, which lie half way between Sweden and Finland and which enjoy a certain amount of autonomy from Finland of which they officially form part. We enjoyed Rödhamn, a small but strategically situated island with an old pilot house which now houses a museum. The little harbour shop is run by Anette Gustaffson, an artist who lives on the island with her young family. She bakes bread and each morning her husband delivers it to the boats in paper bags with the weather forecast written on them.

Our worst anchorage was in Bano-Ø, a large bay which looked as though it should give perfect shelter from any wind. A gale from the north was forecast so we tried to find a secure anchorage on the north shore. The anchor would not bite. We tried over and over again. Eventually some friendly Finns told us that there was enough water to come in close to the shore near some trees. We readied the kedge, and headed straight towards the rocky shore. Alan dropped the kedge over the stern and paid out the warp as we moved forward. Monique and Vanessa flung bow lines to the waiting Finns. We were secured in classic Scandinavian style. It was a perfect spot, the kedge was holding well and we settled down to enjoy a long delayed lunch as the rain poured down.

As it began to get darker (a relative term in these northern waters) a new forecast came in – still a gale, but now from the south. We were tied up to a lee shore. We had to move. We untied all our lines, hauled up the kedge and set about trying to find good holding on the south side of the bay. Again we just could not get the anchor to bite. It seemed that it could not dig through the thick weed on the bottom. At last I felt that we had a reasonable hold, but we had to do anchor watches through the

Quiver

night. Luckily the wind in the bay never rose above F5 and we dragged very little during the night. It was a relief to get going in the morning.

We headed towards our first sauna. Thanks to our special relationship with the NJK, the Finnish cruising club, RCC members are able to become temporary members of the NJK, giving access to the wonderful private islands and anchorages belonging to the NJK and its members. Jill Vasey looks after our relationship with the NJK and she had provided us with an excellent briefing pack containing full details of the etiquette involved in visiting a private island and enjoying a sauna.

As we approached Lillkalvholm we were greeted by some friendly Finns. They checked the NJK pennant at our port crosstree and warned us not to venture too far into the inlet. We dropped anchor close to an attractive wooden hut. We rowed across to the deserted island and found that Jill Vasey's key worked. We made ourselves at home. Alan lit the sauna fire with wood from a pile next to the stove and then started chopping some more wood to replace what we had used. Meanwhile I walked across the island with the NJK ensign, which I hoisted in place of the NJK pennant, or 'wimple', to show that members were in residence. By now the sauna was hot and we had ten minutes in the heat before going down to the shore to cool off in the cold water. Then we had another ten minutes and another chilly dip. We all felt better for it, and wrote glowing enthusiastic comments in the visitors' book.

Back on board we enjoyed a beer and a good lunch and admired the scenery, which included just ahead of us the rocks we had been warned about and which had been invisible two hours earlier. There are tides in the Baltic, even if only little ones.

In the afternoon we continued to a peaceful wooded anchorage in Kramppi, and next day we had a lovely sail to Turku, through a mosaic of islands with charming houses and boats. We tied up to the river bank opposite the marina and enjoyed a relaxing day in this beautiful university city. We found a first rate chandlery, internet access at the tourist office and a convenient Alko wine store. We ate well and sadly bade farewell to Alan and Vanessa.

We continued to Gulkrona, a wonderful island full of nature trails and games for children. We found that Sweden and Finland were very child-friendly, with plenty of entertainment for children of all ages. We were ready for another sauna, and this time we headed for Krakskar, a larger island with some excellent walks, fascinating rocks and wild flowers. We ducked beneath terns defending their nests. We had time for one more NJK sauna and then we started heading back, first to Rödhamn, then Arholma, Rödlöga and Grisselholmsfladden where we zipped ourselves in against the rain and admired a couple of Finnish six metres which were cruising home after their world championships in Sandhamn. We continued to Rano in pouring rain on 1 August; it felt like the end of summer.

Figureheads in the Karlskrona Museum

We left Rano in thick fog very early in the morning hoping to make Visby, 85 miles to the south. It was a good opportunity to try out the radar and to see how its images could be overlaid on the chart plotter. It gave us a new sense of security. The fog lifted as we had our breakfast and a gentle breeze set in. It was an enjoyable sail but hard work to make sure we were getting the best out of the boat. The northwest wind was cold. During the day the wind backed to the southwest and our speed increased. We secured to the wall in the harbour to the west of the marina at 2000.

We spent a day in Visby, a splendid walled city where the highlights for us were the magnificent ruined churches, built in the thirteenth century and abandoned during the Reformation in the sixteenth century. The ruins are beautiful, haunting and very romantic. We ate in a restaurant described in the Rough Guide as massively fashionable. I had my back to the arrivals but Monique thought that was a fair description.

We met the young British crew of a 20-foot Falmouth Quay Punt called *Teal.* Andy her owner had sailed her out to the Baltic last year and laid up in Estonia. This year he had sailed up to the top of the Gulf of Bothnia. He wanted to be at the Arctic Circle for midsummer's eve. The top of the Gulf of Bothnia is 60 miles short of the Arctic Circle, so he had a canoe in which he had paddled up a river to get there. The canoe fitted on the coachroof. At least it fitted once he had cut it in two.

By now the wind seemed to have established itself strongly in the southwest and we found ourselves beating to windward for the next few days. In Kalmar we met the Robsons on *Picaroon* who came for drinks, together with the young crew of *Teal* and a charming French couple alongside us. The poor weather put us off visiting the offshore islands of Christiansø and Utklippen. Instead we sailed along the southern shore of Sweden putting into little fishing villages like Hallevik, where there was scarcely enough water for us and we had to wait while a gale blew itself out, and Skillinge. In Ystad we almost got into the lovely opera house for a performance of *Cosi Fan Tutte*. We listened to part of it in the foyer. More vigorous beating took us round the southern tip of Sweden. Then suddenly as we headed north again the wind dropped, the rain stopped and we were no longer hard on the wind. From now on we enjoyed some magnificent sailing in perfect weather. In Marstrand we were delighted to find John Sharp and Ann Kristin on *Ocean Grace*. It was a great pleasure to spend some time with them.

We visited some more fine anchorages on our way back to Orust. Our favourites were Danholmen, Karlsvik and Storon. *Quiver* is now spending the winter in a heated shed at Martinsson's yard near Henan on Orust.

We have simplified things a little. Old *Quiver* was sold to a charming couple just before we left for the Trafalgar meet. She will be in good hands. The third boat is *Puffin*. She is the clinker dinghy I built during my boatbuilding course. She is in the garage at home, waiting to set sail in the spring.

BABY ON BOARD: *KOKIRI* REACHES THE ATLANTIC

by Peter and Katharine Ingram

The Founder's Cup was awarded for this voyage

Having decided not to sell our beloved *Kokiri* when we reached Vancouver in 2004, we planned to bring her to Europe sooner rather than later. She would then be close enough for weekends and holidays and we might curtail our wayward cruising life before it became too dangerous a habit. To make this trip in a single season ruled out a passage through Panama and the Caribbean, so we chose to truck her overland across Canada. The timing was further hampered by such happy events as two family weddings and the birth of our son, Robert.

In mid-May, after Mary and Daniel's wedding and when Robert was about eleven weeks old, we flew back to Silva Bay on Gabriola Island in British Columbia.

Kokiri had waited patiently for us over the winter and was in excellent condition although we were happy to take our time getting shipshape in such pleasant surroundings. On 7 June we finally waved goodbye to the wonderful staff at the Silva Bay Marina and sallied forth on a short cruise around the Gulf Islands. We enjoyed seeing friends that we had made the previous year and gave Robert a gradual introduction to cruising with settled weather in these sheltered waters. He thoroughly enjoyed our final sail in the Pacific, beating across the Strait of Georgia to the Frazer River where we hauled *Kokiri* at Shelter Island Marina and prepared her for trucking to the east coast. When we had finished she looked shorn and sleek. No mast, sprayhood, pulpit, stanchions or radar arch and with everything wedged, packed and padded down below. We flew home for three weeks for Alistair and Mel's wedding and Robert's christening and left *Kokiri* in the capable hands of Andrews Trucking for her long journey across the North American continent.

When we arrived at the Royal St Lawrence Yacht Club in Montreal in mid-July she was there waiting for us, none the worse for her journey aside from a layer of grime and the splattered mass of bugs on all forward facing surfaces. We spent just over a week putting her back into commission before we were ready to take our Pacific 38 into the Atlantic. We negotiated the shallow Lac St Louis and the last two locks of the St Lawrence Seaway. Where the canal rejoins the river we turned upstream and pushed against a five-knot current towards the rapids and the old port at the heart of downtown Montreal. We arrived just before dark, gave Robert a late evening meal, put him to bed in the pushchair and set off into town. The streets were buzzing with people enjoying the balmy evening and the place had a marvellous mid-summer feel. We soaked up the atmosphere and a fabulous meal.

The long trip down the river was made much more manageable by the strong current pushing us along. We did the 140 miles to Quebec in just two hops, finding anchorage in a muddy creek and surging through the Richelieu Rapids on the way. Quebec is a quaint sort of city with its magnificent walls, citadel and crooked streets but was writhing with a myriad of tourists. It was with relief that we bent on the sails, left the historic battlements behind us and headed for the sea.

At L'Ile aux Coudres we met friends made in the South Pacific who joined us for an excellent sail down to Tadoussac. Here beluga, fin and minke whales abound as the cold nutrient-rich currents from the Arctic mix with the warm river and the Atlantic Ocean. This has made Tadoussac a haven for European whalers and fur-traders since 1600. A beautiful sunny day was ideal for a sail up the stunning fjord of the Saguenay River with pods of belugas and minkes all around. We then had a very fast downwind two-day passage around the Gaspé Peninsula, seeing a number of fin whales on the way, and stopped briefly at Percé and L'Anse-à-Beaufils before a rough, tough and fun overnight sail across the Gulf of St Lawrence to the Iles de la Madeleine.

By this time we were much more used to having Robert on board. When at anchor or underway in calm weather he is very happy in his bouncer, jumping up and down in the cabin, in the cockpit or even on the foredeck from the staysail halyard. Otherwise he can sit in his bucket-like chair strapped to the jib sheet winch or in his high chair clamped to the saloon table and watch the surroundings. We also made lee-cloths to create a playpen for him on the port saloon berth and across the entire focsle bunk. The hammock that hangs in the saloon and used to hold fruit has become the toy box, dangling with rattles and teddy bears like a stuffed mobile.

The Iles de la Madeleine are a wonderfully relaxed group of sandy islets and dunes in the middle of the Gulf of St Lawrence. With their partly British Canadian, partly French Acadian populations they have a very holiday feel. We arrived by chance at the start of the three-day sandcastle building championships, which is taken very seriously on the

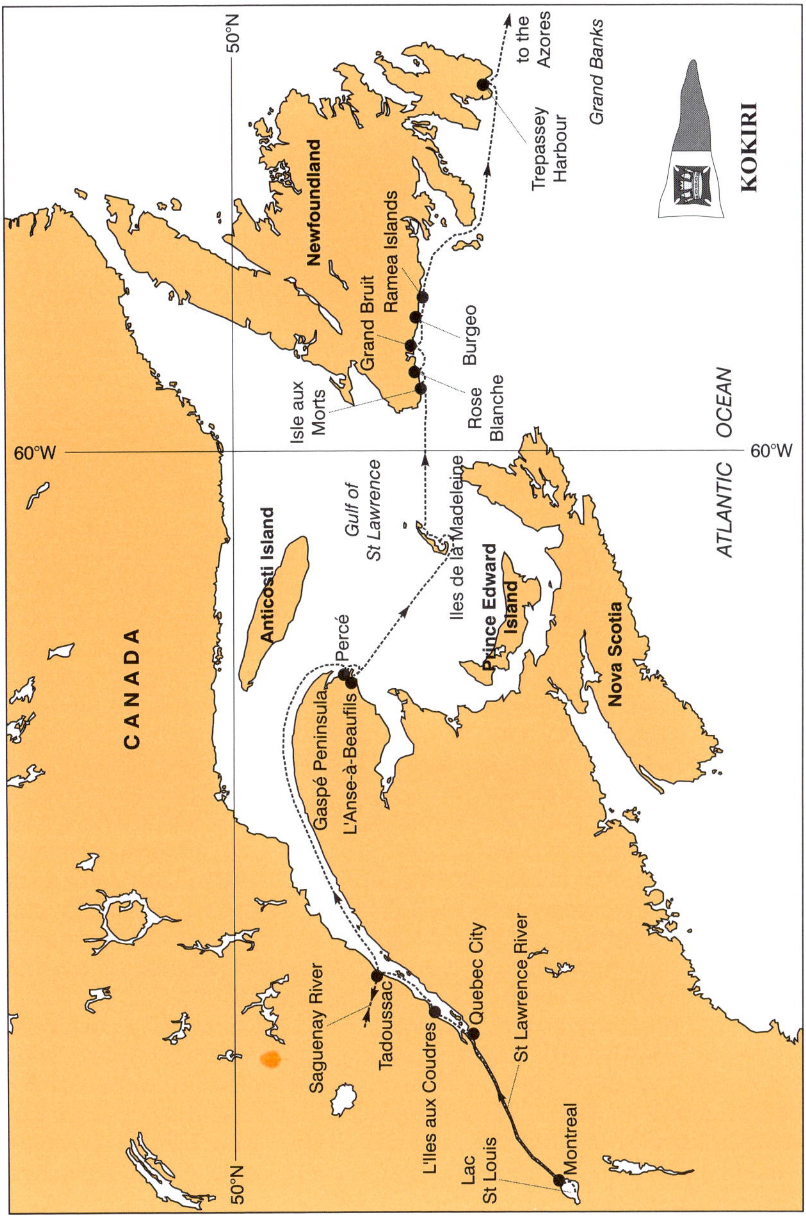
CANADA
Newfoundland
Anticosti Island
Prince Edward Island
Nova Scotia
Gulf of St Lawrence
ATLANTIC OCEAN
Grand Banks
to the Azores
Trepassey Harbour
Ramea Islands
Burgeo
Grand Bruit
Rose Blanche
Isle aux Morts
Iles de la Madeleine
Percé
L'Anse-à-Beaufils
Gaspé Peninsula
Tadoussac
Saguenay River
L'Iles aux Coudres
Quebec City
St Lawrence River
Montreal
Lac St Louis
50°N
60°W
KOKIRI

islands and produces some spectacular constructions. The celebrations for the international Acadian Day on 15 August followed and the whole population came alive for parties, spectacular fireworks and a communal midnight swim. It is peculiar to think that around March each year the pack ice virtually connects these low sand islands to the distant mainland.

As the season marched on we gradually curtailed our plans to cruise northern Newfoundland and a little of Labrador. Instead we headed to Newfoundland's south coast and kept an eye on the Atlantic weather, looking for an opportunity to head for the Azores. But aside from loitering between the laptop and SSB radio picking up weatherfaxes we had some good cruising along this impressive coastline. Newfoundland is nicknamed the 'granite planet', or simply 'the rock', by Canadians and it is easy to see why. Its monolithic landscape of grey granite, scraped over with a patchy layer of vegetation, reflected the grey skies.

Our first walk ashore on Ile aux Morts, named for the number of shipwrecks on the torturous rocks and shoals, was a completely delightful mixture of tiny pine trees, heather, bogs, lakes, great granite slabs and beautiful shining quartz. We had been looking forward to the opportunity for some good walking in Newfoundland and got very used to bundling Robert into *Twofella*, motoring ashore, installing him into the baby-carrying backpack and setting off. He seemed to love the change of scene and was very content, even when he and his father fell thigh deep into a stinking bog!

From the wonderful anchorage at Ile aux Morts we dotted along the coast, stopping at the small fishing harbours of Rose Blanche, Grand Bruit, Burgeo and Ship Cove in the Ramea Islands. They have been devastated in the past decade by the moratorium on fishing and each village, large or small, has the derelict remains of a fish processing plant. It was quite common to be able to walk right through a village without seeing a soul. Many of the villages along this coast have no road connection and the level of depression is evident when you hear that in some places the ferry service is being withdrawn for lack of custom. They are beautiful nonetheless, with brightly coloured shingled houses and small dories tethered to the boathouses that cluster along the shore. The narrow boardwalks and lack of traffic noise certainly add to the charm.

At Rose Blanche Harbour they are making a concerted effort to diversify and attract what few tourists there are. Before Newfoundland joined the rest of Canada in 1949 the dramatic old Victorian lighthouse on the headland was left abandoned and replaced by a cheap modern light. But the local people have restored it as a museum. The last lighthouse keeper lived in this tiny granite structure with his wife, sister and fifteen children. The mind boggles!

To our surprise, our great problem was that none of the villages had good quality drinking water. The boat was still well stocked from Quebec, so we needed very few stores before we set off, but fresh water and diesel were essential. All the villages had a 'boil order' on the tap water and in Burgeo, one of the main centres on the south coast, we found that the supply was usually drinkable but currently unsafe due to work on the pipeline. With no choice and despite its muddy look and taste we reluctantly filled our tanks. We boil anything we give to Robert in any case and hoped the rest of us could make do with whisky.

We had been keeping an eye on the track of hurricane Katrina and watched in horror with the rest of the world as it struck with full force on New Orleans. Its remnants moved north over the continent and, as it drew level with us, would give us a useful push offshore. Having checked the internet weather sites one last time in the small village at Trepassey Harbour on Newfoundland's southeast corner we saw that tropical depression Lee was no longer a threat and was due to dissipate off Bermuda. The five-day forecast showed nothing else, but a long range hurricane prediction showed tropical depression #14, not even formed yet and due to dissipate, way to the south and heading for the Caribbean. On 1 September, with Robert exactly six months old, we decided to go.

We made excellent progress across the Grand Banks despite being close-hauled and although we did not catch a single fish, we found plenty of the other commodity for which they are famous… fog. At one point a container ship came up on channel 16 to advise us we were on a collision course and at about a mile away we could only just hear her engines. Within two days the water turned from a milky turquoise to the deep grey blue of the north Atlantic and the temperature rocketed to 24°C. But then the weatherfaxes began to show that #14, now called Maria, far from dissipating in the south was likely to strengthen and re-curve early. That could put her on a collision course with little *Kokiri*. Our choices were to go back through uncertain weather, admit defeat and maybe try again next year – or to make it across her path in time.

Crossing the bow of a big ship is always a nail-biting experience; continuously taking bearings to check whether you're gaining or losing, not sure whether the captain has seen you, whether it is now too late to cut around her stern, whether the wind will drop a notch just at the critical moment and leave you wallowing. Crossing Maria's path was like this, but played out on a huge scale over three days, like a continental-sized game of chicken. We hardened up and continued on our ear in winds 25-35 knots, setting the tiny No 4 jib with three reefs in the mainsail and later even motorsailing to keep up maximum speed in the steep seas. The weatherfaxes and weather gurus Herb in Toronto and Alistair in England kept us informed of her predicted track. The most pessimistic predictions forecast storm force winds extending 300 miles from the centre that would continue to curve eastwards, meaning that we would not get far enough across her path, particularly for Katharine's liking. Luckily these fears weren't played out and we did not get more than 30 knots of wind.

However, just as we realised the threat of Maria had passed, hurricane Nate, which had been pushing up behind, increased speed exceptionally. We continued our dash for the safety of the marina at Horta on Faial and succeeded in outrunning it, arriving only 24 hours before it passed just north of the Azores group. Phew!

The relief of arriving safe and sound was immense. We had been at sea for nearly ten days and covered over 1450 miles, mostly on the wind, at an average speed of more than six knots. The last entry in the log reads 'A fairly nerve-racking passage – terrifying (Katharine).' Robert, however, had taken the whole trip in his little stride. He was unfazed both by being at sea for so long and by any anxiety he may have picked up on. But even he welcomed the change of scene. So we spent some time in Horta, washing, walking about the town and investigating the VAT situation for *Kokiri*. When finally ready to move on we motored the few miles across to Pico to anchor in the small harbour at Madalena. Time for a treat and we hired a car!

After a visit to the fascinating whaling museum at Lajes we set off for a party in the coastal village of Calhau. It was the village's annual fiesta and included the traditional sport of 'bullfighting on a rope', as well as much drinking and eating. Four angry bulls, having been kept in a box in the sun all day, were let out one by one into the village centre to face the crowd. The villagers looked on gasping and cheering, perched on walls,

Sunny days in Quebec

trees or roofs or behind the white line that marks the end of the rope's reach. For the first two bulls we stayed just on the safe side of the white line, surging to and fro with the crowd as the bulls came our way. The excitement and fear was absolutely gripping. For the third bull we took refuge on the high sea wall close to the middle of the square. A friendly local lady was temporarily holding Robert in a cooey sort of way; the warning rocket went up, the bull was let out of its cage and immediately leapt clean up and onto the sea wall. Panic raged and as it tore towards our group the local lady jumped with Robert down into the village square (read bullring), followed by all the rest of us. We lunged for the limited shelter of a barricade outside the public loos and tried to collect ourselves. Robert was returned but was none too happy among the wailing and screaming ladies. The bull, which had run off toward the sea probably hoping for a refreshing dip, was dragged back into its cage and we were gradually able to recover. We watched the final bull from the top of the cliff that overhangs the village!

The volcanic phenomena of the Azores are magnificent and easily accessible. The great peak of Pico, the recent eruption on Faial, numerous calderas on São Jorge and incredible caves on Graciosa and Terceira are sights to create a budding geologist out of anyone. We had a pleasant sail in light winds across to Velas on São Jorge, encountering three sperm whales on the way, and then had a good reach north to Graciosa with the

Navigating into Newfoundland

Sandcastles at the Iles de la Madeleine

flanker set. Here in the anchorage at Vila da Praia we were somewhat sheltered from the swells and stayed for a few days, exploring the amazing cave of Furna do Enxofre and its stunning caldera. It is unfortunate that the Azores has no really protected anchorages. At this time of year the swells from hurricanes to the south and west and storms to the north mean that rolling is ever present and sometimes severe.

We made a fast passage on the wind to Terceira and tied alongside at the excellent new marina in Angra do Heroismo. We planned to stay a few days, sheltering while a southerly gale passed through, and even hired another car for a day to see the interior of the island. Two interesting caves are easily accessible as well as smoking fumaroles, rustic villages

The painting at Horta

and lovely countryside. The cave of Gruta do Natal is a fascinating lava tunnel and great fun to explore. Robert was happy in his backpack, but as the hardhats provided were not in his size we had to be careful not to hit his head on the razor-sharp spikes and ridges that make up the roof of the cave! At one point we had to pass him, backpack and all, underneath a very low lava ceiling but by this time he was fast asleep and totally unfussed by the strangeness of his surroundings.

Our plan was to meet up with the RCC at Trafalgar for the bicentenary celebrations and then find a winter berth for *Kokiri* in southern Spain. It was already time to leave and we were again watching the weather. The Azores High shifted north, which would have given us head winds all the way, so we waited. Then low pressure formed just north of the Azores offering westerlies and we made ready to leave. Just before the off we picked up one last five-day weather forecast and saw the low intensifying and drifting south, meaning perfect weather for a day or two and then north-easterlies again. We considered trying to get in front of it, but decided instead to take the offer of a blustery run to Ponta Delgada on São Miguel and bide our time there. Thank goodness we did, because the low drifted south as far as Madeira, intensified again and then moved slowly north to hover between the Azores and Portugal in the form of hurricane Vince. We would have been caught right in the middle. Finally after another five days of waiting, the Azores High reformed to the south and a large depression in the north Atlantic gave us the weather we had been looking for.

We made good progress, initially with northerlies and then southerlies. Compared to our last ocean passage this felt like plain sailing and our nervousness began to decline. Many ships and spectacular African dawns broke the monotony. Robert had obviously benefited from the excitement of the Azores and was much more active during this passage, requiring regular entertainment to quell a new level of whining scream. Unfortunately the winds weren't sufficient for us to meet the RCC at Gibraltar on 17 October and instead we made for Barbate, arriving in flat calm at 0700 the next day, Peter's birthday. A shower and a brief tidy up was all we had time for before the fleet began to roll in and by lunchtime we were ecstatically pleased to be able to entertain Katharine's parents on board. What a perfect end to *Kokiri*'s first foray into the Atlantic.

Peter and Katherine bought Kokiri in New Zealand in 2003 and sailed her clockwise round the Pacific to Japan, Alaska and British Columbia.

TARAKI CRUISES THE CHILEAN CHANNELS

by John and Sally Melling

Taraki left Plymouth in June 2002 after having a new engine installed. We wanted to cruise the Chilean channels but decided to approach from the Pacific via Panama, the Galapagos and French Polynesia. The track to Bora Bora via the Panama Canal is now well worn. Many harbours were quite crowded and sometimes too crowded for our taste. We spent time in Spain, the Canaries and Tobago and Trinidad – where one evening when anchored in the beautiful La Vache bay, a young man in a dinghy appeared from nowhere and threatened us with a gun! Happily the situation was diffused but it was rather unsettling. After a few very pleasant days at Bonaire we arrived at Colon to start preparations for our transit of the Panama Canal. We were delighted to find *Troubadour, Nordlys* and *Fortuna* there. They were a great help in making our transit enjoyable but it was still a great relief when we finally arrived safely in the Pacific.

We much enjoyed Las Perlas, the Galapagos, Marquesas and Society Islands but Raraka in the Tuamotus was a highlight. Why did we choose it out of the many possibilities? Firstly the wind blew us there and secondly very few yachts visit. There is no airstrip and no tourism, just copra, fishing and pearl farming to occupy the 80 or so inhabitants.

After reporting to the mayor he invited us to supper, a feast with wonderful fish and plenty of French red wine. The island's only teacher, Bernina and her husband Simon, befriended us and during the 12 days of our stay they invited us for meals, took us to their pearl farm, gave us pearls, got us to plant coconuts in memory of our visit and much more. It is hard to thank such generosity. Fortunately we had a digital camera, so were able to take photos of each child at the school, which they gave to their dads for Father's Day. Then some young women wanted pictures of themselves and their babies. This resulted in yet more presents! The anchorage was not always comfortable as a considerable chop could build up and then the coral helped to strip the galvanizing off our anchor chain.

On 3 August 2003 we left Bora Bora after saying goodbye to *Nordlys* and *Fortuna* and turned to the southeast. A gentle breeze with smooth water and sunshine allowed us to fetch Raivavae, a small atoll in the Australs. Unfortunately the breeze died during our last night whilst we were hove-to waiting for daylight before entering the lagoon and the last four hours were spent motoring.

Raivavae is a gem and quite unspoilt; this however may not last for long as an airstrip opened in November 2002. Development will no doubt follow, as it is a beautiful lagoon with pristine beaches. We were the only yacht there and the gendarme, a charming Frenchman, told us they had about 20 yachts every year. His only concern was that we should provide a picture of *Taraki* and write something in his book of visiting yachts. After leaving Raivavae, sea and air temperatures began to drop, eventually as low as 12–13°C, so our thermals and sleeping bags came out of their long-term storage. In contrast to the downwind sailing we had become used to on our recent long passages, conditions were always changing. Sailing varied from hard on the wind to running before in winds from F0 to F9. Occasionally the waves were quite awesome but when the sun was shining (which it did sometimes) the scene was magnificent and very beautiful.

As our passage progressed there was a big increase in the number of sea birds including the lovely Cape Petrel (Cape Pigeon), other petrels and albatross. When conditions allowed it was always a delight to sit and relax in the cockpit, all wrapped up in oilies, watching the aerobatic and gliding skills of these wonderful birds. Despite our bird books we found identification at sea very difficult.

After 27 days we were beginning to plan our approach to the Canal Chacao. Then the wind blew up. We thought, 'Is this the sting in the tail?' but it turned out we had three stings. The hard blow (F7+) was followed by calm when we had only about 50 miles to go. We wallowed about for part of the night then in the morning decided that if we motored we could arrive before dark. The third sting came as we entered the channel; the spring tides were against us and after motoring hard for two hours in short steep breaking waves our progress was only two miles! Eventually transits ashore and bearings on the Punta Corona light began to change and we anchored in total calm with flat water in the lee of the lighthouse headland just as the sun was setting. There were cows in the fields and the gorse was in full bloom; it could have been Devon. It was bliss sitting in the cockpit, whisky in hand, listening to the geese honking and watching the diving ducks and cormorants.

The passage had taken us one hour short of 29 days with a sailing distance of almost 4000 miles and 13 hours of engine time. We still had another 70 miles to go to Puerto Montt, which took two days of motor-

ing. Conditions were clear and the snow-capped volcanoes of Osorno and Calbuco were visible with the Andes in the distance; magical, just what we had come for. We moored at the Marina del Sur, which we found excellent with friendly, helpful people, hot showers and shore power. Pure luxury.

We spent two months at home, the first time we had left *Taraki*, and returned at the end of November 2003 to start our first cruise exploring the Chilean channels. This was to take us south to Laguna San Rafael with its magnificent glacier. The northern channels were very beautiful with thickly vegetated mountains although often shrouded in mist. The anchorages were mostly small coves with a wonderful variety of trees, totally impenetrable and therefore with no opportunities for walking. Beautiful bird song came from the woodland and small flocks of parakeets flew over. Most days it rained, sometimes all day and night. Anchorages are well protected from most winds and almost always peaceful.

One afternoon after retreating from nasty weather into a snug anchorage and while Sally was roasting a leg of lamb, we were visited by two cheerful fishermen. They presented us with a fish, our favourite *congrio*, so we insisted they should have some wine and chocolates but we were then given another fish. One said, 'It rains 400 days a year here.' On another occasion an Indian family of mum, dad, two kids and a dog arrived in the evening in a heavy rowing boat. Toothless and ruddy faced they offered us two large live spider crabs. First they asked for 'Pisco' then for 'Veesky'. We exchanged wine and chocolate and they seemed happy. It was a struggle getting the live crabs into the pressure cooker but they were excellent eating. The whole area between Puerto Montt and Laguna San Rafael provides wonderful cruising with almost limitless possibilities and friendly people. We spent a week anchored off Castro, Isla Chiloé, in glorious sunshine enjoying visits to villages with their lovely wooden churches, *fiestas*, markets, etc.

Before returning home we flew north for some land travel using 4 × 4s in the Atacama Desert and on the Altiplano in the most northern part of Chile near the borders with Peru and Bolivia. We had wonderful experiences in remote areas at altitudes of 4500m with magnificent scenery and wild life. In Parinacota we stayed with a young Ayamara Indian family.

We returned to Chile in December 2004 and were immediately busy preparing *Taraki*, varnishing, checking equipment and having her out of the water to be scrubbed and anti-fouled. Dealing with officialdom also took its time, getting permission from customs to keep *Taraki* in Chile and from the Armada to sail down to Puerto Williams in the Beagle Channel. Provisioning for four months involved big shopping trips, cataloguing all the items and then finding space for everything. On Christmas Eve we left Marina del Sur for the last time, a little sad to leave an excellent marina where we had been very happy but pleased to start our next adventure. Christmas Day found us beating in F4 winds with bright sunny weather and snow-capped mountains as a backcloth. Except for a few rest days we moved south to a new anchorage every day.

To enter the southern channels you have to cross an open expanse of the Pacific, aptly named the Golfo de Penas (Bay of Sorrows). We rounded the Tres Montes peninsula and entered the 'Golfo' in the pitch black of night with very lumpy seas and gale force winds from astern. Visibility was less than one mile as we approached land and our charts and the GPS did not agree – a little angst making.

We spent two days at Puerto Eden, a small fishing community of friendly people, where we had lunch at a restaurant. Nelda served us crab salad, soup and fried *congrio* with white wine – all delicious. The Navimag supply ship, which ferries between Puerto Montt and Puerto Natales, arrived while we were there so we stocked up with fresh fruit and vegetables. However our most delicious purchase was some local crab, enough for three good meals. We enjoyed some excellent downwind sailing with reasonably strong winds up to 35 knots, but also a lot of motoring.

We woke one morning to find to our horror that the fuel pipe connecting the paraffin tank to our cooker had fractured and could no longer be used. There was a small flood of paraffin but it's fortunate we were not using gas. We have camping gear on board so our little meths cooker was brought into service. Cooking was limited and sadly there was no bread baking. We could make hot drinks and heat up food and Sally was busy experimenting with making *rosti* (grated potato cooked like a pancake) and different types of Indian bread. Quite a challenge!

A small detour to Amalia Glacier was worthwhile. From our anchorage that evening we looked across to the glacier and next morning went

Taraki sailing in the Chilean Channels

ashore to find a profusion of flowers and berries with humming birds flitting from tree to tree.

An extract from our log for 4 February reads, 'Left Puerto Profundo. Talked to Fairway Faro, wind forecast 20–30 knots. In the event we had fast tough sail across Magellan entrance. Paso Tamar then Paso del Mar. Broad reach then run – boat speed surfing! 8+ knots with apparent winds 20-40 knots. Anchored Caleta Mostyn. Trip 52 miles. Lost oars overboard – careless not putting away! Pleasant sunny evening, Good shelter, 2 ropes, some gusts with NW6-8.'

For sometime now it had been our practice not only to anchor but also to use two or three lines to the shore for extra security. Once anchored, ropes and the dinghy were always ready for John to row ashore and tie to a suitable tree. After all this we usually needed a cup of tea or something stronger, but it did mean we could sleep soundly knowing we were secure. We never used tandem anchoring.

Now in the Estrecho de Magallanes we found changes in both weather and scenery; the winds were generally stronger and gustier and there were more clear days when the dramatic mountain scenery could be seen. We passed from the Estrecho de Magallanes to the Canal Cockburn via Canal Acwalisnan without problems. It is the preferred route of all yachts going north and south.

Two anchorages will remain particular highlights of our trip. The first was at Brecknock. On the day we arrived it was exceptionally fine so after lunch, accompanied by Vicky from *Sunstone*, we climbed the nearby mountain (700m) and traversed the ridge overlooking the anchorage. The view from the summit was breathtaking with Monte Sarmiento over 40 miles away. There was an absolutely magic moment when a condor appeared right overhead. Eventually we counted ten gliding around us. We arrived back just before dark having had a superb afternoon. The following day, with copper pipe of the right diameter from *Sunstone*, John was able temporarily to repair the cooker fuel line. After three weeks of cooking on a camping stove Sally baked two loaves of bread, one for *Sunstone* as a thank you. There were celebrations all round on *Taraki* that evening.

After Brecknock we entered Brazo Noroeste, the northeastern arm of the Beagle Canal, sometimes known as the 'avenue of the glaciers' as there are many tumbling into the sea. It has some of the most spectacular and dramatic scenery we have sailed through. Sailing was exhilarating too with between 25 and 40 knots of breeze over the stern. We anchored in Seno Pia when again the weather was kind so we put on our boots and climbed the nearby mountain (1000m). Views of the Cordillera Darwin were magnificent as were the views looking down on large ice fields and the channels beyond. This was our second highlight.

On 28 February we arrived at Puerto Williams, the southernmost town in the world. It was 67 days since leaving Puerto Montt. We had sailed almost 1500 miles with 47 different anchorages. Puerto Williams is a naval base with a population of 2,500. There are basic facilities including some small supermarkets. The marina is centred round the *Macalvi*, an old munitions carrier that was deliberately run aground some years ago. There is a lot of activity with yachts, mostly charter boats and mostly French, coming and going to and from the Horn and Antarctica. Thanks to emails via our newly acquired Iridium satellite phone the spare part for our cooker was waiting.

Ushuaia on the south side of Terra del Fuego was our next port. We left Puerto Williams at first light with frost on the deck and a beautiful fiery sunrise, motoring the 25 miles to Ushuaia. The main street is full of restaurants, internet cafés, clothes and souvenir shops; quite a tourist centre and a bit of a shock after the peace and quiet of the channels. We enjoyed some good restaurants and the Argentinian beef and wine were as good as ever.

Sally Melling climbing above Seno Pia

After leaving Ushuaia bound for Uruguay we had two stops before entering the Estrecho de Le Maire. On our second day out the wind increased to F8 and was on the nose when we arrived at the outer anchorage at Bahia Aguirre. Quite a struggle, but bliss once we were anchored in the safety of a sheltered cove, albeit very wet and cold. We waited two days before attempting the straits, got our timing right and had a good passage through but the next few days gave us a succession of three gales with winds over 40 knots. We also spent 48 hours beating into F6, not very comfortable. In contrast there were sunny days with clear skies when we were able to appreciate the abundant bird life – albatrosses, petrels, prions and shearwaters all circling *Taraki.*

As usual in rough weather John took over all the cooking, producing nourishing meals such as porridge and fried eggs (and that was just for breakfast!). The third member of crew, our uncomplaining Aries self-steering, performed well, needing no sleep or nourishment (except for occasional oiling) and never suffering from seasickness.

An incident occurred on 1 April – this is no joke! Becalmed and going nowhere we were startled by a plane flying low over us, followed by the Argentinian navy speaking to us on the VHF. We were in a firing/danger zone and must move. First we were told to go north, then south (the

Taraki and Sunstone in Brecknock

opposite from where we wanted to go). We could see a naval vessel and what looked like a large hulk with smoke billowing out of it. Target practice? We then found ourselves on collision course with the naval ship but altered course to pass astern of it. The crew were on deck waving to us. We were mystified by commands on the VHF to a fishing boat, 'Get your men to the bridge. We are going to fire at your stern.' We were told, 'We are going to fire at a fishing boat on your stern.' We then saw four of these hulk-like vessels and when one came close we could see it was a very large Japanese fishing boat. We had heard in Ushuaia that Japanese fishing boats were a problem for the Argentinian fishing fleet and presumably these were being escorted off their patch.

We arrived at Piriapolis, Uruguay, on 5 April after a passage of 1500 miles, which had taken just over 11days.

Taraki is a Saltram Saga 40, a cutter-rigged double-ender with a long keel designed by Alan Pape and built by Skentlebery in 1980

MAKING DO

by Meg Clothier

My home, Moscow, has pretty sketchy maritime credentials. Men fish grumpily in the marshy pools by the housing estates; tourists ply the Moskva River past the Gorky Park roller coaster; everyone moans about the hideous statue of Peter the Great that was meant to be Columbus but was judiciously rejected by the Americans as too vile for words.

But a small cluster of my friends discovered that 30 minutes bumpy train ride north of Moscow there were in theory yachts for the taking. The first obstacle was that none of us belonged to an *elitny* set that could claim the acquaintance of an oligarch with a waterfront dacha. Every sailing club we called either had a waiting list of months or wondered whether we could afford their rates. Others promised dinghies but said they were only for children. What about adults? A heavy shrug down the phone: 'They should have their own.' Finally Oliver, with newshound determination, was ping-ponged to a friendlier establishment called Spartak, a popular Soviet name that evokes a sort of smart classicism in an appropriately sod-the-rich way. Yes, they had boats. Yes, we could rent one. Yes, at a price that matched journalists' salaries.

The crew assembled at a pastel train station, loaded to the gunwales with beer, black bread, smoked fish, sausage and mushed-up garlicky aubergines, all wearing their best sea-going outfits. We rattled out of town. The boat was no beauty but it was a good 30 feet long, with a mast that looked as though it would stay up. Sasha, our very gnarly and very disdainful *kapitan*, cast us off. I had been expecting a glorified gravel pit but instead we were let loose on a waterway that stretched further than the eye could see. Rail tracks and motorways soared overhead. Paddle steamers, couples in coracles, a Laser racing fleet, shiny black BMW substitutes. All wallowing, careering, darting, bobbing, basking. Perfect.

Sasha started to set sail, handing the tiller to the most sportsmanlike boy on board, who like a gent handed it on to me in deference to my RCC cadet status. I held her head-to-wind while Sasha peered suspiciously at me and sweated up the main. He allowed me to stay in charge while we bore off and got underway. Every time I flickered off the perfect line to windward he puffed, growled, clutched the tiller and jabbed at the tell-tales. We tried to make friends with him by asking for sailing words in Russian, many of which are mercifully unSlavic as boats only really became fashionable with Peter the Great via Holland. My favourite one is *farvater* – a fairway. Sasha softened by the time the Russo-Anglo-Japanese crew was yelling Ready About, *Po-Ekhaliiiiiiiiiiii* in unison.

We rounded the first point where wobbly *babushki* were sunning themselves on a spit of concrete and copper wires and then the wind filled in. We heeled sharply. The sound of the picnic lurching to leeward magicked up the atmosphere of bigger adventures, as did the shrieks of the non-sailors as the leeward rail dug into the waves. Sasha robustly refused to spill any main and we held our course, north by a little west. A point or two off the bow we saw a RIB with a diver down. '*Tryp*', said Sasha. 'Corpse?' '*Da*.' It wasn't hard to figure out how a crash had happened. Moaning cheerfully at pig-like motorboats is part of sailing but the brutes out that day really deserved it. They swerved helter-skelter at 10, 15, 20 knots. There were no friendly buoys painted with a maximum speed limit and even if there were I doubt the *buzinesmeny* piloting their dubiously funded pride-and-joys would have paid any attention. It's the same on the narrow back streets of Moscow. You hug the edges of the buildings, risking sudden death from falling icicles (admittedly not in July) while Hummers with bulletproof windows steam past.

We tacked away from the maelstrom to calmer waters where a fleet of dinghies was racing in earnest. Masha photographed us in bold seaman-like poses. Oliver passed round beers. Masha's friend from Japan told us about her surfing adventures. Tom lazed on the coach roof with a book grumbling each time a tack meant he had to brace with a different foot. We dropped anchor and handed up our Russian picnic and those less concerned about death by poisoning leapt overboard for race-you-to-the-bow, pretending-to-be-sharks and no-I-can't-shin-up-the-anchor-rope. The stuff of all summer sailing holidays.

The sun wasn't about to set any time soon this far north but the wind was dying and the clock was ticking and it was time to turn home. We had 20 minutes of fruitless goose-winging before Sasha dropped the little outboard into the water and powered us back to base. We paid up and joined hundreds of patchwork-sunburned Russians on the station before squeezing onto the *elektrichka* that was a sweaty fug of vodka-pickled people. Back in the big city we launched into an evening of back-to-land excess that is my favourite part of sailing. We sat in an outdoor café on the grassy Boulevard Ring; a pack of teenagers tried to beat up a passing Tajik; an almighty thunderstorm passed overhead; we argued about Israel and Palestine and I told all my most embellishable sea tales. We went to bed at two o'clock very pleased with our mini-adventure.

A MAN WITHOUT A BOAT

by Bob Shepton

After the disaster in Greenland in January last year I am pleased to be able to write that my insurers, Yachtsure, played absolutely straight and after appropriate enquiries to the authorities in Greenland paid out a full settlement for total loss. This enabled me to look for another boat. It was interesting that I quickly came to the conclusion that, for the price and for what I wanted to do, it would be difficult to find anything better than I had had before. So I narrowed the search and found another 33-foot Westerly Discus. The price agreed with a supportive and honourable owner allowed for a survey that said that the boat had some osmosis which should be dealt with within the next two years.

The only problem was that the boat was in Plymouth and I stay (live) in Scotland. First that guru of Greenlandic sailing, Willy Ker, phoned from mid-Channel on his way home from the Azores and offered his services as crew. Then an acquaintance put me in touch with Clive King, ex-Port Officer of San Francisco for the OCC, and Mike Watling, manager of a heli-ski operation near Whistler and a Yachtmaster (but we promised not to hold that against him). With such a crew how could one fail?

Deeply wounded by huge harbour dues in Plymouth – we are not used to that sort of thing in Scotland – Clive and I set sail on 22 April on the first leg to Falmouth. This was a simple day's sail of course, except the wind was F5-6 on the nose and we had to tack down Channel. We quickly found that my newfound friend, the previous owner, had paid a lot of attention to the inside below but not to the sailing systems above! On the other hand we were pleasantly impressed by the way the boat sailed 'in the groove' with hardly a hand needed on the wheel once she was set up. This was just as well as the Autohelm had a habit of quietly switching itself off without warning.

After this choppy introduction we put into Falmouth and picked up a mooring. We spent a few days equipping the boat and getting an Autosteer windvane steering on board. I had found this worked very well on *Dodo's Delight*. Willy joined us now, as he could not sail before partaking of his homegrown asparagus. We dined Anne Hammick (rather modestly I'm afraid) as a small thank-you for the excellent job she does researching and editing pilots and journals for us all.

The skipper was under a certain amount of pressure; he had not sailed before with a Fellow of the Royal Institute of Navigation. He thought he had better do some coastal pilotage and try to catch the tide around Lands End, and the Lizard as well if possible. In the event he was congratulated on getting the tides right (high praise indeed) though there were mumblings from on high about taking the inner passage round Lands End. 'But I always go that way, Willy', and the aforesaid gentleman duly fortified with *uisge beatha* (the water of life) just about allowed the youngster his way. In fact we motored around in sunshine and calm and with sighs of relief. South coast sailors have my deepest respect and sympathy; I had not found a single creek, river, inlet, bay or harbour where someone did not rush out and charge you. And there were boats *everywhere*. No wonder you'll all be coming to Greenland soon!

It is quite a way across the Bristol Channel and towards the end the increasing wind began to head us and we had to veer off towards Ireland rather than closing the Smalls. There was a newfangled instrument called a Navtex on board. I found it rather unsatisfactory as it usually had detailed forecasts for every area but the one you were in. However this time it did tell us that severe gale F9 decreasing F8 was expected in our area. A strange way to print a forecast but it duly arrived. Fortunately it was from the southwest. We managed to take three reefs in the main even though most of the reefing lines had burst and broad reached before the building seas. At least it bowled us up the Irish Sea at a great rate and as it relented next morning we ran across towards Holyhead. This is where the guru and the skipper had a slight difference of opinion as to when we should gybe approaching the famous North Stack climbing cliffs. But then I remembered one does not argue with a FRIN and retired below. The discussion was spurious anyhow as the San Francisco Port Officer had his own agenda and was enjoying the sleigh ride through the vicious overfalls. I learnt afterwards from a local that we were all wrong. To avoid the race with wind against tide you either stay seven metres off the North Stack or seven miles!

In Holyhead Mike joined us looking as young and fit as you would expect. Four aboard was positively luxurious and in any case the weather decided to be benign with a fair wind for our crossing to Port St Mary on the Isle of Man. Because of the considerable tidal range we got permission to moor alongside another boat to avoid having to tend our lines through the night. Another fine day dawned with the promise of an easy passage though there were slight rumblings again when the skipper cut through the narrow gap between the main island and the Calf of Man.

Fortunately he had looked up the tides. The entrance and the small harbour of Portpatrick always intrigue though the village is rather limited if you want to renew stores. And so on to the Mull of Kintyre. This coastal sailing is awfully hard with all this tidal work but here it really is important to get it right. We had a pleasant sail on the wind towards the Mull, though driven somewhat east by the slant, before tacking past the interesting island of Sanda with its outlying rocks. In fact we were at the Mull a little early but it was reasonably calm and the tide was soon to turn. A pleasant passage up the west coast took us to Ardminish Bay on Gigha, which was unusually full of boats so we had to put our own anchor down.

Gigha is a lovely island and the inhabitants have now taken over its affairs and management themselves. We decided to stay an extra day and Mike, being younger than the rest of us, was able quickly to identify with the local young people, even if this meant *having* to stay out till 0200. So the next day I found we were committed to taking a large party sailing. But this was good; it seemed strange that they had lived all their lives on the island and had never been on a sailing boat, or in some case any boat, before. We duly circumnavigated Gigha under sail with the decks crammed with people.

As happens when sailing, Clive had lost track and suddenly found he was due to take off from Heathrow next day. He left hurriedly on the

Willy Ker strengthens himself for the inner passage round Lands End

small ferry to the mainland. The following day the three of us put out for the Sound of Jura and more tidal work. Another pleasant sail in spectacular scenery before the wind died and we had to motor up to Ardfern Yacht Centre where the boat was due to be lifted out for osmosis treatment and other necessary work. The delivery trip was over and I was without a boat again!

The next venture was a passage to Iceland. A friend here in Scotland had kindly employed me as sailing master aboard his Moody 42 for this, his first ocean passage. We had already had a warm-up out to St Kilda. But now we went through the Sound of Barra, my favourite offing for the Atlantic, for the real thing. But where were those predominant southerlies? We were on the wind against strong northerlies nearly all the way. I have to say I do not find a Moody 42 of that vintage an easy boat to sail with its exposed centre cockpit, winches awkwardly placed on the coaming, mainsheet awkwardly behind the wheel and a big wheel so you have to climb onto the seats to get past. Fortunately the wind moderated on the last day just in time for the owner to take down the For Sale notices and we put into the Vestmannaeyjar. These were extremely interesting with their volcanic islands and hills and with the main island increased by a third by the eruption of 1973. I enjoyed climbing the most modern mountain in the world though I could hardly claim it as a first ascent! There was still no vegetation on it or its neighbour and only a

First time round Nordkapp for the novice Shepton

slightly green sheen on the huge lava field below. At the edge by the shore there is a timber chapel donated by the Norwegians and dedicated to the lost islanders.

The owner's family flew out and we enjoyed a week sailing a little way round the west coast and discovered some updates and useful new anchorages to keep the editor of the Pilot on his toes. One calm evening a school of orcas gambolled slowly around, a rare show and much appreciated by the family. And sitting comfortably outside in the rain in a thermally heated natural pool was quite an experience. We had aimed to return via the Faeroes but in the event there was too much east in the wind. Indeed on the second day out it steadily increased: F7, F8, steady F9 into F10. Now this boat was not really rigged for heavy weather sailing. All I could do was to roll the mainsail right into the mast to trysail size, going up to the mast in stormy conditions to do so, and beam reach across the seas that fortunately did not get too large. The For Sale notices went up again but the wind remained in the north and east and eventually we broad-reached past St Kilda five miles to port and tacked downwind for the Sound of Barra. As we motored gingerly over the shoals to the south I thought I had better confess. 'By the way folks, I suspect I am the only Reverend to have hit rocks in both the Arctic and Antarctica.' Having inspired great confidence, we made our way over the rocks and round the south cardinal buoy to anchor for a night's sleep some distance out from the airstrip, which is on the beach on Barra. We crossed the Minch next day, being able for once to lay the course to Tobermory and then down the Sound of Mull with a fair breeze home.

There was a pause in activity now, punctuated by a circumnavigation of Mull skippering a Westerly Oceanranger for Westward Quest, a Christian charity sailing out of Kilmelford, when I discovered that a group of 13-year olds, mainly girls, was not really my scene! The intention then was to fly out to Svalbard to join the Lomaxes on *Cloud Walker* and help sail her back to Norway but poor David was taken ill and had been rushed to hospital at Kirkenes. This meant the boat was stranded in Vardø and I went to help Judy sail her back to Tromsø. An American friend of theirs, Scott Fraser, dropped everything so we were three.

Poor Judy, I must have driven her mad with technical questions about the boat. And you had to admire how hardy these veterans are. Here was a well-known, well-travelled, well-sailed boat and still all the mainsail hoisting and reefing were done at the mast however boisterous conditions might be. And there was no anchor winch. On the new *Dodo's Delight* I was about to lead all lines back to the cockpit so all reefing could be done from there. And I was certainly glad I had an anchor winch even if it was manual. Clearly I was a wimp, or getting old after all! On the other hand there was a slight divergence of opinion regarding anchoring between what I would call the Norwegian-European attitude, 'It's best to anchor in places that are marked with an anchor symbol because we know they will be safe', and the Scottish-Greenlandic style, 'That looks reasonably well protected and it has sufficient depth; let's try that'. After a couple of 'Scottish' anchorages had been rejected by the skipper, the Reverend had to learn perhaps to rely less on faith and more on care and maybe the lady became a little less cautious. Diplomatic relations continued!

In the event we had an easy passage with little wind and had to motor much of the way. 'Don't worry, Judy, remember it's a delivery trip'. Initially the skipper, having done it probably hundreds of times before, was not too keen on going round Nordkapp as it was further but fortunately the wind blew that day and from the northeast so novices like myself had the pleasure of sailing round the headland with a fair breeze. But which really was the most northerly point? Chancellor seems to have got it wrong.

There was one crisis – there are comparatively few towns in Norway that have a Vinmonopol, the only places where booze can be bought. We had run out and had to get up at 0330 next morning in order to make the next town that had one. On the last evening having caught still more fish almost as soon as we put the lines over the stern, we anchored between some islands sheltered in a small bay from the prevailing breeze. In the night the wind went round 180° and I was forced to eat my thoughts about American-Norwegian anchoring methods, a comparatively short, but heavy, length of chain on the anchor spliced to a long rope rode. It held with no problem. And what a boon it was hauling up a light anchor though Scott being the young man of the party at 53 did most of that.

We delivered the boat safely to Tromsø and I was then able to join their son-in-law Rikki on a professional delivery of a Bavaria 38 from Oslo to Trondheim. Of course I had imbibed all the usual prejudices against Bavarias so it was good to find it sailed well off and on the wind, that it was roomy (perhaps almost too roomy) if rather functional down below and that full vertical battens in the in-mast mainsail had at least improved its performance. For a family getting on the water or for folks mainly sailing coastal and offshore it would be difficult to find anything better for the price. But with that flat dish hull shape I still would not want one for serious cruising. And what a beautiful coastline that south coast of Norway is. Having bashed hard under engine in short seas against F5-6 on the nose we took the inner passage. Passing through a fishing village where the fjord was the village street was unforgettable. After passing the southern corner – it was nice to round both the north and south capes of Norway in one summer – we had F8-9 southerly so we sped up the west coast for a day, before taking the picturesque inner passages once again. And it was great to sail with such a professional and competent skipper.

Unfortunately the grand finale to the season – a trip acting as technical advisor in a 180-foot yacht from Iceland to Greenland to Nova Scotia –

The new Dodo at Ardfern

was cancelled as the skipper was worried by forecasts of depressions spinning up towards Iceland. 'But you always get a couple of gales on that crossing.' He remained unimpressed. Pity, because I needed the considerable fee for fitting out the new *Dodo's Delight*! But, terrible thought, after such a great summer, sailing in a number of places, with delightful people and in a variety of boats, should I have got another boat at all ....?

FEANOR VISITS POLAND AND THE BALTIC STATES

by Jeremy Parkinson

This cruise won Juno's Cup

Feanor arrived at Stralsund, Germany on Friday 3 June having left Weymouth on 8 May. I had been single-handed from Kiel and was looking forward to having a crew again although I had had few problems apart from mooring in the dreaded box berths that they have in Germany. If they are wide enough (and you don't know until you try) they are fine if there are four of you: one on the bow to leap ashore with a rope, one on the helm and one on each side to fend off the posts and lasso them with the stern warps. Single-handed the performance usually ends in farce and you are lucky if there is no audience.

The new crew were Mike Jennings, who has come with me every year for the last ten, and Terry Krasinska who was a physiotherapist at my old health centre. She was crewing with me for the first time and her fluency in Polish was a godsend especially in restaurants. They arrived on Sunday morning after a rather fraught journey from Szczecin where I had arranged to meet them but had failed to make the rendezvous.

After looking over the windjammer *Gorch Foch*, which was in a sad state of repair but restoration has started, we left at 1605 and motored north through the dredged channels between Hiddensee Island and Rugen Island. The wind was a westerly F6 and with an unpractised crew I thought it safer to motor through the well-marked but narrow channels even though the sea was slight. We arrived at Neuendorf at 1920 and, in spite of the strong wind on the beam, managed the box berth fairly competently with the help of a neighbouring yachtsman. It blew F8 during the night and was not much less in the morning so we decided to stay put and explore Hiddensee Island. We walked the four miles to Vitte where we had an excellent lunch of local pike in a harbourside café before walking another couple of miles to the prettiest harbour of the three at Kloster. Fortunately there was a bus back!

Next morning we left Neuendorf at 1020 in a F2 northerly, which again meant motoring through narrow channels until we got out to sea at Rehbergort Point. We then had a gentle sail eastwards along the north coast of Rugen and past the only chalk cliffs in Germany. They are a local tourist attraction but far less spectacular than those of the English south coast. We berthed at Sassnitz, the capital of Rugen, at 1710. Shortly afterwards a steel sloop berthed next to us and her owner from Berlin remarked how nice it was to see a British yacht.

On Thursday we sailed gently south in a F2 northwesterly towards the entrance of the Peenestrom channel between the German mainland and Peenemünde. This is where the German V1 and V2 rockets were developed and there is apparently an excellent museum devoted to this. We were far more enthralled by the scenery as we sailed through the intricate and well marked reed-lined channels. A pair of white-tailed sea eagles was spotted amongst the abundant bird life. We arrived just in time for the 1640 opening of the Wölgast road bridge that we motored through before continuing to sail to a pleasant sheltered anchorage southwest of Gormitz Island.

We left early and kept the engine running to be sure of reaching the Usedom bridge by the 0900 opening. Once through we sailed out into the Stettiner Haff inland sea to Ueckermünde, which we reached at 1145. The pleasant town is about a mile up a canal and we moored to the town quay. After lunch Mike and Terry found a supermarket whilst I walked a couple of miles to a depot to stock up with Camping Gaz before leaving Germany. Ueckermünde is also a good place to clear customs before departing for Poland, as there is a small ferry terminal with a customs post close to the yacht berths.

We left at 1600, motored out into the Haff again and set sail for Buoy 14 where we had been instructed to report to the Polish border control vessel moored there. We were boarded by two border guards in a RIB. They stayed half an hour filling in forms and were very polite. Their English was quite good but they were obviously relieved when they discovered that Terry spoke Polish. They said that a British yacht was very unusual.

Once they had finished with us we motored northeastwards for the Prastowski Kanal leading from the inland sea (which the Poles call Zalew Szczeciński) to Świnoujście. The canal together with a dredged channel across the Zalew Szczeciński forms the approach to Szczecin for commercial shipping. I had hoped to avoid Świnoujście by taking the route from the eastern end of the Zalew Szczeciński to Dziwnów but there is a fixed railway bridge with a clearance of only 12.5 metres and *Feanor* needs 13. The canal is lined with dead trees that have been killed by the numbers of cormorants roosting in them.

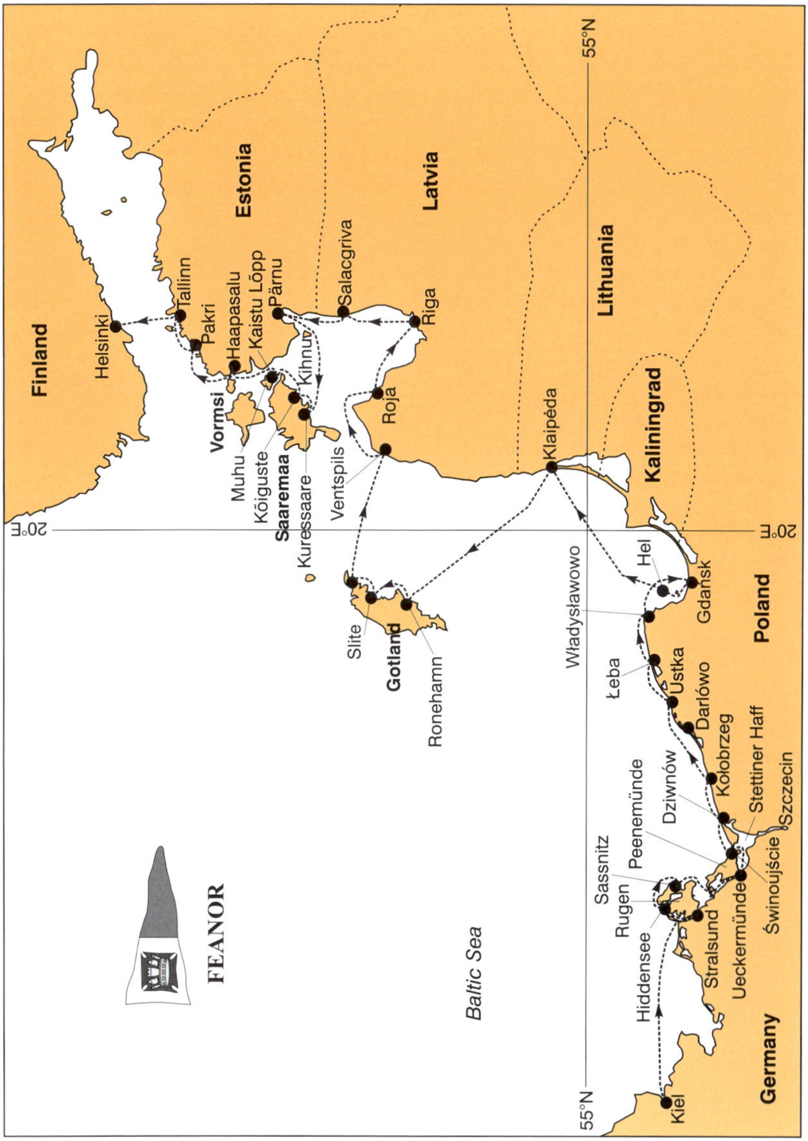
Finland
Helsinki
Estonia
Tallinn
Pakri
Haapasalu
Kaistu Lõpp
Pärnu
Salacgriva
Latvia
Riga
Kihnu
Vormsi
Muhu
Kõiguste
Saaremaa
Kuressaare
Ventspils
Roja
Lithuania
Klaipėda
Kaliningrad
55°N
20°E
Gotland
Slite
Ronehamn
Władysławowo
Hel
Gdansk
Poland
Łeba
Ustka
Darłówo
Kołobrzeg
Stettiner Haff
Szczecin
Dziwnów
Peenemünde
Sassnitz
Rugen
Hiddensee
Stralsund
Ueckermünde
Świnoujście
Germany
Kiel
Baltic Sea
FEANOR

The border guards had told us that we must report to the custom office in Świnoujście. The custom post is at the root of the east pier at the northern entrance and was exposed to a nasty swell from seaward. The berth is well fendered but even so it was on the limit of safety and if the swell had been worse I would have requested an alternative berth. Ten minutes later we were motoring south to the municipal marina at the southern end of Basin Polnocny. We walked two kilometres to the town centre but were unable to find a restaurant still serving so we ended up back at the marina café, which served us a rather strange local dish. We gathered that we would have been more successful had we walked another couple of kilometres to the esplanade.

Next morning we needed diesel but failed to find the fuel berth and moored alongside a quayside garage where we filled up by can. We left Świnoujście at 1220, requesting permission to leave. At all Polish harbours you have to ask port control for permission to enter or leave. The border guards and customs monitor the working channel and are waiting at the entrance to every harbour. There seems to be good communication between harbours and once cleared in, you are not bothered apart from shouting the name of the yacht and last or next port as you pass.

The F3 westerly wind was on the quarter and the motion was uncomfortable as we steered for Dziwnów. Setting the spinnaker made all the difference and our speed increased to six knots. At 1700 we berthed alongside in the pretty harbour between fishing boats. Later we walked to the village and ate a good meal for £5 each including beer. Harbour dues were also cheap at £4 per night.

Next morning the weather forecast from Radio Gdynia gave southwesterly F6 but moderating. We had F4 and an excellent sail to Kołobrzeg. We approached on 148°T as marked on the chart, contacted port control and were asked to call again when half a mile off the entrance, which was difficult to make out because of construction works. At the second call we were told to wait for a 'catcher' to leave but it was still confusing until we saw the fishing boat emerge from behind one of the caissons. Inside there was a pleasant little yacht harbour. Here we met the only other British yacht we saw in Poland. Her owner was preparing to sail home single-handed after his yacht had been laid up on the quay for eighteen months. After supper we walked to the esplanade where they were getting ready for the first of Poland's holiday fortnights. A three-man band was playing and people were ballroom dancing on the pavement – quite delightful.

We departed Kołobrzeg at 0815 ahead of three Polish MTBs that were taking part in a big naval exercise. This was constantly being announced on the VHF along with a string of co-ordinates for the area involved. We made good progress towards Darlówo on a close reach in a F5 southeasterly with two reefs in the main and six furls in the genoa. Between Darlówo and Ustka firing ranges are a problem. Firing times are announced on VHF with the navigational warnings after the weather forecasts.

At 1545 the wind veered to the south and increased to F6 and we noticed some nasty looking weather astern. At 1610 the genoa was completely furled and a third reef being taken in the main when the squall hit us. The mainsail tore about two feet along the leech. It was hastily lowered and we continued under bare poles in a west-southwest F8 and pouring rain. Twenty minutes later we were only five miles from Ustka and I was beginning to worry about entering in a gale as all these north-facing harbours have shallow approaches and you are warned not to enter in strong onshore winds. But by 1700 the wind had reduced and the visibility improved so that we could identify the entrance. The young woman in port control seemed surprised that a British yacht should want to 'come to our little harbour'. We berthed alongside at 1745 and later an Oceanis 343 berthed outside us. We were astonished to discover that her brave single-handed owner was paraplegic and dragged himself round the deck on his bottom. He told us that he had had a very difficult time in the squall. Later still a young German couple arrived in a Folkboat with a torn genoa.

The next day was spent stitching a patch on to the mainsail. Terry did most of the work with Mike and me pulling the needle through with pliers. It was such a good job that the repair lasted for the rest of the cruise and the skipper was so delighted that he took the crew out to

A fishing boat converted for pleasure cruises

supper that evening! During an interval in the mending process I visited Radio Slupsk which is housed in the harbourmaster's office building and broadcasts the firing times on the various ranges. They kindly gave me a printout for the week.

On the Wednesday we left Ustka at 0815 to find little wind so the engine was kept running until 1230 when the wind increased and we were able to tack up the coast to Łeba. Here was a magnificent new marina with pontoon berths, fuel berth, water and electricity on the pontoons and all facilities and it was only a quarter full. It was certainly the best marina we found in Poland. Later we tried to see the spectacular sand dunes in the nearby national park but only got as far the lake. We should have hired bicycles!

We departed Łeba at 1015 next day. We hugged the coast to avoid another naval exercise area. There was only sufficient wind to sail for an hour and a half in the middle of the afternoon. At 1630 Rozewie (Poland's most northerly point) was abeam. At 1815 we berthed bows to at a small yacht pontoon at Władysławowo, a major fishing port. At a café that evening we were served enormous portions of fish.

We left at 0900 and with the spinnaker up sailed gently along the 17-mile length of the Hel peninsula. We then joined the inbound shipping lane in the Gulf of Gdańsk. The wind dropped away so it was down with the spinnaker and on with the engine to make sure Terry had a little time to explore Gdańsk before she flew off in the morning to visit relatives in Warsaw. We followed the deep and well-marked channel into Gdańsk Nowy Port and arrived at 1610. At Westerplatte just inside the entrance is the memorial to the men who died when the first shots of the Second World War were fired by a German battleship. It is the custom to keep the ensign dipped while passing it. We then proceeded southwards for four miles through busy waterways lined with docks and shipyards until we reached the Gdańsk Marina in the centre of the city just opposite the refurbished mediaeval crane, which looks like a tall wooden warehouse. Gdańsk Marina has all facilities and is run by an attentive English-speaking staff. It would be a good place to leave a yacht for a few weeks if necessary. In the evening we had time to explore the city. It is being beautifully restored according to the old plans that were saved when most of the city was destroyed in the war. Later we had an excellent dinner at the Pod Lososiem restaurant, reputed to be the best in Gdańsk.

On Saturday Terry and Mike departed and Joan Whyte and Adam Bird arrived. Joan usually brings her boyfriend but he had opted out this year, thinking that Lithuania and Latvia would be uninteresting. Joan was hoping to prove him wrong and I think she succeeded. Adam is one of my younger and lighter crewmembers and there is usually a job for him up the mast! After they had had a brief look round Gdańsk on the Sunday morning we left the marina at 1345 and motored out through the docks. The wind outside was northeasterly F5 so we put in two reefs and tacked northwards towards Hel. We joked that we were 'going to hell' but it was a beautiful afternoon and was one of the nicest sails of the cruise so far. Berthed next to us was a Polish yacht whose skipper warned us to keep 20 miles off the Russian enclave of Kaliningrad. A few years ago he had been arrested for going too close and had spent a week in a Russian gaol.

We departed Hel at 1630 next day but one mile out we ran into thick fog so we returned. This put the border guards into something of a spin because they had cleared us out and now they had to clear us in again. We left again at 0430 in a flat calm and steered for my carefully plotted waypoint exactly 20 miles off the most westerly point of the Kaliningrad coast. At 1400 we were there and altered course towards Klaipéda. We arrived at the fairway buoy at 0200 still motoring in very little wind. The harbour is formed by the mouth of the Curonian Lagoon, a shallow inland sea extending 50 miles south. Eventually we found the customs post at Pier 41 where two young female immigration officers were waiting for us. They were very efficient and directed us to the Old Castle Marina close by. When we arrived there it appeared very crowded and rather run down so that we reversed out and made for the Smiltyne Yacht Club harbour on the opposite side of the waterway. With hindsight we should have persevered, as the yacht club was adequate but not very convenient. You have to take the ferry to reach the city and the ferry terminal is 15 minutes walk from the marina.

Adam left us to spend a few days visiting Lithuanian friends with his girlfriend. Camping Gas was getting low and as I had two empty Swedish propane cylinders on board it seemed a good idea to pop across to Gotland to exchange them. It is 130 miles but Joan was keen to make longish sea passages and I was getting desperate for gas so off we went. Sadly we didn't have time to visit Nida further down the lagoon. Several people told us how lovely it is in contrast to Klaipéda, which is Lithuania's only seaport and very industrial.

Feanor completed the gas mission successfully. The highlight of the passage was a spectacularly delicious two-pound salmon caught and cooked by Joan. We rejoin them after they cleared into Ventspils, Latvia.

Next morning Adam bade farewell to his girlfriend and we departed under power at 0640 setting a course for the Gulf of Riga. The wind was northerly F3 and as there were 70 miles to go, we motorsailed until we reached the buoy off Oviši Light. The engine was stopped and we bore away into the Irbenskiy Strait. It was busy with shipping and we kept just south of the inbound lane. The wind increased to northwest F6 and we bowled along with two reefs and eight rolls in the genoa. By 1630 Kolka Light at the eastern end of the strait was abeam. We gybed and headed southwards for Roja where we moored alongside the small yacht pontoon at 2015. We were away again at 0750 and set a course for Riga. The wind was northeast F1-3 and we had to use the engine on and off all day in order to let Adam see something of Riga before he had to catch his plane. At 1530 we were at the entrance to the River Dvina and motored against the gentle flow for five miles to the Andrejosta marina on the east side behind the passenger ship terminal. In the evening we caught a tram to the old part of the city, had an excellent meal and saw some of the sights. Children were singing in the cathedral square.

I spent six nights in Riga and enjoyed every minute of it. It is a very vibrant city and part of its charm was the presence of a huge number of schoolchildren from all over Latvia taking part in a festival of song and dance. They were all in national costume and everywhere there seemed to be singing and dancing in the streets until the Sunday when the final parade was held and they all left for home.

Joan left on Saturday and Douglas Meikle and Clem Armstrong, who have both crewed for me for many years, arrived on Monday. They spent Tuesday sightseeing and we left at 0710 on 6 July. We arrived at Salacgriva halfway up the eastern shore of the gulf at 1915, after motoring all day in a flat calm. This was a complete contrast to Riga with one small yacht pontoon almost buried in the reeds at the eastern end of the harbour. There would not have been much shelter in a westerly but in the calm conditions it was fine. A small boy seemed to have been left in charge. He took our fee and gave us the key to the harbourmaster's office where there was a shower. We found a café where we had a cheap but pleasant meal.

Next morning the owner of an Estonian yacht on the pontoon showed me his Estonian charts as I had been unable to purchase any in Latvia. He warned us to beware of the 'stones'. The border guards signed us out of Latvia and we departed Salacgriva at 1210. The wind was only F1 so we motorsailed northwards towards Pärnu. I had thought it would be pleasant to keep to the eastern shore but this was a mistake as we found ourselves in a maze of buoyed fishing nets from which it took a little time to extract ourselves, fortunately without entanglement. We cautiously headed west until we got into the main channel and arrived at Pärnu Yacht Club marina at 2100.

Pärnu is very pleasant with the town only a short walk from the club. In the morning we were able to stock up with stores and I bought two books of Estonian charts from the marina manager who runs a small chandlery. I was very impressed that he allowed me to take away £120 worth of charts on trust. We departed at 1545 and motored down the leading line in a F2 southwesterly. At 1720 the wind veered into the west and suddenly gusted up to F6 only to drop again 20 minutes later. At 1745 we were at the buoy at the mouth of Pärnu Bay and we could alter course towards the small island of Kihnu where we arrived at 2030. We berthed alongside a Swan 37 whose Swedish owner told us he had

Sail repairs at Ustka

arrived just as the F6 gust had blown up and had had a tricky time berthing in the shallow harbour. At least we knew that where a Swan with her 7-foot draft could go, *Feanor* could go too. Ashore the buildings round the harbour had all been washed away during a severe storm last winter.

We departed at 0530 with a certain amount of grumbling from the crew but the wind had veered to the east-northeast and the harbour was exposed to that quarter. We navigated round to the south of the island and headed for Kuressaare. We had the spinnaker up for an hour but by 0900 the wind had dropped and we were under power for the rest of the day. An hour later it was so hot we had to put up the cockpit awning. At 1415 the Allirahu Islands were three miles on the starboard bow and we picked our way from buoy to buoy through the shallow approaches first to Roomassaare and then took a dogleg to the fairway buoy for Kuressaare. The two mile-long final approach to the latter is between banks of mud dredged from the channel. We moored up in the excellent marina at 1815. The very attentive harbourmaster greeted us on the pontoon and immediately gave me a conducted tour of the marina. A German yachtsman had written in the visitors' book that he was 'the best harbourmaster in the Baltic'. In the evening we walked into the very pleasant town and had a traditional meal in a restored windmill.

In the morning I cleaned out the fresh water tank while Doug and Clem went looking for stores. We left at 1415 and motored through 'the ditch', setting the sails briefly before the wind dropped away to nothing and we were motoring again on a northeasterly course along the south coast of Saaremaa towards Kõiguste. We reached the five-mile long entry line at 1930 and steered for the front leading mark. The rear one was hidden in trees and could not be identified against the sun. The Estonian chart showed soundings of only 0.5 metres at the harbour entrance but we found five. We anchored in three metres just north of the buoys marking the approach to a solitary pontoon where two other yachts were moored. The enclosed bay is surrounded by reeds and quite pretty. Ashore there was a small marina building with an office, shower and café but there was no one about in the morning. Later we were told that the harbour is privately owned by a Finnish lawyer.

I took my first swim of the summer before we departed at 1200. With the sun in the south the rear leading mark could now be identified. At 1800 we tacked round the eastern end of Saaremaa and headed up under engine for the south side of Muhu (Moon) Island where we found a sheltered anchorage at Kaistu Lõpp, two cables south of a new breakwater that was not marked on the chart. But there were plenty of 'stones' marked and we crept in very carefully. The anchor was up at 0600 and we motored slowly out of the bay. The wind was northwest F3, on the nose for the passage up Muhu Sound, so we kept the engine on until we reached the northern end when the wind backed and we were able to sail north along the buoyed channel. At 1420 we were back under power. At 1610 I emerged from my bunk to find that the waypoint had been passed and course was altered towards the southern end of Hobulaid Island. We were just looking at the chart and deciding that it would be safer to return to the dredged and buoyed approach channel when we grounded hard on a shallow patch. This was unmarked on my Estonian chart, which had been corrected up-to-date, but was shown as 0.4 metres on a rather dog-eared 20-year-old Russian chart which I hadn't even looked at. We got off without assistance but in the process realized the significance of the term 'stones' when we saw the dense clouds of clay rising from the bottom when the engine was at full power. Much of the bottom in Estonian waters is hard clay on which rocks and boulders are liberally distributed. A significant amount of damage was caused to the bottom of the encapsulated keel but this was not discovered until the boat was lifted out in Finland three weeks later.

We returned to the buoyed channel to Rohuküla and suitably chastened carefully picked our way along the approach channels to Haapsalu where we arrived at 1830. The marina in an old fish dock has recently been taken over by a private company and is in the process of renovation but it has an excellent restaurant. In the morning we took a bus into town for stores before departing for the Gulf of Finland at 1245. We stuck rigidly to the leading lines as we sailed towards the narrow channel between Vormsi and the mainland. A Finnish 40-footer was catching us up and we hoisted the spinnaker to keep ahead of her but as soon as we were in the narrowest part of the channel the wind went ahead and the spinnaker had to come down in a hurry and my hat was lost overboard in the panic. The Finns were laughing as they sailed serenely past! In Arthur Ransome's log of *Racundra's First Cruise* he tacked through this passage swinging the lead and sighting the bottom. Quite a feat even though *Racundra* was shallow-draft with a drop keel. In those days (1922) it was customary to wait for a fair wind if you didn't have an engine. He had one but it didn't work!

Once out into the Gulf of Finland and clear of the shallows we were able to head eastwards towards Tallinn. At 1630 we were at the fairway buoy for Dhirami but we needed to get closer to Tallinn. The wind had now dropped completely and we continued under power. At 2015 we anchored on the west side of the north-facing bay of Pakri. It was a deserted and somewhat forbidding anchorage with rusty wrecks on each side of the entrance and some very large boulders along the eastern shore. However it was a lovely evening and we spent a peaceful night until we were woken at 0630 by a northerly F3 blowing into the bay.

We sailed then motored towards Tallinn, passing south of the island of Naissar, and made our way to the eastern side of Tallinn Bay where the Kalev Yacht Club has a marina at Pirita on the site of the 1980 Moscow sailing Olympics. The wooden visitors' pontoon was full but we managed to find a berth elsewhere which was lucky as there were many visiting Estonian yachts preparing for a major race round the Estonian islands starting that weekend. They seemed to be holding all-night parties every night but by Sunday evening all was quiet and the marina half-empty. Kalev Yacht Club is very friendly but next time I might choose the Olympic marina as the facilities appeared to be better.

Friday was spent sight-seeing in Tallinn and on Saturday morning Douglas and Clem left and my new crew arrived in the evening. They did their sightseeing on Sunday and we started for Finland the next day. They remained with me for the very pleasant fortnight we spent cruising the waters round Helsinki until *Feanor* was laid up for the winter at Emsalö Yachtyard 30 kilometres east of Helsinki.

Feanor is a standard Contessa 28, designed by Doug Peterson and built by Jeremy Rogers in 1981.

SLOWLY SOUTH FOR TRAFALGAR

by Roddy Innes

In July and August 2005 after the Fleet Review, *Jessamy* sailed south for Trafalgar. On 7 July, as we were at the fuelling pontoon in Gosport, they said the harbour was being closed because of the London bombings. We didn't wait to find out, legged it and had a brisk sail over to Alderney. The crew were old hands, David Adams and Julian Livingstone who had been with me to the Azores and further and Jerry Cobban, a sometime naval engineer. After a picnic on the cliffs and supper at the 'First and Last' we sailed on the tide shortly after midnight and reached to Ushant. Then as the wind veered to northeast F3-5 we had a lovely run across the Bay of Biscay with spinnaker and boomed-out headsails, taking just over three and a half days to La Coruña, with our faithful Windpilot, Georgina, steering most of the way.

Although I had stopped at Bayona on the way to Madeira and the Canaries in 1998, the Atlantic coast of Spain and Portugal was a totally new cruising area. It also seems to be ignored by the Brit holidaymaker – well, virtually no one speaks any English!

Just before I left home I heard that Anne Hammick, who is in the process of up-dating the Pilot for the area, was unable to do northwest Spain, so I offered to do what I could to help, visiting in the end over 40 harbours and anchorages. Little did I know…! An early discovery was that practically every harbour in northwest Spain has had substantial improvements since 1999, when the 2000 edition was researched – new breakwaters, new marinas, new pontoons and new *clubs nauticos* with facilities and often a good restaurant. A whole new world! So that is where all the EU money goes. In fact as the marinas are full of motorboats, not much is for the benefit of the visiting yachtsman but there are spin-offs.

Commercial fishing in Spain and Portugal is a very serious business, however much one may resent their fishing fleets, and small boat fishing is also a passionate pastime. That sets the scene for the cruising

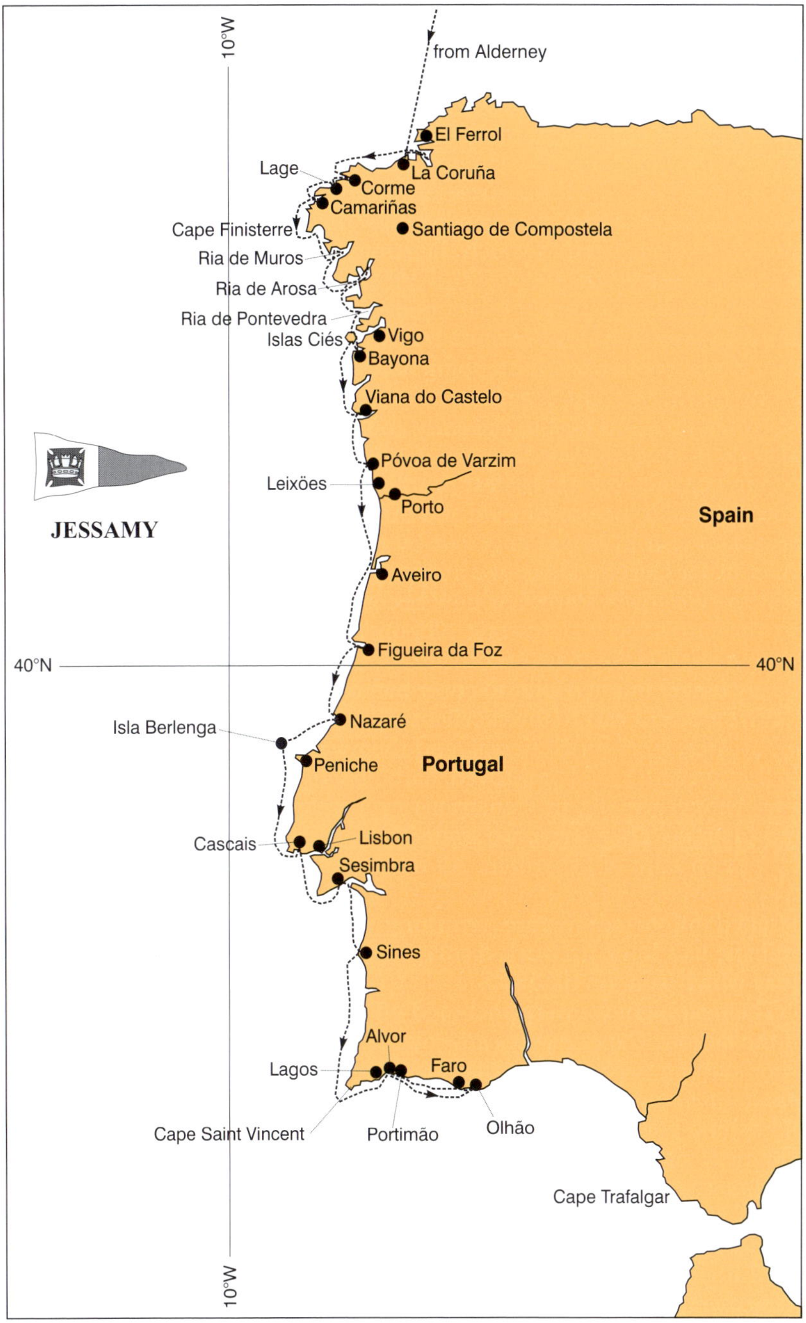
10°W
from Alderney
El Ferrol
La Coruña
Lage
Corme
Camariñas
Cape Finisterre
Santiago de Compostela
Ria de Muros
Ria de Arosa
Ria de Pontevedra
Islas Ciés
Vigo
Bayona
Viana do Castelo
Póvoa de Varzim
Leixöes
Porto
JESSAMY
Spain
Aveiro
Figueira da Foz
40°N
40°N
Nazaré
Isla Berlenga
Peniche
Portugal
Lisbon
Cascais
Sesimbra
Sines
Alvor
Lagos
Faro
Cape Saint Vincent
Portimão
Olhão
Cape Trafalgar
10°W

yachtsman – fishing vessels give no quarter to yachts and their quays and fuelling facilities are not for us either.

But the locals are very friendly, the seafood is excellent, the wine cheap and drinkable and the scenery, particularly in the Spanish Rias, is often stunning, spoilt only by wind farms. Also all the harbour and marina developments mean that there are now numerous refuges as you cruise slowly south. On the Portuguese Atlantic coast harbours and anchorages are more limited but you can happily day sail from one to another, though you may need to watch the strong tidal streams and rough water in the river estuaries.

There is also the very relevant question of weather. All the way down this coast, mist and fog are quite frequent and so radar is a great comfort even if you are inside the shipping lanes. The other major feature is the strong northerly wind, which tends to get up at lunchtime and is blowing F6 by teatime. It is best to sail early and arrive by early afternoon, especially if you are going north.

Our landfall was the oldest working lighthouse in the world at La Coruña, said to be pre-Roman and built by the Phoenicians. By the time we got to visit it, it was engulfed by fog and we missed the tram stop! Most of La Coruña looks like a concrete jungle but the fishing harbour near the old town centre has now become the new marina. This is ideal for the attractive and historic old town, the excellent ancient history museum at Castilio San Anton and for eating out. We would have liked to stay longer but had a lot to cover before the crew change at Portosin.

First we went east to the excellent new marina and *club nautico* restaurant at Ares, south of El Ferrol, and then west towards Finisterre, taking in the attractive and improved harbours of Corme and Lage on the way, before arriving in Camariñas to a welcome of rockets, fireworks and hooters. They were, we understood, celebrating the saint's day of the patron saint of fisherman. All the fishing boats and their crews were dressed overall, so we did too, Then, after a 'Blessing Ceremony', they paraded off to sea before returning for more festivities including a brilliant half hour firework display at 0100 and a rock concert on the quay which went on till 0500!

The next night we were anchored off the town of Finisterre, just south of the famous Cape. As we came out of the restaurant after supper, they were starting a display of folk dancing, with a story we didn't understand, on a stage on the quay. It was absolutely stunning. Finisterre is an old fishing port and not exactly attractive but it had a nice atmosphere. The next night we retreated round the corner for a quiet anchorage off Sardineiro.

Our next Ria was Muros, with the attractive old town and harbour on the north side. Again there is a proposed marina in the old inner harbour but I hope there won't be as it would probably lose its charm. It is an attractive town. As we arrived there was a coastguard helicopter picking

The outer basin of the new town centre marina at La Coruña

up and dumping water on a nearby forest fire, apparently successfully, though later we were to see weeks of failure.

Our first crew change was at Portosin, an excellent new marina and *club nautico* on the south side of the Ria and fairly close to the airport at Santiago de Compostela. The small town is about a mile from the marina and doesn't live up to its promising name as a run-ashore but the marina staff were excellent and arranged taxis to the airport. They also helped repair our broken rod kicker.

Unfortunately the weather now rather let us down and in the Ria de Arosa it dampened what might have been a memorable visit. As we left it we went in to Porto Pedras Negras, a small marina on the southern tip, where we were stormbound for a couple of nights. As often happens when things go wrong this meant that we explored further than we would otherwise have done. There were boardwalks along two miles of lovely coves and outcrops of rocks and we met some most entertaining company.

This was followed by Ria de Pontevedra and in particular the old fishing village of Combarro at its head. It had been recommended to us by a number of people as an unspoilt gem, though it might better be described as 'the old part being sympathetically restored'. Unfortunately, as we arrived at lunchtime, the heavens opened, the anchor wouldn't hold in the thick weed and we didn't get ashore till the evening, though then it was worth the effort not least for the fresh grilled sardines on the quayside. The next day we inspected the progress of work at the new seriously big marina at Sangenjo and then poked our nose into Porto Novo, to find a whole new marina not even mentioned in Reed's.

We were nearing the end of Spain and that evening secured in Bayona at the *Monte-Real Club de Yates* below the fortress. The brand-new and still being developed marina to the east will try and lead you there (and it does have finger pontoons) but despite the hated 'bows-to and stern line' moorings at MRCY, this is where you should go – a lovely position with good facilities and a good restaurant. That, the fortress and a nice town, is no doubt why Bayona is an old favourite with the Brits.

In Bayona we met *Rapscallion* with John Button on his way quickly south for the Trafalgar meet and Cormack McHenry, Commodore of the ICC, single-handed in *Island Life* sailing slowly south. Along the way we had also met David and Sarah Price on a mid-life gap year or two, on their way to Croatia in their smart Nicholson 35 *Natian*. They had no idea where the name came from but Cormack was sure she had been an ICC boat! Our paths crossed many times, though they almost invariably anchored off while we often 'researched' the marina facilities, partly genuinely and partly because the rolling crew wanted an easy run-ashore! We later had a farewell cockpit dinner with them off Olhão before they went east and we went west to Lagos.

From Bayona we went back to Islas Ciés, off Ria de Vigo, for a day and a night anchored off these attractive islands before running south with a fresh northerly, to Viana do Castelo, our first stop in Portugal. Up the estuary we secured in the very full marina just below the Ponte Eiffel (of the Tower). That evening we enjoyed more folk dancing, this time Portuguese, in the nearby park.

The next crew change was planned for Leixöes, just north of Porto airport, but after a serious industrial accident there last year the marina was closed while a thorough clean up and restoration was carried out. So we changed at Póvoa de Varzim, a few miles north, though with very cheap buses and trains the leaving crew were still able to enjoy a good day in Porto. After here the wind ran out, even in the afternoon, and it was nearly all motoring.

We arrived at Aveiro in two minds as whether to go the six miles up the river to the town or to anchor in the harbour a mile or so up the estuary, off San Jacinto. In the event, we were hastily ushered by the Marine Police into the San Jacinto anchorage, because seaplanes were about to 'land' to scoop up water for fighting forest fires to the south. All afternoon two seaplanes came in every fifteen minutes or so, just yards away on the other side of the low breakwater – quite exciting as they lumbered off fully laden, barely getting airborne! For the next couple of days we could see the smoke from the fires away to the east, and smell them, but fortunately the wind remained in the northwest blowing it away. The smoke and haze meant that the sun didn't rise until it was about ten degrees above the horizon.

After a night in the unexciting marina at Figueira da Foz, which we left in very dense fog, Nazaré was the next friendly small marina and from there we went on to anchor for the night off Isla Berlenga, an attractive high rocky island northwest of Peniche (which we were advised against visiting because of apparently unfriendly fishermen and berthing difficulties).

At this point I should say that we *never* encountered unfriendly Spanish or Portuguese fishermen but they have a serious job to do and it is understandable that they don't want to be messed about by yachties obstructing them on their quays or picking up their moorings, which are in regular use. At Muros we saw a fishing raft *(viveros)* towed by two tugs secure to a buoy with a visiting yacht, whose crew had gone ashore, still on it.

The delightful town of Cascais, near Lisbon, was a return to the big time, with a large new marina and hypermarket. We made a crew change before the last leg to the Algarve. But we weren't there yet! Sailing on south, we spent a very hot lunchtime anchored below the cliffs some four miles east of Sesimbra and a lovely evening and night five miles further on off Arrábida, before stopping at Sines, birthplace of Vasco da Gama.

As we left early the next morning our feathering propeller broke. It had stripped its teeth internally, if that is the right description! It was early Sunday morning and when I went up to the marina office I was told that Monday was a saint's day and a holiday. The marina manager tried to get someone to help, but without success. He suggested we move to the slip at high water to dry out, which we just managed to do. We eventually found one of the propeller blades 'disengaged'.

Unbeknown to anyone else, for seven years I had carried the original fixed prop under my bunk. Furthermore, I had an Engineer Rear Admiral (always carry one, though God knows what for) in the crew! Waiting for the tide to go down was like watching paint dry, but eventually we started to get the damaged prop off. In spite of undoing everything it wouldn't come. At low water, with the shaft just six inches above the water, help arrived. We needed heat and the chap went off to get a blowlamp. When he returned, the shaft was still just above the water and shortly after we had lift-off! In no time the fixed prop was fitted. Well, our largest spanner wasn't large enough but a friendly Oyster, *Shakura,* obliged.

That night we floated off and sailed for Cape St Vincent and the Algarve. Unfortunately our lost day meant that we missed spending the night at an apparently stunning anchorage below the cliffs at Arrifana, some twenty odd miles north of the Cape, which we finally rounded in a flat calm the next morning at 0800, anchoring round the corner for breakfast.

Suddenly it was hot and not only did the locals speak English, it seemed that half of them *were* English. For the next ten days we cruised back and forth along the Algarve coast as far as Faro and Olhão. Three times we went up through the shifting sands to Alvor, eyeballing it with no problem on the top half of the tide, and I had even written up my notes saying as much, when on the way out at low water springs, having navigated the channel with no problem and reached the 'no worries' zone between the harbour entrance and the first channel buoy, we grounded! 'Won't be long', I said. Half an hour later a Sadler 34 came out. They tried to feel their way past us, gave up and anchored. There we stayed for two hours on what is clearly a bar of the wrong sort.

We also investigated the new Marina at Olhão, but concluded that it was 'not for visitors' – well, 'no office, no staff, no keys for pontoons, no facilities, no anything'. It wasn't promising. On the way back to Lagos we stopped off at Albafueira, where a new marina has been dug out behind the hills to the west of the sea front and a way in cut through the hillside. The scale of this project was amazing.

Portimão had been our original destination for before and after Trafalgar but although it was more expensive we preferred the atmosphere and more central position of the marina at Lagos, so we decided to leave *Jessamy* there for the winter. The railway station is right next to the marina and the Faro Flyer runs every couple of hours to the airport!

As to Trafalgar, we shall have to wait and see. The night after the battle there was a hurricane that blew for four days, resulting in 16 of the 20 French and Spanish ships captured either sinking or being wrecked on the coast. At the time of writing, in the last month the Gulf of Mexico has already had the two worst hurricanes ever recorded!

Jessamy is a Rustler 36 built for me in 1990. She did the Atlantic circuit in 1998-99.

THE NORTH ATLANTIC IN BLONDIE'S WAKE

by Paul Heiney

Crossing the north Atlantic under sail from east to west is, arguably, a mug's game. It is certainly not a cruising man's preferred option. If you track too far north you face certain headwinds from bad-tempered depressions, even in summer. Head too far south and you may be entrapped in the balmy but lifeless Azores high-pressure area. Either way, you have to confront the Gulf Stream and its offspring the North Atlantic Drift. And if you attempt to wriggle free by hitching a ride on the southwest flowing Labrador current – assuming you have achieved 2000 miles of beating to get within its grasp – then you enjoy fog so thick you could stab it with a marlinspike and the possibility that an iceberg or two will drift by in the night to allow you no rest. If this is not sufficiently taxing, you then choose to make the passage single-handed and, for ultimate wear and tear on both skipper and boat, make it a race as well. Welcome to the 2005 OSTAR in which two burgees crossed the starting line in Plymouth this year, one flown by me from *Ayesha*, the other by Mervyn Wheatley at the helm of *Tamarind.*

In 1960, when the first race was held, it was considered a lunatic adventure. Many would agree that it still is. Strangely for a sailing event that defies all the logic of good cruising practice, its founder Blondie Hasler was a member of this Club. From speaking to those who knew him, it becomes clear that he was never a man to assume a conventional way of thinking, hence his building of the junk-rigged *Jester*, so named because 'everyone thought she was such a bloody joke'. It was also his inspired idea, in the late 1950s, to pin a note to the board at the RORC inviting those who were interested to join him in a race from Plymouth to New York. Famously, Francis Chichester was eventually to take up the challenge but not until after David Lewis and Val Howells had expressed interest. This is no place for a portrait of Blondie and anyway Ewen Southby-Tailyour's biography cannot be bettered. Suffice it to say that he shunned the idea of radio communications, believing that all those who went to sea should be presumed lost until they arrived and threw his barometer overboard because it only ever presented him with depressing news. He also loathed spinnakers and enjoyed baking bread. I find it difficult to disagree with any of those sentiments.

So if we assume that this perverse way of crossing the Atlantic is some kind of illness, first brought into the Club by Hasler, then it is an infection that has spread widely. Lewis and Hasler were pioneers, joined in subsequent years by such names as Jock McLeod, Mike McMullen, Richard Clifford, David Scott-Cowper, Desmond Hampton and Clare Francis. And here I hesitate because there will be some names I have overlooked and I apologize but to this list must be added Jonathan Virden who claims the Club's longest crossing at 56 days to Bermuda and seven more to Newport, while Mary Falk has won the under 35-foot class and set a new record of around 21 days. And last (literally in the case of OSTAR) but certainly not least, must come Mike Richey, who admits to 13 single-handed crossings of this ocean. We are indeed a broad church of sailors.

Since there was not the slightest possibility of my winning this race, it is worth asking why I ever wanted to enter. Some who take part are clearly set on line honours but a glance at the entries over many years shows that they are far outweighed by those who might as well be riding donkeys in the Gold Cup. The answer to this conundrum comes from Blondie himself who wrote of no desire to be faster than any other individual but rather of sailing against himself, knowing how well he and his boat should be performing and trying at all times to achieve that standard. Mike Richey also speaks of the satisfaction of the voyage well made. It was with this last intention that *Ayesha* and I turned up in Plymouth in May this year. Richey came to wish us well, and remarked, 'Whatever the outcome, you will never forget your first voyage'.

I had what might be grandly called a two-pronged strategy. I hoped to stay out of trouble and if possible I wanted to get there within the official finishing time of 40 days. *Ayesha* is a well-found, heavy old ketch who under Miles Quitmann's previous ownership faced many an ocean storm with equanimity. His father described her to me as having great vigour – this is not quite the same as speed. Much to my relief the start took place in light, westerly airs, which faded to calm over the first 24 hours. Wheatley, on the other hand, said he wanted a 'good old force seven, bang on the nose, to sort things out', but he is a Royal Marine and must be excused such desires.

It was not long before the southwesterly wind filled in, strengthening by the hour to give me three days of heavy windward work, still not fully accustomed to the motion of the boat, uncertain where to grab and leap. It was during this prolonged rough spell that the full enormity of the job ahead became apparent. The course is 2,800 miles and undoubtedly to windward. I was aiming for a position 45°N, 35°W known as Waypoint Weld after the 1980 winner, Phil Weld, who was given the strong meteorological advice that by passing through that point the worst of the storms would be avoided. I liked that idea. From there I planned to make west to the tail of the Grand Banks and then to the finish off Newport spending as much time as I could in the favourable Labrador Current. It

Trouble ahead

is hard to be the only boat plodding relentlessly south while all the others are on a Greenland tack, cheeringly coming on the radio to tell you they are hoping for another gale, stronger than the last. However within the first week some of those twangy, tuned-up individuals who had chosen the head-banging northern strategy were regretting it, as news came through of retirement after retirement. In the end only half the fleet was to make it across the Atlantic. Amazingly after seven days at sea, an easterly wind took hold of us and blew fair for three days. 'This is *not* OSTAR' boomed Wheatley on the SSB. 'This is *not* what we signed up for.' It suited me fine.

There is no event quite like this race for revealing every weakness in both skipper and boat. Boat first. After two weeks of pounding to windward the plastic fitting that held the log impeller came loose, causing first a dribble and then a torrent of water. This was discovered at 0300 on a rough night when I swung my leg out of the bunk to find my feet stepping into bilge water. Oily scum was slopping in and out of the food lockers. The engine-driven bilge pump did not work. I can confirm that the proverbial frightened man with a bucket is the best pump ever invented. Later, south of Halifax, I discovered that a U-bolt through the deck that held the starboard lower after shroud, had snapped – classic metal fatigue. By chance, I noticed this on a calm night; in stronger weather the mast would probably have been lost. In a frenzy of DIY I unbolted the broken through-deck fitting, removed from the cockpit a U-bolt we use for harness attachment, drilled the deck, made a backing plate and had the entire rig re-tensioned within an hour and a half. All this with a torch held between my teeth as the boat slopped along in a foggy calm. You could have mopped up the spare adrenalin with a rag.

The skipper, if I am honest, fared less well than the boat. I spent far too long wishing to get there instead of enjoying the passage and extracting from it everything that it had to offer. How I now regret never getting the sextant out of its box, learning the ways of the stars in the sky or relaxing into the contemplative, almost transcendental, frame of mind that some ocean voyagers seem to achieve. I poured over too many weather faxes, which unnerved me – I really don't like deep depressions spinning in my direction. Then one night, a fortnight out of Plymouth, I suffered both a bad weather forecast (Blondie was right to throw his barometer overboard and I should have done the same with the fax receiver) and a lousy supper of reconstituted dried food bought from Poland on the internet. Depression coupled with poor digestion overtook me and I decided to retire. The rules of the race required us to carry satellite phones through which I could send emails. My first was to the race office, the second to Libby. The warm embrace of the Azores was only 250 miles to the south and a drink in the Café Sport seemed the best invitation on earth. I wouldn't even have to alter course; I was aiming right for it. I'd had enough. The Atlantic had beaten me.

I got no response from the Royal Western (it was the middle of the night) but Libby, who had been keeping an internet vigil, immediately reminded me that it was as far to sail home as it was to go on, along with other well-tempered words of encouragement. I slept on it and woke certain that I wouldn't be able to live with myself if I turned back. I thought of the effort of preparation, and the cost, and the dream of this race that I had carried with me for nearly 30 years. And anyway once that Polish slop had worked its way through my system life might feel better. I sent another message to the race office withdrawing my retirement. This confused them as they'd never received the first.

It took two whole weeks to Waypoint Weld and a further week to the Grand Banks. By now, winners were already across the line. It was only as the Nova Scotia coast grew nearer that the old cruising instincts started to surface. I became curious about the harbours and read Pam Kellett's FPI as keenly as if it were a page-turner of a novel. How frustrating to have to sail on.

In the last fortnight, I suffered days of fog so thick that it swirled in the cabin yet found great pleasure in the changes in the weather as we sailed in and out of the tepid Gulf Stream and the icy Labrador Current; T-shirt to thermals in a couple of hours. I might wake one morning to find the sea temperature a balmy 18°C; by teatime it might have dropped to a chilly 10°C, the fog would be gathering and I would be reaching for sweaters. For the last five days, the incessant fog became unbearable. In this damp, grey world there was no demarcation between sea and sky, except at night when stars directly overhead would pierce the shallow but dense layer of fog. On the very last night at sea, with less than 100 miles to go and wracked with frustration at the lack of wind and the dampening fog, the temptation to fire up the engine was almost overwhelming. But I took an hour's sleep and woke to a new world. Like a silver dome lifted from a serving dish, the fog and cloud rolled back, the air became crystal clear, the lights of Nantucket beamed out and I had my first glimpse of America. Even better a breeze filled in from the northeast and blew me home.

I arrived at eight that evening, crossing the finishing line 3,787 miles and 35 days after leaving Plymouth. I was met by Robin Wallace, former Commodore of the Ida Lewis Yacht Club, and as his launch pulled alongside to lead me to the Newport Yacht Club's dock, he dropped into my fist a hot, roast beef sandwich. Fresh food never tasted so good. Then the sky lit with dazzling fireworks, a stunning display which filled the horizon for what seemed like an hour. 'For me?' 'No,' said Robin. 'In case you hadn't realised, it's the Fourth of July'.

I had always expected to be last – in the '*Jester* position', as Mike Richey called it – but a Dutchman beat me to it, arriving five days after me. Mervyn Wheatley sailed a remarkable race and *Tamarind* was not only class winner but also the first monohull on handicap. There were

Jester at the start of the 1968 OSTAR with Mike Richey at the helm

several boats in our class that would never be thought of as racing boats; indeed they would look more at home at the Beaulieu Meet than on the starting line of an ocean race. But in the event all of them made it across the Atlantic while many of the racier designs limped home broken. I suspect Blondie would have been amused.

Ayesha of St Mawes is a Biscay 36 ketch designed by Alan Hill and built by Falmouth Boat Construction Company in 1982.

SECRET MAINE

by Roland Lennox-King

Maine is America's secret cruising ground. It is arguably one of the most beautiful cruising areas in the world and it is easy to see why it has its share of artists and galleries. With 5,500 miles of scribbling coastline doodling across northern America towards Nova Scotia, dotted with 68 lighthouses and thousands of islands and tiny bays we saw less than a dozen foreign yachts in three months of cruising.

American artists know Maine; in many villages half of the buildings are galleries, while the other half house a post office, library, and maybe a general store. In this part of the world art seems to be more important than food and when you are here you want to paint, photograph or write about it.

Think of Maine and you think of lobsters. We saw photographs of a 25lb lobster but there are restrictions on size and you can only catch lobsters with a permit. A lobsterman told us they are limited to 800 pots, which explains why the channels are crowded with the brightly coloured buoys; each lobsterman has a different colour-combination.

Some villages have been settled since the 1600s. There are impressive beach-houses with turrets, lighthouses, sweeping lawns, guest cottages and private docks with beautiful wooden boats, most of which have been in the same families for generations.

We sailed up the eastern seaboard and arrived in Boston mid-June in time to meet our daughter Olivia and Tim and Ginny Le Couteur from New Zealand, with their list of 5-star must-see Maine beauty spots. We sailed to Manchester on 23 June, where we looked up Anne and Tom Walker, who hosted us to our first lobster dinner. The Cruising Club of America welcomes RCC members to share many of their members' guest moorings and the Walkers were very helpful in their advice of how to get the best out of cruising in Maine.

At 0530 next morning we set off for Maine and arrived in touristy Booth Bay Harbor, Muscongus Bay, at 2000, assisted by the prevailing southwest wind and Mr Perkins. The next morning after a quick trip ashore we sought the quiet of Seal Cove, a delightful 'hurricane hole' on the Damariscotta River. That night the tranquillity was broken only by noisy seals! Lack of wind and a favourable tide took us next day to Round Pond, which *Taft's Cruising Guide* noted had been visited by Joshua Slocum in 1895. We stopped for another night between Harbor Island and Hall Island and saw Outward Bound teenagers preparing for a damp, cold night ashore. We walked around the tiny unoccupied cabins left completely open; something we were to learn was normal in Maine, where houses, boats, and even cars are left unlocked.

A pleasant sail next day was interrupted by one of many fog banks we were to meet and we retreated into Port Clyde where we took a rest from the fog and stayed the night, going ashore to eat lobsters at a cosy dockside restaurant, the Dip Net. We met lobstermen who had seen puffins on nearby Eastern Egg Rock but we were not lucky enough to see any.

The next day we felt our way through persistent fog, past pot-buoys, rocky ledges, islands and boats. It was a relief to arrive safely at Tenants Harbor, in Penobscot Bay, where the Cod End fish shop will sell you cooked or live lobster. We bought a live one to cook aboard with Ginny's delicious paella. The next day we motored and sailed through still more fog to Cabot Cove, in Pulpit Harbor on Northhaven, and on 30 June sailed to Buck's Harbor. This stop had been a much-cherished dream of Ginny's who had read Robert McCloskey's books to their children.

Tim ironed out our C-Map problems as we motored through pea-soup fog to Sylvester Cove, where we knew Ed Kendrick has a home but we could not make contact. It was quite spooky to hear waves breaking and then see a line of pine trees above yet not to be able to see more than 20 yards at sea level. Next day we seldom saw the shore 100 yards away and our planned trip to Rockland was postponed. Olivia sat on the stern while two baby porpoises tickled her hands and feet in the icy cold water. Roland had an icy swim each morning, to prove that some can do it.

Luckily the next day was clear and we had a pleasant passage to Rockland. For many years this has been a fairly tough out-of-the-way fishing town but now with an up-graded airport and tourist facilities it is a good alternative to the overcrowded port of nearby Camden. After a last dinner at Contes restaurant on Rockland town dock with several schooners tied up alongside, readying for the Fourth of July schooner race, the Le Couteurs flew out the next day.

We then prepared for the arrival of Rory from New Zealand and his son Rob from Canada. It was the Fourth of July and we sailed along with many schooners racing past Rockland lighthouse to Castine for the fireworks. However our excitement was short-lived. The fireworks were cancelled because of a pyrotechnical injury the previous evening. We had

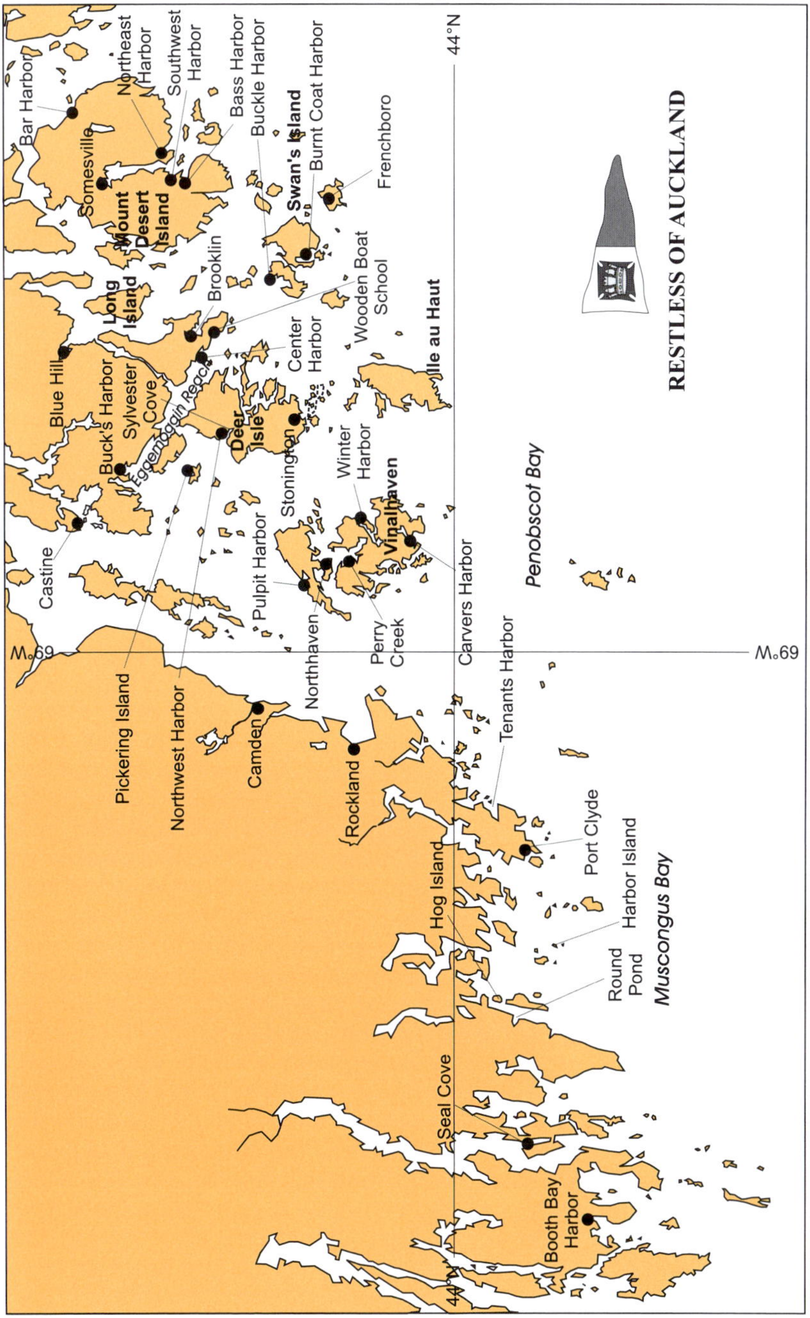
RESTLESS OF AUCKLAND
Bar Harbor
Northeast Harbor
Southwest Harbor
Bass Harbor
Buckle Harbor
Swan's Island
Burnt Coat Harbor
Frenchboro
Somesville
Mount Desert Island
Brooklin
Long Island
Wooden Boat School
Center Harbor
Isle au Haut
Blue Hill
Buck's Harbor
Sylvester Cove
Eggemoggin Reach
Deer Isle
Stonington
Winter Harbor
Vinalhaven
Castine
Pulpit Harbor
Northhaven
Perry Creek
Carvers Harbor
Penobscot Bay
Tenants Harbor
Pickering Island
Northwest Harbor
Camden
Rockland
Port Clyde
Harbor Island
Hog Island
Round Pond
Muscongus Bay
Seal Cove
Booth Bay Harbor
44°N
69°W

a lovely walk around Castine, one of the oldest communities in North America. Founded in 1613, it had been fought over by the French, Dutch and British and was now home to the Maine Maritime School. After re-provisioning at the market, we sailed on to Pumpkin Island where we anchored next to the lighthouse in a glorious sunset.

The next day we sailed to Buck's Harbor and on to Center Harbor and to the Wooden Boat School. After looking at all the workshops, we sailed on to Swan's Island, past Burnt Coat Harbor lighthouse, an old Quaker settlement, where we bought five enormous lobsters, clam chowder and crabs and had a huge cook-up aboard. Next day we moved on to Frenchboro, a tiny picturesque settlement that is often painted. This island has no store, only a café, museum/library and a church.

Another foggy morning and we motored to Southwest Harbor. The fog got denser and colder and in the afternoon a friendly US Coast Guard boat came along and led us into a mooring area, making a spot check of our documents. We woke up to a wet, cold, foggy day, so decided to stay where we were. The men went into the village for bread, milk, eggs and vino and then climbed up one of the nearby hills in Valley Cove, Somes Sound to get a different perspective on the fog.

Fog is the main hazard of cruising in Maine, together with the millions of pot-buoys. Even with care, we caught six buoys in the three months. Luckily we have a lifting rudder (to go with our lifting centreboard) but manoeuvring through the buoys means very slow motoring. Lobsters are a major industry; an estimated 20 million pounds are harvested each year. We found it easy to buy them direct from the lobstermen for about $8 a pound and everyone was eager to instruct us on how to cook them: drop into boiling water, bring back to the boil and cook for a further five minutes. You are limited only by the size of your pot.

It was time for Olivia, Rob and Rory to leave so we hired a car from Bar Harbor Airport and drove to Boston leaving *Restless* on a mooring in Abel's boatyard on Mount Desert Island. We visited the Museum of Fine Art and Harvard University and walked the streets of Boston.

We returned to find *Restless* covered in bird-poo from gulls and cormorants resting on our spreaders and spent the next day scrubbing the boat before Roland's brother Oliver and Jane arrived. The fog had set in again so it was a good time for sightseeing and mountain climbing around Mount Desert Island, a huge national park. Three million tourists a year visit this area, mostly Americans. The Rockefellers have a beach house and boatshed and they have had roads built to reach the whole island. There is a free bus service and bike and horse-riding paths. We went by dinghy into Southwest Harbor, hugging the shore in the fog, walked around the village and bought 4 (more) huge lobsters. On 20 July the sun shone and we set off with some leftover strands of fog past the Hinckley Boatyard, past Bass Harbor lighthouse and into Bass Harbor, a very picturesque spot partly because there is a huge lobster fleet. Then we had a gentle sail to Buckle Harbor. Oliver and Jane are keen bird-watchers and were excited to see ospreys nesting at the tops of the pine trees and to watch a pair of loons diving.

We experienced another Maine hazard at Blue Hill. After carefully following the marker buoys to get into the mooring area, we went ashore to the town dock, tied up and went for a walk, picking blueberries. On returning we found the tide had gone out – a long, long way. Why would we think the town dock might be a safe place to tie up? We went off and had a lobster dinner in a nearby café, returning about 2030 but still no water. We went to a bar as it was by now dark and cold and we were in shorts and tee shirts. Full tide would be at 0300, we persuaded the bartender to stay open until 2230. Oliver asked him what a person from Maine is called and he said a Mainey or a Mainiac! We finally got back to *Restless* and a disturbed night; the disturbance was a pair of grumpy seals lying on a raft nearby. We woke to discover we were in what looked like a giant rock pool. The tidal variation is about 10 to 12 feet, so it is important to note where the rock ledges are before the tide goes out! With our centreboard up we draw 3 feet 10 inches; we were very close to the bottom. We then headed back to Mount Desert Island and Oliver and Jane set off for their long drive back to Toronto.

Maine lobstermen

Consie's twin Feyona and her husband Andre van Stom joined us on 1 August for three weeks, arriving by bus at Bar Harbor. We anchored in Somesville and took the free Mount Desert Island bus to collect them and bring them back to the boat. The next morning we sailed west to Brooklin boatyard where we had our generator checked.

We stayed in the area for the Eggemoggin Reach Regatta and over the next couple of days about 100 wooden boats of all ages and sizes showed up. Roland was lucky enough to be invited to race on *Cuilaun*, a varnished 55-foot McGruer ketch, owned Brian Smullen. We also went to the barbecue at the Wooden Boat School and Roland chatted to 97-year-old Olin Stephens who had been racing on *Falcon*. Olin was the designer of *Restless* and also of *Reverie*, the 40-foot wooden yawl that we cruised around Hong Kong and the Philippines and then sailed to England in the 1980s and 1990s.

On 7 August we motored to Buck's Harbor, where we anchored, got water and bought the only two packets of cereal in the general store and the next day we motored to Castine where friends loaned us a car to drive down to Stonington. On 11 August we sailed to Camden, a beautiful harbour, full of superyachts. We woke up to the smell of a skunk, which alerted us to the most wonderful fiery red sunrise we have ever seen.

After a quick motor around the harbour, and a hullo to *Cuilaun*, we sailed on past Curtis Island and Rockland lighthouses into Rockland, where there was a New York Yacht Club get-together with 100-odd superyachts and also the Maine boat show. This was a great chance for Roland to speak to all the local dealers and order new dodger and awnings. We left on 14 August, past Rockland, Owls Head and Brown's Island lighthouses to Northhaven, another picturesque village, and up Perry Creek, a protected bay on Vinalhaven. Here we watched a small family of seals fishing for dinner and dinghied up to the hurricane hole at the head of Perry Creek.

On 16 August some locals (Mainiacs?) invited us to join them at a picnic at White Islands. Then we went on to Carvers Harbor, Vinalhaven, with about 600 lobster-boats in the harbour; we had been warned that at 0430 each day there is a lot of activity. We went on to Winter Harbor, on the east coast of Vinalhaven and close to Stonington where we were due to pick up friends for a day's sail around Isle au Haut. We went ashore for a lobster and blueberry pie birthday dinner in Stonington.

On 19 August we went alongside Billings Marine, Stonington, to get our refrigerator serviced. This yard services about 350 lobster boats. A number of superyachts came in to re-fuel as the New York Yacht Club motored up the channel, on the way to their next rendezvous. We sailed over to a group of nearby islands, famous for being one of the best anchorages in Maine, and it was gorgeous with guillemots swimming in rows, seals fishing around us, and a few kayakers. We anchored for a peaceful night at Coot Island, with Camp, Bold and Devil Islands and 'Hell's Half Acre' nearby, and roast lamb on board for dinner. The days were already getting colder and shorter and we had been told that many of these bays would be frozen solid with a foot of ice by Christmas. In the past much of the material for the huge beach houses had been towed miles across the ice by horse-drawn carriages. We felt lucky that in New Zealand we can sail all year round.

The next day we motorsailed to Deer Isle and anchored at peaceful Northwest Harbour, where there was a fireworks display from one of the beach houses We woke to dense fog and cooler temperatures. We walked around the village but could not find any bread or milk. (Yes, there was an art gallery, ice cream parlour and two antique shops). We found a churchyard full of wild raspberries and blackberries and had to hurry back before the bay turned into another giant rock pool. We needed to get back to Rockland on Monday for the Van Stoms to get their flight. Feyona was struggling to understand why we are living aboard for the foreseeable future. We are identical twins but our lives are very different, with hers as an artist really taking off. She has had over a hundred exhibitions and has been invited to exhibit her sculptures in New York, Philadelphia, and Chicago.

We left *Restless* at Brooklin Boatyard for a fortnight to have new windlass, windows and hatches fitted. We flew to San Francisco for Roland to race in the Etchell Worlds. We returned mid-September and sailed south to Rockland, to pick up our new dodger and awnings and to carry on south to the Cape Cod Canal, flying south with the birds to warmer weather. We were sorry to leave Maine and wonder how many places in the world can boast so many anchorages within such short distances of each other.

Roland and Consie Lennox-King bought Restless of Auckland, a 51-foot Sparkman & Stephens De Riveur centreboard ketch in Grenada and since February 2005 have sailed some 3,000 miles up the east coast of America to Maine.

JURA IN PERIL: A WHALE OF A TALE

by Bill and Pam Kellett

In 2004, after trucking *Jura*, our 35-foot Wauquiez Prétorien, from the Great Lakes to the west coast, we set off to see the best of British Columbia. This year we planned a 'blitz' run through British Columbia to reach Alaska with adequate time for exploration before returning to Anacortes, Washington.

Planning for cruises is part of the fun and we tackled the task of assembling the necessary pile of charts and cruising guides with enthusiasm. Fortunately CCA member Sandy Weld lent us his charts, collected over several summers in these waters. At $20 for a new chart this was a welcome saving especially as they were primarily back-ups for the chart plotter. We completed our navigation suite with the latest *Exploring Southeast Alaska* by Don Douglass, the Canadian Tidal Current Tables and Atlas and several new charts as many of Sandy's were verging on antiquity

Our main objective was to explore the 4,400-square mile Glacier Bay National Park with its 20 glaciers, 15,000-foot high mountain ranges, protected coves and plentiful wildlife. It needed sharing and Bryan and Dorothy Collins, long-time sailing friends from Scotland, quickly accepted our offer of a two-week cruise. They would fly into Juneau, join us at Auke Bay then depart from Sitka in a ferry back to Juneau. We hoped to provide a cruise exciting enough to justify their 4,000-mile trip. Unanticipated events ensured that we had no worries on that score. Now, we will begin the story of this leg of the cruise at Auke Bay.

For those who may follow us, Auke Bay not Juneau is the logical jumping off place for Glacier Bay. This marina, with 6,000 feet of berthing, doesn't take reservations or give berth assignments; it just maintains a ten-day maximum stay rule. The entire marina is for transients. Yachties, fishing vessels and commercial whale-watch boats all battle for space. If you do not spot an empty slot on the way in there is a short stay berth where you can tie up while roaming the docks looking for an opening. It's a real scrum. Pam befriended Lew, a commercial fisherman, who not only gave us a large coho salmon but also went over our charts to point out little-known anchorages along our route to Sitka.

The National Park Service strictly enforces rules for vessels entering Glacier Bay. Exactly 60 days before your desired entry date (and not a day earlier) you must apply for a visitor's permit stating how many days you wish to stay (maximum of seven), providing details of the vessel and crew and giving alternate dates in case your first choice is not available. This is a little stressful as only 25 boats are allowed in the park at one time. So normally three new boats enter as three depart. With our crew flying in from Europe, we were concerned about locking down our permit dates!

When we entered the bay, two humpback whales breached nearby in welcome. Landing at Bartlett Cove for the mandatory briefing, we were told of areas for unpowered vessels only and restrictions regarding the minimum one-mile distance from shore and a quarter mile from humpback whales that must be complied with to ensure that feeding whales are not disturbed. Perhaps the best way to convey the nature of this National Park is to quote portions of the US Coast Pilot description:

'Glacier Bay is about 50 miles long to the head of Muir Inlet, 54 miles to the head of Johns Hopkins Inlet and 62 miles to the head of Tarr Inlet. Above Willoughby Island, both shores of the bay are steep and foul and should be avoided. All shoals of less than 6-fathom depth are covered with kelp part of the year, but this kelp cannot be depended upon to indicate danger as the strong current tows the kelp under most of the time.'

'Currents: The tidal currents from Point Gustavus to Willoughby Island at times can attain a velocity of 6 knots or more. Heavy rip tides and swirls occur abreast Beardslee Islands…'

'Ice: Numerous discharging glaciers enter the bay and glacial ice is always present, sometimes in enormous quantities in Muir Inlet, Tarr Inlet and Johns Hopkins Inlet… When the ice falls from the faces of the glaciers, it may create waves 30 feet high. Therefore, small boats should not approach closer than 0.5 mile to active glaciers. Icebergs are unstable and should not be approached closely because, if disturbed by swell from the small boat passing, they may roll over or break apart at any time…'

'Vessels are advised to carry extra propellers aboard when navigating Glacier Bay and single screw vessels should not attempt to navigate the bay at all.'

Following the briefing, we walked to Glacier Bay Lodge to see the tiny but interesting exhibit of flora and fauna before getting underway for North Sandy Cove. The ensuing 37-mile run past South Marble Island offered an amazing collection of wildlife: more breaching humpbacks, Steller sea lions, sea otters, tufted puffins, pigeon guillemots and nesting kittiwakes. To end the perfect day, there were three brown bears and a moose in the meadow by the anchorage.

In our self-allotted five days, we could only cover a small portion of this wonderland so we took the Douglass Cruising Guide most picturesque glaciers recommendations: Margerie and Grand Pacific in Tarr Inlet, Johns Hopkins in Johns Hopkins Inlet, Reid in Reid Inlet and Riggs and Muir in Muir Inlet. We visited the first four as they clustered together but gave Riggs and Muir, 40 miles away, a pass.

After a peaceful night, the crew was up early for the traditional *Jura* Sunday breakfast, pancakes and maple syrup, and then a timely start for Reid Inlet. The usual anchoring problem of water too deep or too shallow put us on a narrow shelf close to the beach. Bryan and Dorothy inflated the Avon for a jaunt ashore in spite of the warning by the Bartlett Cove ranger that recent kayakers had had their camp 'tossed' by a bear looking for food. Luckily, the only bear encounter was with tracks during their hike to the glacier face.

The following morning cold air and wet mist hung over Margerie Glacier. Intermittent rain and fog added to the artic feel, a truly miserable day – but no one noticed! The only concerns were keeping the cameras dry and avoiding damage from the ice. When first seen, a calving glacier is a disorderly jumble. Hugh blocks of ice break away from the face and plunge into the sea with thunderous explosions and sizable waves. Besides the big growlers, thousands of bergy bits float around requiring a slalom course to navigate the mess without prop damage. Dodging larger pieces of ice kept the helmsman on his toes and necessitated spotters on both sides. As we got closer to the ice face the skipper said, 'Enough!' The ice density represented too much risk to the propeller. Just then we discovered the head's water inlet pump was nearly inoperative. After some thought, we realized the cause was extensive glacial silt in the water. It was probably hard on the engine cooling water pump impeller as well but there was no apparent increase in the engine temperature.

Next on the agenda was a 'cruise by' of Johns Hopkins Glacier. Bill had fashioned a custom 14-foot pole in Prince Rupert and was eager to practice his iceberg-pushing technique on the small bergs in the bay. In the continuing rain, we ran past Lamplugh Glacier before returning to Reid Inlet for the night. The sun finally appeared as we worked southward looking for our last Glacier Bay anchorage. A distant view of snow-capped mountains behind Grand Pacific Glacier was breathtaking. We dipped into Blue Mouse Cove but dismissed it as marginally attractive and too deep for easy anchoring. Fingers Bay with its rock-strewn entry was much more appealing.

The anchor was dropped as close to the south end as possible while allowing for a few more hours of ebb tide. We were quite close to the mud bank but this vantage point provided front row seats. Two black bears soon wandered by searching for edibles in the shallow creek. Early the next morning a black bear was back together with a female moose

and her calf. The young moose paid no attention to the bear nor the bear to the moose but nonetheless mama moose watched nervously.

Going back to Bartlett Cove to clear out, we found that the admonition that currents could run six knots or more was quite true. It was close to springs and we could barely stem the flood. Even with the throttle advanced and the log showing 6.8 knots, we were going nowhere. Edging closer than the minimum one mile from shore in an attempt to find less current or even a back eddy, we were startled by a VHF call directing us, in no uncertain terms, to get further off. Sheepishly we moved out into the current again feeling fortunate that we had escaped detection until past the worst. Finally, the quiet anchorage at Bartlett Cove, a great dinner at the Lodge and a top up of the fuel tanks at 20% over market price. The consensus was very positive for the Glacier Bay experience. While the glaciers may not be as impressive as those in Tracy Arm, the wildlife more than compensates.

After a very early departure, we headed south down Chatham Strait for Tenakee Springs in what was predicted to be favourable wind and current. Not true. We copped out at Pavlof Cove, tired of light wind motoring. If it had not been for Lew we would never have known of this attractive anchorage. The only disappointment was that the perfect bear/salmon stream and waterfall had neither in view this day.

Civilization! Tenakee Springs, known for its hot springs and written-up as quaint, looked like a good stop; we did not know what we were getting into. The town, really just a jumble of small buildings, seemed occupied by escapees who wanted to live the frontier life. To set the

Elegant living for the Tenakee Springs harbourmaster

tone, the harbourmaster's floating home, with a Harley-Davidson poster showing dully through a window, was one of the first sights as we walked along the pontoons. Then we met the harbourmaster himself complete with silver ponytail, tooling around the dirt paths in his mini vehicle patriotically draped with the national stars and stripes. True to its name, Tenakee Springs has a hot spring in a small building off the main street. It's a central gathering point for the locals. Ladies' hours are mid-afternoon and after dinner, men's during the morning and late afternoon. Inside it looks like something from a horror movie and smells like sulphur, not too good. However, the townspeople use it to exchange gossip and bathe – no swimsuits allowed, naked all the way.

All this aside, there is a certain charm about the place. There is a single six-foot wide dirt road through town. Two or three wheeled trail bikes, a couple of small-motorized hauling carts and feet provide transport. A walk took us past the Blue Moon Café (about as appealing as the hot springs), the general store (quite good) and the tea room/art gallery (nice). Everyone is exceedingly friendly. There is a path through the woods to a stream crossed by a miniature suspension bridge built by the US Army Corps of Engineers. It is really a bridge to nowhere and due to its size looks like a school graduation project.

One night at the Tenakee docks was enough so another early start for the 40-mile run to Peril Strait and Appleton Cove. Just as we were turning off Chatham Strait into Peril Strait, we were amused to see multiple seals resting on the Morris Reef bell buoy. We rolled up the jib to slow down for picture taking then saw a group of seven humpbacks milling about. More pictures as we realized they were bubble feeding. This is an individual or group activity where the whale(s) swim around a school of small fish making a net of bubbles to keep them together. When the corralling is complete, the whale(s) come up in the centre with mouths open wide to scoop up their prey. It is an impressive sight to see these enormous mammals simultaneously rise far out of the water in an amazing feat of teamwork before crashing back with a tremendous splash.

After 45 minutes of oh-ing and ah-ing, we left the humpbacks to look at some orcas. We were all jabbering about what we had seen when Bill exclaimed, 'Look at those bubbles!' With horrified fascination, we watched the line of bubbles head for *Jura's* starboard side. They disappeared under the hull and seconds later all seven whales shot out of the water within a boat length of our port side. Tremendous confusion ensued with whale tails and whale bodies thrashing the water. Total shock and awe on our part. Imagine a near miss by seven school bus-sized monsters. With a quiet expletive, Pam put the engine into reverse hoping to get clear of the mêlée. However, the light wind in the mainsail pushing us towards the whales while we were trying to power backwards made for a slow escape. Finally, surrounded by enormous bubbles, the whales

SAMBA DANCING FORTH FROM LOCH MELFORT

by Lorne Byatt

Samba is a Seamaster 925, a Holman and Pye design built in 1979. She is a sister ship to Simon Butler's *Apprentice*. Having always been impressed by Holman and Pye designs (and having been hoping to buy a boat for at least two years) I bought *Samba* in Loch Melfort on the west coast of Scotland in mid-August 2005, perhaps a bit late in the year! This simple log records the fun we had in bringing her to Granton on the Firth of Forth.

We left Kilmelford Yacht Haven with a pretty full family crew at 1430 on Friday 19 August – a bit later than planned after one or two unexpected jobs. (Some members of my family occasionally utter a minor swearword, 'Oh, Boat!'). My father Hugh, son Douglas (16), brother Duncan and his children Letty (9) and Harry (7) all enjoyed a first proper sail on *Samba* down to the Dorus Mhor and thence to Crinan. The skipper made tea; there was a pleasant westerly F3-4 so we made a happy five plus knots over the ground with the tide beginning to get under us. Apart from the slight doubt, 'Would we be at the Crinan sea lock in time?' all was right with the world. Even the threatened rain held off. We roared round the Dorus and called up the sea lock on VHF. 'Och aye, ye'll be fine, come away in'. The engine, an elderly but well maintained Volvo Penta MD7A, started when it should. I had observed the previous owner's starting procedure: decompress and crank to get oil circulating before the engine fires up. Having propelled us happily out of Loch Melfort with the wind on the nose, it had already done a bit of work.

Into the sea lock with two other yachts (somewhat after the usual closing time of 1700) and up into the basin – what a joy to be back in the Crinan Canal. We quickly realised that, with *Samba's* tumblehome, the maximum beam (9′10″) is well below the toe-rail, so fender positions need to be carefully considered. More family arrived: my wife Harriet,

Duncan's wife Alexandra, my mother Fiona, my uncle Robin and aunt Jilly Byatt. Drinks at the Crinan Hotel were a great celebration of *Samba's* first modest passage under my command, even if some found it necessary to keep the washboards in the hatch to keep the midges out!

Douglas and I had an excellent supper on board, carefully planned by Harriet (and aided by some Piper's Ale brewed in Argyll; try it). We then spent our first night on board, very peacefully in the canal basin. The skipper snored – he is not unknown for this. We woke to a glorious and absolutely still Saturday morning, with perfect reflections across the basin. Our first problem became apparent – the auxiliary battery (which runs instruments, VHF and a fresh water pump) was weakened by our modest use of power the previous evening. I investigated and found battery cells more or less empty. *Okavango,* with whom we would be making the canal passage, gave us some distilled water that had been bought when she was in Greek waters the previous year. The problem began to reduce and running the engine through the canal all day undoubtedly helped to put some charge back in.

Douglas and I set off with *Okavango* and *Drumbeat,* a Bavaria 36 that had been taking part in West Highland Week. Some locks were a tight fit

Crinan Canal

for the three of us but good humour prevailed and *Drumbeat* was fully crewed and provided much of the manpower needed to operate the locks. My parents brought my daughter Emma (13) to join us and we began to make good progress. With our bow line led through a block on the toe-rail back to a sheet-winch in the cockpit, I could handle bow and stern lines together, while Douglas and Emma stood by to fend off. Emma had been working sheep at home so there was no problem looking after the boat.

It was a beautiful day. Since I was a boy I've always had very happy experiences going through the Crinan Canal and this was no exception – made even better by the fact that we were under way in *Samba*, only our second day on board. There was no time to stop after Cairnbaan to have a picnic lunch; our hope was to reach Ardrishaig and even lock out into the sea if we could. To speed our passage, Douglas and Emma played their accordions together on the foredeck with the RCC Song Book acting at least as a musical score. On the long reach free of locks after Cairnbaan the concert entranced cyclists and walkers on the old towpath. We arrived at Ardrishaig in good time to lock out and I surrendered the first day-ticket from my 16-day Explorer book, bought from the British Waterways Scotland office at Crinan; good value at £224 giving us access to all the BWS canals for a year.

Samba had no burgee halyard but with binoculars we could see that there was a suitable fixed block at the masthead. So outside the sea-lock and alongside the new pontoon, with one eye on the falling tide, we sent Douglas in a bosun's chair to the masthead with a line. He took a digital camera and recorded the (reasonable) condition of various things at the masthead that I had not had the opportunity to inspect. 'Dad, it's such a good view, can I stay up here for longer?' Finally I was able to hoist my RCC burgee for a glorious quiet late afternoon sail in sunshine down to East Loch Tarbert with my father, Douglas and Emma. The wind dropped away so it was necessary, with family commitments in mind, to use the engine a bit to maintain our planned ETA. I had hoped that with the wind on the beam we might have been able to set the cruising chute (a very large sail) but this was not to be. *Samba* went very happily nonetheless, dancing with pleasure at being back in the sea. Alongside the pontoon in East Loch Tarbert more family arrived to see *Samba* for the first time – Harriet and I had a very happy supper on board with about five children. There is a surprising amount of space down below, for smaller people at least; the generous beam helps. I'm nearly 6′5″ but there is six-foot headroom in most of the main cabin.

Douglas, Emma, my nephew James and I spent the night on board. James said the pilot berth was great. Staying alongside the pontoon at £14.50 a night was the best we could do, as there were no visitor moorings available. Sunday morning came the rain, rain and more rain. Time to leave the ship and start other jobs that needed doing at my parents'

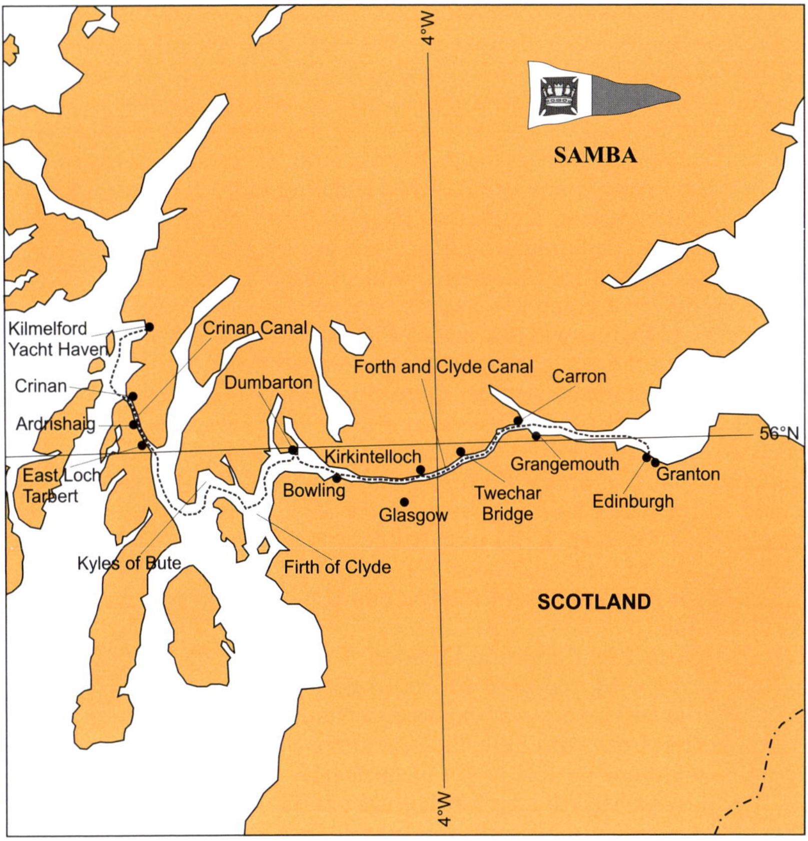

home on Loch Stornoway (on the west side of Kintyre and just to the north of West Loch Tarbert) before we could set off for the Clyde, to enter the Forth and Clyde Canal at Bowling.

The forecast for 23 August was awful, with southerly F9 expected so it was much better to stay put in Tarbert where Douglas and I could do some necessary jobs rather than essay a night at anchor in Blackfarland Bay in the Kyles of Bute, which had been part of my initial passage plan for a Tuesday departure. *Samba* has a 25-pound CQR. It made no sense at all to try a first test in F9, especially if it came as forecast in the middle of the night. My crew (Douglas, my cousin Amanda and a local friend, Damon Kenneil) were all set to leave promptly on the Wednesday if the low had passed north and east.

I had an early start at my parents' home on 24 August, consulting all the available weather forecasts to update the picture from the previous

Admiralty Bay, Marlborough Sounds (Mitchell)

Previous page: *Iron Bark* (Hill)

Cloud formations near Nuuk as storm brews (O'Grady)

Spring skiing in Greenland (Hill)

Icebergs almost block the entrance to Illulisat as the supply ship makes harbour (O'Grady)

Monique steers *Quiver* up the Stockholm Skagard (Browne)

Penelope's Ark, Lyon (Vasey)

have been recent instances of vessels trying a short cut, with dire consequences. We got in safely, dodging the flotsam that was resolutely wind-driven into the sea lock despite the efforts of the canal staff to remove it with something like a dragnet.

The Forth and Clyde Canal was built from east to west starting at the Carron River in 1768 and reaching Bowling in 1790 after various financial delays. It closed in 1962 because of declining use and the perceived need to build new roads across the canal and opened again in May 2001 as a Millennium project after some three years of repair work. It is 31 nautical miles long with 39 locks and several lifting/retracting bridges. I had seen parts of it but had never used it. The passage we were to make, crossing Scotland's central belt, was obviously a huge saving in time compared to going through the Caledonian Canal. However, there were many unknowns – not the least of these being the reportedly troublesome parts of Glasgow through which it runs.

The canal staff, led by Billy, was great. They were patient with us when we were nervous getting the mast down for the first time (the crane facility is excellent) and were full of helpful advice. With the mast strapped along the coach roof and supported by miscellaneous timbers and fenders (all well below the canal's maximum air draught of 9′10″), we could relax. It was a peaceful evening in the basin although passing trains make a lot of noise. Not enough to blank out the snoring, said Douglas.

We were asked to be ready to move at 0845. There were three members of the canal staff helping us through the locks. Best of all, our cheery escort George (not a BWS employee but a volunteer) had sensibly been provided with a bicycle so that he could keep us company all the way along the canal past Maryhill. Riding shotgun would be an exaggerated description – George's calm good humour spoke volumes about his good sense, more than sufficient armament. Then we were left on our own until the Twechar Bridge the next morning when the east coast BWS team took over.

Unlike the Crinan Canal, the arrangement in the Forth and Clyde is that the staff does most of the work for you, taking lines, opening and closing sluice gates. The aim was to get through the Clydebank and Maryhill stretches by lunchtime – a prompt start, we were told, would tend to find troublemakers still asleep. In the first two years or so after the canal re-opened, it was reported that there was a lot of damage done to vessels passing through, stone-throwing and the like. But now I guess the novelty is wearing off and it would be great to see more vessels using the canal. In late August I had expected to see at least a few other yachts heading back to the east coast. However, we were the only vessel moving on the western half of the canal. We had no trouble whatever in Clydebank or Maryhill, perhaps aided by the frequent rain-showers. We attracted some interest when we stopped at 'the world's only sail-through chippie' in Clydebank for excellent bacon rolls (expect strong crew demand here) but there was no hostile action.

We were also constantly watching for bottom obstructions. The claimed maximum navigable draught in the canal is 6′ but the advice I had heard is that 5′6″ draught in salt is a practical limit. At 5′ in salt and probably 5′4″ in fresh water, *Samba*'s long fin keel touched many times, but we think mostly on mud; we left a methane trail quite often. Bottom hazards included several submerged shopping trolleys but we managed to avoid these if we saw them in time. There was quite a lot of weed and occasionally it seemed to help clear the prop (fixed, two-bladed) if we ran the engine astern. We also kept a lookout on the bow for plastic bags and similar rubbish that might block our engine water intake. We either took avoiding action or fished the rubbish out with a boathook. All this led to a sense of adventure, not frustration or worry. The canal is a great industrial monument and it is good to see it being respected once again by BWS, if not by all the people living nearby. Eighteenth century construction feats such as the Kelvin Aqueduct and the Maryhill flight of locks are matched by twenty-first century marvels such as the Dalmuir Drop Lock (taking vessels under a main road by pumping out many tons of canal water – a slow operation, there was plenty of time to make tea for the canal crew) and the Falkirk Wheel, which lifts boats 110 feet from the Forth and Clyde to join the Union Canal running into Edinburgh. Our destination, Granton on the Forth, cannot be reached from the Union Canal basin in Edinburgh and anyway there is a draught restriction of only 3′6″ in the Union Canal. Maximum beam and LOA for vessels using the Forth and Clyde are quoted as 19′8″ and 63′ respectively. Perhaps the ideal in a yacht much larger than *Samba* would be to have a centreboard with less than 5′ draught when retracted.

Moving steadily east from Glasgow, the country alongside the canal makes it a pleasure to be there. We had been warned that one stretch was especially shallow; indeed it was. BWS says it does remove obstructions but water levels can vary. This had not been an especially dry summer. We stopped for the night alongside a pontoon at Kirkintilloch, the 'Canal Capital of Scotland'. Harriet and Emma came from Edinburgh by car and eventually found us. We still had not seen any other vessels moving on the canal, apart from a BWS weed-cutting barge. Supper ended with some members of the crew much enjoying chocolate pudding that was supposed to feed eight but actually fed no more than the three who ate it (no names, no pack drill). It started to rain but we had the use of a well-appointed BWS shower-block right by the pontoon so no need to wash on deck.

A better morning greeted us on 27 August and we were keen to get going, even though there was little chance of getting out into the Forth that day. We waited in a pool just before the Twechar Bridge for the Carron sea lock team to take over; they arrived more or less on time.

Then the traffic flow was disrupted, just for us. Onward and eastward, still in sunshine. The major excitement was passing the Falkirk Wheel. When Emma, Amanda and Douglas all wanted to stop for ice cream, the skipper relented and had some too. More vessels were underway on this eastern portion. They were mostly canal boats, some of them hired and not entirely under control or certain of the collision regulations.

The Carron sea lock team were good – but less vocal than their Bowling colleagues, perhaps marking in a small way the difference between west and east coast attitudes. We pointed out that our warps were not long enough to be passed round canal-side hooks and back on board. Please could we keep that bowline on the end (the Bowling crew had understood this very quickly)? Usually a good flick of the warp would free it after working the lock, rather than a member of the canal team having to lift the bowline off the hook.

Amanda had to leave us at Falkirk as she and her family were going to the Edinburgh Tattoo. She had been an excellent member of the crew. With Douglas on the helm and Emma and I as crew, we continued peacefully through the last few locks, once again very empty of other vessels. We arrived at the Carron sea lock at 1530. As at Bowling, there were a number of vessels here that looked as though they had not moved for a while. Because of tidal restrictions in the River Carron running

Near Falkirk Weir

down to Grangemouth it was too late to lock out, so we occupied ourselves doing jobs such as re-fuelling (an impressively economical engine had run for about 15 hours since Tarbert on only nine litres of diesel). Donald, the friendly BWS manager at the sea lock, had worked on the Crinan Canal for some years so was pleased to hear of our passage. He cross-checked my tidal calculation for the next morning and confirmed that we could lock out about 0845.

Sunday morning saw us up early, with a sense of excitement not dampened by the rather wild and wet morning. The forecast was for southwest F5-6 in the Forth. I had been strongly warned against using the mast-stepping facility in the River Carron near Grangemouth, partly because it uses a crane on a pontoon. As we went past it, I was glad that we were not attempting to step the mast there nor was it possible to have the mast stepped at Port Edgar near the Forth road bridge, because the crane operators were on holiday. Either location would charge while the use of the crane at Bowling was free. BWS had tried to get planning permission for a similar crane at the Carron sea lock but had failed for some reason.

Anyway there are bridges between Grangemouth and the sea lock for which a mast has to be lowered. So we went under power out of the River Carron at Grangemouth and down the Forth, in rather unpleasant conditions. Forth Coastguard acknowledged my on-passage report made from a hand-held VHF (the main masthead aerial of course being unusable). The wind was on our quarter, there was a short steep sea building and since the mast was necessarily well off the centreline to starboard, *Samba* started rolling. I put some extra lashings on the mast to keep it with us. It started to rain hard and visibility became less than good. We stayed on the (much rougher) north side of the shipping channel as required, then crossed the shipping channel to the south side of the Forth (rather more sheltered) and went past the familiar landmarks of Hopetoun House and Port Edgar and under the bridges. We made good speed with the wind and tide in our favour. I was listening carefully to the engine all the time but it seemed to be running happily. Douglas and Emma were the watch on deck as I was down at the chart-table with the washboards in (it was still raining, and the sprayhood was folded down under the mast). Rather than open up the hatch, I signalled the course to steer through the navigator's porthole, which they found amusing. The worst part of the trip was when we turned southeast, some distance after Hound Point, to cross the edge of the Drum Flat towards Inchmickery and Granton. The short, steep beam sea made the motion really sharp without the steadying effect of any sail. However, I judged this was better than going rather further down the Forth and then having to fight upwind with much resulting strain on the engine.

Finally, with a sense of relief and achievement, we tied up alongside the Royal Forth Yacht Club's pontoon in Granton Harbour at 1315. Harriet met us and we all went home for a late lunch. A week later, it was possible to step the mast again using the RFYC crane. It took us a long time, but it was great to complete the task.

Samba's passage from Loch Melfort to Granton, although not a huge distance, had given me an excellent opportunity to get to know the boat and appreciate her good qualities. We had a lot of fun too. Much better than having her transported by road! After a number of excellent day-sails on the Forth during September and into October with family, friends and work colleagues, she is now wintering ashore at Granton.

I have of course, a 'jobs list' ... but I am also much looking forward to the 2006 season. Douglas and I hope to take her up to Inverness and into the Caledonian Canal in the early summer, then through to the west coast – a great advantage of doing this is that we would not need to un-step the mast!

Samba to the Isles of the West in 2006:

From the lone shieling of the misty isle, mountains divide us and the waste of seas: but the blood is strong, the heart is Hielan' and we in dreams behold the Hebrides. (Anon, Blackwood's magazine, c.1880)

We look forward to meeting other RCC members there.

WINTER HOLIDAY

by Annie Hill

Annie Hill was given the Goldsmith Exploration Award

Some cruises are born of long-held desires: 'I *will* get to New Zealand, some day'. Some are born of a moment's fancy: 'Let's crack the sheets and head for Nova Scotia instead of Ireland'. And some insinuate themselves until one day you're drawing up lists, poring over charts and committed.

Which is how I ended up going to Greenland. I've always loved snow and wanted the chance to play in it every day. Three years ago, we spent the winter in Baddeck, Nova Scotia, but being in civilization rather spoilt things. I would play in beautiful, white snow then 'they' would plough it into dirty brown heaps; I'm sure the Northern Lights burned brightly in the sky, beyond the orange glow of the street lamps.

Trevor had spent 1999 in the Antarctic and his tales made it hard to believe that he'd enjoyed it. The approach passage from New Zealand sounded horrible, with the 11-metre *Iron Bark* down on her marks with stores for Trevor's sojourn. With insufficient fuel to run a heater, he lit a fire once a week to dry his laundry and otherwise lived in temperatures well below freezing. He claimed that it wasn't bad. His suggestion that we go on to Greenland and spend the next winter there wasn't entirely unexpected. Nor was it appealing. But a year later he managed to persuade me, bribing me with promises of heating oil, tempting me with new and wonderful cold-weather clothes, seducing me with visions of pristine snow under the pink wash of an Arctic twilight and unmarked save for animal tracks.

When I finally agreed, we immediately set about organising the 'exhibition' as they are endearingly known in Labrador. This was a surprisingly straightforward operation because Trevor knew what equipment was needed and after three decades of provisioning a boat for long voyages I could handle that aspect. Nova Scotia could meet all our requirements.

Eric Hiscock stated that adventures are a result of bad planning and implementation and we were determined to abide by this tenet, especially as we intended to be completely isolated; if anything went wrong, we might pay the ultimate price. We endeavoured to ensure that nothing did go wrong, but we also considered strategies in case we bungled, for example allowing for an extra high-calorie meal every day and buying thick sleeping bags and liners, in case the heater broke down. Selecting suitable clothes was a real boost to my morale because they were so obviously superior to the wool that had previously been my normal cold-weather gear. Wonderful windproof and waterproof outer garments, snug layers and best of all, a down pullover. I knew that I would be a lot happier if we could keep *Iron Bark* comfortably above freezing but at least now I was convinced that I wouldn't die of cold if we couldn't. Although I might die of misery!

We planned to get to Greenland as quickly as possible, find a wintering site and then spend the rest of the summer exploring our surroundings. The desiderata for our winter home included being well above the Arctic Circle; around corners that the sea ice couldn't penetrate; away from the shoreline, where ice pressure would cause the ice to rise in chaotic ridges; sufficiently small that we could take lines ashore from all four corners; shallow enough that we could anchor until the ice came, but deep enough that it wouldn't freeze to the bottom; near a stream, but not right next to a large lake which might burst dangerously come spring; protected by high ground, but not so high as to produce downdraughts or block out the light. It seemed a tall order, but Trevor, looking at the charts, said there were dozens of possibilities in our chosen area. And if we couldn't find just what we wanted, we'd try somewhere else.

We had a number of friends in Canada who now cheerfully made space for our summer clothes, spare sails, paint and excess gear and lent us cars so that we could buy books, a crowbar, food for 450 days, charts, jerry-cans with 300 litres of paraffin, pick and shovel, clothes, candles, sleeping bags, tents, half a ton of miscellaneous gear and, in spite of outrageous Canadian prices, whisky, rum and wine for the long, cold night. When we left Baddeck on 1 July 2004 the poor, little ship was staggering along, well down on her marks.

Heading up the west coast of Newfoundland, we intended to sail non-stop to Disko Island, which is about 70°N. As we approached the Strait of Belle Isle our Aries self-steering gear jumped a cog, so we sailed into the outport of Flowers Cove to sort it out. A few hours later, we were clearing Belle Isle and its icebergs and heading for the Greenland.

I'd made this passage in 1991 and warned Trevor that we would be plagued by calms and bedevilled by fog but although we did more motoring that we'd have chosen, wishing to avoid heavy weather with *Iron Bark* so heavily laden, we had relatively little fog. This might account for the fact that we saw rather more icebergs than I had before. Sails went up and down, the engine went on and off and the crosses on our chart crept up the Labrador Sea and into the Davis Strait. The desire to be there had the usual effect of making all delays irritating and the passage seemed tedious and unusually drawn out. It was also cold and damp because we can't use our heater under way. Telling myself that this was good training was as ineffectual as such stern talk generally is.

On the morning of 21 July, after 18 days at sea, we sighted Disko Island. This was our first proper sight of Greenland although we'd had several tantalising glimpses. The sea between it and ourselves was strewn with a spectacular number and variety of bergs and we looked forward to sailing gently between them. Breakfast was barely finished when the wind picked up and in less than an hour, it was blowing an honest F9. To say we were shocked would be an understatement. With a maze of bergs to weave through, there was no sensible alternative to dropping all sail and lying a-hull until the blow passed. We didn't anticipate it lasting long and it was all over bar the shouting by lunchtime but it had blown long enough to knock up an extremely unpleasant jobble. As we got underway again, *Iron Bark*'s sails crashed and banged in the rapidly dying breeze. We ended up motorsailing, weaving our way through the ice and finally got the hook down in Fortune Bay, Kikkit just before midnight.

The next morning, we climbed a hill to marvel at over 200 icebergs drifting across Disko Bay before making their way anticlockwise around Baffin Bay and down the Canadian coast. Some would make it to the Grand Banks reminding any who saw them of the ill-fated *Titanic.*

Back on board, we were eager to continue north and have a look at Laksefjorden, which runs eastwards into the Greenland coast for several miles, winding around islands and ending up in a large area of shallow water. It was close enough to the settlements of Upernavik and Kangersuatsiaq (Prøven) to permit us to buy our winter fuel, but sufficiently isolated that we would be entirely on our own.

The Vaigat, between Disko Island and the mainland, is stunning with massive bergs debouching from three fjords, so we took that route north, discovering one or two good anchorages along the way. Now we were experiencing more fog, which when combined with ice, makes for particularly tense sailing. Lack of wind forced the choice between extremely slow progress and motoring and because we felt that finding a safe winter berth was a priority, *Iron Bark* became a motorboat. I could hear the sound of my illustrious predecessors whirring in their graves and considered lowering the burgee for the duration but Trevor consoled me by reading passages from Tilman who also motored for hours over glassy seas. 'You can't have 'Greenland Days' and good sailing,' he reminded me.

The afternoon of 2 August saw us rounding the Kangeq Peninsula and entering Laksefjorden. Initially its shores were dark, steep and daunting but it became increasingly lower and more attractive and I noticed a

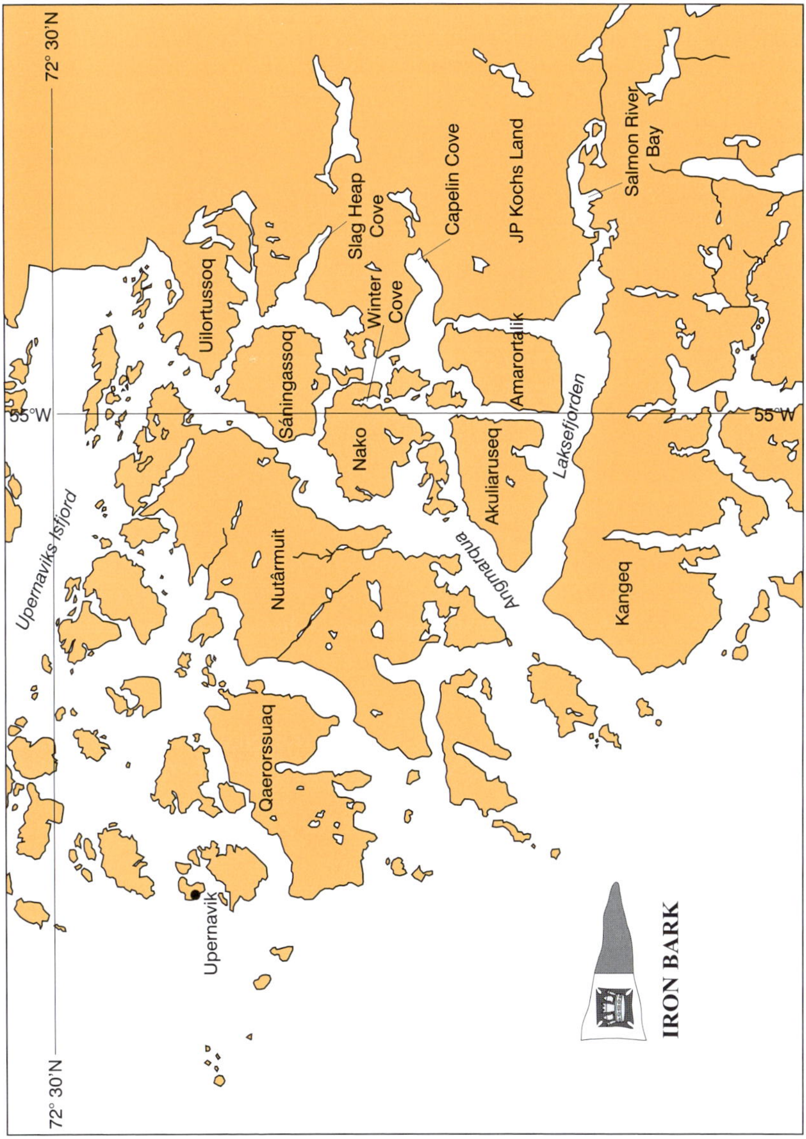
72° 30'N
55°W
Uilortussoq
Slag Heap Cove
Capelin Cove
JP Kochs Land
Salmon River Bay
Winter Cove
Sâningassoq
Amarortalik
Laksefjorden
Nako
Akuliaruseq
Angmarqua
Upernaviks Isfjord
Nutârmuit
Kangeq
Qaerorssuaq
Upernavik
IRON BARK

tempting array of islands to the north – the Nordre Sunds. We were excited at the prospect of finding our winter harbour and had a lot of fun working our way down the fjord, getting lost in a blind end and then having to pick our way among islands, skerries and rocks. We concluded the day by almost running aground as the silt bottom rose up sharply from 12 metres to three in, it seemed, as many seconds. Deciding that we'd had enough for one day, we dropped the hook. To the south was a bay marked 'Salmon River' on the Admiralty chart, which had an 'Eskimo encampment', some of whom visited us later. Having no language in common, communication was limited to offers and acceptance of coffee and cake, smiles and handshakes. It appeared that the families were here for the arctic char fishing and they readily located themselves on our chart, indicating the routes they used to and from their villages.

Next day we continued to the far end of the fjord, taking to the dinghy on several occasions to sound our way through the shallows. We finally found a route with a least depth of 1.5 metres (*Iron Bark*'s draught) at low water, which snaked its way eastwards and finally led behind an island into a small bay that appeared perfect for our needs. We stayed here for a couple of days and I celebrated my birthday by the side of the river that ran into the bay, having had a successful morning picking bilberries and wild mushrooms while Trevor hooked a couple of fish.

We were delighted with our find and planned to start settling in but it was not to be. The area was closely patrolled by a fishery protection officer who was puzzled by our presence. When we had attempted to 'enter' Greenland, in Qeqertarsuaq, no one had been at all interested in us, we had not asked permission to stay and nobody had enquired as to the proposed length of our visit. We felt that it would create fewer problems for all parties if we didn't mention our plans, so after a second interview from this gentleman we decided that we'd better move elsewhere.

We had briefly investigated several of the attractive-looking islands that we'd seen and we set off to explore them more thoroughly. The Nordre Sunds are covered by a 1:400,000 Danish chart, too small scale to show much detail and largely innocent of soundings. Instead of wandering aimlessly around the area, we decided systematically to chart it. With innumerable fjords, islands and passages, it is a perfect miniature cruising ground and we had no real problem with the thought of getting to know it better, although there was a nagging need to locate a safe winter haven, especially as snow was already settling on the hillsides. Our first anchorage reassured us. Although there were high and gloomy cliffs on one side and it was a long way to a stream, it was a possibility and further exploration revealed a number of other potential sites. We had added 'unvisited' to our desiderata and on 4 September came across the perfect spot. It had everything a wintering visitor could desire and no sign of humanity, not a piece of rope or a shard of plastic to indicate

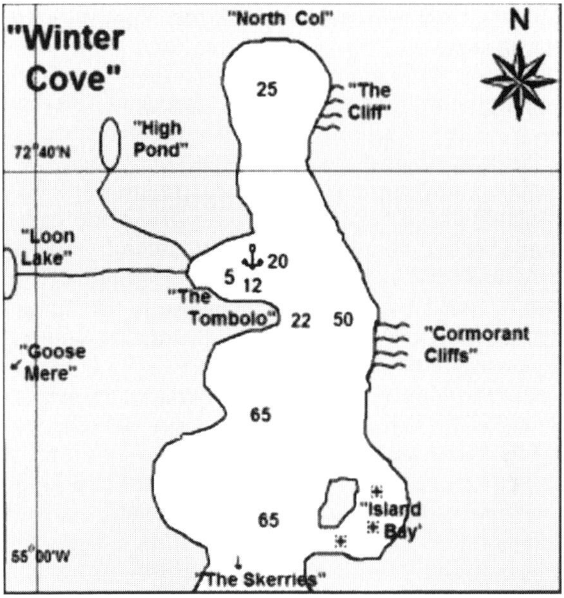

Winter Cove

that anyone had ever been there before. Winter Cove (72°39.9′N, 54°58.6′W), as we called it, was tucked away on the east side of Nako Island up a blind fjord and round a corner. We'd be as inconspicuous as we could wish. All that remained was to stockpile 800 litres of fuel and we could settle in for the winter.

We bought this in Upernavik. To transport it back, we needed several 44-gallon oil drums and finding a pile in the middle of the town, went into the adjacent building and asked if we could buy some of them. When our request was finally understood, the manager came out with us and selected five of the better looking drums, apparently taking our request entirely for granted. We took them back to the boat and filled four from a truck on the wharf. We had sufficient paraffin for cooking and melting ice; this was for keeping Annie warm. Upernavik is a dreadful harbour and we left immediately and made our way round to a bay to the east, where we had perfect shelter during a nasty little gale. With such a deck cargo, we could only move in fine weather, but the following day saw us steaming back into the Nordre Sunds, with our final major hurdle crossed.

With this reassurance, we explored our surroundings with added enthusiasm. As we made our way along the sounds, Trevor meticulously noted the soundings, which I transferred to charts, 'drawn' on my laptop computer. Together we wrote up directions and eventually had a fairly complete survey of the whole area. Such a delightful cruising ground deserves to be known.

A week after finding Winter Cove, we decided to settle in. By now, there was frost and ice where the sun no longer penetrated and grease ice in the mornings. Those final days before the equinox were a delight as we walked over the surrounding hills, gathering bilberries and enjoying the last of the warmth with no mosquitoes to torment us. It had been calm and sunny for so long that this seemed the norm. We shifted *Iron Bark* further into our little cove and spent several days adjusting and readjusting lines, balancing the several factors of moving ice, strong winds and breakout. Eventually, the boat faced west, into the worst of the winds. The first of the sun would pour in through the south-facing galley windows, an attractive prospect.

As we established ourselves, I was frankly apprehensive of what was to come, particularly the low temperatures. Cold frightens me. I knew we had to ration our fuel carefully and common sense told me that our tiny heater was not going to keep us warm when outside temperatures were −30°C. As the days shortened and the cold increased, our heater struggled to keep the cabin at 6°C. I had worked out a fuel ration and at this time we were only permitted to use one litre per day. Careful observations showed that on its lowest setting the heater burned as little as 180cl an hour, giving six hours a day heating, or at least gentle warming. This was less than the manual suggested and was a cheering consideration while I waited until 1600 when I could light the heater. I worried how I'd cope when it got seriously cold and was quite literally counting the days that we'd be there. Chilblains appeared on my hands and feet and the only time I felt warm was in bed.

Our bay froze and then broke up. At first, the ice formed on the fresh water from the stream. One day this blew out entirely and we were back in the open, wondering if we'd ever freeze in. Trevor had told me that once this happened we could relax and I could well believe him. Every time we got a good build up, a howling gale would sweep down the valley to the west of us and blow it all out again; the ice made a terrific din as it banged against the boat and it was hard not to worry. I reminded myself that *Iron Bark* had been through much worse in the Antarctic but we were both heartily relieved when the wind died away.

The snow crept down the hills until it covered the foreshore and the ice clung increasingly tenaciously, creeping across bays and spreading out from the shoreline. Each day was noticeably shorter than the previous one and on 22 October, we stood on deck at noon and watched the sun slide over the hill northwest of us for the last time that year. Daytime temperatures were below freezing and ice was encroaching into lockers inside the boat. We used pieces of closed-cell foam to isolate the lazarette. There was ice under our mattress in the morning and on the bulkhead at the foot of the bed. Condensation would drip on us as we slept. I un-

Annie Hill

rolled a couple of camping mats and put them either side of our bunk. At the foot, I used foam from a cockpit cushion and secured a blanket to the deckhead to mop up condensation. After that we were comfortable and the bed was snug and dry all winter, although a hot water bottle made the first 20 minutes less of an ordeal. We also put cling film under the hatches, which made effective double-glazing. Whenever there was snow on deck, its insulation properties made a noticeable difference and we started to wish for it for warmth, as well as for making travelling more fun.

As the ice advanced, we drained the seacocks and blew through the pipes, clearing them of water that might freeze and split the ball valves. The engine is keel cooled, so could be run periodically, which helped prevent the batteries from going completely flat. At −10°C a battery's capacity is about 20 per cent of what it is at 25°C. We had insufficient fuel to keep the batteries charged for lighting, the solar panel was obviously useless and in the calm conditions that prevailed for most of the winter and spring, a wind generator wouldn't have been much better.

Strong winds were thankfully becoming less frequent and the ice was extending further and further into the bay; already we were engaged in the winter-long chore of lifting up the shorelines so that they didn't get frozen into the ice and dragged down. Ice forms from above not from below as the weight of snow depresses it and floods the sea ice,

of a bruise. Trevor took advantage of this to empty the buckets and I'd often go for a short walk on the ice or over to the Tombolo. It didn't worry me if I stayed on the boat for two or three days at a stretch; in many ways, it was like being on a long passage.

The previous year, we had bought boxes of wine in the Canaries; I eked these out over the winter, allowing one box per weekend. This little treat gave shape to the week and influenced our decision to celebrate the solstice, rather than Christmas because 22 December was a Wednesday. We had a branch of willow for our tree, which I decorated with icicles and snowflakes I'd made from the tiny beads that Eskimo women use for their traditional dress. We had hoarded presents and wrapped these up and placed them under our tree. I iced the Christmas cake that I'd baked in October and instead of the orthodox turkey, made all sorts of little dishes to nibble at over the day, which were much easier to keep hot. We had loads left over, so could then celebrate Christmas as well, drinking toasts to absent friends who might be thinking of us.

In January, we finally had sufficient snow to cover the boat properly. Trevor cut blocks of snow, laid them around the windows and then shovelled snow over everything, while I chinked any holes. The result was a strange looking igloo with a mast. Inside the difference was instantly noticeable and it was easy to keep the boat at a comfortable 9°C. Even more to the point, when we went out for several hours, it was still above freezing when we got home. Previously the temperature had plummeted as soon as we left, in spite of our insulation and the snow on deck. Once or twice we had left the heater on but the worry that something might go wrong frightened us and spoilt our pleasure; we'd rather have a cold boat than none at all.

We were looking forward to the sun's return and by mid January, the twilight was extending. One day the stars disappeared for a little while at midday, we saw a mountain peak glowing pink and then several. We had just started using our skis and were complete beginners. Now it was bright enough to see where we were going, we were eager to become more proficient. After a couple of overcast days, 1 February was beautiful, still and clear so we skied across the sea ice to 'North Col'. It was a long haul up the valley but well worth it when we turned to look down the fjord. It was suffused with pink and the glow of the sun was bright behind the hills. As we watched it, we realised that it might possibly show through a notch in the mountains south of us and we quickly climbed higher.

We waited and then the sun slid out from behind a cliff face, shining on our faces, dazzling our eyes, flooding the fjord with light. We gazed at it, unable to look away as it moved across the gap and disappeared behind the cliff on the opposite side. We hugged each other, laughing and dizzy with joy. As I made my precarious way down the steep slope back to the sea ice, my mind was filled with the satisfaction of having made it. Despite the fact that the coldest weather was yet to come, despite the fact that we had the difficulties and dangers of breakout ahead, I felt that the worst was over. Indeed, after the sun returned, I stopped counting the days until we would leave.

The days lengthened rapidly and the temperatures fell to −35C°. When it was calm, it never felt bitterly cold but as soon as there was the slightest breeze, we needed to keep moving to keep warm. Those beautiful sunny times when we went skiing into the hills were just wonderful. Everything was pristine. The sky was a deep, transparent blue and often the sun would pick out crystals in the snow which, through our ski goggles, were transformed into tiny prisms, flashing rainbow colours. It was breathtakingly lovely. Our only disappointment was that the fjords always had breaks in the ice, where there were upwellings. This meant that we could not travel long distances unless we were prepared to climb very steep hillsides. Although we were within 40 kilometres of both Upernavik and Kangersuatsiaq, it would have been almost impossible to get to either of them. Our isolation was complete.

There were also days of total whiteout when it was extremely difficult to walk. The lack of shadows made bumps and hollows invisible and I once found myself taking an inadvertent ski jump over a two-metre drop because I simply hadn't seen it. Winter was at its height and *Iron Bark* completely buried in snow.

At about this time I amused myself with working out how much our year was going to cost. I'd kept the receipts for everything: food, fuel, equipment, clothing and all the sundry items we'd bought. Our expedition would cost just over £10,000. If not low budget, it was scarcely extravagant. There was obviously going to be a fair quantity of food and fuel over and much of the clothing would be used for years to come. It's satisfying to know that you don't need vast resources or sponsorship for more ambitious undertakings.

During the winter, we'd only seen and heard ravens and ptarmigans, but now other birds appeared. Great cormorants came back to their cliff to nest and occasionally we saw the outlines in the snow of where they had crash-landed on the sea ice. They had probably forgotten that the water was solid. They were quickly followed by black-backed gulls, glaucous or Iceland gulls (I never worked out which), snow buntings, eider ducks, mallard, mergansers, redpolls, black guillemots, Canada geese and Lapland longspurs. Their presence was a delight after so much stillness and silence.

Although the land was still covered in snow and the fjords frozen, spring was coming. Warm sun heated the rocks and slowly patches of brown started to appear. One day we heard dripping water – the sun was melting our snow cover. Foxy was finding her coat too thick now and would sprawl in the cool snow, panting. A tiny moat appeared on the south side of the boat, where the hot steel melted the ice, and we could

Trevor clearing the lines

sense the ice loosening its grip. We cleared the snow from our decks and as the weight came off the boat, she started to rise in the water. Trevor assisted by breaking the ice around her and suddenly she gave a great leap before settling back, higher than she had been. We ran the engine in forward and astern and after a few more shudders and jumps she was floating back on her waterline. A line along the hull showed that she had been pulled down a total of 35 centimetres into the ice.

I spent a day digging out our dinghy *Lisa* from her snowdrift while great, big fluffy flakes of snow fell around me – *proper* snow, such as we rarely saw in this near desert. Trevor dragged the sails from under *Lisa* and brought them back on board, then returned for the dinghy, hauling her over the ice to *Iron Bark* and looking like a re-enactment of an *Endurance* photograph. It was fun bending on the sails in anticipation that we might soon be sailing. We hoped we weren't being too optimistic, because there was no water in sight. I scrubbed and cleaned inside the boat, the bright sunlight revealing the grime from the cooker, heater, lamps and candles. The ice inside the boat melted, producing half a ton of water that we had to bale out until the pump thawed.

A couple of days later, we awoke to find water flowing down the valley. We hurried our breakfast and ran over the ice to see it. Water was boiling and roaring as it tumbled down the hillside and vanished into cracks in the ice, reappearing as a brown stream that crept along the shore lead. We followed this torrent up to where it appeared from under a snowdrift.

Further yet and we could see water flowing over the ice on the lake and way up the Big Valley we could see a huge cataract leaping from the edge of the mountain and crashing down. A lake must have burst its dam of ice, releasing tons of water to career madly down to the sea. We couldn't tear ourselves away.

We felt that all this water should affect the sea ice but for days nothing seemed to happen. *Iron Bark* was pushed back in her cradle and every now and then we'd slack off the forward lines but the ice in the bay appeared as solid as ever. However we no longer heard sounds like explosions from ice pressure and the fresh water was making holes in the shore leads. Then holes started to appear in the sea ice and our beaten path from the bow to the shore flooded and then vanished. Foxy had to pick her way ever more carefully to come for her breakfast; overnight the snow became too soft for skiing or even snowshoeing and we floundered thigh deep, falling through holes and filling our boots with water. Shorelines snagged on moving ice and Trevor started taking our plastic, folding dinghy with him in case he fell through.

On 7 June, we climbed a nearby hill to look out over the ice. It was full of holes and there was open water only about a mile away, extending as far as we could see. We had to floe-hop getting back to the boat and Trevor broke through the rotten ice into the freezing water while digging out the shore lines. I was worried until I saw him scramble back into the dinghy. Back on board the sun was so warm that he stripped off his clothes and dried himself. I gave him a large medicinal rum.

The next morning, Foxy had a real struggle getting to us and had to jump over several wide leads. After breakfast, Trevor went to clear some shorelines, which were under considerable tension, and fell through the ice again. Dried and dressed, he said that he would have to cut the starboard stern lines. The result was dramatic. Suddenly, our stern slewed across to the south side of the cove and big sheets of ice started moving out on the north side. This reduced the pressure on the rest of the ice, which now started jostling and moving. Some of the pieces were pushing against *Iron Bark* and I fended them off, which then allowed other pieces to shift. As I pushed and heaved and the boat swung back and forth, other floes twisted and escaped, floating for several metres before getting trapped once more. Trevor was back on the other side of the bay, freeing those lines and I was grateful for the fact that it was flat calm. In fact, I was enjoying myself hugely because there was no risk to *Iron Bark* and it was wonderful to see the ice breaking up around us. Trevor came back aboard to help me with a big pile of ice jammed around the bow. We broke lumps off and pushed them to one side and then a huge piece split off. This slithered down our port side and all the ice to starboard started moving. Within a few moments, the whole mass in Winter Cove was streaming out and into the main part of the bay so that soon only isolated floes remained. Our dinghy, which a few hours ago had been sitting on the ice alongside, now floated serenely astern on her painter; mallard, a pair of mergansers and black guillemots swam nearby. It was almost beyond belief. We sat on deck in the warm sunshine revelling in the feeling of once again being truly afloat.

A few days later, we moved out to anchor. A number of our lines were still encased in thick ice and after a futile week of digging to free them, we let the sun and meltwater do the job while we went off for a few days' sailing. We left with the plan of spending the night at Akuliaruseq, a favoured spot to which we'd skied during the winter. We sailed down an ice-free fjord, but found the anchorage choked with ice. The nearest alternative was Winter Cove, so we returned home somewhat ignominiously. The exhaust system, which is dry, developed a leak filling the cabin with exhaust fumes. Trevor patched it as well as he could but the repair could only be regarded as temporary.

The next day we had rather more success. We explored an unpromising-looking fjord on the north shore of JP Kochs Land but near the end we saw a magnificent waterfall tumbling down and a well-protected cove opening up. We found depths of eight metres and Trevor suggested anchoring in this pretty spot and going ashore. Surrounded by small fish jumping and swimming, we rowed up a little stream to find a landing – most of the shore was still solid ice three metres high. It was grand walking ashore with lots of tiny white bells in the heath and half a dozen other pretty little flowers.

When we came to the river, we found a truly raging torrent, which had obviously flowed over the ice before cutting through to the rock below, leaving a frozen fall at one side still blocked by ice. We continued up the narrow gorge, climbing and scrambling with great pleasure. The river was a delight, running between three-metre walls of ice and flowing under precarious-looking snow bridges. It was all splendid. We named our find Capelin Cove (72°37.3′N, 54°35.9′W).

The following day we carried on, to explore the next inlet north. The chart showed a narrow slot with a rock at the end. The rock proved to be an extraordinarily symmetrical mound of glacial till that looked exactly like a slagheap, with a bay on the far side. We anchored and sounded around in the dinghy, finding enough water for *Iron Bark*, so we took her in and had the hook down for teatime. We went ashore and I got my first mosquito bite of the year. Summer had arrived. Although the anchorage wasn't pretty, Slag Heap Cove (72°41.4′N, 54°32.9′W) as we called it, is well protected and another good find.

We got away next morning at about 1130 and made our way north to the island of Uilortussoq. Our plan was to go along its south shore and see if we could get up a narrow channel shown on the chart to the ice cap. It was perfectly calm and warm in the sun. Once we entered the fjord to the south of Uilortussoq, we encountered quite a lot of ice. We steamed along and at last could see the ice cap coming down to the sea.

As we continued, we realised that it has receded three or four miles from its charted position. It was exciting, proceeding into the unknown. At last, we were off the chart! We chugged along following the shore and tried to go right round an island but backed off when the depth fell to three metres.

We then continued to head north and west, following the ice face round. Some of it was exceedingly grubby but it was interesting to see one or two newly emerged islands with their own private ice cap. A lot of the glacier front was quite lovely. We could see that it went miles to the north but we couldn't follow it because the route was blocked by masses of ice jammed between the ice front and islands near the head of Upernaviks Isfjord. We tried motoring west, which had the advantage of going back a different route, bringing the dinghy on board because of the brash. We alternated steering and piloting from the ratlines. To my surprise I felt quite comfortable up there.

After some time, the way out became increasingly choked with ice. We wove between everything from massive bergs to tiny bits of ice the size of a teacup but eventually came to a dead end. Rather than continue deeper into the packed ice, we turned back to look for another way out. The first possible exit was completely blocked with ice but as we continued I remembered seeing another possibility and suggested that we head that way. We did, I spotted a gap between the ice and the shore that look

'Some of it was exceedingly grubby'

passable and we managed to squeeze through in 13 metres of water. The constant twisting and turning to avoid ice and skerries was disorientating but after some consultation with the chart, the GPS and each other, we made our way back to where we had started. This was the highlight of our time afloat in Greenland and we reckoned we might as well start heading south.

On our way back to Winter Cove, the wind suddenly picked up and soon things were getting unpleasant. It was quite wild, gusting F9, but we only had a short way to go and as we passed the Tombolo the wind was cut off and we anchored without difficulty. We'd perhaps chosen our haven better than we'd realised. In the morning we found that most of our lines were now accessible. Trevor dug the remaining one or two out of the ice that still clung in the shadows and we went ashore for a final walk to High Pond before heading south. A red-throated diver had taken up residence and as we walked down the hillside, we heard the eerie call of a common loon. It was a fitting farewell.

There were two major headlands to pass on our way to Disko. Svartenhuk has an unpleasant reputation and Nuussuaq had a tricky-looking harbour that would be fine in settled weather but was open from the west. After so long in sheltered waters, we were a little apprehensive of this passage and indeed had a false start, turning back when the wind picked up and headed us. On 25 June, we tried again and soon made all sail to topsail, trundling happily along with a fair breeze. This fine weather continued and although the wind occasionally faltered, we sailed past Svartenhuk and had Nuussuaq abeam at midnight on Monday. We turned into Nordfjord as the wind started to fill in, sending fog before it. This was probably a wise move insofar as the fog was concerned but we had the greatest difficulty finding any sheltered spot to drop the hook. As usual the chart was devoid of soundings. The east end of the fjord was extremely shallow and the rest very deep; the putative anchorage mentioned in the Pilot was 25 metres only a few metres offshore and part of our shelter was provided by a grounded iceberg – not the most reliable of breakwaters. It was, as I noted in the log, a 'sad conclusion to a delightful passage.'

The next morning, our iceberg took itself off on the rising tide and we hauled everything in and motored over to a spit to the west. If we went within two or three boat lengths of the spit, we could anchor in just over 12 metres but would be pushed aground should the wind turn easterly. It was, as Tilman would quote, 'a berth to be chosen from necessity and not from any hope of tranquillity,' but as long as the wind stayed west, we had good shelter. We left at the first opportunity for Diskofjord, enjoying a couple of anchorages in this attractive area. We stopped at the small hamlet of Diskofjord on 2 July and spoke to a delightful man who was cleaning out the fish factory. His English was surprisingly good and he explained that some 20 years previously, he had spent six months on

STS *Danmark*, where he had learned the language. He hadn't spoken it for several years but had not forgotten it because of the number of American and English films that he watched. It was only after we were back on *Iron Bark* that we realised this was the first person we'd spoken to in 10 months.

We sailed to Qeqertarsuaq in the hope of fresh food but it was so expensive and of such poor quality that we decided to stay with vitamin pills for another few weeks. After sailing across to Kronprinsens Ejland to take on water, we headed towards Newfoundland. It was a sparkling day; Disko Bay was filled with impressive bergs, many more than we'd seen the previous summer; they positively scintillated against the bright blue sea and sky. We had a fine topsail breeze from the north and were more than pleased to carry this until we were out of sight of land and bergs, particularly as the temporary repair to the engine exhaust had failed and we were now without a motor. To our astonishment, this breeze lasted the best part of six days, by which time we were abeam of Kap Farvel. In that time, there had been neither fog nor ice. For the next week we had a mixed bag of winds. While it was getting noticeably warmer, the increasingly dark nights seemed strange after the glorious, perpetual sunshine of Greenland. As the wind died away again on 18 July, we headed inshore to a small anchorage on the Labrador we'd visited some years previously. St Francis Harbour basked in hot sunshine and several million mosquitoes descended on us with whines of delight as we dropped the hook 12 days out from Disko Bay.

We left a couple of days later and after an unpleasant night dodging shipping in the fog sailed into St Anthony Harbour, busy with fishing boats, surrounded by houses and with cars driving along the roads. We were back in civilisation. At 0640 on 21 July, we dropped the hook, a year to the day from our arrival in Greenland. The ordeal that I'd dreaded had turned into a wonderful winter holiday.

Iron Bark is an 11 metre steel gaff cutter, designed by Nick Skeates, built in Australia by Trevor Robertson and launched in 1997. She is possibly the only yacht sailing that has over-wintered in both the Antarctic and the Arctic. For all that, she is also a comfortable boat to sail in warmer climes. Electronics consist of a hand-held GPS, echosounder and VHF. She has no radar.

A HIDDEN PARADISE: *NATANIS'S* INTERLUDE IN NOVA SCOTIA AND NEW BRUNSWICK, 2005

by Michael Lewin-Harris

The Bay of Fundy is a place with a reputation. The head of the bay has the greatest tidal range in the world (the Bristol Channel comes next), the water is cold (even Andrew, my die-hard swimmer crew, declined to go in for more than a few seconds) and fog abounds. We had just made the entire 35-mile passage from Brier Island at the southwest side of the entrance to Digby up the southeastern shore in thick fog. Thank heaven for GPS and radar. Luckily there are compensations. When the fog clears the scenery can be spectacular. Wildlife abounds and the inhabitants are almost embarrassingly friendly.

On 12 August the sun shone warmly, not altogether surprisingly as the latitude is roughly the same as Bordeaux and slightly south of Venice. What is more, we could see our destination of St John, New Brunswick (not to be confused with St John's, Newfoundland) some 30 miles across the bay. True there was little wind, but there were whales, seals and seabirds, the trusty Yanmar helped out when needed and after a relaxing day we arrived to be introduced to the Reversing Falls.

St John is at the mouth of the river of the same name, which is navigable for some 150 miles. It finishes through a narrow canyon, 120 metres across at its narrowest point, having passed over a ledge little over 5 metres deep. This confines the river water to a tidal range of less than half a metre, as against around 10 metres outside. The result is spectacular at both high and low waters, but at around half tide the levels meet, all goes quiet for about 15 minutes and passage may safely be made. There is an additional hazard in the form of separate road and rail bridges, the centres of which line up neither with each other nor with the centre of the channel flow. This is of little consequence unless, like *Natanis*, you have a mast height of 18.5 metres to a charted clearance of

21, so accurate timing is all. The whole setup provides entertainment to visitors who can watch the antics of those who have mistimed by a few minutes or later on ride the standing wave in a speedboat. This is not advisable in a yacht.

Once safely through the narrows the scenery is magnificent, with a deep gorge opening out into the wide Kennebecasis Bay at the back of the city. The temperature goes up several degrees and was matched by the welcome we received from CCA member Ernest Hamilton and the Royal Kennebeccasis Yacht Club. As we settled to our cocktails in the dusk on Ernest's mooring, the rest of the world and its troubles seemed far away. *(Please note the spelling of Kennebeccasis as in the yacht club is not a typo, but differs from the Bay. This is to do with the Victorian paperwork for the grant of the Royal charter. The Palace accidentally put in a second 'C' and by the time it was discovered it was far too late to change it!)*

The next morning (Sunday) there was rain and thunder but Ernest had offered to run us into the city so we blew up the dinghy and went ashore in oilies, whereupon the rain promptly eased off. Ernest duly appeared in his comfortable American car and took us to the chandler, (we needed a river chart) and on to his favourite café for breakfast and chat whilst we waited for the market to open. This was the first traditional indoor market we had met. It had a magnificent collection of fresh vegetables, meat and just about anything else you could need.

Reversing Falls

Humpback whale

Returning to the Yacht Club, we filled with diesel and water and set off up the river, by then sailing in brilliant sunshine and a pleasant breeze and spent much of the afternoon 'racing' a similar sized boat. In places the river widens out into lakes, some several miles long and a mile or more wide. We finally set the spinnaker to lose our opposition and finished up at anchor in a creek about 25 miles up the river. We ate our supper accompanied by distant music and fireworks from a party across the valley, followed by a peaceful night.

We spent a further day going on through much gentler country with farms and grazing cattle more reminiscent of the upper Thames, but on a huge scale. We went as far as Gagetown, a pleasant place set in rolling agricultural (cattle and fruit) terrain looking almost like something out of a Constable painting. The impression is of a big country, with scattered dwellings along the river and on the surrounding hills. The whole is an enormous catchment area with a number of lakes and connecting waterways, wide and narrow. They normally freeze over in the winter and there is ice yachting, skating and so on – a bit like the northern Germany we once knew.

We spent a final night at the RKYC, having much enjoyed our peaceful interlude. It would have been good to stay for longer, but time was limited, a crew change was due soon and the gunk holes of Maine were calling. I hope to return.

CERES IN SCOTLAND, JUNE 2005

by Jim Pitts

A coward cannot pretend to be brave at sea,
Nor a fool to be wise, nor a prig to be a good companion,
And any venture connected with the sea is full of venture
And can pretend to be nothing more.

(Hilaire Belloc)

The Hebrides was our intended destination and once more I was lucky to have my faithful crew of the past few years, Geoff, John and Michael. We are all maturing quite rapidly so a decision to have no hard and fast plans apart from joining ship and an end of cruise date reduced the pressure to meet deadlines. We decided to sail across the Minch and see where the wind might take us.

Leaving Ardfern on 12 June we had a fine sail to Loch Aline which I think is my favourite anchorage on the whole of the west coast of Scotland. There are other wonderful places of course but the gentle green scenery, great walks ashore, friendly locals and its safety as a bolt-hole in all weathers puts it at the top of my list by quite a margin.

Although only a day out Michael found that we could be short of one or two items for the galley. As this could not be tolerated we left Loch Aline for the major sail of 11 miles to Tobermory, arriving in time for lunch and fortunately found a vacant buoy. They used to be free but now we pay about £12 for 24 hours. They are well serviced and have a handy pick-up buoy, instead of the dreaded shackles that at the mere sight of a boat hook fall absolutely flat and are virtually impossible to pick up from a high foredeck.

Moonbeam was lying on the next buoy and soon we had David and Lynn Wilkie aboard for a drink and this turned into lunch as the heavens opened and looked like staying that way all day. Anyone who has had the good fortune to sail up to Ardfern will need no introduction to David and Lynn. Taking advantage of our relaxed schedule we came to an arrangement whereby we would all assemble on *Moonbeam* for supper; we would provide the chicken and the wine and Lynn would do the work!

Next morning there was quite a fresh wind blowing through the moorings but conscious of our burgee we managed to sail off from a fairly tight situation and feeling pretty pleased with ourselves headed away bound perhaps for Eriskay, some 50 miles to the west. We began with a fine reach out past Ardnamurchan, the Cairns of Coll and then Hyskeir. The visibility deteriorated slowly and it was not until we were about two miles off that the misty isle become visible. We sailed slowly into Acairsaid Mhor carefully lining up the leading marks and finding one of the two visitors' buoys vacant.

Next morning dawned fine and clear and we could see back over the Minch to Rum and Canna that had been invisible yesterday. As the sun rose higher but was not yet over the yardarm, we set off in the dinghy for a mussel hunt. In spite of rowing all around the harbour it proved entirely unsuccessful. However the skipper of a small lobster boat told us they would be in at the pier at 1400 and would probably have some lobsters for us. With this prospect we returned to *Ceres* and paid due respect to the sun's position over the yardarm, whilst lunching on a smoked salmon salad. True to his promise the skipper returned and we bought two fine lobsters and were given a huge basket of squat lobsters as well. For those who are unaware of squat lobsters, they are rather like chubby prawns but without long claws. They are truly excellent eating.

After this culinary work we set off for a walk ashore on what was once the island of Eriskay. It now has a causeway joining it to South Uist and has lost the island status. It rather shows this by a general clean up of the old abandoned cars and other domestic waste that used to disfigure the island. The architecture still leaves you wondering if somehow the planners and builders might have had rather more respect for traditional Scottish buildings.

We enjoyed our walk over to the west and eventually came to the pub, the *Politician*, named after the whisky ship that was wrecked off Eriskay in World War II, much to the joy of the locals who harvested an unusual crop from the sea. Compton Mackenzie wrote a delightful book, *Whisky Galore*, about this episode of the island's life. We walked back to the boat with a hearty appetite that was satisfied with a first course of the squat lobsters and a cold bottle of Chardonnay, followed by fillet steak and a fine red wine. This is cruising in fine style, at least according to us!

We planned to sail to Loch Skiport next day but after leaving Eriskay and clearing the Hartamul Rocks that lie in waiting for the unwary, we sailed into Loch Boisdale for no other reason than that the crew had never been there. We thought it would be better to lunch whilst tied to a buoy, thereby able to give the lobsters our full attention.

We left mid afternoon, and began with a fine reach to Usinish Point, where it became quite a lively run into the loch. Finding Wizard Pool full with one other yacht, we sailed on past and beat into the narrow entrance of Coalas Mhor. During the next three hours the wind, fresh at first, blew itself into a frenzy no doubt aided by the high ground of Hecla. I kept anchor watch until 0200 when the wind faded. The rest of the crew were more confident of our grip on the bottom and slept the sleep of the unjust. Who said this was cruising as it should be?

I think we ate the last of the kippers before we set sail, bound for North Harbour on Scalpay. After a very pleasant reach the wind died, a fog bank rolled up and a fine Scotch mist enveloped us. In a very short space of time we had come from fine sailing to dismal motoring. We relied heavily on the radar and the chart plotter, both giving us a great sense of confidence, as by now we were very happy with the complete accuracy of the latter and the ability to see other shipping with the former. There will of course be discussion among members of a certain age as to the wisdom of placing one's trust in electronics. We saw two very large radar reflections that we assumed were either a Calmac ferry or a large freighter, but neither was within a couple of miles of us.

I thought that we might relieve the monotony if we found a safe haven for the night. Loch Finsbay was a good deal nearer than our planned

Ceres leaves Tobermory bound for Eriskay

Scalpay anchorage. It looked fine on the chart but in very poor visibility we had to rely completely on instruments to find the narrow and rock encumbered entrance. We managed the double bend past unseen rocks and came to in a lovely sheltered pool with just a slight swell gently rolling us as we lay at anchor. For those not familiar with this anchorage it is a peaceful haven far from the crowds and civilisation. The rest of the day was given over again to food, drink and conversation, with nothing to see beyond 400 yards.

We awoke to a bright clear morning, which enabled us to discover what a wonderful spot this is. We left around 1000 and found a fresh southerly giving us fine sailing past Scalpay, Kebock Head, Marivaig and into Loch Leurbost, entering this loch at perhaps rather greater speed than the navigator would wish but all the leading marks fell into place. The tide race in the Shiant Sound kicked up a nasty sea, but *Ceres* coped in her usual steady and comfortable style.

As the shelter gradually flattened the sea we sailed more slowly up to our chosen anchorage, Tob Shuardil, about half way up into Loch Leurbost. Believing that we had a firm grip on the bottom the more serious and vital part of the day began by preparing supper. On the point of sitting down to what was gong to be a grand meal one of my crew thought that perhaps we weren't where we thought we might be. What a joy to have observant crew! Supper was put on hold, the wayward anchor hauled on deck and a fresh anchorage sought near the head of the loch. We came to in the very same spot that Bill Speirs had chosen for the rolling meet in 2000. Supper was resumed once we confirmed that we were holding well.

Loch Leurbost is a bit of a contrast to most of the Hebridean lochs. It is more pastoral and the grassland looks as though it is farmed with a bit of effort and skill. It is a welcoming area in contrast with the bare and occasionally bleak scenery on this coast. The holding on a windy night was excellent. On Monday we sailed into Stornoway – there was no point in going there on Sunday! Leaving Loch Leurbost we hove-to for a while to watch a spectacular display of gannets diving very close to us. We felt almost able to touch the birds as they folded their wings and darted into the water, most of the time surfacing with a fish. Cameras were clicking away.

Earlier there had been awesome noises coming from the 24v alternator so apart from running the engine to recover the anchor it was given a whole day off. We sailed into Stornoway with a stiff southerly and came alongside the main pier. We could not berth in the marina at the head of the harbour as we were said to be too big. The pier is not the best place. It is noisy, constantly disturbed by passing vessels and to cap it all we were next to a freighter discharging cement. But the harbour-staff are very friendly and Bill Speirs took me off to find an engineer who promised to fix the alternator next morning.

High ground over the Sound of Raasay

That evening we invited Bill and Audrey to supper. Nigel Wollen and Simon Wilkinson had just come in on *Wish Hound* and they were soon aboard *Ceres* for a drink before supper. It was a great evening, and Michael as the head chef did us all proud. Next morning the engineer arrived and I showed him the problem but in spite of spending about six hours he was unable to fix it. We spent another great evening with the Speirs in their house. Cruising again as it ought to be.

The next morning was just as bad as could be. The wind blew us hard against the piles of the pier, whilst the rain was in top gear. The forecast was lousy and it didn't take long to decide to hire a car and do the Hebrides in rather more comfort. We managed to hire the last available vehicle, a large people carrier. Michael was the only one of us who had his driving licence so drew the short straw. What a good decision to be ashore. If anything the rain fell even harder, the wind joined in so not to be outdone and at times we wondered if the roads, which were under major repair, would be washed away before we returned. We had lunch at Tarbert, tea at Rodel and supper back aboard whilst the rain continued. It could only improve.

I think we all felt that Stornoway does not do a great deal to attract the visiting yachtsman. There is almost no room to anchor, the pier is not very comfortable whilst the marina is cannot cope with much above a

35-foot yacht. This is a great shame as it is a major jumping-off place for places north and northeast. If it were not for calling on Bill Speirs I doubt if we should return.

We awoke next morning to a much brighter prospect even though the fresh wind held us hard alongside. With some difficulty we managed to spring off, although losing a fender in the process, which then cunningly evaded recovery by drifting under the pier. With two reefs in the main and a third of the jib rolled away we had a fine sail over the Minch, laying Loch Gairloch close hauled on starboard and making the 40-mile crossing in just over six hours. We looked about for an anchorage, finally coming to right at the head of Loch Sheildag behind one of three small islands. This is a fine spot, sheltered from every direction, except possibly the northwest. It was pleasantly wooded and made a welcome return from the bleaker Hebrides. There was a huge gin palace at anchor with a very strange name, *Parraffin*, but I don't think she was a purveyor of that liquid!

The wind had shifted to the north and with this new direction Portree on Skye was our next day's intention. After a fine breakfast we set all sail on a glorious morning. Everything was very special; the wind was just perfect at about 17 knots from a favourable direction, the sun shone, the sea sparkled and the coast all around looked very fine. Sailing into the Sound of Raasay was as exciting as usual. The wind stirred up by the high ground of Skye came from all over the place, demanding constant attention to sheets and steering. Sometimes we had no wind and then 25 knots!

Portree is the principal harbour on Skye and used to be much busier with shipping but I suppose the bridge has taken its toll – no pun intended! Even the toll on the bridge has now been discontinued. Some of the crew rowed ashore to attend to the commissariat, always a number one priority on *Ceres*. They returned with a large bag of prawns and expectant smiles on their faces.

The weather gods were still kind to us and allowed us another great sailing day over the Inner Sound to Plockton. This is a wonderful place to lie at anchor. There is always something happening and today was race day for the local dinghies. I believe one class is called the Plockton One Design. There are several visitors' buoys and you are on trust to pay at one of the shops or hotels. Plockton is one of our favourite places and we could easily spend a week just watching the comings and goings, whilst the provisioning opportunities ashore are very good.

However the next morning we sailed off our buoy, beat to Kyle Akin and under the Skye Bridge, which never looks high enough! Isn't this the same with all bridges when viewed from a boat? A strong head wind plus a following tide stirred the waters in Kyle Rhea and a frustrating and fluctuating wind right down the Sound of Sleat made us alternate between beating or motorsailing, but once past Eigg we had a fine sail into Tobermory. We only saw four yachts underway all day; this is high summer!

We arrived at 2200 and were busy preparing supper when there was a tap on the hull. I found a fellow Royal Highland member saying rather smugly that it was past 2100 and we were still wearing the ensign. Well of course he was right, but as he had been in Tobermory for the past few days I thought it a bit rich. We left Tobermory under sail and enjoyed the Sound of Mull on a lovely bright morning. There was some excitement as we rounded Duart Point with wind against tide. This is an extraordinary patch of water. The tide races and currents, although clearly charted, almost always catch you out when sailing south. I suppose that is why you nearly always see yachts motoring round the point. But you may as well have a motorboat if you are going to do that!

We made the entrance to Loch Spelve and Geoff sailed us in whilst I was off watch. It is very narrow and under sail care is needed. It was difficult to stay below but good for my crew to con us in and they did so very competently bringing us up to anchor in the northwestern arm. John and I went ashore to the mussel farm and came back with perhaps rather too many. The farm is always willing to sell mussels and they are very reasonably priced.

Our last day afloat was 28 June. It was a lovely day, as long as you did not want to sail. The water was as calm as the proverbial millpond. We left under power and once out into the Firth of Lorne raised sails, more in hope than expectation. We sailed, then drifted with the tide, then sailed a while. In this manner we went west about Scarba because Michael had never been through the Corryvreckan. It was about half ebb as we approached the Great Race and even though there was little wind, the waters fairly boiled and at one point our GPS gave a speed over the ground of 13.6 knots!

Miraculously the wind filled in and we sailed over to the Dorus Mhor, tame by comparison, but nevertheless still swirling away. We came into Loch Craignish and anchored in Bagh na Cille on the west shore for lunch. This is a fine spot about a mile in from the Dorus Mhor and is little used. Reluctantly we hauled up the anchor for the last time and slowly sailed the last three miles to our berth at Ardfern. I think we achieved all we set out to do. We sailed a lot, we ate a lot, we drank a lot and we laughed a lot. And we saw some new parts of Scotland's magic coastline. We decided that it really was, to use a well-known RCC phrase, *Cruising Without Fuss*!

Ceres is a Hallberg-Rassy 45. She was built for Jim Pitts in 1990

SMALL PIRATES TO THE CARIBBEAN

by Anna Brunyee

This voyage was awarded the Irish Cruising Club Decanter

Marguerite is a 53-foot ex-Bristol Channel pilot cutter built in 1893. We bought her in March 2000. Four years, two boys (Jonathan and Matt-matt) and a new keel later, Rob and I decided to take a year and cross the Atlantic.

The deadline of reaching Brest for the six-day festival for traditional boats, starting on 9 July 2004, was only just reached. The house was emptied and sorted for holiday lets. The boat was filled and chaotic. Miraculously we were only two days late at Brest. Jonathan enjoyed his fifth birthday at the festival with a trip to the nearby aquarium. He was suitably impressed that someone had laid on spectacular fireworks for him and even managed to stay awake until midnight to enjoy them.

Siobhan (now 23) had joined us in the summer for each of the previous four years (including last summer in the boatyard) and planned to be with us for the year. Being good with the boys, an excellent sailor and happy to get stuck into any job she was a somewhat useful crew. Various other friends came and went during the year but to have Siobhan always around was great – at least someone knew where everything was stowed!

From July to November we cruised down to the Algarve. Rob kept up his work in the Merchant Navy, two weeks away and two weeks on *Marguerite*. In the times he was away Siobhan, the boys and I explored Bayona, Cascais and the Guardiana River settling into boat life and trying to get on top of the endless job list.

Bayona was the start of Alfredo's wonderful rally, which we thoroughly enjoyed. This took us on a ten-day cruise of the Rias and included special permission to land on Isla de San Martiño in Islas Ciés and on Isla Sálvora off Ria Arosa. The boys met and enjoyed playing with Hugh and Jenny Clay's Matthew. Back in Bayona Rob returned to work and we continued the maintenance, enjoyed the castle and small beaches, took bus then train to Santiago do Compostela up in the hills and camped on the beautiful and sandy Islas Ciés for a bit of a change.

Rob returned on 9 September with Jonathan and Brenda and we set off south. The west coast of Portugal we found extremely interesting, historical and conveniently littered with a good supply of beaches and play areas. We mostly day sailed to Cascais with strong northwesterly winds falling light or calm over the week. We stopped first at Viana do Castelo (small busy marina with a tight entrance), then Leixöes (good harbour anchorage though the marina was closed) and visited Porto by bus before sailing overnight to Peniche. Just inside the harbour entrance at Peniche there are some pontoons, reputedly subject to swell, but with no room at that time for us. We took the only alternative we could find – a fishing boat steel mooring buoy. The fishing boats are tied up to the new quays, which seemed only for their use. We survived the steel buoy, enjoyed the nearby sandy beach and left for Cascais the next day.

We treated ourselves to a night in the new large (rather expensive) marina before anchoring in the bay while Rob returned to work. The weather was calm and hot although it was the last week of September. The boys, Siobhan and I really enjoyed our time here. Cascais has all facilities including a particularly large supermarket, a nearby park and maritime museum, beaches plus easy 30-minute train links to Lisbon. We spent several days in Lisbon. The maritime museum was a favourite with the boys as well as Siobhan and me, as it was particularly well laid out with a lot of models and maps. We started our study of the Discoverers here, finding further references to the Portuguese explorers at various points on our route especially the Henry the Navigator's navigation school on Punta de Sagres, close to Cape St Vincent.

We took a two-hour bus trip into the hills to the north of Cascais to Sintra, the Portuguese royalty's summer retreat. It was wonderful with a Moorish castle, palace, gardens, a siege engine exhibition and a toy museum. Plenty to keep the boys busy for two days afterwards filling their scrapbooks. Jonathan and Mattmatt were sad to leave Cascais when Rob returned with Greg and Theresa. They had made several friends among the 30 or so anchored yachts, even learning a word of two of German and Dutch along the way.

We headed south in light westerly winds to Sessimbra, a lovely town with a small fishing harbour and fairly exposed anchorage, before sailing overnight around Cape St Vincent to Alvor. One or two recently placed buoys helped us up the channel to a rather tight anchorage off the town. It was disconcerting to find everyone here speaking good English after several weeks attempting to make ourselves understood with our poor Portuguese. After a day we sailed along the coast overnight to Tavira, a lovely old town a mile up a river from the sea. The anchorage is just in from the sea where two rivers meet but there is little space or depth,

Sorting, checking and stowing stores

Marguerite needing a little over eight feet. After three attempts we managed to anchor clear of other boats, without obstructing the passage of a regular dredger and without going aground...just! As well as the town there is good walking across the spit of land protecting the harbour to a long sandy beach on the seaward side. We had an evening barbecue here before Greg and Theresa left.

Two days later Rob left us anchored on the border between Spain and Portugal at Alcoutim, 20 miles up the Guardiana River. Information on the river was limited but after ascertaining that the road bridge just up river of the Spanish town of Ayamonte was 22 metres (we need 19.5) we proceeded upstream. Advice of 'follow the water flow and avoid where the tributaries join' seemed to work.

Nearly three weeks later Siobhan and I had moved the boat back down to the marina at Vila Real de San Antonio, just five miles in from the sea on the Portuguese side. Rob arrived back laden with 'things', mostly for *Marguerite*, along with our crew for the Caribbean: his eldest son David (20), his cousin's son Peter (21) and his girlfriend Laura plus our friend Sally Visick, taking time out from family life and her business to sail the Atlantic.

Siobhan's and my efforts of re-stowing and space creation (with boys helping?) were put to the test as somehow everyone and everything slowly disappeared below. A couple of days later on 10 November we set off

westwards along the coast towards Lagos. Our shakedown turned into a shake-up in the night when a sudden strong head wind tossed us all about a bit. Not such a bad thing at this stage even if it did add to the list of things to be secured more securely!

Lagos was a handy spot for last minute stores, to knock more jobs off the list and enjoy the nearby beach. Rob and David completed a pole for booming out the staysail that proved invaluable. Our idea of making a square sail on twin poles had come to nothing but this little thirteen foot pole proved its worth, fitting our larger staysail and also working well with the heavier and flatter smaller staysail. It was attached to the 'contraption', a three-foot pole it could slide up or down that was clamped to the mast and the gooseneck fitting. The pole then clipped to a separate sheet put on the staysail and led outside the shrouds. Once set up the only way to remove the pole or gybe was to drop both pole and sail on deck. This proved very easily and safely done by one person if necessary. We had worried about dipping our long boom in the sea in the swells but in the end the passages in the trade winds were relatively quiet.

Sunday 14 November, 1700. 'Leaving Lagos and Portugal' noted in the log by Jonathan. This is what we had worked all summer for. We felt fairly confident in the boat but before we left Cornwall I had had all sorts of concerns about the boys. What if they became ill at sea or hurt themselves even if they did not fall overboard? How best to entertain them and manage to cover the basics of schoolwork? I had originally thought it might be better for everyone if they and I flew to the Caribbean.

By the time we left Lagos I had met other cruising families, including North Americans who had crossed to Europe during the summer and had observed the boys adapt to living aboard over four months. There were moments of worry and despair but in general they learnt to make the best use of what space they had and to make the most of each other. At this stage Mattmatt still asked when we were going back to Quarry House. It was not until we were part way up the Caribbean island chain and he was approaching four that he seemed really to start taking an interest and to be involved in all that was going on. At about this time his and Jonathan's relationship took off too and their play and imaginary games were brilliant to observe, to the extent that often they were not interested in going ashore as it would interrupt what they were doing. By November however, Jonathan had been very closely involved and taken a big interest in all the preparations from buying, cleaning, stowing and listing food, securing things, making space for extra water and so on. I felt that it would have been too much of a disappointment for him not to have then done the passage, so off we all sailed.

The five-day passage south to the Canary Islands was a brilliant introduction to ocean sailing especially for Peter and Laura who had not really sailed before but were full of enthusiasm. The winds were mostly northeast F3-4, falling light or even calm at times. The pole was tried and its sheet leads sorted out, Rob and Sally started practising sights, two small turtles were seen (identified as hawksbills in Siobhan's book) and we caught a perfect-sized tuna as we came up onto the Canaries shelf approaching Graciosa. At this point the wind became south to southeast and our planned anchorage on the south side of Graciosa was untenable. The harbour looked busy and rather small so we nosed into a sandy bay on the Lanzarote coast (no obvious name on our chart). The beach was lovely, the sea warm and the tuna delicious – not a bad start.

The next afternoon, 20 November, we left for an overnight passage to Tenerife. The wind was calm so apart from a stop for a swim we had to motor all the way to Marina del Atlántico at Santa Cruz. The marina facilities were poor but it was useful and being close to the city centre was popular with all. We had arranged a one-day lift out at the small boatyard of Varaderos Anaga at the head of the Dársena Pesqueira (fishing dock) three miles to the north. It seems that you cannot spend a night here easily as the marina is for locals and the boatyard has just one pontoon. However, they were friendly and helpful and lifted *Marguerite's* 43 tons skilfully for a four hour blitz on a couple of leaky seams and a coat of antifouling. (Their showers were much better than the ones at Marina del Atlántico too.)

This done, it was on to La Gomera on 26 November to finish stocking up and wait for the rather odd weather to do something more normal (preferably to go into the northern quadrant as a change from the persistent southeast to southwest winds). We enjoyed La Gomera with its fresh fruit and vegetable market, helpful and friendly marina with good facilities, interesting small museum and its link with Columbus. You can see the well where his ships filled with water. We also had a fun day out in a hire car, or rather bus as there were nine of us including the boys.

We left on 1 December and decided to head south to the Cape Verde Islands, as the mid-Atlantic weather still looked variable and light. This was a popular decision with David and Peter as Ilha do Sal is apparently a good surf spot and in anticipation of surf somewhere they had brought boards along!

During the six-day passage the wind went from northwest F3-4 to a good F6 from east-northeast. The beam seas were particularly uncomfortable for 24 hours and we reduced the mainsail further than ever before on the roller reefing gear. On the last day we saw flying fish and several joined the watch in the cockpit in the rough seas. A turtle was spotted and a rather large fish (we assume) took off with the end of our fishing line. We anchored in the afternoon of 7 December in Baia da Palmeira, the main anchorage on Sal. A small village of squat one-storey houses and cobbled streets sat at the northern end of the small bay where a breakwater had been built. The land around looked rocky and arid. We joined the queue at the village water tank to fill our cans, which we used for laundry and showers and then refilled for the same on the next leg. Rubbish seemed to be dumped by the harbour where it was sorted and either recycled or burnt in a 40-gallon drum by a group of local women. Police and immigration were very friendly and Zidare, a local guy who made his living helping visiting yachts, showed us their location and changed some euros for us so we could pay their fees. There were some small shops and daily at 1700 bread was delivered to a couple of women who sold it in the square. For anything else you waited on the edge of the village for a high speed ride in the bus to the main town, Espargo, about ten minutes away.

We thoroughly enjoyed our three days in the harbour which included some surfing for David and Peter and an interesting meal which Zidare's mother-in-law cooked for us and the crews of four other boats, for a set fee per head. However the difference between the development round the surf beach in the south of the island and the village of Palmeira was rather alarming. We were not sure what the future holds for this island.

On 10 December we lifted the anchor, secured the deflated dinghy on deck next to the hard dinghy (mostly full of 40 gallons of water in small cans), hoisted the main and jib and headed west to southwest with a pleasant north-northeast F3-4. Sally was in danger of missing her Christmas Eve flight back to Northern Ireland from Tobago. As it turned out

'Rob determined not to miss the opportunity to become proficient at sun and star sights'

she did miss it as the winds, though easterly, were light even dropping to calm for the last four days of what turned out to be an 18-day passage.

The crossing was relatively comfortable and uneventful. The pole was put to good use and we sailed most of the way goose-winged with main, topsail and staysail set. We consumed a fair number of flying fish and one dolphin fish, which did not manage to get away. Rob and Sally had time to become proficient astronavigators, the others consulting the GPS for 'miles to go'. With a larger than usual crew we set up a watch system with one person not standing a watch and being responsible for feeding us all, then getting a full night in their bunk. This proved popular and we all ate remarkably well. We usually work a five-person rolling watch system with two people on at any one time. Each person is awake for four hours and off for six. My job as the seventh adult was to keep the boys occupied and to fill in where needed. Each person also had a daily job. Sally updated the chart and organised happy hour and Siobhan took the French forecast. David checked for chafe and adjusted halyards. Rob was responsible for the batteries being charged either by the towing generator or the engine. Peter and Laura had the un-enviable task of sorting fruit and vegetables so we had a regular supply.

As we sailed south and west heat became a problem below especially sleeping in the unventilated double bunks. Bodies started appearing on deck or on the saloon floor at night in an attempt to find a breeze. Mattmatt was more comfortable under the saloon table than in his bunk above Jonathan. During the day we rigged a sheet to shade the cockpit and when the swell eased, blew up our second inflatable and filled it with seawater for all to cool off!

As the wind died we realised Sally would definitely miss her flight (she reached home on New Year's Eve instead) and we would be at sea for Christmas Day. The boys had a great time making Christmas decorations, a crib and crackers and everyone helped turn the mast below decks into a Christmas tree. Father Christmas was sent a message in a bottle and there was some concern he would not fit down the diesel stove chimney, but at least it would not be on! There was also debate as to which watch was most likely to see his sleigh!

We all had a very enjoyable day. The more athletic leapt into the sea to grab a fender on a long rope towing behind before we stopped to check the engine and for all to have a swim. After failing to catch another fish we roasted the last of the potatoes with tinned steak followed by a Christmas pudding Sally had miraculously thought to buy in Santa Cruz. We shared various presents, pulled our crackers and generally lay around the deck passing around a large tin of sweets that appeared from somewhere. All very normal but particularly stress free.

From 19 December we had started seeing more wildlife, the red-billed tropicbirds being the most striking. There were a few dolphins then a lone (young?) whale that played around the boat, barrel-rolling and eyeing up those watching in the rigging. Quite spectacular. The last few nights of the passage were lovely with a full moon. The boys and I were now sleeping on the foredeck, which we all enjoyed.

Twenty-four hours of cloud meant that we did not sight land until 2230 on 27 December. Jonathan was determined to see us arrive and was woken at 0200. He joined in as we gybed for the anchorage in Man o' War Bay on Tobago's north coast. The anchor was dropped at 0445 (ships time) on 28 December. The sweepstake was won by Siobhan who was the most pessimistic as we left the Cape Verde Islands! It was lovely to sit in the cockpit and share a celebratory bottle from Gavin and Georgie McLaren (*Margaret Wroughton*), generously given back in July for safe arrival. Some chocolate and crisps were rustled up and handed round by Jonathan, still wide-awake.

We woke some time later to daylight, lush green scenery, birds, boats and fishermen leaving and arriving along the beach. The community was strung out along the shore and back into the hills a little. We all headed ashore to check in and explore. Customs and immigration are conveniently together and close by the police station. We managed to change some US dollars for Trinidad and Tobago ones in a shop (there is no bank) and all met up at Jane's kitchen. This was a small wooden building with a tiny kitchen on the beach where we found excellent food.

During the next two days David, Peter and Laura set off to explore Tobago and look for surf before they had to head home. Sally also went home to celebrate New Year with her family. Rob, Siobhan, the boys and I found ourselves alone. At this point it started to rain – and we got to know Charlotteville well. We settled into a different routine for island cruising and once the rain stopped (or rather we gave up after two weeks and moved north to Grenada) things picked up.

Despite the rain Tobago was well worth the visit as the people are very friendly and the island full of interest and wildlife. By the time we had been in Charlotteville two weeks we were known to many as we went around with Jonathan and Mattmatt. The new library was fantastic (especially in the rain) and shops were adequate with the daily fish market and the killing of a bullock at New Year as extras. Jane's kitchen was voted the best place of all being, like everything in Tobago, very good value.

However time goes too fast and we had set ourselves quite a task to reach the Virgin Islands by Easter and head back to Antigua for the Classic Yacht Regatta in mid-April. It was different cruising with the boys. The Grenadines and the volcanic islands of Grenada and St Vincent are long time favourites of mine. Despite its being a winter of light trade winds the swell still found its way around the islands. The beaches were fantastic and popular but the swell at the water's edge put the boys off swimming. We had not managed to get them to be confident swimmers

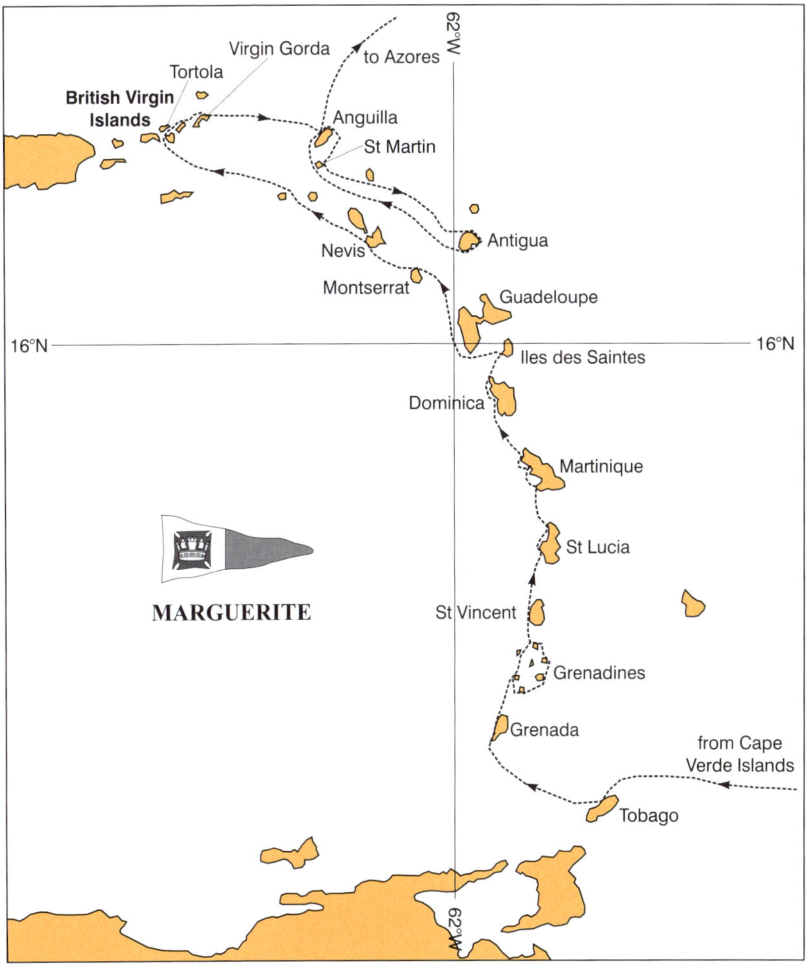

before we left. The light trade winds did give us easier passages north, often overnight, though we did motor more than we had expected.

Highlights in the Grenadines included Tyrell Bay on Carriacou. Here there was a calm beach and mangroves plus local and cruising children to play with. There is also a good small boatyard with a 50-ton hoist and some pontoons. Sandy Island, on Carriacou's west side, is a lovely spot with a brilliant sheltered snorkelling pool protected by a reef of washed-up broken coral. Sadly the off-lying reef looks as if it has mostly died and the palms have been washed or blown away. Efforts to regenerate the vegetation have been made. Hopefully the island will manage to hang on.

Bequia is a very pleasant island. The boys went to a small school and pre-school here for a week, which they loved and where they would have liked to stay longer. The Sunshine school is independent, follows a Canadian system and actively encourages visiting children to join them even if only for a week.

Friends Diccon and Jan (who have pilot cutter *Peggy*) joined us in Bequia. While the boys and I stayed on the island they sailed with Rob and Siobhan to St Vincent. From the anchorage at Wallilabou (the set for *Pirates of the Caribbean*) they climbed the Soufrière volcano at the north end of the island. This was a highlight for everyone though not for the faint hearted, as the 3000-foot mountain has to be climbed from sea level.

We re-joined in Marigot Bay, St Lucia, on 19 February, Siobhan's birthday. Marigot Bay is famous for having hid the whole English fleet, with palm fronds in their rigging, while the pursuing French sailed past. As we sailed up through the islands we became interested in their history. There are forts at Pigeon Island at the north end of St Lucia, Fort Shirley at Portsmouth, Dominica and Fort Napoleon in the French-owned Iles des Saintes, not to mention Nelson's Dockyard in Antigua and HMS *Diamond Rock*. This was fortified with cannons, somehow hauled up its rear vertical 570 feet, and commissioned just a stone's throw from the shores of French-held Martinique. The British held the rock for 18 months from early 1804 before Villeneuve was sent to re-take it. Nelson chased Villeneuve from France but went to Trinidad by mistake. It was shortly after this that the two faced each other in the Battle of Trafalgar.

History lessons were interspersed with geography as first at St Pierre on Martinique and then in Montserrat we saw the devastation caused by volcanic eruption. St Pierre was the commercial and cultural centre of this part of the Caribbean, was known as Little Paris and had 30,000 inhabitants. In 1902 the nearby Mont Pelée erupted and wiped out the city. It has never really recovered and the capital of Martinique is now Fort de France, more centrally placed and with a larger, more sheltered harbour.

In Montserrat the Soufrière volcano erupted between 1995 and 1998. This volcano is above the capital Plymouth at the southern end of the island. The flows of ash and lava completely covered the town and changed the shape of the coastline but with warning the town was evacuated and no one lost their lives. You now have to anchor in Little Bay, in the northwest of the island, where customs and immigration have re-located. Most of the other services are nearby and consideration is being given to building a new town. However around 7,000 of Montserrat's 11,000 population have left.

We were taken on a fascinating tour of the island by Sam in his taxi. We were able to go towards the southern end and look down on the

Leaving the Caribbean May 2005

devastation. There are large tracts of land near the volcano that have been evacuated even though they were not destroyed. These areas are not yet considered safe so are just abandoned and the houses are starting to deteriorate. This gives a rather eerie feel. Hopefully this lush and rather beautiful area can be opened up before long and some will be able to return to their houses – and catch some of the wild pigs and chickens.

After two days we moved north to Nevis using the engine again. The weather was still quiet. We anchored off the quay at the capital Charlestown, moving a mile north the next day to anchor off the lovely sandy Pinney's Beach. History lessons returned with a visit to the Nelson museum. Nelson's wife Fanny was from Nevis. We also filled in some of *Marguerite's* history. Les Windley rescued her from the Hamble mud in the 1970s, sailing to the Caribbean a few years later where he stayed, selling her in 1991.

By now it was 19 March, nearly Easter and the time Edward (Rob's 17-year old number two son) was to join us in the Virgin Islands for his Easter holiday. We left that evening and 24 hours later anchored in the dark off Norman Island, British Virgin Islands (one of the few times we used our radar). We had a lovely sail with a northeast F3-4 sending

Marguerite along at five to six knots with all sail set. This was much enjoyed by Siobhan, Rob and I as we took our watches during the night.

The next day we moved to Sopers Hole at the west end of Tortola to clear in. Procedures here seemed particularly rigorous and quite expensive if you want to use the National Park's mooring buoys by the good snorkelling sites. We enjoyed the British Virgin Islands for two weeks collecting Edward from the airport by anchoring 100 yards off the end of the runway at Trellis Bay at the eastern end of Tortola. The winds settled into the east around F3-4 allowing us some very enjoyable short sails between islands. We found a variety of anchorages mostly with lovely sandy beaches and no swell.

We returned to Trellis Bay to collect Phil and Gillian from Cornwall and left from Virgin Gorda on 6 April. It was lucky the easterly trade winds failed to blow allowing us a quiet motor rather than the anticipated 80-mile beat to Anguilla. The anchorage at Road Bay and village of Sandy Ground strung along the shore were much enjoyed. The local boats are quite something being 28 foot on deck with 40 or 60-foot masts, depending on conditions. Conditions also dictated crew numbers and the number of bags filled with sand placed as ballast once the boats are hauled down the beach and launched.

Anguilla is northwest of Antigua and we had hoped for a northeasterly wind. However, we got a southeasterly and had to take Edward to St Martin to catch a plane, as we were not going to make his flight from Antigua in time. We left the next evening once the wind had eased a little and had a fairly uncomfortable motorsail to Jolly Harbour on Antigua's west coast. We had arranged a two-day lift out, only enjoyed by the boys who spent most of the time in the small Avon paddling pool. With *Marguerite* looking very smart we sailed around to Falmouth Harbour in time for the start of the Classic Yacht Regatta.

Here we were suddenly surrounded by lots of yachts, pontoons, chandlers, shops, bars and people. We soon got into it all and had three great days racing, supplementing our crew with Colin, from Cornwall, and friends we had met during the winter who came to Antigua. These included another previous owner Scrim (a scrimshaw artist) and a Dominican boat builder. The winds blew up to F4-5 giving some great sailing and a wonderful spectacle of all the boats including two J-class.

The boys enjoyed the racing but enjoyed more the novelty of being alongside for several days. We were first on pontoons in Falmouth Harbour courtesy of the Antigua Yacht Club Marina then stern to at Nelson's Dockyard in English Harbour. In the Dockyard they built up enough confidence to take themselves off to the museum or nearby bakery and even on one occasion to the bar to order themselves a drink. *Marguerite's* 112th birthday fell part way through the regatta and was celebrated with a deck full of people and plenty of music – and rum.

However all good things come to an end and as Phil and Gillian left and Luke and Liz joined it was time to sort everything for the passage home. Even after the short time we had been in the islands, about four months, there were a lot of goodbyes. We enjoyed regularly sharing anchorages with David and Peta Kimber (*Moon Song*) and exchanging chat, laughs and drinks. We finally said goodbye to Colin, leaving Siobhan, Liz and Luke with us for a shakedown sail to Anguilla. The local boats were racing over the weekend and we thought it would be a fitting finale to stop there before we left for the Azores. Luke and Liz had done a reasonable amount of sailing before and everyone settled into a watch routine well. The 120 miles were not very pleasant with sloppy seas, showers and cloud. The weekend made up for this. Both Siobhan and Liz found boats to race on in the yacht classes. After final fresh stores, spending our last East Caribbean dollars and saying goodbyes to several friends who had also sailed to Anguilla, we finally left at 1700 on 10 May.

The boys were surprisingly happy and relaxed about the prospect of time at sea. The boat really was their home now. Also on passages they get a lot of Mum and Dad's attention. On this one we got through two more *Swallows and Amazons* books. Luke and Liz settled in well. Liz was entertainments officer, thinking up plenty of reasons for parties at happy

On the wind for two weeks as we head towards the Azores

hour on our route back. She also had the boys in her bunk teaching them songs as she practiced the penny whistle. Luke excelled at Lego much to Jonathan's delight and between them they built some amazing things. As everyone was fairly experienced we did watches on our own with two hours on, six off during the day with eight off at night when I did watch at midnight. Everyone took turns cooking the evening meal and the boys and I mostly made bread and lunch.

The trip to the Azores took 23 days, 14 of which were on the wind with the strength varying from F3 to F6-7. Our track was north turning slowly to the east just before it looked as though it would be sensible to stop in Bermuda. The first hurricane, Adrian, was forecast on 19 May. The American NOAA forecasters predicted it would track to Bermuda. Luckily this did not materialise. It was interesting, though not very helpful, to realise that the weather was behaving oddly again. In his forecast and chat with cruisers on the SSB radio Herb admitted that none of the models agreed with each other and the weather was hard to forecast. The Caribbean weather centre's forecaster was equally mystified. Their skills however did allow them to predict that Adrian would fizzle out rather than head north.

Mattmatt's fourth birthday was 22 May and the wind increased to F6-7. Neither boy was at all concerned about the motion but they were upset to have spray over them every time they ventured into the cockpit. The requested chocolate cake never made it to the complete stage and was eaten in bowls as sponge and sauce. *Marguerite* sails herself well on the wind and can also be easily set up on most points with a rope on the tiller. We blessed the Appledore roller reefing gear as we rolled the main in and out around the boom to keep her balanced and driving in these conditions yet comfortable below.

There was much joy on 24 May when the wind eventually went into the northwest coinciding with a halfway party. Rob produced a bow tie and got out his accordion while Liz sang her own version of a well known sea shanty. From then on we had mostly free winds, mainly from southeast to southwest and at last started covering the miles to the Azores.

We arrived at Horta on the island of Faial in the early hours of 3 June and anchored in the harbour, with a forecast southerly gale close behind us. In daylight the greenness of the island was quite startling after the more arid Caribbean islands. We all loved the Azores and our 18 days among them are almost worth a log of their own. Suffice to say we visited Pico by ferry (Liz even climbed Pico itself) before sailing on to Terceira with our new crew Chris settling in well.

We went to the harbour of Praia da Vitória and hid in the new fishing harbour from a southwesterly gale. The marina is a bit exposed in such conditions and the pontoons a little light for us. Once the wind eased we could not stay in the fishing harbour and went to the marina. The manager was extremely friendly and spoke good English. It was he who

30
13

Harbour at Vestmannaeyjar (Shepton)
Previous page: *Iseult* at speed off Falmouth (Bourne)
Sisimuit, Greenland's second largest settlement (O'Grady)

Mina[2] outside Vadstena (Barker)

The restored mediaeval crane at Gdańsk (Parkinson)

Flight of eight locks at Berg, Göta Canal (Barker)

The Pritchard-Barrett family

organised our berth in the gale rather than have us anchor in the bay. Everything in the Azores was very reasonable including car hire. We hired a minibus for a day and enjoyed the island including the other main town, Angra de Heroismo. This is where the Portuguese discoverers stopped to do repairs and stock up on their way home.

We did the same before squeezing in a 24-hour visit to the small island of Graciosa a day's sail to the north. Here we visited another volcano, going down inside. Nearby the lava had followed a weakness horizontally before flowing out and down the volcano, leaving behind partly exposed round lava tubes in the ground. After a lovely walk back to the anchorage at Vila da Praia we had a meal aboard and left for Falmouth as the sun was setting. This was 21 June.

The forecast was for a large high to develop between us and Britain so we had made sure our diesel tanks and cans were full. In the end this did not happen and after good southwesterlies for the first 24 hours the wind went into the north, varying from northwest to northeast for the next week. This was slightly frustrating as progress was slow as we tried to go north or at least not too much to the east. Sometimes it looked on the chart as though *Marguerite* did not want to go home and was trying to return west. Persistence eventually paid off and on 28 June the wind went into the southwest. It then oscillated from southwest to northwest and from F3 to F6 as we romped off towards the Western Approaches.

The wind died as we approached the Lizard and we spent a very pleasant last night at sea sailing slowly towards Falmouth in the lee of the Lizard peninsula. It allowed us to savour our return to the Fal and reflect on the last year. We were all on deck, except Mattmatt cosy in his bunk, as what seemed a very cold dawn broke as we passed St Anthony lighthouse. We drifted in to anchor in Falmouth Harbour at 0740 on 4 July.

THE ART OF CRUISING: COWES TO IRELAND BY WAY OF CHERBOURG AND THE ISLES OF SCILLY

by Colin Ford

Nandisa was gale-bound in Glengarriff and by way of diversion Marylyn and I decided to take the bus to Bantry rather than trust to the uncertain anchorage behind Whiddy Island. A literary festival was closing with Seamus Heaney signing books and Mary Kenney busy behind the bookshop's counter. The tourist office leaflet *What's on in West Cork* indicated other arts festivals and that set the pattern for our cruise.

Earlier more prosaic matters had occupied us. The passage from Cowes to Cherbourg had been cold and grey with a mean little following breeze which pointed up the benefits of the new flame-safe cooker. After provisioning at a wine warehouse we departed at 0600 on 2 June in foggy conditions. Our intention was to take the early west-going eddy to the Raz and so catch all the ebb and be in the West Channel for the weak flood. Our destination was the Fastnet Rock, the Isles of Scilly or Falmouth, as the weather served. This timing can give a bumpy ride across to Alderney and so it did. The wind died three miles north of Braye. Being sucked into the Swinge or drifting into the shipping lane did not appeal so the engine was started, and stopped. Oh no! The new filters were filthy with black treacle. Hang the expense and ask the harbourmaster to arrange a tow into Mainbrace Marine. The lifeboat was crew training and with no fuss tweaked us in. Over the next few days Steve sorted us out and roundly told me off while selling me some de-bugging stuff.

We had a sunny, rolling passage to Falmouth. The forecast on 10 June had too much north in it for the Fastnet. This time it meant what it said so we bore away for St Marys. The course now passed close by Wolf Rock and a good photo opportunity as *Patricia* was hove-to with a working party on the light. On a previous unscheduled visit to St Marys our chosen mooring buoy ended up looking like a porcupine with all three boathooks jammed between the links of the heavy pickup chain. This time Marylyn stretched out on the side deck and slipped a stiff nylon line through a link, easy. We exchanged drinks with *Margaret Wroughton* who was conducting checks and research for the pilot. Poor weather kept us but it was no hardship with such lovely walks ashore.

Crookhaven has long been our preferred port of entry in southwest Ireland and after 170 miles of following wind, motoring in a foggy calm followed by a headwind, we picked up a mooring in the afternoon of 19 June. Behind schedule? No, we are retired. Walking past the church of St Brendan the Navigator we recalled a previous visit to this jolly port. We were enjoying O'Sullivan's hospitality and discussing the little church when we were offered us the loan of the large key to the building. What would we do with the key after our visit? Why, just leave it behind the bar, of course. Moving on to Bantry Bay we had a solitary anchorage in beautiful Adrigole and watched the cloud shadows changing the face of Hungry Hill. The shop closed last October but the pub's landlady kindly drove us to Peg's general store. Phil Harrington welcomed us to Lawrence Cove Marina where we made good use of all facilities. Returning from a long walk we saw *Ghoster*, the lovely 57-foot Nicholson ketch, built in 1927, being manoeuvred skilfully into a tight berth by Bent and Ulla-Britt Lyman. *Halcyon of Hebe* was also there, gearing up for some serious walking in Galway.

Church of St Brendan

Art installation at Charles Fort

With the intention of moving on west we positioned ourselves in Castletownberehaven where there are now no facilities for the visitor. A kindly shopkeeper relieved us of our compacted rubbish bag. A few trawlers are still working out of the port and we bought some excellent shellfish from the co-operative. An unhelpful long-term forecast encouraged us to stay in Bantry Bay and enjoy the company of the seals and black guillemots at Glengarriff. When conditions eased we had a beat down the bay and rolled around Mizen Head in boisterous seas. Off Brow Head Marylyn waved merrily at a fisherman until she realised he was guarding his net, which we avoided in the nick of time. Last summer Schull was very busy with the ICC cruise in company. This year *Holly* alone flew the burgee and was off to join the Classic Boat regatta at Glandore. Ashore, the Arts Festival was opened by the local TD, himself a published poet. There were paintings in the butcher's window, photographs at the pharmacy and most pubs exhibited pictures. There were poetry readings and a performance by Ed Malone, a great comic actor from Cork. In bright sunshine a rowing regatta was strongly contested with Castletownshend winning overall. It was revealed that training was apparently the secret of their success.

In fickle breezes we drifted past the Stags and the cardinal buoy marking the wreck of the bulk carrier *Kowloon Bridge*. How she came to be on that course is a mystery. Mary Ann's pub beckoned following a long dinghy ride up to the head of navigation, as the ICC Sailing Directions put it. Herons and curlews stalked the shallows. Then it was off to Glandore, avoiding Adam and hugging Eve as the pilot instructs. It was busy with the regatta but we anchored well clear of the unmarked channel, out of which we had been gently asked to move on another visit.

The big Kinsale Arts Festival was about to open and we had a nice sail for the 30 miles past the Old Head to the River Bandon. At the Charles Fort extraordinary art installations sprouted from the walls and there were more inside. We anchored off the marina but there was little swinging room so we picked up a buoy as squalls came down the river over the spring tide. There was great deal of activity ashore. We particularly enjoyed the photographic exhibition, jazz at Acton's Hotel and a thrilling Irish traditional music session. A day out by bus to Cork, 2005 City of Culture, topped off our arts cruise.

The passage back to the Scillies on 20 July was similar to the one to Ireland, a light following breeze, calm and a fresh headwind finish. We hopped home via Falmouth and Salcombe, now in mid-season and very busy. In the latter we found good anchorage in the Bag, away from the rafts on the visitors' buoys. The final port before Cowes was Cherbourg as somehow the drinks locker had almost emptied itself. *Nandisa* enjoyed a good sail home in sunshine and we thought how lovely the Isle of Wight looked from seaward.

Nandisa is a Biscay 36 ketch designed by Alan Hill and built by Falmouth Boat Construction Company in 1980.

CLOUD WALKER'S ARCTIC CRUISE TO MURMANSK

by David and Judy Lomax

Busting a gut to get to Murmansk

It was perhaps not surprising that *Cloud Walker*'s ambitious plans for a vast arctic triangle would have run into trouble sooner or later but in Tromsø in June's eternal sunlight neither of us could have predicted how dramatically they were to be frustrated. We had wintered afloat in a marina just north of the ice-free harbour and found the yacht in satisfactory fettle when we returned for a refit. The hull seemed clean after its immersion in cold water so we did not have her lifted out and after a few days of simple preparation and provisioning we were joined by our long-standing crew, Jim Reeves, and set off in threatening drizzle along the grey fjord to the north. We were aiming to reach Murmansk then to revisit Svalbard before returning to Tromsø for another winter.

The first stage started satisfactorily in spite of much motoring across a flat oily sea with glimpses through the mist of distant snow-covered peaks. Next day with a rising wind we shortened sail, horsed past Loppa and finally reached a semi-derelict quay in the harbour at Hasvik on Sørøya. Fortified by the mate's splendid dinner of whale steak and mushy peas, we then explored the windswept village and discovered that a Lebanese entrepreneur married to a local girl had bought the island's three hotels. Over Turkish coffee Ahmed told us of the German tourists who came hunting the world's biggest cod.

Next day we had a gentle 30-mile goose-wing with the spectacle of ice-riven mountains on all sides and later, from the top of the hill overlooking Hammerfest, an uninterrupted view of a new gas terminal on a nearby island. Oil company publicity notices boasted that four special tankers were being built to supply much of America's natural gas needs. However we did not have to go far to return to north Norway's rugged isolation.

Away from Hammerfest there is an air of decline in many of the coastal fishing villages. We nosed our way into the pool at Bustadhamn and found only grazing reindeer around the summerhouses. Ten years ago the island of Masøy near Nordkapp had a thriving primary school with 14 pupils. We made a detour to revisit it and met a woman delivering waffles for her fisherman husband's breakfast. She told us there were now only three children left and the school would soon be closed. There are simply no jobs. The people who bought the local fish-processing factory had gone bankrupt and disappeared. Others had given up and gone south.

Because the weather was suspect for the open sea rounding of Nordkapp, we chose to take the inside passage south of Magerøya and soon discovered that we should have paid more attention to advice about the tidal streams. For much of the Norwegian west coast tides are insignificant but here we were taught a lesson and for a couple of hours had to negotiate huge evil swirls through water that was on its way at up to 6 knots in the opposite direction. Once through this harsh looking sound with bare cliffs on either side, a brisk westerly bowled us into Honningsvåg where we tied up in the new small boat harbour. Honningsvåg survives on the passing tourist traffic visiting Nordkapp but there are still the remnants of a fishing industry and we were able to find a mechanic who could advise about a worrying leak from the innards of our engine's water pump. We did not have a spare for the culprit, a broken aft seal, so the yard called their man in Hammerfest who put one on the next plane. It was fitted and we were on our way again all within four hours.

The coast from Nordkapp to the Russian border changes in character from the grandeur of the more familiar fjords of the west. Rugged cliffs and headlands replace towering mountains. Along the shores of the Barents Sea the landscape is barren and the settlements small and isolated. Norway's Finnmark province is as big as Denmark but only has a population of 70,000. At Mehamn, we saw immigrant workers from Poland stacking dried cod, ready for shipment to Portugal. This was always the biggest trade along these shores but nowadays there are few other jobs.

In the Second World War the Germans occupied this coast, using Serbian and Russian prisoners of war as slave labourers to build fortifications and anti-aircraft batteries. We climbed the cliffs at Kongsfjord and inspected what must have been one of the loneliest of the occupier's positions. It is surrounded by steep shale cliffs and looks out towards the North Pole and the routes taken by the Murmansk convoys. You can still see the bases where the guns once stood. On a nearby cliff is the rusty hulk of a tank. When the Germans withdrew they ordered the inhabitants of every settlement to leave and then, to impede a feared advance by the Red Army, burned their houses. Kongsfjord for some reason was spared. We were able to explore an ancient wooden fish warehouse untouched for 50 years and were shown round the manager's house by one of his descendants who had restored it when he wasn't on his yacht in the Caribbean or running his business at the southern end of the Oslo fjord. Somehow in this friendly, hospitable and slightly eccentric part of the world it didn't seem surprising that he had a pony tail, tattoos and a Harley Davidson.

In another windless day we motored past the bird cliffs at Syltefjord. The noise of hundreds of thousands of sea birds was deafening. Every imaginable species was here, swooping, fighting, feeding, diving and making such a cacophony we needed earplugs. Above them all circled four stately fish eagles. However as we motored further into the fjord we noticed a worrying new sound, a sort of coffee-grinding rattle from the drive shaft. We handled the engine gently after this and decided that the only solution was to have the yacht lifted at the earliest opportunity.

The first chance was at Vardø, Norway's most easterly port on the Russian border. Judy's sister, Sally Lawson, was due to join us and arrived on schedule in a small plane. We negotiated with the owner of a huge crane who promised he would lift us onto the quay as soon as he and his crew had finished demolishing a nearby house. For two days we wandered around Vardø until the crane was available. Unfortunately its strops would only fit a fishing boat shape so in a spanking northwest breeze we set off across Varangafjord to a shipyard at Bugøynes where we'd been told there was a helpful manager and a trawler slipway.

This was a most satisfactory stop. The rattle, as we suspected, turned out to be a loose anode. A passing Finnish diver soon tightened it. He refused payment but did accept with glee a half bottle of scotch. Then Danish friends we had met the year before arrived in their Nicholson 45, *Lady of La Mancha*. We had an excellent impromptu barbecue together next to three rusting Russian trawlers that were being converted for the new Kamchatka crab trade. On Stalin's orders millions of these monster spider crabs had been transferred to the Barents Sea in the 1950s as a food source for the gulags. They were now multiplying, eating all other forms of fish life and moving west at 20 kilometres a year. A local fisherman gave us a quarter of one to sample and we then saw why it's such a delicacy in the Far East and the USA. It made a delicious starter to our arctic reunion dinner.

Next day I noticed annoying stomach pains and at first blamed the crab. But by the time we reached an anchorage on the way to Kirkenes I elected to stay in my bunk while the others dinghied ashore and climbed through a stunted wood to view the surrounding fjords and idyllic anchorage which I wasn't in any mood to appreciate. I was similarly laid low during our visit to Kirkenes where we exchanged Jim and Sally for Judy's cousin, Janet Thumim. The general advice was that my stomach pain was something the body would deal with in time and with rest and aspirin so I decided to continue towards Murmansk. It seemed perverse

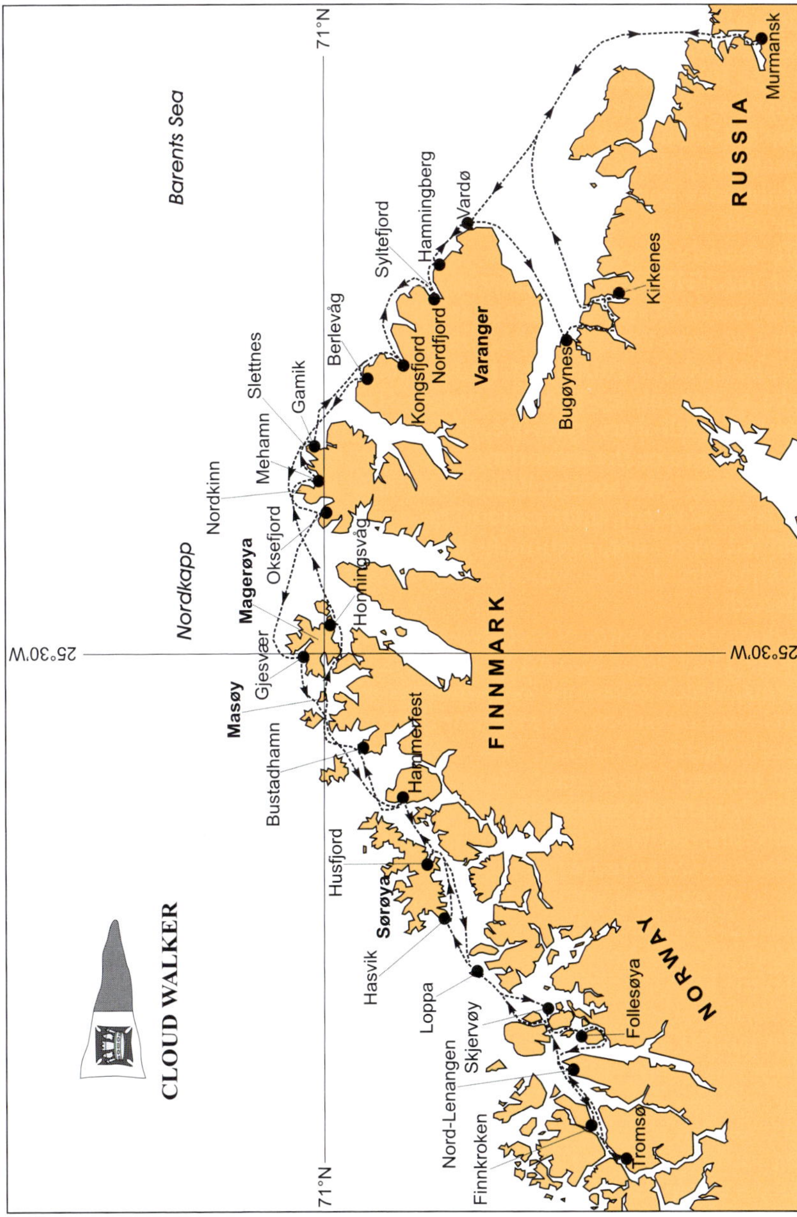
Barents Sea
71°N
25°30'W
Nordkapp
CLOUD WALKER
RUSSIA
Murmansk
Kirkenes
Bugøynes
Varanger
Vardø
Hamningberg
Syltefjord
Nordfjord
Kongsfjord
Berlevåg
Gamik
Slettnes
Mehamn
Nordkinn
Oksefjord
Magerøya
Honningsvåg
Gjesvær
Masøy
Bustadhamn
Hammerfest
FINNMARK
Husfjord
Sørøya
Hasvik
Loppa
Skjervøy
Nord-Lenangen
Finnkroken
Tromsø
Follesøya
NORWAY

having come all this way not to look round the corner. In any case we had gone to considerable trouble and expense in negotiating all the necessary permissions.

The Russian authorities wanted us to give a precise ETA and position where we intended to cross into their waters. We did this, making sure that we would stay offshore for 12 miles from the sensitive ex-military areas along the Kola Peninsula and only turn south when abeam of the Murmansk fjord. The conditions could hardly have been better, a calm sea with a gentle warmish wind and good visibility and sunlight all night. We thought of calling up on Channel 16 to announce our early arrival but the VHF was jammed with many different and apparently urgent conversations so we motored onwards down the chart's entry corridor until we were far into the harbour and only then were we challenged.

The harbour authorities told us to proceed at minimum speed and take a compulsory pilot on board. Half an hour later a large launch covered with lorry tyres steamed towards us. I was worried that this was going to be the most dangerous moment in the whole cruise but the manoeuvre was accomplished with skill and a pilot leaped cheerfully aboard. 'Captain, information,' he said, and pointed in the direction he wanted us to take, eventually leading us to a rusting pontoon next to a floating dry dock in which a vast nuclear ice breaker was being shot-blasted.

A reception party of assorted officials was waiting for us on the pontoon. They came aboard in droves and presented us with sheaves of forms, which asked us for a most comprehensive series of apparently irrelevant questions. 'We are not a cargo ship or oil tanker', I protested, 'just a yacht on holiday.' The officials were all pleasant and courteous but blamed 'the system'. From time to time they made mobile phone calls apparently seeking clarification of some point or another. Eventually after all our papers had been examined and everyone consulted we were told we were free to explore the town. A Murmansk TV crew then came aboard and asked for an interview. 'Why have you come to Murmansk?' was their first question. Later we were told there was a TV report about a boat from the Queen's Yacht Club visiting Murmansk, the first for a couple of years.

Several officials had warned us that we should not leave *Cloud Walker* unattended and that there should always be someone left on board to deter thieves. At this stage of grumbling pains I wasn't much in the mood for energetic exploration but Judy and Janet walked ashore and managed to find their way across the bridges over the sprawling railway marshalling yards and into the town centre. Later we took turns to explore the streets around the busy railway station and have showers in a luxurious suite in the main hotel. I was still in some pain and was feeling unsteady so did not venture far. Then it was time for us to leave so that Janet could catch her flight home from Vardø. Again the same army of officials

Murmansk approach

swarmed aboard and presented us with forms to record the amount of fresh water we still had in each tank and many other pieces of information. Finally the pilot came aboard and we motored out to sea past the docks and cranes and the few naval ships under way, all sending huge clouds of black oily smoke into the still blue sky, as if the engines hadn't been maintained for years – and they probably hadn't. Finally it was time for the pilot to leave. He was courteous and friendly and shook our hands before leaping across to the approaching launch, which we again managed to avoid.

It was liberating to arrive back in Vardø where there were no formalities. Sverre Kraemer and *Quest* soon joined us, fresh from Archangel and the White Sea. In a mini-meet we swapped stories of the bureaucracy we had experienced. He and Per then left for Tromsø while Judy and I considered our next moves. My grumbling stomach pains were just about tolerable but obviously not getting better. I was persuaded to postpone our departure to Svalbard and to visit the local clinic. A Serbian doctor – Norwegian medics are apparently reluctant to work up here – prescribed an antibiotic and when this had no effect advised that we should leave the yacht and fly to Kirkenes hospital where I could have tests. Sixteen days later and minus a bit of infected bowel, I was discharged to fly to Oslo with Judy who had been camping out in the nurses' hostel and to recuperate at our daughter and son-in-law's house. I will leave Judy to continue this turbulent tale.

'No wind, and no condensed milk' round Nordkapp

The silver lining to David's cloud was that I got to be skipper for the 10-day passage to return *Cloud Walker* to her winter berth in Tromsø from Vardø. My crew was Bob Shepton, who was banned from any attempt to mend the heater, and Scott Fraser, who flew from Boston. Our 0230 arrival on board (it should have been 2030) after a long bus and taxi diversion from a fog-bound flight was celebrated with Scott's malt whisky and bacon and eggs that had been on board for several weeks.

It was the first time I had sailed *Cloud Walker* without David and therefore my first official experience of being her skipper. Both crew made frequent, and usually helpful, suggestions of what I should decide and how it should be done. They had other things in common: bedroom slippers, which I had never seen on a boat before, and faith, in God if not necessarily in the skipper. Bob however was alone in his passion for condensed milk and golden syrup.

The wind for our first few days, when it blew at all, was from the northwest, from Nordkapp, which we had to round though whether by the outer route or to the south (it is on an island) was a matter of some discussion. We made gentle progress towards decision time, with leisurely hops up the bleak foreboding coast of the Varanger peninsula and across the top of Nordkinn, Europe's most northerly mainland. Bob sent David a text, 'Norway is no good. No wind, and no condensed milk.'

Our first night was spent at anchor near the top of Syltefjord, inland of Nordfjord where we had tied up on the way east. For our second night, we squeezed with a fast-flowing current through a narrow entrance into a lagoon at the head of Kongsfjord, again bypassing the harbour. It was a wonderfully tranquil unmarked anchorage, populated only by seals.

Gamvik, on the northeast corner of Nordkinn, added a new entry for the Norway cruising guide I was researching. The area northwest of Gamvik is the lowest large protrusion off the north coast. Slettnes light stands guard over rock-strewn shallows, which have claimed many an unwary ship and have been the cause of at least one death by burning when a witch was accused of wrecking three Dutch ships.

The cliffs at Kinnarodden, west of Slettnes, were a grandiose contrast. Continuing in rain into the mouth of Oksefjord, Bob was keen to invent a new anchorage behind a rocky ledge. Its anchor-holding properties looked distinctly suspect to the more cautious Scott and its shelter did not seem to the wimpish skipper to promise a good night's sleep. The surroundings of the marked anchorage, beneath steep slopes shrouded in mist a wet hour on at the head of the fjord, were surprisingly rural and gentle. There were even a few trees; the first we had seen. They were also the last.

It was cape-rounding decision time. Conditions, although damp and overcast, were ideal with a gentle wind from the north. After a detour under raucous bird cliffs to investigate an anchorage at an abandoned village – in any other wind it might have been enticing – we set course round the top. At last *Cloud Walker* was able to show Bob, and to remind Scott, how well she can sail. It was our longest passage so far, just over 50 miles round the sheer impressive cliffs of Nordkapp and the less impressive and pronounceable but more northerly Knivskjellodden. We broad reached at five knots just over half a mile off Nordkapp, almost close enough for the less trepid crew.

Just over two hours later, we had woven our way through a complex jumble of islands, quite different from the bare bluff eastern approach to the cape, and tied up outside a small fishing boat on the tourist pontoon at the busy little lagoon harbour of Gjesvær. An early start was called for next morning, not because of tide – although noticeable, this was not appreciable enough to dictate departure times – but to be sure of reaching Hammerfest during Vinmonopol and fuel dock hours. There had been much precise measurement of wine and whisky levels in our glasses each evening.

Our 50-mile mission was accomplished, mainly by motorsailing, in brilliant sunshine (at last) and with breakfasts served at intervals by Bob. It was still warm, calm and sunny when we motored out of Hammerfest,

Judy Lomax off Lyngen

having replenished our stocks and with no desire to spend a night in town. Sørøysund, between large islands west of Hammerfest, is as beautiful as any sound on the west coast, with grandiose bare mountain and fjord scenery on either side. I was pleased to be able to show Bob the 'real' Norway at last, and to remind Scott of its attractions ten years after he sailed from Svalbard with us.

The south coast of the island of Sørøya is deeply indented with small fjords, many of which are accessible only from the sea. We chose Husfjord for a night at anchor, in a pool behind a small island beneath steep mountain slopes. The temptation to squeeze on into an inner pool was resisted in the evening and aborted on the second attempt in the morning. We rose however to the secondary challenge of an alternative exit. There was just enough water at low tide between our sheltering island and a single house, wharf and landing stage to which there was no road. Northeasterly gusts poured down the hills inside the fjord but outside in the sound the wind was from the southwest, the direction in which we wanted to go.

The area between Nordkapp and Tromsø was proving once again a Navtex-free zone but David was texting me from Oslo with warnings of impending strong southwesterlies. We made an overnight stop at anchor in the open harbour on the southeast side of Loppa, a foreboding island above which an eagle was being mobbed as we approached. More eagles soared over twin mountains behind the harbour. By morning a rising southwesterly had set in. With a reef or two, *Cloud Walker* had an opportunity to show how close she could sail to the wind on her way to the shelter of Skjervøy, the biggest harbour and town (but still small) between Hammerfest and Tromsø. This time I made a better job of coming alongside. We tied up on a guest pontoon just inside the inner harbour and paid our money into the honesty box outside the boat club.

The next morning's wind was funnelling fiercely from the west directly through the sound north of Skjervøy as we battled our way west then turned south down the Lyngenfjord with two reefs and a scrap of jib. By the time we anchored between the two small low bird refuge islands of Follesøya, it was idyllically calm. More eagles soared over us. Lyngen's mountains peaks, which had been hidden by glowering cloud on *Cloud Walker*'s way east, revealed their alpine snow and glaciers. We were already several weeks past the midnight sun of midsummer.

Tromsø was in easy reach, but although it was a delivery trip none of us wanted to get there early. So we circumnavigated the island of Uløy before emerging back into Lyngenfjord, which we goose-winged down in perfect weather glorying in the sailing and the scenery. Our last (of several) fresh fish suppers was caught by Scott while we drifted with the current between the Finnkroken islands. Scott's meticulous calculations decreed exactly where the anchor should be dropped to give us swinging room should the wind change during the night. When it did indeed change, rising as it did so, we all emerged in the dark to make anxious observations. The anchor was holding, and *Cloud Walker* had pulled back to exactly the position Scott had predicted.

It was a gentle four-hour morning motor to Tromsø, where we tied up in the sun at our usual shopping spot in the middle of town for the first showers of the trip in readiness for a celebratory meal ashore. Heavy rain delayed our four-mile passage to the marina at Skattøra, where an afternoon proved just long enough to pack *Cloud Walker* up for the winter. Thanks to Scott's folding expertise, the main and jenny were packed into a smaller space than ever before, ready to be freighted to Oslo for a winter overhaul. He and Bob did an excellent joint job of winterising the engine and I was given an instant lesson in diesel and battery maintenance. All that remained was to replace the anode, which had again worked loose and was rattling unpleasantly. This was done a couple of weeks later by a friend in Tromsø, who for the second year running is keeping an eye of *Cloud Walker* during the winter.

Scott is now back on his own boat enjoying the warmth and sun of the Caribbean. Bob has revised at least part of his opinion of Norway, which still has no condensed milk. I could not have wished for better crew.

Cloud Walker is a Beneteau First 345, launched in 1985.

QUAILA'S HEBRIDEAN CRUISE, 2005

by Sandy Taggart

Quaila left Craobh Marina on 17 July and sailed to Tobermory, Coll, Canna and Barra where Sandy Taggart joined her at Castlebay. The crew was Hugh Morrison (skipper), Ian Michie and Katie Christie

Quaila took water at the pier before heading through the Fisherman's Passage to Vatersay. The Clyde Cruising Club barbecue was extremely well organised by the Commodore, his wife Elizabeth and other helpers in a sheltered corner at the north end of the beach. It did not go on too late which was fortunate as an early departure was planned for Monday morning. Andrew and Anne Fleck and the girls aboard *Malouine* joined in the festivities as well as Jen Guinness on *Alakush* and Bill and Rosemary McKean on *Siolta*.

It turned out to be a bit grey with little wind as preparations were made to sail. There was also little or no wind forecast so the skipper decided on a short leg south and then out between Sandray and Pabbay. Once the passage to the west was completed the course was set for St Kilda. The sky cleared and any wind there was almost completely disappeared. The main was left up as a steadying sail but in fact there was little or no swell. Motoring on in sunshine watching the Outer Hebrides sink below the horizon astern and to starboard it was not long before Hirta and the Stacks were spotted. There were a few fishing boats about. It comes as a surprise to find buoys in the middle of nowhere but it is the tanker route after all.

Good time was made to the St Kilda group, arriving about 1700. As the sea was slight and hardly any wind a circumnavigation of Dun Soay and Hirta was undertaken. An evening breeze filled in as *Quaila* passed round the north and east of Hirta and into Village Bay. The warden called on the VHF so the evening meal was delayed for a quick trip ashore.

We were welcomed at the pier most courteously but the news was

The main street, St Kilda

broken that the Puff Inn was out of bounds. The shop would be open shortly for a brief period. Not only could three members of the National Trust and one of the St Kilda Club not get that much prized trophy, a pint in the most westerly pub in Britain but it was also not possible to use the only pay phone as it too was out of bounds in spite of there being no mobile reception. The shop visit completed, it was the consensus of the crew to repair aboard for drinks and dinner and hope that the weather would allow time ashore the next day.

There was a bit of swell in Village Bay during the night but conditions were right in the morning to spend time ashore before a noon departure. The whole St Kilda scene is fascinating and once again the warden was most helpful. Apart from the civilian team now manning the base there were the usual National Trust work parties and a sheep monitoring team doing their periodic count of the Soay sheep. The time is probably now right for many of the military eyesores to be removed or at least covered up or made to blend in with the rest of the old buildings. Most of the native wildlife was spotted in the pleasant sunny conditions.

The wind had got up from the north and was scheduled to increase. Before heading back east an attempt was to be made to have a look at Boreray, Stac Lee and Stac an Armin. The breeze was still filling in so *Quaila* motorsailed close in to Boreray and Stac Lee. Even after the quiet weather of the previous few days the swell was high. The wind was increasing all the time so in the lee of Boreray a reef was taken in the main and the genoa set. Once clear of the land *Quaila* stormed along on a broad reach. The options were the Monach Isles, Sound of Harris or Taransay so a middle course was taken with the final decision yet to be made. The wind from the north finally settled in at between 25-30 knots and strong winds were forecast from that direction for the next few days. Half way in, Taransay got the vote and with a few rolls in the headsail a new course was set.

Large black clouds building up over the hills of Lewis and Harris did not come any further south. Having left Village Bay at midday and stooged around the stacks for a while, *Quaila* was securely anchored in Taransay off the magnificent white beach before 1900. All signs of the television programme paraphernalia have been removed but it is obviously a popular place judging by the campers and walkers in evidence. The northerly winds were cold but the evening turned out most pleasant with a lovely sunset.

Next morning the wind was fresh and cold but the sky was almost cloudless and clear. Conditions were ideal for negotiating the Sound of Harris. The pool at Rodel had been surveyed for the sailing directions by Sandy from *Starletta* in 1964 with a check-up ten years ago so an inspection was called for. The tide was not right for entry to the pool so the anchor was dropped at the head of the bay for a lunchtime break. After lunch with the tide flooding and the wind well and truly in the north a bumpy passage was endured until sheets could be eased after Scalpay to head into Loch Seaforth. Surprisingly the land killed much of the wind in the loch and the sea was flat. *Quaila* came alarmingly close to the bottom at one point before anchoring in the pool just south of the entrance to upper Loch Seaforth.

No real distances were planned for Friday as Ian was due to catch the ferry from Tarbert on Saturday morning. Starting slowly from the head of Loch Seaforth a series of soundings were taken to help the editor of the Sailing Directions. (The new CCC edition of the Outer Hebrides is excellent.) Taking passage down the loch, passing north of the large island, Katie's suggestion of lunch on Loch Claidh was jumped at. Just *Quaila*, some seals, terns, cormorants and another excellent lunch in magnificent surroundings. Cruising at its best. Crew replete and full sail set, all enjoyed a delightful downwind passage under the bridge to Tarbert where only one other yacht was anchored.

More stores were acquired ashore and a short walk to the west loch helped to loosen the 'muscle-bound shanks'.

All was set for Ian's departure on the morning ferry. As it came to view he was put ashore and *Quaila* was prepared for the sail to the Inner Sound. The breeze was still holding strong from the north and *Quaila*

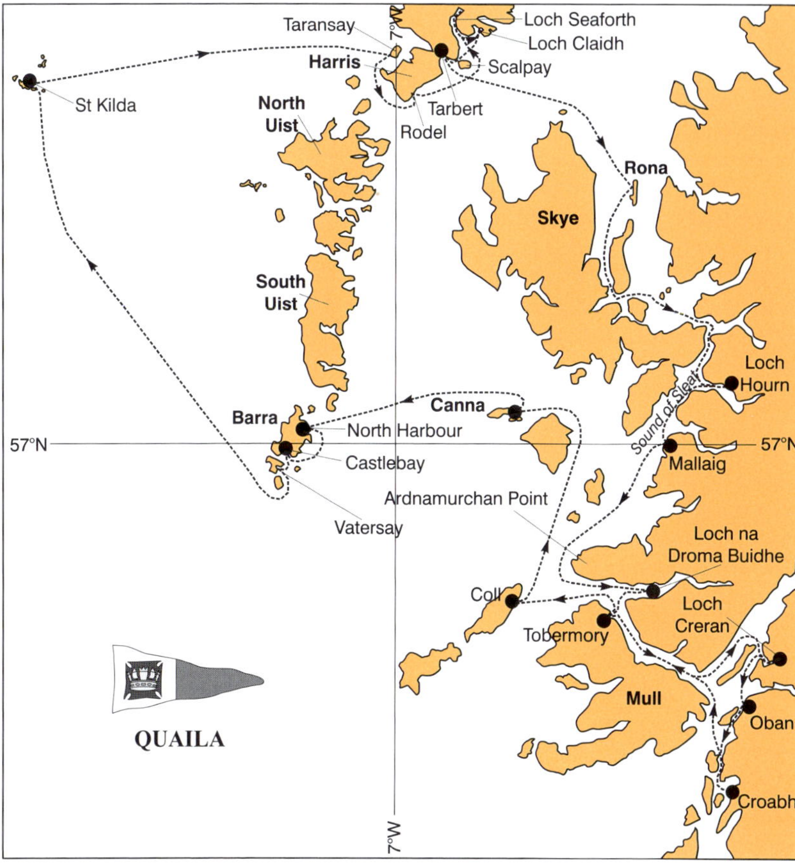

was well out from Tarbert by the time the ferry passed to leeward. Only three ships were seen in the Minch on the passage to the north of Skye. It was another fast trip and all the rough tidal spots on the chart and chart plotter came up on cue. A super sail ended in mid-afternoon at Acarseid Mhor, Rona. This pleasant and peaceful place was later invaded by yachts making many attempts to anchor. It turned out to be the Gordonstoun Summer School fleet. Laurie Mill came aboard from one of the yachts with two shivering Japanese girls who were quickly plied with warm drinks. The evening did turn out to be peaceful amongst the largest number of yachts seen together since Vatersay. The tide in Kyle Rhea was a factor for Sunday's sail so a leisurely departure for a downwind sail on another sunny day made for continued good cruising.

The skipper's calculations were perfect and after a fast sail *Quaila* entered the sound on the first of the ebb. Loch Hourn was the chosen destination and Arnisdale the anchorage. The light and the shade on the mountains were beautiful and totally belied the opinion held by many that it is a gloomy and foreboding place. There were many stags and hinds on Knoydart that morning as a slow passage was made out of Loch Hourn into the Sound of Sleat in a light breeze. On arrival at Mallaig the inner harbour was full of fishing boats so the best spot for water and fuel was in the new fishing harbour. The owner of the classic *Ada and Mary* welcomed *Quaila* alongside. It was so hot in Mallaig that the tar was melting on the roads. Honestly! The town was buzzing with holiday-makers. Amongst general replenishment of stores, some shellfish and fish were purchased for lunch and the evening meal. There can be no better cruising pleasure than a seafood lunch with wine in the cockpit rounded off with ice cream in the boiling sunshine. Could it last? Alas, not!

The forecast was not good for the next few days. Thoughts of a night in Muck gradually changed to Loch na Droma Buidhe as a pleasant passage was made towards Ardnamurchan. It hardly seemed possible that there could be such a dramatic change in the weather after the past week but during the night it came in and blew hard. The morning was still wet but with less wind. It was Sandy's birthday and he had invited the crew to join him for dinner in Tobermory that evening. We had a jaunt up Loch Sunart to Salen for lunch aboard. The rain stopped and the day cleared up. Tobermory was busy as the West Highland Week

Stac An Amin and Stac Lee, Boreray

competitors were due on the following day. A most enjoyable time was spent ashore and an excellent meal savoured in the evening.

More unpleasant weather was due on Wednesday when the fleet from Oban would be beating up the Sound of Mull. *Quaila* cleared the anchorage in good time and with a strong stern wind was past Loch Aline by the time the leaders came through. The racing fleet was having a hard beat up the sound. Attempting to enter Port Ramsay it was decided that the depth was not right. The next option was Loch Creran where the anchorage at South Shian was comfortable overnight.

The final day of the cruise was windy again from the southwest with heavy showers. Fortunately there was a short break in the weather when Sandy was dropped off at Oban to collect his car. Hugh and Katie brought *Quaila* to Croabh pushing the tide for part of the way. Sandy's journey was the more comfortable. Apart from the last three days the cruise had been carried out in excellent weather but cold at times in the northerly air stream.

Quaila is a Moody 42 built in 2000

PINCH THE BABY (AND OTHER WAYS TO FIND SAILING SOLITUDE)

by Jamie Pritchard-Barrett

Picture this – we have just found an unspoilt cove, the perfect place for the skipper, mate and junior ratings to swim, snorkel and relax in peace. The anchorage was steep-to but just shallow enough to anchor with a long line ashore and swim in glorious solitude with nothing but the usual chatter from the children as they frolicked about. It was an idyllic spot: a tiny strip of a pebble beach, a dash of turquoise on the edge of a blue sea and a spectacular view to the east of the mountains on the Greek mainland. Well worth the effort to get moored up; a place we could linger a while.

A yacht edges across the panorama, followed shortly by another then another – this one motoring flat out in the gentle following wind. We detect a change of course. Oh no! It's coming this way. They have spotted us and our little paradise. Soon a 45-foot platform of white plastic steams in, along with wash, diesel fumes and a full complement of oiled-up sun worshippers. They anchor right next to us, politely remembering to put over some fenders in case we touch. Within moments our idyllic swimming spot is awash with diving bodies and loud bobbing heads. It is the deserted beach syndrome; when you are trying to find some space people always come and camp right next door.

Within moments a day-hire dinghy comes buzzing in. 'Nudist alert!' shout the children with great hilarity. Our newest neighbours have leapt onto the beach and have stripped off, their bodies flopped like streaky bacon on the white-pebbled strand. 'Back to the boat!' I shout whilst untying the line ashore. We swim back, up anchor and move on again.

We are in the fabulous and beautiful cruising area of the Inland Sea as they call it in the Ionian Islands around Levkás but it is August and the height of the season. 'Perhaps we should re-paint the boat in camouflage and drape cam nets from the masthead, so they can't spot us in future' I suggest to Bella. Co-incidentally we are passing the cave of Papanikolis

Swinging Papageno

on the island of Meganisi where the Italian Navy reputedly hid a camouflaged submarine in the Second World War.

'We missed the opportunity to pinch the baby this time,' laughs Kiki, our 11-year-old daughter. 'Pinch the baby' has become a family joke – a euphemism for making us look like the neighbours from hell. We are embarrassed to admit that in the past we have gone to shameful practices to try to put off other yachts from mooring close by or rafting up to us. A few years ago we made the most of having a baby on board – draping the boat with children's clothing, nappies and other unmentionables to indicate to any would-be neighbours that they wouldn't get much peace with three rampaging children. A particularly undesirable-looking crowd made overtures to come alongside. 'Pinch Theo!' Bella cried. 'Get him crying – that will put them off!' Ollie (then 5) was only too delighted to tweak Theo (2) and get him roaring. It worked! The boat had second thoughts and rafted up elsewhere. How desperate we have become in our quest to find peace and solitude afloat.

Now don't get me wrong – we love meeting kindred spirits anchored up in bays anywhere in the world but this sort of holiday cruising is different. It is a bit like too many queues for the ski lift. We do rank finding some solitude away from the mad world we live in as one of the principle reasons we go cruising.

Actually we became quite good at sniffing out our own idyllic anchorages this summer in the Ionian Sea. We found Kalamos and Kastos and ports on the mainland much less crowded with some really beautiful spots. In the busier places we found that if you are prepared to anchor a distance away from the mêlée and perhaps accept a little swell you can normally find your own space. We anchored in the lee of the small harbour of the unpretentious working town of Mitikas, opposite the stunning pine clad vista of north Kalamos. It was perfect; calm, good holding and we had a fabulous and incredibly good value meal ashore and provisioned the boat cheaply the next morning.

From Mitikas we had a cracking sail in a good breeze to the perfect but undoubtedly popular One House Bay on Atokos. We hoped the lively breeze would have put off the charterers. The children whooped for joy as yet another wave smashed the starboard bow and sent spray flying, soaking us all in the cockpit. We had a good beat, shaking out not only the cobwebs but also most of our poorly stowed cabin. Boats were crammed into the bay when we got there. They looked entombed by an entanglement of lines and crossed anchors after the gusty night. We started skirting the island. We didn't have to look far. Immediately south of the bay was a cove complete with a cave. With plenty of scope we might just be able anchor and put a line ashore. However gusts were alternately shooting down each side of the cove, making the rocks look precariously close.

Now here comes the detail of the secret weapon in our bid to find unspoilt anchorages – the Rope Reel. Before leaving England we had a large reel welded out of stainless. It takes 300 feet of 18mm warp, sits on the stern locker and will pay out a very long line ashore PDQ. Holding station pulling astern against the anchor I can whizz ashore in the dinghy and get a line around a rock or tree in less than a minute. We have seen so many people having nightmares fumbling with piles of tangled rope that we now consider the rope reel the most essential piece of kit for cruising in the Mediterranean. Most importantly it means you can get into places that others can't.

Heading north from Levkás up to Paxos at the end of August we found it much less crowded, mainly because after 24 August the multitude of Italian boats had gone. We were alone in Longos half way up the east side of Paxos (listed in the Rough Guide as amongst the top ten must-see places in Greece).

Corfu was even less crowded. In fact we found beautiful bays in Gerald Durrell's northeast part of the island where we were all alone. Kouloura bay was one of the most picturesque, complete with one of the best tavernas. The serenity of the place was made complete on our

last morning when we sailed out of the bay to the glorious sight of a Tall Ship making her way down the Corfu channel.

We left *Papageno* for a month in Gouvia Marina, returning with a blokes' crew to sail up to Croatia at the end of September. With my cousin Andrew, my brother Alexander and Sam West, a yacht surveyor, we were a scratch crew making it a fast and well-rested passage. We had a cracking sail and stupendous landfall on Dubrovnik under genniker, sailing past the walled city making over seven knots.

We were enjoying the conditions so much that we beat into the port of entry of Gruz, tacking close to the line of cruise ships and mooring stern-to amongst other yachts just past the customs building. Little did we know that this would unleash the wrath of a furious harbour official. We were berated by this enraged Slav for sailing in the harbour, tacking too close to the cruise ships and for mooring illegally past the customs building. 'Yoo hav gon beyont ze vire' he shouted, pointing to the fence at the end of the customs quay. 'Yoo are illegal in Croatia'. He aggressively demanded we move our boat immediately and moor alongside the quay by the cruise ship. After this first terrifying brush with Croatian officialdom things got better; on checking in for our cruising permit the harbour master was blasé when I apologised for the incident. 'He is always like that, he wants to fill my shoes' he said.

Cruise in company, Papageno style

We were pleased to get into Dubrovnik Marina as that night the infamous bora struck with a vengeance. We had horrendous rain, thunder and gusts to 40 knots blasting down the hillsides throughout the night and the following day. Many charterers were stranded as the airport was closed for all flights. Finally released from the spell of bora-dom we had a cracking good sail up to Polače on Mljet on the tail of that northeast blow. Then on to Vis, sailing past the stunning view of Korčula in the soft autumnal light. On 3 October we had a wonderful final sail of the season from Vis to Kremik in a 25-knot 'yugo', covering 36 miles in less than five hours.

It was great to be in a whole new cruising area again after two years in Greece. However my hopes that we might be able to find solitude in this myriad of islands have yet to be fulfilled. We were amazed at how many boats we saw sailing in early October. Both Dubrovnik and Kremik marinas were heaving with people and there were long queues for the showers. We were told that the charter industry was up 20% from the previous year and the marinas were full. Croatia is now well and truly discovered. It looks as if we will need to employ our solitude-seeking tactics once again next summer. We were lucky to get into Kremik where the staff efficiently arranged for us to be hauled out for the winter.

Papageno is a Dorne 39 sloop, designed by Alan-Williams and built by North West Marine in 1996

AND THE DUCKS ATE BLACKBERRIES

by Tony Vasey

I last wrote in 2002 when we had made our way as far south as it is possible to get in France without going to sea. And going to sea is not an option with our flat-bottomed barge that would take fright at the smell of salt water and roll her decks under in the slightest swell. We had spent three seasons on the Canal du Midi but were growing tired of this 300-kilometre crowded waterway, despite its abundance of attractive plane trees and cheap wine and the equable weather that extended our cruising season from April to November. So we decided to move north again. In her centennial year we planned to return *Penelope* to her birthplace in Holland for a much-needed refit. We had failed to find a yard in France where we could get reliable work done on her corroding iron. But there lies the rub! The only way north is back up the Rhône and Saône, some 500 kilometres against the current and with our modest 8kph cruising speed we could be reduced to a crawl by the dreaded mistral.

Our Canadian partner had left *Penelope* at Beaucaire, on the Rhône some 30 kilometres from the Mediterranean but now cut off from the river and requiring a 60-kilometre diversion to get to the other side of the closed lock gates. Jill and I arrived at the end of July in blistering heat with the temperature just reaching 100°F and making our iron box quite untenable when stationary. We had intended to victual and get away quickly but were easily dissuaded when we found the town *en fête* with the annual bull-run and Portuguese bullfight. A hundred bulls were released to run through streets that were lined for about a kilometre with high steel fencing. Intrepid youths could slip through the bars before being overtaken by the young bulls that were doubtless more frightened than their tormentors. The bulls were then corralled in the arena where they were cut out by horsemen and herded into delivery trucks for return to their pastures in the Camargue.

The following day brought the bullfight, Portuguese style. The caballeros fight from horseback, the toreadors only providing diversionary antics during a change of mount. Beautifully turned out Portuguese horsemen on magnificently caparisoned steeds gave us a breathtaking display of horsemanship. The horses clearly enjoyed themselves as much as the riders. The highlight of the evening was a young local girl who eclipsed the men with her daring and skill. She was one with her mount, who taunted the bull as much as she did by dancing to the martial music in front of the snorting bull, changing tempo with the band and swinging its rump only inches from the horns.

All good things must come to an end so the following morning we made a dawn start, heading southwest into the Petit Rhône then east to gain the Rhône itself at Arles. We were dreading the current but were pleasantly surprised to find not more than 2kph against us. After a 12-hour non-stop plug we made Avignon. It was more than we had dared to hope for and morale was high when we swung round the *Pont* next morning to start on the journey proper. We knew what to expect as we had brought *Penelope* down the Rhône three years previously but descending is altogether less challenging. This time we were armed with Jeremy Bradshaw-Smith's log from his journey up the river, which gave us useful information on stopping places.

The Rhône is canalised throughout and dredged to reliable depths but is still very attractive where it winds through the hills of southern France. There are a total of seven locks varying in depth from 40 to 83 feet, the latter being the deepest in Europe. They are 200 metres long and will

Rocher du Roi

hold two euro-standard barges but would allow us through alone if there was no other traffic. A quarter of a million tons of water to lift a 20-ton pleasure boat is hardly economical but we had paid our €300 *vignette* for the season so did not agonise over such profligacy. Every lock has a hydroelectric station that when it is generating produces a strong current in the cut below the turbines, sometimes reducing us to 4kph. Then we would skirt the bank as close as we dare prompting Jill to accuse me of trying to pick blackberries whilst under way.

On the second day the northerly wind began to brew but we hardly dared to breathe the dreaded word 'mistral' till we called at the Valence marina. There in black and white the forecast was for winds of 40-60kph with higher gusts but mercifully the winding river gave us some shelter. It was hot with a clear blue sky so we could persuade ourselves that it was like a good Caribbean beat in bathing suits with a reef down. Well not quite, but the temperature in the middle 90's was made acceptable with the strong breeze over the decks. The flying spray gave the wipers plenty of exercise on the more open stretches. The wind decreased as we clawed north so that the day before Lyon, when we passed the Rocher du Roi, it was once more calm and hot. This mid-stream flat rock, no bigger than *Penelope*, was in dispute when the river was the boundary between the Holy Roman Empire and Royalist France and to this day you still hear reference to the *peri* and *reiaume* banks. A wily riparian on the west bank heard that Louis IX was on passage down river to the crusades so laid a banquet on the rock and invited him to dine. Thus the humble rock gained the royal appellation. Despite the wind, the current and these historical diversions we averaged 60 kilometres a day, making Lyon, the confluence with the placid Saône, in five days from Avignon. There we tied up on the shady tree-lined quay in the middle of France's second city for a well-earned day's rest. On the Rhône I suffered badly from the what-ifs? What if the engine died on a windy open stretch miles from civilization? What if the wind was so strong that we couldn't make shelter for the night at one of the infrequent stopping places? Well, it didn't and we did but it was a blessed relief to enter the tranquil Saône.

After the valley of the Rhône the country opens out into pastoral plains where the locks are so few and far between that we even saw sizeable sailing boats, admittedly all tied up in marinas. The flat country is dotted with flooded sand and gravel quarries that have access to the river through narrow cuts. Showing complete lack of imagination, most are deserted except for prominent *interdit* notices though they could provide perfect bucolic anchorages. Carefully averting our eyes we motored into one to find 50 acres of deep tranquil water without a building or any other sign of civilization in sight. There we enjoyed our most peaceful night of the whole passage. Much to our surprise, breakfast was disturbed by a sand barge that disappeared behind dunes that hid an in-use quarry. But

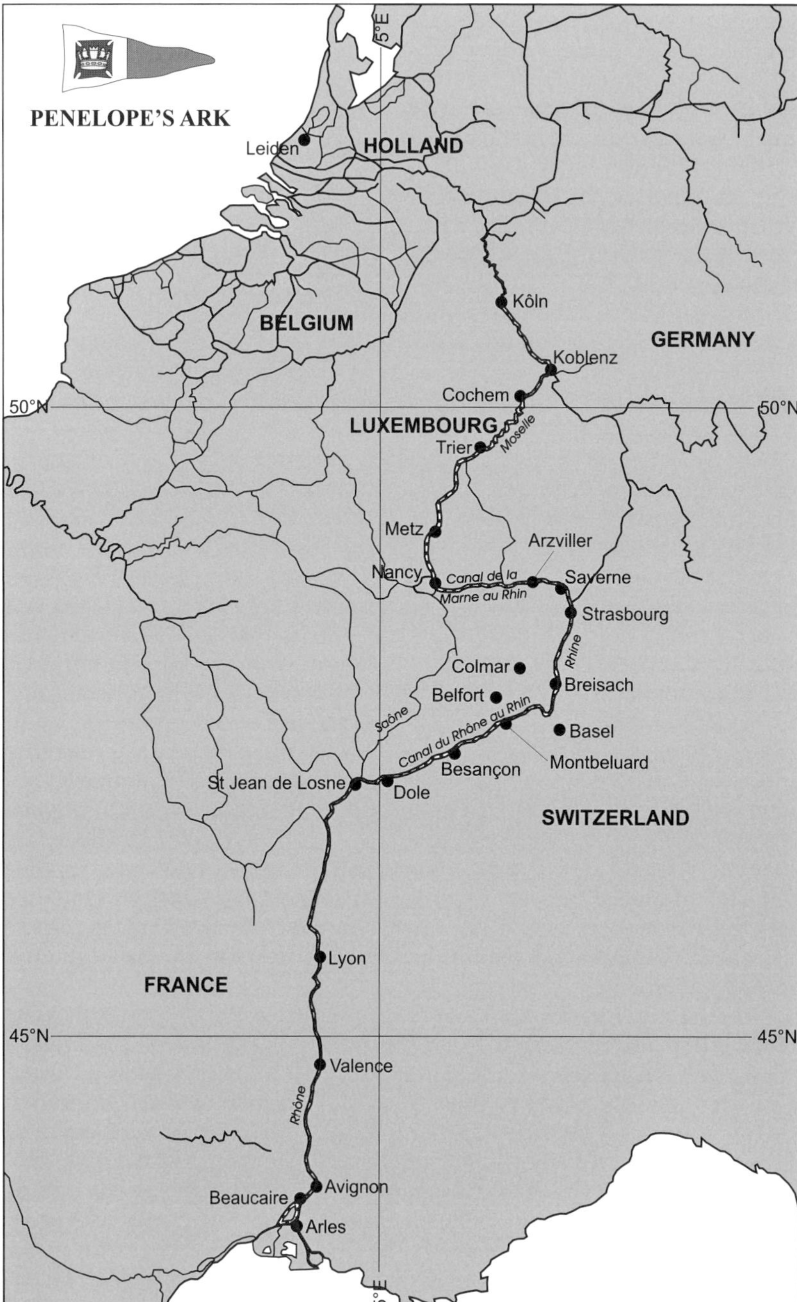
PENELOPE'S ARK
HOLLAND
Leiden
BELGIUM
GERMANY
LUXEMBOURG
Kôln
Koblenz
Cochem
Trier
Moselle
Metz
Nancy
Canal de la
Marne au Rhin
Arzviller
Saverne
Strasbourg
Rhine
Colmar
Belfort
Breisach
Basel
Saône
Canal du Rhône au Rhin
Montbeluard
Besançon
St Jean de Losne
Dole
SWITZERLAND
FRANCE
Lyon
Valence
Rhône
Avignon
Beaucaire
Arles
50°N
45°N
5°E

the French working man's ethos is live and let live and my wave was returned with a pleasant *bonjour* by the bargee.

Four short days took us the 200 kilometres to St Jean de Losne, the one time hub of commercial barging. Five waterways meet there so small tramp barges could pick up a cargo from the large river boats and transport it almost anywhere in France. There are still echoes of the past with the barge-ways on the water front but it is mostly given over to pleasure boats with sheltered mooring for several hundred in the large artificial harbour cut from the peat bogs. We had hardly got a line ashore when we spotted the inimitable Bill and Laurel Cooper who had just sold *Hosanna* and were making last minute repairs before handing her over. After a meal together we repaired to *Penelope* for a gam, catching up on the several years since we had last met. As usual, Bill and Laurel were full of ideas and showed us a model of their planned new barge to be built in Lowestoft this coming winter.

Going north from St Jean de Losne we had three options. The Canal de l'Est would take us through pretty country to the Moselle, but we had done that before. A more torturous way would take us into the Marne and through Belgium but we thought the quickest route would be to climb up to the Rhine and take the fast current through Germany into Holland. So after a day's R and R we set forth up the Canal Rhône au Rhin that winds through the Jura, parallel with the Swiss frontier, till it meets the Rhine just north of Basel. It is 250 kilometres with more than a hundred locks and in mid-August we expected it to be crowded with hire boats.

The Rhône au Rhin is not the most attractive canal but has the great merit of having interesting towns at two-day intervals and we regularly took a day off to explore. The locks are now automated. You are supplied with a zapper to alert the unmanned lock from about 200 metres. When it is ready the gates open to let you in and a manual handle inside does the rest. If there is a problem a small screen advises you in your language of choice but the English is at times a little quaint. Once we were told that there would be a delay as the lock was 'undergoing an operation'. We dreaded reading that it was in intensive care but that never happened.

The first sizeable town is Dole that we knew well from previous visits so we didn't linger. Next is Besançon that occupies a large loop in the canal. The amazing citadel is perched on a 200-foot high promontory through which the canal tunnels. It is a beautifully restored limestone town that glows in the sun and seems to radiate back at you on even the dullest day. Here we enjoyed our only manual lock that allowed a short-cut from the marina back into the main canal. We thought we were being clever going through behind a Frenchman who we assumed would show deference to our age and operate the lock but he pleaded heart trouble so Jill had laboriously to work both ends whilst the men tended the boats.

The stage through the gorge to Montbeliard is the most attractive of the whole route but we had our first wet day so it was very dismal where the canal cuts through the steep hills that at times narrowed the passage to a slit. The unkempt banks with overhanging trees closed it even more and the ducks ate blackberries, treading water and sucking the ripe fruit from the brambles. We had never seen this before and wondered if it was a new trend that would spread through the duck population like when tits discovered how to steal the cream from milk bottles.

We secured to the modern Nicholls hire-boat marina in Montbeliard and there lay the answer to the almost complete absence of the charter boats that we had so dreaded. They were virtually all tied up, mid-week, mid-August. The manager said they were having a disastrous season so perhaps the oversupply that caused so much crowding down south was beginning to work against them.

We took the train north to the historic town of Belfort that guards the famous Belfort Gap between the Jura to the south and the Vosges to the north. It was heavily fortified by Louis XIV and through the centuries invading armies have been held up by a relatively small defence force. In 1870 a force of 16,000 resisted an invading German army of 40,000 for more than 100 days, delaying the fall of Alsace-Lorraine. We had particularly come to see the massive stone lion erected on the slopes of the fortifications to commemorate this heroic defence. It is 72 feet long

All alone

by 36 feet high and was carved by Bartholdi, who also designed the Statue of Liberty.

On the approach to Montbeliard we had passed a derelict steel ketch lying forlornly on a rickety jetty and remarked that it must spell some one's broken dreams. To our amazement, that evening the derelict motored in and tied up in the next berth, sporting a German ensign. The next day was to be the final assault on the summit for which we had booked itinerant *éclusiers* to work us through the 27 locks that take you over the top. We were a little surprised when the Germans asked if they could sail in company as they were in a hurry to get back to Germany. We could both just fit into the locks together and lock-side conversation revealed that Frederick and Martina were on their way home for a much-needed refit after 15 years in Elba and that their ketch, *Seehund*, drew six feet, more than is prudent for this canal. Sure enough in the pound before the summit they failed to appear round the bend behind us so we hovered to allow them to catch up. We couldn't turn round as the canal was too narrow and shallow so gingerly went astern till we found them aground. They had anticipated problems so had come well prepared. A 60lb anchor was swung out on the spinnaker pole and some 20 large containers in the scuppers were filled with water giving them just sufficient heel to get off. It was therefore a double celebration when we passed the next lock into the *bief de partage*. The two of us, aggregate age 150 years, had humped our 20 tons of old iron up from the Mediterranean to nearly 1200 feet by nothing more than basic hydraulics and it was now all downhill to the North Sea.

The flights of locks down from the summit are very closely spaced, just allowing passing room between them. To the Germans' dismay the first commercial barge that we had encountered emerged from the second lock, forcing them to take the ground to avoid him. By then Frederick had sent in his anchor and emptied the buckets so this time we got a rope on them and hauled them into the lock. The descent was very quick and efficient with one *éclusier* working us through a lock whilst the other went ahead to prepare the next. That evening a grateful Frederick and Martina entertained us aboard *Seehund* in their halting English and our even more hesitant German but we did learn that he had twice sailed Solings in the Olympics. The language practice was a good primer for the Rhine locks that were all radio controlled in German.

A night in Mulhouse failed to secure a pilot book for the Rhine so we sailed the next day chartless depending on *Seehund* to show us the way. We now left the Rhône au Rhin and entered the commercial Kembs-Niffer canal. It was planned to go right through to the Rhône, allowing 2000-ton barges access from the Rhine to the Med, but the project was abandoned in 1999. It was wide, straight and dull, but the lovely morning and the goal of the Rhine only a few kilometres ahead made it seem like Shangri La.

We had heard such tales of doom about the Rhine with its fierce current and bureaucracy that it was with some trepidation that we entered it through the massive Niffer locks. It was wide and tranquil with delicious light blue glacial water from the Swiss mountains not yet polluted by the lower muddy rivers. Not the hair blowing back stuff we had expected but a magic smooth ride, rather like an airport moving pavement and equally un-intimidating. We were held up at two locks waiting for commercial vessels but made the 40 kilometres to Breisach by evening where we squeezed into a sheltered marina, out of the wash of the all-night river traffic. This far up the river we actually encountered very few commercial vessels. This river has been an artery since Roman times, supplying the empire that stretched as far as the Elbe and it is said that Germanicus employed 1000 vessels on the Rhine in his campaign in AD14.

From Breisach we wanted to make a diversion but *Seehund* was carrying on down the Rhine as they were working folk who had to get back to the office. Frederick, bless him, lent us his chart of the river as he had sailed it many times and knew well the 300 kilometres down to his home near Mainz. We went up the short, narrow canal to the medieval city of Colmar where we spent a very wet weekend exploring this incredibly beautiful old town.

On return to the Rhine we just made closing time at the last lock on the Colmar spur and spent the night on the waiting pontoon beyond the lock, just out of the wash from the main river. We were lucky that traffic was minimal on this Sunday night but later met a Dutch boat that suffered heavy damage on this berth from wash reflected off the wall, smashing them against the dock. We hurried away when the first traffic of the day spoiled our breakfast and once again climbed onto the magic carpet that in six hours took us to Strasbourg. There the lock keeper at the southern entrance to the port told us that there would be a long delay, but gave us no reason. Our suggestion that we should go round to the northern entrance was accepted with alacrity but we found that the current in the cut between the two locks was faster than our steaming speed so there was no going back should the northern lock-keeper be equally intransigent. He could not have been more pleasant, working us through without delay.

We were being joined by Jill's brother Peter and wife Ruth in Strasbourg so worked our way through the extensive port to the Club Plaisance just south of the city, where we had arranged to meet them. We were made most welcome and when we asked the cost were told that it was up to us as it was a private club with no fixed charges. Despite being several hundred miles from the sea, 45 years ago Strasbourg was France's fifth largest port, handling 10,000 ships annually. To reach the marina we passed miles of empty wharfs, road transport now having largely supplanted the smaller vessels.

Penelope sports a handsome mast that we were able to carry raised in much of Holland with its many opening bridges but in France it was inconvenient to have it cluttering the deck so we had left it on top of a mountain in Alsace five years before. We just had time to get there and back in the week before Christopher and Valentine Thornhill were due to join us in Strasbourg, so when Peter and Ruth arrived they were given five minutes to stow their bags before we were off again.

We have sailed the Marne au Rhin canal several times so hurried passed the opulent EU buildings and across the dull plain in the hinterland of Strasbourg but after about 40 kilmetres you are confronted by the northern foothills of the Vosges, that from a distance appear impenetrable. We had a run ashore in the attractive town of Saverne before tackling the winding climb up the narrow valley leading to the modern lift-lock at Arzviller. Whilst queuing for the lift we met a Dutch couple on their way to Holland and told them of our plans to ride the Rhine to Rotterdam. They were aghast! Had we not heard of the horrendous floods in Switzerland that would render the Rhine dangerous any day now? We paid attention when they described how the gorge below Strasbourg would become a boiling torrent where only the most intrepid professional would venture. This clearly called for a rapid reappraisal of our plans.

Penelope's Ark

At Arzviller, 17 locks have been replaced by an inclined plane up which a box of water, holding three boats of our size, is hauled sideways for 230 feet. It takes about ten minutes where the staircase that it replaced took commercial barges a whole day. At the top you enter a 2.5 kilometre tunnel that leads to the level pound crossing the plateau separating the Rhine, the Saar and the Moselle. There we found our mast, a little dusty but all intact. After an exchange of cross words with the owner of the yard about the unconscionable time we had left it and a certain *pourbois*, the mast was restored to its proper place.

Then came the question of which way to go. Three days ahead was the charming city of Nancy from where we could navigate the torturous Canal de l'Est Nord to Belgium and the Meuse. But that would take far longer than our remaining time and was going away from the rendezvous with our American partner. Back to the Rhine did not seem to be an option so on we went to Nancy, where we bought a chart of the northern route and prepared for the long slog over the Ardennes. In our innocent days we had thought of barging as cruising across flat plains with distant vistas but here we were confronted by our third mountain range in as many weeks with the flatlands of Holland still half a continent away.

We made good time to Nancy giving us a day once again to explore the legacy of inter-royal exchange. François III had inherited the dukedom of Lorraine but preferred his seat in Tuscany so Louis XV supplanted him with his father-in-law, the Polish King Stanislaus, who had been driven out of his own country by Peter the Great. A keen patron of the arts, Stanislaus poured his money and energy into beautifying his new capital and it became one of the most elegant cities in Europe. Peter and Ruth took the train to their car at Strasbourg, collected Christopher and Valentine and drove them back in time for us all to dine al fresco at the edge of the square on a glorious summer evening. The surrounding buildings were bathed in the golden twilight that gradually gave way to subdued illumination.

We had hardly briefed the Thornhills on the rigours of the Canal de l'Est when a small German boat pulled out of the marina in front of us. They said that they were going down the Moselle to the Rhine then north to Germany. What of the floods I asked? 'All over,' they said, and departed with such confidence that we had little option but to follow. The Moselle is a 350-kilometre slalom through vine-clad hills from France to Luxembourg and thence to Germany, and we had a week before our American rendezvous. It is a wide river and after a dry summer was fairly shallow. There is little provision for itinerant boats and the frequency of commercial barges and passenger ships makes tying alongside the bank an uncomfortable option. We squeezed into a small slot at Metz for the first night but had to leap for the shore over our four foot barn-door rudder. It was worth it to explore this ancient city but we could not linger as we needed to average 50 kilometres a day with 17 locks to hold us up.

Although half the river is in France or Luxembourg, the language for the locks is German. I was concerned that my bachelor German, with vocabulary limited to the garage and the pub and 50 years of rust, would not be adequate so was delighted to learn that Christopher had spent time at Strasbourg University and was anxious to de-rust his. This he did to good effect but found the local accents a little difficult. Indeed, at the very first lock there was great confusion when we thought we had been directed to the *sportboot* lock, only to find on arrival that it was dinghy-sized. What they were really asking was our dimensions but in such colloquial German that neither of us understood.

On the third day France gave way to Luxembourg on the port bank where we were anxious to fill with cheap fuel. After much delving in the locker we unearthed what we took to be the appropriate courtesy flag and were delighted when the fuel attendant congratulated us on our choice. It appeared that ours was the ancient ensign that whilst strictly correct is now rarely flown. Perhaps our regalia is as old as the boat? At Schengen we finally crossed into Germany on both banks but were not challenged despite our red ensign advertising our non-compliance with the treaty of that name.

We particularly wished to explore the ancient town of Trier but throughout its 4-kilometre waterfront there was not a single visitor quay. There were dozens of passenger boat moorings but we were shooed away every time we approached one. In desperation we secured to the rowing club launching raft that allowed about an inch under us but fouled our bow-thruster in the abundant weed. Christopher and Valentine had done their homework and beetled round taking an intelligent interest in the many ruins. But after nearly six weeks of wandering Jill and I were 'ruined out' and took more interest in hotdogs and ice cream.

We motored on into the evening in search of a sheltered mooring and eventually let go the anchor in the cut below a lock. There was a rock hard bottom at two metres but with no current and absolute calm we judged our 100lb CQR would confine us sufficiently as it grumbled over the stone. It did, but in the morning we found that the head was jammed and had not uncocked so we were never really attached to the bottom. We got away early on a glorious morning with a shallow mist over the water and the first rays of the sun flooding down the steep vine clad slopes. Christopher was determined to try the local wine at every stop and we were treated to some delicious whites whose names were plastered in large letters across the hill-sides.

Having had such a comfortable night at anchor previously we thought to try again, this time behind an island where there was a yacht club marked on the chart. We had hardly left the main channel when we went hard aground on a very firm bottom. By judicious use of astern and the bowthruster we were able to screw her round to face deep water but she was still firmly on. Then our erstwhile antagonists the fast pleasure boats

Quiet anchorage

came to our rescue. With the crew on the foredeck and the engine full ahead their wash lifted us clear but we still had nowhere for the night. There was said to be a river authority harbour at Alf on the neck of a particularly tight loop where we covered nine kilometres to make good 500 metres. It was a Sunday and we could find no one from whom to seek permission so at last light we sprung her to the bank but had a very disturbed night when a fast pusher barge sent wash clear over the bund.

On our penultimate day we reached the pretty town of Cochem where we moored in the only visitor harbour that we found on the whole river. There were four cruise ships in so the attractive narrow streets were crowded with sightseers but we escaped the throng by climbing the steep 200-foot path to the castle above the town.

The next evening we arrived at Koblenz on the Rhine after a 500-kilometre diversion to take us round the infamous Rhine Gorge. That was the bit of the Rhine that we had been looking forward to since we planned this trip and had regaled Christopher and Valentine on the thrills and dangers of shooting these rapids, lest they should think this form of boating too sedate. However we were justified in our decision to avoid it as we learned at Koblenz that the river had been closed to private vessels and had further confirmation when our American partners arrived with film taken the previous week of barges making 23kph through the gorge with buoys almost towed under by the current. They were so alarmed that we feared they would not complete the journey to Holland as arranged and hastily changed our plans so as to accompany them.

It certainly was a thrilling ride. This far north the traffic was thick on the water with as many as a dozen large commercial barges in sight at one time. When all were adhering to the conventional rules, navigation was manageable but it got quite hectic when upcoming barges 'blue flagged' round the inside of bends so as to get out of the strength of the current. This is so called by the requirement to fly a one metre square blue flag to indicate that you wish to pass starboard to starboard. The opposing traffic must then reply showing that they understand their intention. This is fine until the next up barge does not wish to 'blue flag' so you must pass between and is further complicated when you are being overtaken at the same time by a fast down-stream barge. We were quite breathless after covering the 90 kilometres to Köln in six hours and were looking forward to finding a berth in the marina when we found a dredger on long anchors virtually blocking the entrance. There was a mass of unfamiliar flag signals that appeared to require us to go below the dredge and all its attendant vessels but as we were making 16kph at idling revs we should have had a struggle to get back up-stream inside the dredger. Judging the angle of the anchor wires we crabbed through between the vessels and shot into the calm waters of the dock.

From Köln our American partners took her the last few hundred kilometres to her birthplace at Leiden whilst we flew home after our 1600 kilometre passage. Since the 220 locks had reduced us to an average walking pace, we rated this a fair six-week cruise for two in their seventies whose ship was entering her second century.

Penelope's Ark is a 46-foot iron barge built in 1904.

THE FINAL CRUISE

by Donald Tew

For some decades Mother had been telling her five sons, Donald, Ian, Edward, Malcolm and James, what she wanted doing when she died. 'You're to scatter my ashes half way between Old Harry Rock and the Needles. You must sail me out and not use the engine or else I'll come back and haunt you'.

Helen Tew

Mary Helen

James and Donald had had a previous warning about engine use, because when taking *Mary Helen* with 'her' on board back to Beaulieu after the launch of her book *Transatlantic at Last*, the engine would not start. After about four minutes James and Donald looked forward and said 'Mum, we are not taking you out yet'. The engine promptly started! It is certain that had they turned right and not left at the Lymington River entrance the ticker would have played up.

So at 0900 on 11 June 2005, Mother was taken by car from the boat to her house on the Solent shore, where James waited for *Mary Helen* to arrive. She anchored off Thorns Beach at 1140. It was fitting that James swam out to *Mary Helen* with Mama as she had swum off her beach for many decades. She would have approved. Just her five sons were on board, probably for the first time together at sea. There was of course no wind to speak of at this point, nevertheless full sail was made, the engine sealed and the anchor lifted. Very slowly (against the tide of course) and in bright sunshine *Mary Helen* inched ahead, a quarter of a mile in the first hour. Mother's neighbours at Durns House came out and waved a final farewell. Eventually the wind came in from the southwest, the tide turned and she sped through the Solent and out through the North Passage. The wind lightened, stretching the final sail for as long as possible. However at 1800 in position 50°39.5'N, 01°45.5'W *Mary Helen* hove-to and Donald formally assumed command to recite the committal as her ashes were scattered on the sea. It was a sad moment and a time for reflection. The final cruise was over. She was where she wanted to be surrounded by all she loved.

THE 2005 AWARDS

Judge's Commentary by Jonathan Trafford

November is the low tide of the English winter. The boat is laid up, the evenings draw in. Pleasure is lighting the log fire. This year, I had another task. On 1 November I received a box of papers from the Editor. I stoked the fire and settled down to judge the year's logs.

Jonathan Trafford

The Journal always provides vicarious armchair enjoyment. For the Judge the enjoyment is of a higher order: he has to live each voyage as a member of the crew; he has to read the log once, twice and again, to satisfy himself that he has got to grips with the story, its highs and lows, its achievement, its difficulties. He then has to measure each cruise against the spirit of the criteria laid down for each award.

So this year the Judge, in the wake of earlier Judges, has circled the globe and penetrated the Arctic north and the southern wonders of the Beagle Channel. He has learned the skills of the South Seas pearl farmer. Nearer home, he has relived the pleasure of a cross channel passage and the challenge of a wet and windy Shetland. And much more besides.

There are eleven prizes to award. The quality of the cruises that have won can be gauged if I begin with a resume of those that have not. In home waters, William Bourne describes a cheerful circuit from Newhaven via Falmouth and north Brittany in his 30-foot cat-rigged *Iseult*. The objects of the cruise were to inspire two teenagers in the joys of cruising (clearly achieved) and to buy some waders, they being cheaper in France than in Cornwall (object also achieved, albeit with difficulty). William's other satisfactions were to resist motoring if a breath remained on the water and to beat his young crew at Cheat. Keith Holland-Gems sailed his 28-foot shoal draft cutter *Jan Van Gent* in cold November northerlies from St Malo to Christchurch and then in May (still cold) the 320 miles from Christchurch to Waterford.

In Scottish waters, Lorne Byatt took his newly acquired 28-foot *Samba* through the Crinan and then the Forth and Clyde Canal, originally built in 1768 and reopened in 2001. Avoiding submerged shopping trolleys contrasts with fending off bergy bits which features in other logs. We then have two unashamedly gastronomic cruises on the Scottish west coast – a circuit of Mull in *Brown Bear* with Mary Max in command and to the Outer Isles in *Ceres* with Jim Pitts, who as you would expect of a recent Hon Steward cruised 'in fine style'. Lobsters beware.

Further afield, the Vice Commodore and Judy Lomax went north from Trømsø to Murmansk in *Cloud Walker* but had to abort their plan of revisiting Svalbard as David required surgery at Kirkenes. Judy sailed the boat back to Trømsø minus David but with Bob Shepton and one other. These two, wrote Judy, 'shared faith in God if not necessarily in the skipper'. James Nixon sailed his 43-foot *Scilla Verna* from Trømsø to Belfast Lough via the inner leads to Ålesund and thence to Shetland, Fair Isle, Orkney and the Hebrides. A fine six-week cruise.

The Lennox-Kings bought the 51-foot *Restless of Auckland* in Grenada and sailed to the US Virgins and later to Maine, which they much enjoyed despite the ubiquitous fog and the lobster pot hazard. Peter and Gill Price in the 37-foot *Lectron* joined the East Mediterranean Yacht Rally for a cruise along the coasts of Syria, Lebanon, Israel and Egypt. Although describing themselves as 'not rally people' they nevertheless contrived to have much fun and saw an astonishing range of interesting places.

Jamie Pritchard-Barrett treats us to an entertaining account of a model family cruise aboard *Papageno* in the Ionian Sea. Happy days indeed, well recorded with evocative photographs. In Alaska, Bill and Pam Kellett explored the 'shore-side wonders' of the dramatic Glacier Bay National Park in *Jura*. Their account leaves the reader breathless with whale encounters, sightings of moose and bear and a 6.8-knot tidal stream. Sunday breakfast of pancakes and maple syrup comes as a relief. The Kelletts then trucked the boat to Connecticut, the last leg of 16 years cruising in foreign waters, as their UK friends well remember.

John and Sally Melling sailed their 40-foot *Taraki* from Puerto Montt through the Chilean canals and the Beagle Channel, ending a fine cruise three months later in Uruguay. The fascination of this cruising ground is evident from the Mellings' photographs but the narrative is disappointingly sparse. By contrast, Tim Barker devoted 33,000 words to his 4-month Baltic circuit and exploration of the Danish islands in the 45-foot Oyster *Mina*^{2}.

Tony and Jill Vasey offer a very readable account of six weeks covering 1600 kilometres and 220 locks from the Rhône via the Rhine and the Moselle to Köln. This was a considerable achievement, both for the vessel, which was 100 years old, and for the Vaiseys who clock up over 150 years between them.

The Awards

In the best tradition of RCC ocean voyaging, Richard Clifford sails to New Zealand in the 35-foot *Warrior Shamaal*. His cruise, full of variety and much of it single-handed, is an inspiration. He combines fine seamanship with thorough enjoyment; he fraternises with islanders to understand and share their way of life; he explores and records for FPI and does all this with panache. Essential reading for young and old alike. To Richard, I award the Challenge Cup.

Graham Morfey brings *Flight of Time* back to the Mediterranean from New Zealand. A thoroughly assured voyage in a fine vessel. There is a sense of relaxation throughout, with fascinating excursions ashore, but members will know that such a voyage, completed without significant problems, indicates a mix of notable modesty and commensurate skill. An outstanding cruise that commands the Romola Cup.

Peter and Katharine Ingram in the 38-foot *Kokiri* feature large in contemporary Club voyaging. We now have another immaculate cruise which combines all that the Club holds dear: a visit to the St Lawrence River, seldom explored by members, a taste of Newfoundland, a dramatic race across the north Atlantic against the threatening tail of a hurricane, the relief of the Azores and a perfectly timed arrival at Barbate for the Trafalgar Meet. All this within three months – just right for the Founder's Cup (for the second time).

I award Juno's Cup to Jeremy Parkinson for his cruise in the 28-foot *Feanor* to Germany, Poland and the Baltic States, waters which, in the terms of this award, I regard as 'out of the way'. *Feanor* is a refreshingly small boat and Jeremy communicates well his pleasure in exploring this still bureaucratic but friendly region. Much motoring, interspersed with windy intervals, prompts the dire warning that if you can't enter the north facing harbours of Poland, you'd best head for Bornholm. Heavens!

David Mitchell has real talent for presenting a log tailor-made for our Journal. This year, again in the 35-foot *Ondarina,* he visits the north of New Zealand's South Island and mixes 'excitement with terror' in sometimes testing conditions. Adventures are packed into a one-month cruise, which renders the Judge's task straightforward. David wins the Claymore Cup.

Andrew O'Grady, a master of the art of cruising in demanding waters, entertains us (or amazes us, depending on your point of view) with his account of a voyage from Labrador to Ireland via Greenland, an iceberg collision, the sentiment that 'we got off lightly with only F9 winds and a day lying a-hull' and the towing of a rudderless Swedish yacht for 80 miles in the north Atlantic. He provides valuable sketch charts and descriptions of harbours on Greenland's west coast. All this marks him as a clear winner of the prestigious Cruising Club Bowl.

The Irish Cruising Club Decanter goes to Rob and Anna Brunyee, who sailed their 53-foot pilot cutter *Marguerite,* built in 1893, from Falmouth to the West Indies and back. In 12 months they visited the Canaries, the Cape Verdes, the Azores and the Virgins as well as the Windward and Leeward Islands. A well-organised, cheerful cruise, which introduced two small boys to the joys of shipboard life and was executed without any disasters.

In his Rival 36 *Borealis*, David Vass and his wife Moira circuited the Shetlands, calling at Foula, Out Skerries and Fair Isle. These are home waters but by no means easy and it is a joy to share the enthusiasm that David and his wife demonstrated in achieving their project. I award the Royal Cork Yacht Club Vase to David.

The potential of our future membership is demonstrated by Christopher Clothier who made a single-handed passage in *Brown Bear* from Stornoway to Ålesund. He waved goodbye to his father on the Stornoway dockside, forcing him to make the same journey by other means of transport. The Sea Laughter Trophy is awarded to a delightful account by an able young seaman, from whom we can hope for further contributions in the years ahead.

Annie Hill's singular account of the 36-foot steel cutter *Iron Bark's* voyage from Baddeck to the west coast of Greenland and back a year later to Newfoundland, having meanwhile wintered in the Arctic ice, must be as far removed from most members' notion of a restful season aboard as could be imagined. Annie ('cold frightens me') and Trevor Robertson conducted surveys of numerous anchorages north of 72°N and produced much original information and beautifully drawn chartlets. Their documentary sources were the Danish charts, which were 'largely innocent of soundings'. Annie wins the Goldsmith Exploration Award.

Finally, the Grace Cup. Robert Ingram, 5 months old, boarded *Kokiri* in Montreal. His enterprising parents then took him on an arduous 3-month voyage to Spain. Robert's mother, Katharine, to whom this Cup is awarded, demonstrates in generous measure her courage and the special qualities of seamanship and loving care prescribed by this award.

Ladies' Cup (awarded by the Commodore)

One of the most enjoyable privileges of the Commodore is being able to award the Ladies' Cup. There are many fine and accomplished women in the Club but this year the most deserving is Valentine Thornhill. She has worked tirelessly alongside Christopher in his various roles in the Club, including most recently as Commodore. Valentine and Christopher have sailed together on all their cruises in *Sai See*. When Christopher suffered his stroke early this year, Valentine's unstinting support and energy made sure that the Club's affairs remained on an even keel and that Christopher made an excellent recovery. So much so that they were able to enjoy a busy summer, culminating in the Trafalgar Meet. Well done, Valentine, and thank you very much from all of us.

Seamanship Medal

A few years ago a young woman from Kent, who had been a tomboy and keen athlete in her teens, contracted a degenerative illness and gradually lost the use of her legs and arms. She became more and more depressed and at one point even contemplated suicide. But then she was introduced to sailing. She joined a club and learned fast but soon wanted to be more than just a disabled passenger. Last summer she found a sponsor who lent her a 26-foot yacht and helped her to install a control system with parts salvaged from two old wheel chairs. The mechanism was activated by the skipper puffing or sucking air from two plastic straws while being held upright in a specially moulded racing driver's seat. Last summer *Malin* set out from Dover and crossed to Calais in 6 hours 13 minutes, setting a record. Her skipper was the first quadriplegic to sail solo across the English Channel. She says she wanted to change the public's perception of disabled people. 'We do not need wrapping up in cotton wool and can go out and do silly or dangerous things if that's what we want to do.' To prove this she is now planning to sail round Britain. The Seamanship Medal is awarded to Hilary Lister.

Medal for Services to Cruising

During the depression in the US a 19-year-old engineer and designer joined forces with a successful yacht broker and formed a company to design and build yachts. The new company survived the depression when his father ordered a design for *Dorade*, a now famous yacht that won the 1931 Transatlantic and Fastnet Races. Since then the young designer and his company have produced more than 2600 designs, many for cruising yachts, and gained a worldwide reputation. He designed America's Cup yachts including *Ranger, Columbia, Constellation, Freedom* and the two times winners, *Intrepid* and *Courageous*. Three of his yachts have won the Whitbread. Many others have cruised round the world and set new standards for cruising yachts in general. The man who made all this possible is not young anymore – he's 98. It's about time that the Medal for Services to Cruising should be awarded to Olin Stephens.

Bluebird Cup

The Bluebird Cup (for innovation, renovation and restoration) was presented to the Club by a previous Commodore, Lord Riverdale, who was himself a keen designer and builder of yachts. He had an early bilge keeler called *Bluebird,* which was later renamed *Inversanda* and is now owned by an RCC member. Some time ago *Inversanda* sank off Jersey. Her new owners were not dismayed. They organised the salvage and then set about a magnificent and comprehensive restoration project which ended with Lord Riverdale's old yacht looking youthful again as she enjoyed a place of honour in the main trot at the last Beaulieu Meet. It seems fitting that the Bluebird Cup should be awarded jointly to the two who were responsible, Mike and Michael Allo.

Tilman Medal

We heard of many fine cruises in high latitudes but none with the outstanding flair and dash of near lunacy that is usually associated with this award. The committee has therefore decided not to award the Tilman Medal this year.

Vice Commodore's Prize

When he lost *Dodo's Delight* in the ice off Greenland the skipper was so upset that he even offered to resign from the Club. I told him that I'd never heard anything more ridiculous and that the RCC was packed with his admirers who all knew that accidents happen. Since then he has bought another boat only to find ever-escalating osmosis costs, which he's trying to meet by hiring himself as a delivery skipper. He's not had the best of luck. Last summer when I was laid up in hospital in north Norway and *Cloud Walker* had to be returned to Trømsø, he crewed for Judy cheerfully and at his own expense. He has borne his recent difficulties with characteristic courage and good humour and I hope will be cheered to learn that the Vice Commodore's prize has been awarded to Bob Shepton.

Dulcibella Prize

Anyone who takes on the challenge of the north Atlantic, single-handed and racing, in the same year as he embarks on the equally demanding commitment of producing the newsletter deserves the sympathy and admiration of the Editor, who awards the Dulcibella Prize to Paul Heiney.

THE BEAULIEU MEET, 2005

10 and 11 September

The 2005 Beaulieu Meet was a happy affair. The weather was moderate and the only interruption of the proceedings was from the wash of passing boats in the river. The Commodore ensured that efficient organisation was mixed with a relaxed atmosphere.

37 boats gathered, a smaller number than usual. Several people had already left for the Trafalgar meet and both rising mooring costs in home waters and the Easyjet factor are no doubt encouraging more members to keep their boats at long range. Whatever the reason, smaller numbers made for less of a crush of people on the raft and for time to visit other ships.

Rafted together for partying were *Balæna, Flycatcher, Inversanda, Quicksilver, Marguerite, Mina*^{2} *and Skat.* In support were *Albatross, Astros, Bleuet, Blue Fox, Bonney, Couvache, Dorigen, Firedancer, Frances, Galliard, Holly, Jacson, Kariat, Libertà, Mahjong of Taipei, Mary Helen, Nandisa, Nirvana, Ostara, Salvation Jane, Sarakiniko, Satellite, Southern Comfort, Squander, The Otter, Tioman, Tiptoe, Westernman and Zazu* (Michael Burnford). Two other boats had been borrowed or chartered and there were a few RIBs about. Several people came by road, which is to be recommended, *faute de mieux.* You don't need to bring a dinghy. A mobile phone is enough.

This was the first Beaulieu meet since the war without Helen Tew, apart from the year of her Atlantic circuit. But Donald and James were there in *Mary Helen,* smart as paint. Those who have not been below in *Mary Helen* may not understand the extraordinary feat Donald and Helen achieved in so small a boat or what comfort we take for granted in our boats today.

The customary race in Lasers against the Beaulieu River Sailing Club took place after lunch on Saturday, organised by the Vice Commodore. Although our team of Colin Campbell, Simon Wood, David Mathews and David Reynolds was strong, the offshore team was beaten by the canny longshoremen, as is also customary.

The weather was balmy for the evening party and the Commodore set the tone in shirtsleeve order. Senior Members in evidence included Mary Barton, Gill Lloyd and Oliver Roome. Christopher Thornhill, in full fig, including his unique Club bow tie and the new Club socks, was in admirable form.

A gathering of RCC boats is always an interesting guide to the nature of the Club. The Blue Book reveals that the average age of boats attending the Beaulieu meet in 2005 was 25.8 years, not including *Mary Helen* and *Kariat*, John Power's Victorian steam launch. Evidently high, wide and light factory-built boats with no sea berths and no chart table have had little impact on the Royal Cruising Club.

WHR

The Raft gets bigger

OBITUARIES

George Bastard

George bought his first boat in 1957 and cruised in home waters during his career in the Royal Air Force. When he retired he was able to sail further afield and cruised as far as Gibraltar. In 1987 he completed the AZAB single-handed. Between 1992 and 1994 he and Anne made a classic north Atlantic circuit, visiting the Caribbean and Venezuela.'

Such few words may summarise a cruising lifetime, at first glance a modest one compared with those who circle the globe or explore high latitudes. They entirely fail to do justice to an outstanding man, albeit one of great modesty – a distinguished and much decorated aviator, a

George Bastard

courageous and determined sailor, a loving and dearly loved friend, husband, father and grandfather.

George was elected to the Club in 1986 and many members only knew him as a yachtsman. But between 1941 when he joined the Royal Air Force on his eighteenth birthday and 1977 when he retired as a Group Captain, he had a remarkable career. Originally a fighter pilot, he converted to bombers and commanded 25 missions over Germany. On one occasion his aircraft was so badly damaged that it had to be scrapped on reaching England. He flew operations in Burma and Malaya, made 300 trips to Berlin during the airlift and flew bombing sorties over Egypt during the Suez conflict. He commanded 9 and 617 squadrons, the latter operating V-bombers that carried nuclear weapons. His many decorations included the DFC and AFC. He had a dry sense of humour, particularly where his name was concerned, and would often disconcertingly answer the telephone with the single laconic word 'Bastard'. When younger he sported the most magnificent handlebar moustache.

As a cruising yachtsman George was supremely competent in the most unassuming way. He and his first wife Joe sailed in home waters as often as his career permitted. Sadly she died in 1981 and for the next few years he sailed *Skyjack II*, his Westerly Conway ketch, mainly single-handed. A great supporter of the RAFYC, he served as its Commodore from 1980–2. As he himself said, 'In 1987 I was fortunate enough to marry Anne and after more than five years as a widower, my life changed very much for the better, both at home and afloat.' They were ideally suited and cruised extensively together. Their Atlantic circuit represents all that a proper cruise should be: well planned, perfectly executed, unpublicised and thoroughly enjoyable. Anne had grown-up children of whom George was immensely fond and supportive. His grandchildren gave him great joy and they loved him dearly.

George was admired, respected, yes even loved by all who knew him. Those who worked for him gave of their best because he made them want to, the hallmark of a real leader. He was a true friend, a proper cruising yachtsman, a man of the highest standards in all that he did and a perfect gentleman. He exemplified all that the RCC stands for. It was a privilege to be proposed for the Club by him.

GHMcL

Donald Beswick

Donald exuded bonhomie and humour; he was tremendous fun. He and Peggy were friends with my parents and he was the father of my chum, Andrew, who sadly is also not with us anymore.

Donald was born in Newcastle under Lyme and wanted to become an engineer and join his father's firm. But it was the time of the slump and business was not good so he joined his uncle's firm of solicitors. After serving his articles, he qualified in 1939 and went straight into the RNVR.

He commanded ML 295 in the Mediterranean on mine sweeping duties and was awarded the DSC. His brother, a Royal Marine, also won the DSC and they were decorated in the same ceremony. Donald was demobbed in November 1945 but retained his interest in the Navy as a volunteer and joined HMS *Wessex*, based in Southampton.

In the meantime, he had married his teenage sweetheart, Peggy, in 1941. They met at dancing class where Peggy excelled but poor Donald struggled. He was away at sea for three years and Janet was born after he had left; she did not meet him until she was two years old. Back in Civvy Street, Donald was invited to an interview with solicitors in Southampton. Seeing the Hamble River with its yachts, he said, 'This is for me!' and accepted the job. He remained with them and was eventually senior partner.

Their first boat was a Hamble Star, in which Janet and Andrew, who arrived in 1946, learned to sail. She was followed by a Morecombe Bay shrimper, and then by *Raumati*, a Virtue 5-tonner built for them in 1962 by Elkins. She was a delight and deceptively quick; both Peggy and Donald used to say of her, 'Lovely boat ...but only for two!' She was replaced by *Knotty*, a Moody Halbadier, which was fitted out in Aberdour. On taking delivery, they sailed down the east coast, through the Caledonian Canal, hopped around a few islands on the west coast before returning to the Hamble, all in three weeks. Which perhaps explains why Donald drove a very fine Alvis!

After retirement, he and Peggy cruised in *Knotty* far and wide but their big task, in 1978, was to revise Blondie Haslar's *North Brittany Pilot*, the copyright of which Adlard Coles had just given to the newly formed RCC Pilotage Foundation. Donald was thus the first of a long line of authors who have written books for the Foundation.

Not only was Donald a great raconteur. He was also a medal winning skier. He put this down to being short so he was closer to the ground for extra stability. In fact, that's how I remember him: down to earth and practical, not a typical lawyer, and very competent and able in all he did. And always with that irrepressible humour and twinkle in his eye.

RJMB

Bob Dibben

Bob grew up at Sarisbury Green and Bursledon on either side of the Hamble River. Sailing was his parents' great enjoyment and the three brothers, Bob, Johnny and George, carried that on. For Bob this meant a lifetime of racing and cruising all over the world. Possibly his greatest pleasure was hoisting the RCC burgee (a king-sized one on his last boat *Ipsilante*), as he had done on so many other boats throughout the years at home and abroad. He loved sailing and, typically, shared it with everybody and particularly with his family so that Emma, Andrew and Francis became very competent sailors.

In 1970 and 1971 he raced *Jumping Jack Flash*, a Quarter Tonner that he owned with his brother. Two years in Australia allowed him to cruise the New South Wales coast in *Hunter*, a 26-foot Tucker cutter. In 1979 he bought *C.T.*, a 24-foot First sloop, which he again shared with his brother. For several years he cruised the south coast with his young family and later chartered mainly in the eastern Mediterranean. In the late 1980s and early 1990s, Bob raced an X-boat at Yarmouth and Lymington and then crewed on a Daring in Cowes. Sailing with his brother he also had an enviably successful record in the Round the Island race.

A chartered accountant, at work as in all things he was indomitable, hard working, ever supremely optimistic and ingenious. He touched the lives of many. He was well known to bankers, quickly realising that debt did not dilute, and was popular with his shareholders. This is not altogether surprising in the light of the family motto which translates to 'Never knowingly under borrowed'.

Bob made no secret of his views whether on saving the pound or a game of rugby. There can be few who have not received the benefit of his opinions, quietly or otherwise, afloat or ashore, before or after midnight. He enjoyed the cut and thrust of debate.

Bob served as honorary auditor of the Club for nearly ten years. He performed this role with enthusiasm, efficiency and good humour and was always ready to help the Treasurer. Anthony Browne fondly remembers many enjoyable, cheery debates with Bob about the Club's accounts. Each year Bob chose a different West Dorset pub as the venue for these important discussions. He will be greatly missed.

GD

John Donaldson

John Donaldson, a senior member of the RCC, reached the top of his profession, becoming Master of the Rolls in 1982. At forty-six he was the youngest High Court judge. He was a highly distinguished lawyer but is probably best remembered for his energy as an administrator and reformer; his advanced thinking combined with deeply conservative instincts inevitably made him enemies and caused some unevenness in his career. The Labour party disapproved of his presidency of the Industrial Relations Court and blocked his promotion for several years but Mrs Thatcher thought highly of him, sent him to the Court of Appeal and nominated him as Lord Denning's successor, a most difficult act to follow.

His professional life is well documented but the title that he took, Lord Donaldson of Lymington, gives a clue to another side; he loved boats, sailing and the sea. The sea featured strongly in his professional career. As a barrister he was much involved with shipping and after his retirement from the law, he chaired some important enquiries into shipping disasters in which lack of available salvage tugs and divided chains of command exacerbated the situation. His response, through his commissions' reports, led to wider deployment of salvage tugs (referred to by some as Donaldson Tugs) and to streamlining the responsibility for control of potential disasters by the creation of a single government authority.

In the 1940s, shortly after they were married, he and Mary took up sailing as an antidote to their busy professional lives; she was as high-powered as he and was the first woman to become Lord Mayor of London (see her obituary in the 2003 Journal). Together they sailed small boats then graduated to cruising yachts. John was elected to the RCC in 1969 and Mary became a full member in 1971. They owned a succession of yachts, always small enough to be handled easily by two people and they habitually sailed together. Their joint entry in the Millennium Record bears this out: 'Never take anyone else with you except grandchildren without parents.'

They were not ambitious sailors; the English Channel was their cruising ground and they frequently visited the West Country, Normandy and Brittany. Occasionally they ventured further afield to Sweden, Holland and Denmark but their one cruise towards Spain ended in disaster when *Rogger* hit a Breton rock, sank and was not raised for two tides before being towed to Guernsey for rebuilding. This adventure prompted their only contribution to the Journal (1978) a light-hearted account of the catastrophe; characteristically it was under their joint authorship.

It was sometimes rather daunting for younger members to meet a man of such power and intellect, but a few minutes' conversation revealed a fellow member with a real interest in people, modest and charming. *Final Fling* was to be their last yacht but she was followed by a *Final Fling 2*. Even that was not conclusive because in 1995, their golden wedding year, they bought their really final boat *Golden Folly*. How many couples, even among the doughty RCC, acquire a new yacht for their golden wedding? Ten years later John sailed with his son Michael just two days before he died.

CJHT

Philip Fox

Philip, a member since 1969, died in October 2005 at the age of 83. Although to his chagrin he had been born on the wrong side of the Tamar he came from a Cornish family and grew up in the family home at Glendurgan on the Helford River. So it was not surprising that he took to the sea at an early age and as a young man achieved the remarkable feat of capsizing a St Mawes One Design discovering that it will sink if subjected to such an indignity. He read engineering at Cambridge but his studies were interrupted by the war and he was commissioned into

Philip Fox

the Scottish Horse. After the war he joined his father in the family firm of GC Fox & Co, ship agents in Falmouth.

In 1951 he was a member of the crew of *Morvah*, a large and good-looking Falmouth based ocean racer, which won the RORC Brixham to Belle Isle race. He then went into partnership with his cousin, Tony Laity, to buy *Pintail*, a Falmouth Sunbeam. Sunbeam racing has always been a very competitive sport and every week she could be seen against the quay at the Royal Cornwall Yacht Club having her bottom scrubbed.

With growing families, the partners decided to buy something with a cabin and offshore capability and acquired *Bluetail*, a sloop not much bigger than the Sunbeam, the tender inevitably being called *Tailpin*. *Bluetail* certainly looked the part but in practice proved to have too much mast and not enough freeboard. After some scary experiences in heavy weather off the French coast the partners went to the other extreme and bought the aptly named *Cautious Clara*. She was a double-ended Harrison Butler design with a cabin that although spacious had all the ambience of a third class railway compartment. She needed half a gale to get her moving and realising that they had made a mistake, they finally got the right balance between performance and comfort by buying one of the first Nicholson 32's. Named *Quaker Girl*, reflecting the partners' family heritage, and painted an appropriately sober shade of grey she was actively raced and cruised and became a frequent sight in West Country and Breton waters.

To Philip cruising was not just getting from A to B but a means of meeting old friends and making new ones. That unusual person, an Englishman who actually liked foreigners, he built up a remarkable range of friends along the Brittany coast. The description of him in the local paper as 'Falmouth's finest ambassador' was apt. Anyone who sailed with Philip came back for more and his regular crew sailed with him for many years. In particular, Roy Coote, a Falmouth tug master, crewed for Philip for the best part of 40 years and together they made a remarkable combination.

Philip was involved in many local organisations and played an active role in the life of Falmouth. He held many honorary consular positions, representing at various times the Netherlands, Sweden, Norway, Denmark and Spain. He served Cornwall as a Deputy Lieutenant and as High Sheriff and generously gave Glendurgan to the National Trust. He was predeceased by his wife, Rona, and leaves three sons and five grandchildren.

JGF

Sam Hammick

Sam was a sailor of great distinction from early days on the Hamble in *Wendy*, an International 14, through a naval career that started at

Sam Hammick

Dartmouth in 1935 and ended with a DSC, two Mentions in Dispatches and the rank of Captain. At Cowes he sailed in *Cyclops* and *Sea Otter*, both Fifty Square Metres, winning the Britannia Cup. He married Betty Westmacott in 1943 and after the war they restored and sailed *Amethyst*, an old six-metre.

His naval career included service in HMS *Brooke*, which rammed the boom at Algiers in 1942 to land American troops and was sunk soon after leaving harbour. After taking an Asdic course, he served as an anti-submarine warfare expert in HMS *Woodpecker* and in HMS *Kite*, a Black Swan class sloop. He won his DSC in 1945 for the sinking of a German U-boat in home waters, not far from the Nab tower in the eastern Solent.

With his beloved wife Betty he spent nearly eight years in Italy, first as Adjutant in Naples and then as Naval Attaché in Rome. Sam was a linguist with fluent Italian and excellent French and was for some years RCC Foreign Ports Representative for the western Mediterranean. He bought *Catspaw*, a 34-foot teak-on-oak Laurent Giles design with an eccentric profile, built in Italy in the 1950s. Betty and he remained faithful to her throughout their sailing days. They sailed, always together, sometimes with family members but mostly *à deux*, in the western Mediterranean, the Bay of Biscay, north Brittany and the West Country. They made many friends through their warm-hearted affability, their interest in others and their great hospitality. Betty is a cordon-bleu cook, even on a boat. Arriving cold and wet in a foreign anchorage and finding *Catspaw* already there was a great lift to the spirits, and the latter were poured unstintingly.

Although Sam could appear formidable on first meeting, he was a great raconteur and always good company. Elected to the RCC in 1980, he was also a member of the RYS. This was on his doorstep in Cowes and in later years they could watch the racing in Cowes Roads from the balcony of their home in Castle Road.

ROR/KR.

John Lancaster-Smith

Born in Hampstead in 1921, John's family soon moved to North Fambridge, Essex. His earliest experiences afloat were with his father on their duck punt on the Essex marshes. It wasn't long however before John had spotted the punt's potential and fitted it out with leeboards, rudder and a mast. This was the beginning of a love of sailing that lasted over 75 years.

On leaving school he worked briefly for a boat yard on the River Crouch but an interest in wireless and things electrical led him to the London School of Wireless Telegraphy where he gained his Post Master General Certificate. At 18 he joined Alfred Holt as a radio officer. On 3 September 1939, while familiarising himself with the wireless equipment aboard his first ship *Idomeneus* he caught the announcement that Britain was at war. He subsequently sailed in other Blue Funnel ships, *Prometheus* and *Pyrrhus*. When *Pyrrhus* was torpedoed off Cape Finisterre

John Lancaster-Smith

by *U-17* on 17 February 1940, John was almost the last to leave, leaping into a lifeboat as she sank.

After service in *Denbighshire*, he joined *Breconshire* on the convoy run to the besieged island of Malta. He made a number of trips in her before she succumbed to air attack during a desperate convoy battle in March 1942, first disabled by bombs and then sunk in Marsaxlokk harbour. John's next ship was the armed merchant cruiser *Queen of Bermuda* on Atlantic patrol. On his return to Britain in May 1943, he was commissioned and was trained on HF/DF equipment used to intercept enemy signals. After a period based in Londonderry, he went to the sloop *Leith*, patrolling the Strait of Gibraltar. Subsequently posted to the Far East, he became an expert on Japanese communication.

In 1946 John joined Cecil Tress as manager of the marine department supplying component equipment to overseas shipbuilders. Here he met his wife Jean. He had by now also met Peter and Anne Pye and crewed on *Moonraker* whenever possible. He had also bought his first proper boat, a 16-foot half-decker called *Halcyon*. The production of two new crewmembers, Jane and Jill, saw the purchase of *White Seal*, a 22-foot Robertson sloop and cruises to the Dutch canals and Amsterdam. With the appearance of additional crew (a third daughter, Jo) came the need for the larger 34-foot sloop *Grace*. Annual summer cruises to the Netherlands, Brittany and the Scillies followed.

The imminent arrival of further crew (John) led to the purchase of *Marlin*, a 36-foot gaff cutter. She stayed in the family for 33 years and not only enabled the continuation of summer cruises with the entire family (now joined by Jemma) but was also the focus of John's retirement plans. Tragically the months before John's retirement saw the death of his beloved Jean after a brief battle with cancer. After this bitter blow, although some months later than originally planned, John set off for the Med.

A three-year odyssey followed and *Marlin* travelled as far as Antalya and back to Lisbon. Sadly on the final leg back home she started to ship water at an alarming rate and they had to turn round. The decision was taken to bring her back by road and years later John spoke about the odd sight of seeing his 1935 gaff cutter doing 70mph along the M4. The next year he set off for a season in the Baltic.

In 1996 came the difficult decision to downsize. *Marlin's* upkeep was proving hard going and she was replaced by a 28-foot Sterling sloop. He was never completely at ease with her somewhat more nimble performance but she served him right up to his death at the age of 83. Just a week before he was diagnosed with cancer he called sounding almost euphoric with his day's sailing, the culmination of a season that saw him make two cruises across the Channel and his becoming a life member of the RCC.

He is greatly missed by both his family and the many that have been deeply touched by his friendship and enthusiasm.

JPL-S

John Lawson

John Lawson packed punch into his small frame. As a midshipman at HMS *Ganges* he adorned the flagpole with ladies' underwear before an important parade; he water-skied behind his first command, HMS *Pellew*; as captain of a squadron of frigates, he drove his ship with terrific verve.

John was born at Banchorie on Deeside. His father died aboard HMS *Prince of Wales* in 1941. As a teenager, he fished the Dee and learned to sail dinghies. He played rugby for the Navy at Twickenham and unsettled his neighbours in Newton Ferrers by driving golf balls from his lawn, over their houses, across Noss Creek and into the woods beyond.

John joined the navy in 1946, a career choice which offered full scope for his resourcefulness and leadership. He trained as a gunnery officer and had his first command in 1961. Later he was appointed Naval and Air Attaché in Athens. He based *Rinaldo* there and developed a love for retsina and the Aegean. He cruised those waters extensively with Anne, whom he married in 1959, and his two children Emma and Angus. On return to the UK, he commanded HMS *Charybdis*.

Retirement from the Navy presented new opportunities: the Sail

John Lawson

Training Association appointed him as sailing master of *Sir Winston Churchill* and later *Malcolm Miller*. He also skippered the ill-fated *Marquese* and when, after his spell aboard, she was lost off Bermuda, he devoted serious energy to clearing the names of those involved. When eventually he came ashore, he dedicated himself to the Royal Western Yacht Club, of which he became Commodore at an important stage of the club's history. He led the move to new premises and developed the club's lead in running ocean races with a difference.

John enjoyed racing and campaigned his boats successfully. His cruising was likewise thorough: if he said he was leaving at 0600, he did so, regardless of weather or petty officialdom. He baffled an irritating Turkish harbourmaster who because of some minor dispute denied him the right to sail, by cutting his warps and going full ahead.

One of John's crew praises his talent as a seagoing chef and recalls that his fish pie, normally selected for the first night of a bumpy passage, was a masterpiece. He never allowed his crew to go hungry; the rougher it got the more he thrived. He was also an accomplished entertainer on the accordion and edited the first RCC song book. His last naval appointment was as Chief of Staff to the Flag Officer, Plymouth, and he will be remembered for the band which performed on his barge for the benefit of visiting warships as they entered the port.

Competitive at sea, John was equally so in his garden. When his neighbours were catching up with his skills at growing carrots and potatoes he had already moved on to his prize winning artichokes.

John's contribution to the work of the RCC Pilotage Foundation was stupendous. He wrote a brand new seventh edition of *South Biscay* and joined the Management Committee bringing a high level of technical knowledge. Then came a major rewrite of *North Brittany* and as soon as that was published he took over the revision of *Atlantic Crossing Guide*, published in 2003. Then he turned his mind to the effects of developments in electronic navigation on the RCCPF books and in no time had produced a series of prototype electronic pilot books which were of enormous value in helping to indicate the direction in which electronic pilotage might develop. By now John was seriously ill, but this only served to increase his determination. He conceived an innovative Passage Planning Guide, now freely available on the RCCPF website. John was twice awarded an Archie Black Prize for his work for the RCCPF.

John was one of those people whose range and level of skills was constantly surprising. We entered the church for his funeral through beautifully carved gates of his own making. He was accomplished on the accordion. He completely disproved the theory that anyone over the age of thirty can't understand computers: working on his computer (beside a museum-quality model of an eighteenth century warship that he had made himself) he could devise book layouts, draw harbour plans, create websites and many other tasks that would defeat people half his age.

John didn't wait to be asked – if there was something he thought worth doing, he had usually done it before the rest of us had even thought about it. With determination and mental energy he would fight his corner hard and then wholeheartedly support whatever course of action was agreed. His impish sense of humour never left him and sustained him through his last, debilitating illness which he bore with characteristic fortitude.

CDP, JHT

Mike Manzoni

Mike Manzoni had an infectious enthusiasm for sailing in any vessel and a keenness to share it. He will be remembered for his comradeship and consideration for his crew; he and Julie unselfishly always ensured that the crew's enjoyment came first.

Based for much of his life in the Midlands he raced Fireflys at the Barnt Green Sailing Club where he was a respected Commodore. He was the driving force behind a number of members joining forces to buy *Sea Thrift*, a Rival designed by Peter Brett. Unable to spend as much time cruising as he would have liked, he continued to race at Barnt Green, crewed by Julie or one of his children.

With an engineering degree from Cambridge, Mike worked for the Port of London Authority and briefly for RM Douglas before a spell

Mike Manzoni

in Canada. Returning to England, he rejoined RM Douglas where his stature grew on the back of successful motorway construction projects. He joined the main board and then became managing director of RM Douglas Construction. He expanded the business overseas by focusing on areas where living conditions were particularly arduous – in order to limit the competition. Two notable projects were the National Exhibition Centre and the Symphony Hall and Conference Centre in Birmingham.

During this time Mike cruised both Channel coasts and western France in *Sea Thrift* but after his retirement he bought a Bristol 45 in the US. He sailed *Blue Sonata* on the US east coast to Bermuda and then south to explore the eastern Caribbean, for which he took on the responsibility of compiling the club's FPI notes. His report in *Roving Commissions 38* describes, with delightful self-deprecating humour, the selection of elephant grass as a stick for the burgee and the continuing search for a reliable fan belt (hinting at Mike's pleasure in the increased time under sail). After exploring Venezuela, *Blue Sonata* completed a circuit of the Caribbean via Cuba, Cayman, Guatemala, Belize (*Roving Commissions 41*) and Mexico.

With *Blue Sonata* abroad he demonstrated his enjoyment of the simple pleasure of being under sail, buying a Folkboat that was as much for his use in the Solent or to go to the Beaulieu Meet as for his children to race.

Always one to avoid the more populous places the distinctive feature of his cruises was his ability to engender a happy ship and to play to the individual strengths of each crewmember. Life on *Blue Sonata* was never dull. Mike frequently provoked what he called 'discussions' on a wide variety of subjects. One crewmember was heard to remark that 'Mike could start a riot in an empty room'.

Mike demonstrated a quiet excellence in all that he did afloat and ashore. He did it with a genuine interest in those around him that endeared him to all who met him. Perhaps those who did will join me in remembering him when listening to the Birmingham Symphony Orchestra on the radio.

HC

George Millar

After the war, George like everyone else must have had to take stock. He had undergone a lifetime's worth of experience, knew what people could do to each other and knew himself. He emerged a war hero and a writer of rare ability, who related events 'like it was' but with extraordinary perception and rich detail. He had proved his courage, his self-reliance and that he could write more than just journalese. Now he had to find occupations that replaced the life 'on the edge' that he had found so stimulating. People were eager to read what he had to say and luckily he did not have to stoop to anything as banal as an ordinary job. Isabel, his spirited new wife, was an ideal companion for adventure.

George had an instinctive love of the sea and, egged on by Isabel, bought a boat with proceeds from wartime best sellers *Horned Pigeon* and *Maquis,* planning to take her through the French canals and eventually to Greece. They chose the hefty motorsailer *Truant.* Isabel liked her because she looked good and solid and because the saloon was almost as big as a drawing room. George did know a little about navigation, having navigated army vehicles in the desert, and the two of them set off for an epic voyage to Greece wonderfully described in *Isabel and the Sea.* This was the start of his sailing career.

His next boat *Serica,* was in complete contrast to the straight-stemmed and heavy weight *Truant.* Her sailing qualities were infinitely better, though it was a wet ride, and this time George took the ocean route to the Mediterranean. This voyage bore fruit in the delightful book *A White Boat from England.*

In 1955 George and Isabel owned the 50-foot *Amokura,* quite a handful for two people but by this time they were outstandingly competent seamen. George was elected to the RCC in 1951 and the RYS in 1957. His next sailing book was *Oyster River,* recently reprinted, based on a summer in the Morbihan and as riveting a boating adventure story as any.

George had a good summertime occupation in sailing but come the autumn Isabel and he had another exciting hobby, fox hunting in Dorset, finding the jumping of Cattistock hedges as much of a challenge as the sea. He had to go one further and rode in local point-to-points with some success. They bought Sydling Court with 1000 acres and becoming farmers could no longer spend all summer sailing in the Mediterranean.

They then kept a bigger-than-ever yacht *Irene* at Castletownshend in Ireland but were forced out by the IRA, who objected to her white ensign. 'George, we'll burn your boat if you continue to fly that flag.' So they moved *Irene* to the west of Scotland, an even better and more challenging cruising ground. Isabel was tragically killed in a car crash in 1990 and George moved from Sydling Court to Uploders Place, where he spent the rest of his days, often sailing with friends in the Mediterranean.

George had an enviable life. He served his country and France with great skill and extraordinary courage in the war. He put his numerous talents to good effect. He wrote brilliantly, had an amazing memory and was a distinguished and prodigious author. He was an honourable gentleman of the old school. He leaves behind numerous books, which are a fitting memorial. Luckily if we want to remember George, we just need to read his books again.

PB

Dick Moger

Elected to the RCC in 1979, Dick Moger was a colourful, popular and thoroughly gentlemanly figure on the River Dart for over 40 years. He was part of Dartmouth's traditional sailing scene and of a civilised era that is slipping away.

Born in 1918, Dick spent his early years at Milverton, near Taunton. After Sherborne School, the first Dartmouth links were forged, when he became a trainee manager at Philip's Shipyard on the Dart. The yard built minesweepers and Dick found himself in a reserved occupation, unable to join the navy. After much lobbying, he was commissioned as a sub-lieutenant RNVR – a Saturday night sailor, he used to say. As second-in-command of the naval tug *Growler*, one of his tasks during D-Day operations was towing huge sections of the Mulberry harbours across to Arromanches.

After the war Dick started farming, an occupation that absorbed him for the next 20 years, initially back in Somerset. By then he had acquired the 32-foot gaff cutter *Athena*, in which he cruised whenever he could escape from the farm. In the early 1950s Dick moved out to Kenya, where he ran Brooke Bond's large farm supplying the company's tea estates. Even here, in the middle of Africa, there was sailing on Lake Victoria. After independence in 1963, when the Kenya government requisitioned many farms, Dick managed the Brooke Bond Tea Hotel at Kericho, which went from strength to strength under his sociable direction.

Dick Moger

Returning to Devon in the mid-1960s, Dick settled in Dittisham and started a successful yacht charter business on the Dart, which grew to a sizeable fleet. He often shipped aboard *Matawa* with Robert Franks, cruising to Brittany, Spain, Scotland and Norway. In the 1970s Dick owned the 32-foot Contest *Lakwet* and later a North Sea class sloop, *Rockabill*. In 1980–1 he sailed on *Drumbeat* with David Cole in the Caribbean Race to Antigua. Dick was a long-standing RORC member.

His last and perhaps favourite yacht was the Folkboat *Maestro*, which he cruised with his second wife, Gerlinde, who was such a mainstay of the charter enterprise. From their Dartmouth house on Ridge Hill, they enjoyed fine views of the estuary that had been so important in their life together. Dick's great good humour and zest for life were infectious. He always cheered you up when you met him on the quay. His jaunty gait, smiling eyes and inimitable tweed cap will be much missed on the Dartmouth waterfront and by all who knew him. His superb home-brewed beer, made to a secret recipe from Gerlinde's family, was renowned and I was privileged to have drunk his very last bottle.

PGC

John Savill

Back in December, just before going for his operation, my grandfather uttered the memorable, but not entirely surprising, comment, 'It's funny,

John Savill

but I'm not nearly as nervous as I was rowing up to the start of the Boat Race.' It is somehow fitting that he died three months later on the morning of this year's race. John's time at Cambridge was particularly significant in shaping his life. He rowed twice in the Boat Race and was one of the greats in a famous era for Jesus College Boat Club.

John had friends from Radley, Cambridge, the Irish Guards and the Masons and was very faithful to those institutions to which he belonged. He coached Jesus' crews for many years, inspiring them through his presence and reputation as much as through his quiet but expert advice. He was a dedicated Freemason, who rose modestly through the ceremonial ranks. He also served on various committees and boards, ranging from the youth club in Odiham to important Masonic institutions.

He served in the Irish Guards during the war when he lost an eye. He was evidently a strong and respected officer, as well as a resourceful one. The Guards History of World War II tells of his learning from previous errors of British Army night-time navigation and enlisting a young Belgian boy scout to lead him and his line of tanks from Brussels to Woluwe.

Sailing was one of the great passions of his life. I remember gentle trips around the Solent with the whole family on *Saint Radegund* and one less gentle occasion when I was at the wheel absolutely petrified as she bumped over waves at what seemed to me to be an impossible angle, while my grandfather just sat grinning, in his element in what was probably in reality only a slightly strong wind on a slightly choppy sea. My father and I took John sailing a year or so ago and although he was not particularly mobile and couldn't see well, he seemed to gain a spring in his step and looked years younger with his battered skipper's cap and toothy grin. Also, it goes without saying that, despite the failing eyesight, poorly stowed ropes were spotted from a distance and swiftly dealt with.

Around the Solent, *Saint Radegund* was renowned not only for being a beautiful, immaculately presented boat but also for pink gin. The quality, or should I say the strength, of John's pink gins was such that they once even warranted a mention in *Yachting Monthly*.

This habitual aperitif is also frequently mentioned in connection with the Henley regatta, a highlight of every year. Apart from the obvious rowing connection, he was in his element in the convivial, yet formal and traditional, atmosphere of the regatta. He enjoyed ceremony, dressing up for occasions and the old fashioned conventions of the church, masonry and indeed the regatta. But alongside this often imposing air of formality was a great sense of fun and of humour and a remarkable aptitude for conversation. He had strong, considered views and was able to express and defend them delicately and articulately. He was also a mine of poems and ditties, of which there seemed to be one to fit any topic. And when he declaimed, it was always in an atmosphere of rapt attention created by his slow, sure, sonorous baritone and exemplary use of the pregnant pause.

The motto on John's coat of arms was *Esto stabilis* (be steadfast). He lived up to this, a strong and imposing presence in every sense. He was a figurehead for his family and provided love and strength to his wider family and many friends.

MH

Dick Tizard

Dick was a distinguished engineer involved in successful wartime efforts to design a gyroscopic sight for anti-aircraft guns and in the infancy of computer controls. As was mentioned by all the speakers at his Memorial in Cambridge, he had two passions. The first of these was Churchill College where he was a much respected Senior Tutor, recruiting assiduously from state schools and leading the single-sex college into becoming amongst the first mixed Cambridge colleges. However, a close second to Churchill College was his passion for sailing.

He sailed in *Firefly* (an Albert Strange yawl owned by Sir Henry Clay) before the war with both Gabriel and Jim Clay but he must also have had a boat of his own as there is a theory that Arthur Ransome modelled Jim Brading in *We didn't mean to go to Sea* on Dick.

Like many other RCC members he started as a racing man and was part of the Oxford team pre-war and later President of the Cambridge Cruising Club. Until he died he cruised regularly often with one or more crew press-ganged from among his students or colleagues. His post-war crews could quickly add up 11 boats that he had owned, though there may have been more.

He always tried to improve each boat he bought but at some stage would decide that a particular fault could not be cured and he would buy another. For a time he was a partner in a yard on the Fal estuary and, as this was primarily so that his boat would be well looked after, he kept her there and cruised to France. However his favoured sailing was on the east coast and he would sail for preference to Holland and from there up to the Baltic.

That he was a meticulous and very competent sailor is born out in two among many stories. The first was when sailing in *Fubbs* and the mast went over the side. I enquired from Gabriel Clay whether he carried bolt cutters to which the response was, 'No, but I had Dick Tizard'. Apparently Dick, as soon as the mast hit the water, organised the whole crew in freeing the shrouds in very quick order despite, in common with most of them, suffering from seasickness brought on by the fiendish motion of the boat without the mast. The second was sailing his own boat with another Clay as crew. They had left the Solent and fog had closed in. Dick proceeded for some hours with no sight of any navigational aid before saying, 'Right, this is where we wait'. Five minutes later, out of the fog, came the pilot boat to take them into Rye – all this well before the advent of GPS.

Dick continued to go afloat as long as he could even, towards the end, being lowered by crane in his wheelchair to be dropped into the cockpit. He was a very considerable man in many ways.

JMC

FLEET MOVEMENTS 2005

Anatina	David Cole	Barcelona ad Balearics
Albatross	Richard Burnett	Normandy, Brittany, Channel Islands
Arcadia of Glaven	Stephen and Sue Lennane	Canal du Midi, South Coast of France, Balearics, Spain, Morocco
Ayesha	Paul Heiney	OSTAR from Plymouth to Newport
Balæna	Andrew O'Grady	Labrador, Greenland, Ireland, UK, Germany, Denmark, Sweden, Norway
Black Velvet	Ewen Southby-Tailyour	West Country
Blue Heeler	Paddy Carr	East Finland and Lake Saimaa
Borealis	David Vass	Shetlands, Fair Isle, Orkney
Brown Bear	Jonny Clothier	Scotland and Norway
Ceres	Jim Pitts	Western Scotland
Cloud Walker	David and Judy Lomax	Norway
Cresting	David Brooke	Turkey, Greece, Sicily, Balearics, Gibraltar, France, UK
Dafony	Mike Redfern	Denmark, Sweden, Finland, Estonia and Latvia
Dodo's Delight	Bob Shepton	West Country, Isle of Man, western Scotland
Feanor	Jeremy Parkinson	Northern Germany, Poland, Baltic States, Finland
Fillipene	Nick Bailhache	North and south Brittany
Flight of Time	Graham Morfey	NZ to Turkey via Australia, Indonesia, Malaysia, Thailand, Red Sea
Foxtrot of Rhu	Bill Ludlow	West of England and Isles of Scilly
Halcyon of Hebe	Jeremy Gurney	Southwest Ireland, Scillies
Harrier	John Marsh	Croatia, Venice
Harrier of Down	Julian Mustoe	Uruguay, Argentina

Holly	Peter Poole	Chichester, west and south coasts of Ireland and return
Iron Bark	Annie Hill	Greenland
Iseult	William Bourne	West Country, North Brittany, Channel Islands
Jan Van Gent	Keith Holland-Gems	Southwest Ireland
Jessamy	Roddy Innes	Spain, Portugal, Trafalgar Meet
Jesta IV	Stuart Carnegie	Croatia and Venice
Jura	Bill and Pam Kellett	Alaska
Kokiri	Peter and Katharine Ingram	Montreal, Gulf of St Lawrence, Newfoundland, Azores, Spain
Kwai Muli	Kit and Julian Power	Ionian Islands
Lectron	Peter and Gill Price	Turkey, Cyprus, Syria, Lebanon
Libertà	Sandy Watson	Western France and northern Spain
Malouine	Anne and Andrew Fleck	Western Scotland, Western Isles
Marguerite	Anna and Rob Brunyee	Caribbean to the West Country via the Azores
Mina[2]	Tim Barker	Baltic circuit
Namaqua	Leslie Jones	Algarve, Gibraltar,Balearics, south Spain, Morocco, Trafalgar Meet
Nandisa	Colin Ford	Cowes, Cherbourg, West Country, southwest Ireland
Natanis	Michael Lewin-Harris	Maine, New Brunswick, Nova Scotia
Nirvana	Sarah Watson	Channel Islands and North Brittany
Ondarina	David Mitchell	New Zealand, Malborough Sounds
Oriole	John Lytle	Caribbean from Antigua to Trinidad
Ostara	Charles Nodder	West Country, Scilly, North Brittany, Channel Islands
Papageno	Jamie Pritchard-Barrett	Greece, Croatia
Pemandia	Peter Fabricius	Southwest Spain and Portugal
Penelope's Ark	Tony Vasey	French and German canals
Quiver	Anthony Browne	West coast Sweden, Denmark, Baltic coasts of Sweden and Finland
Rafiki of Lymington	Bill Keatinge	Kusadasi, Turkey to Preveza, Greece via Cyclades and Ionian Islands
Rapscallion	John Button	Guernsey, Portugal, Gibralatar and the Trafalagar Meet

Restless of Auckland	Roland-Lennox King	Carribean, eastern USA, Maine
Saint Radegund	Joe Fraser	Solent to the west coast of Scotland and Western Isles
Samba	Lorne Byatt	Loch Melfort via Crinan, Forth and Clyde Canals to Firth of Forth
Scilla Verna	James Nixon	Norway, Shetland, Fair Isle, Orkney, Hebrides and Bangor, Co Down
Stella	Mike Barron	South Brittany and west coast of France
Sundance of Suffolk	Colin Barry	Croatia and Venice
Surgical Spirit	Alan Gardner	Bordeaux to south coast of France via canals, Corsica, Calvi, Bonifacio
Tao	John Guillaume	Gokova Korfezi, Turkey
Taraki	John and Sally Melling	Chile, Argentina, Uruguay, Brazil, Trinidad and Tobago
Tijdtverdrijf	Sandy Taggart	Netherlands, Waddensee, Ijsselmeer, Markermeer
Twilight	Michael Pocock	South Brittany
Upshot	Foster Swetenham	Sardinia, Tuscan Islands, west coast Italy, SE Italy to Dubrovnik
Wandering Moon III	Christopher Buckley	Southwest Ireland
Warrior Shamaal	Richard Clifford	Carribean to New Zealand

ROLLING INDEX OF CRUISES 2001 – 2005

CHART INDEX

INDEX

OFFICERS OF THE CLUB

2005/2006

Commodore
A.G. Browne

Vice Commodore
D. Lomax

Rear Commodore
A.E. Wells

Trustees
His Hon. A. Phelan
Maj. Gen. O.M. Roome, C.B.E., D.L
J.H. Trafford, D.L.

Hon. Secretary
Sue Lennane

Hon. Treasurer
S.L. Nockolds

Hon. Steward
W.H. Read

Hon. Journal Editor
J.C. Clothier

Hon. Newsletter Editor
P. Heiney

Hon. Solicitor
Mrs J.L. Bracegirdle

Hon. Secretary
Foreign Port Information
S.F. Carnegie

Hon. Cadet Members' Secretary
T.H. Trafford

Hon. Librarian
Prof. J.C. Hayward, C.B.E.

Hon. Cadet Captain
T.G.S. Bourne

Committee

H. Clay
J.F.C. Hodges
C.T. Nodder
Miss P.S.J. Scott-Bayfield
Mrs J. Twyman
Surg. Capt. D.A. Cunningham
Prof. J. Nixon
S.C. Perkins
D. W. J. Tew

Club Rooms
60 Knightsbridge, London SWIX 7LF
Tel: 020 7235 2121
Fax: 020 7235 5672